The Enneagram:
Pathways to Happiness

An Extraordinary Guide to
Realigning Your Life & Becoming Your Best Self

Veronica Croft and Chris Croft

BALBOA.
PRESS
A DIVISION OF HAY HOUSE

Art Credit: Chris Croft

Balboa Press books may be ordered through booksellers or by contacting:

Balboa Press
A Division of Hay House
1663 Liberty Drive
Bloomington, IN 47403
www.balboapress.com
1 (877) 407-4847

Because of the dynamic nature of the Internet, any web addresses or links contained in this book may have changed since publication and may no longer be valid. The views expressed in this work are solely those of the author and do not necessarily reflect the views of the publisher, and the publisher hereby disclaims any responsibility for them.

The author of this book does not dispense medical advice or prescribe the use of any technique as a form of treatment for physical, emotional, or medical problems without the advice of a physician, either directly or indirectly. The intent of the author is only to offer information of a general nature to help you in your quest for emotional and spiritual well-being. In the event you use any of the information in this book for yourself, which is your constitutional right, the author and the publisher assume no responsibility for your actions.

Any people depicted in stock imagery provided by Thinkstock are models, and such images are being used for illustrative purposes only. Certain stock imagery © Thinkstock.

Print information available on the last page.

ISBN: 978-1-5043-3193-7 (sc)
ISBN: 978-1-5043-3195-1 (hc)
ISBN: 978-1-5043-3194-4 (e)

Library of Congress Control Number: 2015906473

Balboa Press rev. date: 06/26/2015

Contents

Introduction

Your Inner World

Discovering Your Number

The Nine Types

Clarifying Typing Confusion

Pathways To Becoming Your Best Self

Acknowledgments

This book was in the development stage for a long time and we are most grateful to all who have helped it come to fruition. Most notably, we wish to express our infinite gratitude to our teachers in spirit, the Collective, for the continued blessing of their teaching, support and love. Our special thanks also go to Dorothy Chitty who channelled the Collective for us for many years.

Our warm thanks go to Amelia Rowes, Leonie Ashe and Rebecca Muddeman for their valuable help in assessing and proof reading the manuscript. And we would also like to express our appreciation to all the wonderful people we have had the privilege to teach, who have enriched our understanding and provided valuable insights about the nine personality types which we can share with others.

Preface

Ever since the human mind evolved enough to think freely, there have been those who have sought to understand themselves. All of us, at one time or another, have pondered the nature and purpose of life. We ask questions, such as these: Who am I? Why am I here? What is my purpose? Why am I like this? Why are others the way they are? Why is life so hard?

Finding the answers to these eternal questions has proved so important to us that we now study the nature of the mind through the field of psychology, a science developed for the purpose of understanding why we are the way we are. While psychology has given us many valuable insights into the human psyche, it has also created great complexity where there should be simplicity. We are not nearly as complex as has been made out, yet we appear so because we have not possessed the necessary understanding. Without the right tools of knowledge, human behaviour would appear to be a perplexing and tangled web, the mind's intangible depths seemingly impossible to make sense of. Yet once the true wisdom of the Enneagram is understood, this vast and complex puzzle becomes simple and logical.

Since the re-emergence of the Enneagram into Western consciousness in the middle of the twentieth century, a great deal of hugely valuable material has been written about it. There have been many authors and teachers who have brought a variety of approaches to this important work from different sources. Many of these approaches have attempted to apply 'pre-existing' models of human understanding to the Enneagram. Psychological archetypes, theologies, religious dogma, and other literary concepts and systems of human classification have been assumed to 'fit' what is known of the Enneagram. These attempts – to make sense of the Enneagram through what is already known – have unfortunately led to many misleading ideas or proposals, often creating complexity and confusion where there was never intended to be any.

Until now, it has not been possible to go beyond these ideas because the true wisdom of the ancient Enneagram was lost in the eons of time. Before there was such a thing as psychology, the quest for self-understanding was a spiritual journey. In earlier times, you would consult your priest or spiritual elder for guidance on life's journey. These wise ones were highly enlightened beings with a strong knowing of their true Essence, and the deep and powerful wisdom they taught included that of the Enneagram. During these periods in human history, knowledge about our true nature was considered of paramount importance to self-development and personal growth, and the Enneagram was the key to this. By its very definition, the road to self-knowledge is a spiritual one – since our true nature is that of the spirit – but while modern interpretations of the Enneagram have focused on understanding the mind, its deeper, more profound spiritual emphasis has often been overlooked.

The true, ancient knowledge of the Enneagram teaches us not just about the structure of the conscious mind, but also enables real understanding of the subconscious and even the deep spiritual nature of the higher or super-conscious. It shows the process of growth that is held within all of us, explaining past and present experiences, and even showing glimpses of where your particular path is headed in the future.

We have now reached a period in the spiritual evolution of humanity where the true and whole nature of the Enneagram wisdom needs to resurface. For various reasons, the spiritual truths of the Enneagram that were taught during ancient times became lost as we entered a darkened period in human existence. For thousands of years it has lain dormant, awaiting a time when we were once again ready to embrace its wisdom. Now, as we enter a new phase in human spiritual development, the light is once again beginning to shine, and the true knowledge of the ancient Enneagram is ready to come forth to guide us towards it.

Despite the fact that we seem to be alone here in the physical world, left to cope with the difficulties and challenges of life unaided, this is not actually the case. Each of us has unseen helpers, guides and angels who silently walk beside us, ready to guide our footsteps if we stray from the path.

The authors have worked very closely with those that oversee and aid the progress of humanity from higher dimensions, in order to gain the full understanding of the way in which the wisdom of the Enneagram was used in ancient times. For many years, a collective of highly evolved non-corporeal beings called 'The Educators' have been conducting a dialogue with the authors through a spiritual medium. *The Collective* – as the authors refer to them – are beings of extremely high vibration who reside in the twelfth dimension and whose purpose is to help souls in physical form (including humans). Most of the material in this book is based on the teachings from the Collective, and as a result, this groundbreaking book contains much material that cannot be found elsewhere.

Humanity is now ready to take the next step in its spiritual evolution. It is now once again time in our society for the great power of the Enneagram to resurface into human awareness. For a long time now, human beings have been traversing their life in darkness, tripping over unseen obstacles and falling flat on their faces over and over again, but only because they did not understand about the Enneagram.

The Enneagram only reveals itself to those that are ready to take responsibility for their lives and embark upon a journey of personal transformation. This is why you are reading this book. Regardless of how you have happened upon it, the time has come to allow the Enneagram to illuminate the remainder of your journey in this life, to show you how easy it can be and let it guide you to a future you could not possibly imagine.

It can be tempting to pick up a book such as this and only read about one's own personality, seeking to only discover one's own personal truth. However, it is by experiencing the full picture that so many other things about our lives fall into place, so we would urge you to read the whole book. It is only through having complete knowledge that the potential for meaningful growth gifted to us by the Enneagram becomes available.

The Enneagram is a universal truth, not an invention of man. It is not a typology system or profiling model, as many have said; the Enneagram simply *is*. It is present throughout the universe, underpinning the cycles of all life on all planets. *The Collective* has spoken of how the Enneagram exists where they are in 'the higher realms', of how they use its wisdom to understand their own existence and the existence of other dimensions of life that they oversee. As humans, it is fundamental to our existence and our experience of the world. It is the map that charts our inner terrain, and its influence dictates our thought patterns and drives our emotional and behavioural responses. Simply put, the Enneagram is, and has always been, the **Blueprint of Life**.

A Message from
the Collective

*The following is a direct extract from our conversations with the Higher Beings who refer to themselves as the Collective. The purpose of the message is to express the love they have for humanity and to explain why they have chosen this time to bring us their great teachings. When it was originally received, this complete spoken dialogue from beginning to end lasted exactly **nine** minutes.*

"We are a collective. We are not the only collective, for there are many. We are part of a collective that is not only planetary but also universal. We are souls; just as all living creatures have souls, so it is in the Outer Universe. We are expanded intelligence.

The understanding we have of your world has its limitations, for it is the understanding of your *world* that we have, not necessarily of its *inhabitants*. It is with the understanding that we *do* have that we recognise a need for our work with these souls (the authors) to now be spoken of. We are the Educators, as you would understand us, and as such, with our knowledge of what you understand as ancient times, and of your planetary system, we have brought forwards the [knowledge of] numerical power, for there is power beyond humans' comprehension at this time in the number Nine. Nine is the number of the Universe.

Through each of your lifetimes you will choose to be a particular personality type. We do not say this to typecast any one of you - let us say that it is for you to be able to step out of your own typecasting [and] to give yourself freedom in knowing how to understand self and your interactions with others. It is to bring about understanding of self on a physical level, an emotional level, and a deep, subconscious level, for you are multilayered souls and it is only when you open your layers that you can understand yourself.

The purpose of these teachings is to help humankind discover their qualities in a positive manner; it is to help interaction with not just individuals, but as it will grow, it will be with nations. For when humans understand themselves – both their positive and their less positive side – and find their own balance honestly, harmony begins to replace disharmony in their world. It is to this effect that we came forwards to speak, to create harmony and balance within your world. This will, of course, not be the only method, yet it is a very important one as far as we are concerned. Thus, we have chosen these souls to work with in honesty, for they have had to strip away some of their negative side in order to become teachers of this.

There are implications of these numbers at this time that are beyond human thinking, implications that will heal nations. For everything is numerical in your world; everything *beyond* your world is also numerical. Numbers have an energy, and with each number the energy is enhanced when an understanding of self dawns. Our teaching is to nurture that which is within you all – the knowledge that is stored within your soul. Our teaching is born out of what you would understand as love. There is love aimed at your planet, your world, through individuals and through your animal kingdom.

If each one of you reaches out with love from your heart, you will change the energy of your world."

The Collective

INTRODUCTION

CHAPTER 1

The Blueprint of Life

"The Enneagram is about the blueprint each soul writes for themselves, the blueprint of things that need to be addressed in this particular lifetime. This work brings the blueprint out of the world of spirit into the world of form in order for it to be understood."

The Collective

The True Self

There can be no doubt that the world in which we live is an incredible place. You need only to look around you in order to observe the masterful and ever-changing patterns of life unfolding with breathtaking harmony before your eyes. Most of us cannot begin to conceive of life's underlying complexities, yet its simplicity truly leaves us in awe: the astonishing biological genius of our own bodies, the mesmerising beauty of a blooming flower, the life-giving warmth of the sun, the sculptural magnificence of our planet's landscapes, and the inexpressible joy of being in love. Words are not sufficient to express the extraordinarily exquisite nature of our planet. Nature's silent life-supporting details are unimaginable, and the number of elements that coincide with such unerring perfection in order to produce life are simply inconceivable.

For human beings, this world is a utopian wonderland, with the potential to bring us unbounded joy and fulfilment. Our world is a playground where we can, during our lives, choose to act out any experience or role that we could wish. Anything is possible here. You can choose to be, do or have anything that you desire, and your time here can be 'heaven on earth.'

Unfortunately for so many of us, we do not perceive the world in this way. We see life as an enduring struggle that is filled with suffering, pain and difficulties. Life is neither easy nor enjoyable but is experienced as an attritional fight for survival. Consequently, you might say that the experience of life for so many of us is actually like 'hell on earth.'

This part of you that struggles with life and is forever doing, striving, worrying, or achieving is often referred to as the 'self.' This is your personal identity, your sense of 'I am' which has emerged, perfectly normally, from your need to find purpose and ultimately survive here in the physical world. However, this is *not* who you truly are.

**The 'you' that struggles with life and is
forever striving is not who you truly are**

Beyond the sense of self that has formed through our ongoing relationship with our mind, our physical body and our emotions, there is another aspect to our existence. Most of us are aware of something that exists that is larger than our self – a higher, deeper facet to our experience that has been ever-present throughout our lives. It is a silent force that has fed our instincts and guided our behaviour; it is indefinable yet undeniable. This is the higher part of your being, the part whose gentle whispers you so often reject in favour of what your mind is telling you. This is your Soul, your Spirit, your Essence. *This* is who you really are. The 'self' is nothing more than a temporary, but extremely convincing, identity that your soul has assumed in its desire to know itself, a role that you are acting out in the physical world.

The Embodiment of Essence

Although most of us perceive ourselves as individuals, separate from each other and separate from our Source, our higher self or soul is an integrated part of all of these aspects. It is part of the All That Is (referred to as God, Source, the Creator, and many other names throughout various traditions).

When the soul chooses to take form here in the physical world, the illusion of being separate from the divine and infinite Source is experienced so that the soul may know itself experientially and experience itself in relationship to all the other aspects of Essence that exist. This is the role of the self – as a tool for expansion of the soul. *It is an unfortunate necessity that the same physical state that allows our soul to discover more about itself has led us to forget this truth and believe that we are nothing more than human – limited, flawed and finite!*

The soul is eternal, and its very nature is pure Divine Essence; this 'forgetting' that is experienced while in physical form offers the opportunity to rediscover and remember – through the process of human experience – every tiny aspect of the true state of being. This is a process that is achieved over many, many lifetimes – hundreds, perhaps thousands of different journeys as a human being – each one embarked upon with the specific goal of experiencing a certain aspect of the Higher Self.

In order for the soul to experience what it desires in a particular lifetime, there are choices to be made before taking physical form. (These choices set the overall format of each life, but they do not make that life predestined, for we have complete freewill when here in the physical body.) The soul will first choose what will be 'worked upon' in this lifetime and what sorts of human experiences will give the best opportunities for growth and expansion. Then, for these experiences to become available, the most suitable environment into which to be born is decided upon. Agreements are made with the souls who will provide the parenting environment as well as the other major 'players' in this life, each of which will help the soul *realise* – that is 'to make real' – the desire for experience and growth. The exact date and time of birth is also chosen so that the alignment of the planets will provide the necessary astrological influences.

Now the most fundamental soul choice is to be made. Although the soul embodies all that is Essence, before this new journey in physical form is embarked upon, the soul chooses which specific aspects of Essence to work with in that particular lifetime. There are essentially *nine* different aspects of Essence, so there are *nine* distinct 'vehicles' through which Essence is expressed in the physical world. The nine aspects of Essence are thus the origin of the nine personality types of the Enneagram.

> **The personality is the vehicle of consciousness**
> **through which the Divine Essence of the soul**
> **is expressed into the physical world**

Because each expression of Essence is slightly different, each of the nine personality types experiences the world slightly differently. Each of the nine types literally has a different sort of journey through life with different sorts of experiences and challenges; thus, each of the nine personality types offers the soul different opportunities for growth and expansion.

It is clear then that the choice of personality is the most important choice to be made and has the most influence on the shape of the life that is to be lived. The personality determines the way in which the new physical being processes and copes with its environment and the people in it. These 'coping strategies' evolve into the habitual patterns of behaviour displayed throughout that life, and the conclusions about self, other people and life that are formed ultimately become the beliefs that unconsciously drive these patterns of behaviour.

So it is only through the sensitivities of the personality that the soul choices can be fully transformed into the unique human experience desired by the soul. Having made these life choices, the stage is now set for the soul to embark upon the journey of human life.

The Development of the Personality

The debate of *nature* verses *nurture* has been around since the advent of psychology. Those who emphasise a psychological approach would have us believe that we are born as a blank canvas and that the way we are is a result of our upbringing, that we are a product of *nurture* and not *nature*. So it may come as a surprise to many to discover that we are born with the personality in place and that the choice has already been made before we enter the physical form. (Of course, the fullness of the personality has not yet developed; it is in the embryonic stage, as a 'seed' ready to come into flower.)

Any parent with more than one child will be well aware that their children seemed to be very different from the moment they were born and, despite their best efforts to parent them the same, they have developed very different personalities. Many women who have carried two or more babies even remark that their children were different in utero. This is because they *were* different. By the time the child is in the womb, the budding personality is already in place, so each unborn child is already processing their world slightly differently.

Once born, each child instinctively begins to use its personality 'vehicle' to process the environment it finds itself in. Although there are both positive and negative traits within each of the nine personalities, each of us began life expressing our personality through our inherent positivity; the negative aspects of the personality are only acquired through the experiences we encounter in the physical world. It is these negative aspects that develop that give us opportunities for growth and expansion, so we need to transcend them in order to move back into the highest expression of our personality.

Although the parenting environment *does not create* the personality of the child, it can certainly affect the development of the personality. It can determine whether a more negative path or positive path is followed in that lifetime, and there will also be many later influences that can affect which path is followed, because each soul is a constant expression of its own freewill. Clearly, the personality will develop differently where there is neglect to where there is love, and neglect or lack of love can result in the child assuming more of the negative traits of their personality type. But contrary to what might be expected, this can also happen where there is too much love. A child who is suffocated with love and comes to believe that he or she can do no wrong may also go towards the negative, and a soul who does not receive enough love may go towards the positive. There are no absolutes; it is all choice, and it is all by the soul's design.

**Each soul will discover themselves in a
different way; it is the essence of Being**

How each soul chooses to express their Essence through the experiences that they have is down to their freewill. Each of us has our own path to tread and challenges we must meet, and we cannot know what other souls have chosen to experience this time. For this reason, we should be careful not judge others for the choices that they make and the life that is lived. Every soul must experience some lives of negativity, for it is the soul's desire to experience all that it is to be physical. There are no right or wrong ways to express our personality, and ultimately all paths lead back to our Source.

Weaving the Canvas of Life

How often have you heard someone proclaim, 'I've always been like this; this is just the way I am' or 'I can't do anything about the way I am; it is because of my childhood'? As we have discussed, the early years of childhood set the overall pattern of the life, but we all have freewill, and the choices we make throughout our lives result in changes in the way our personality develops. Your negative patterns of thought, emotion, or behaviour are not 'just who you are'; you are experiencing them because your soul desired to experience, to learn and to expand. The negativity you experience need not be viewed as negative at all because it offers you opportunities to grow and become more of who you truly are – your positive self – so all experiences and the way you react to them are in fact, positive.

In every moment, we are creating our lives via our personality – with our thoughts, words and actions. We create the pattern of our lives like a pictorial story woven into our individual consciousness through our many and varied experiences as a human being. It is this canvas that provides us with our inner picture, the filter through which we view our world, and the beliefs we hold about who we really are.

**The personality is the thread with which
we weave the canvas of life**

Interestingly, the word *cosmos* (the term used to refer to the outer universe) derives from the Greek *kosmos*, which means 'embroidery.' Clearly, the ancients understood that this is not an accidental world filled with chaos but a harmony of woven patterns, a tapestry of life.

At any time, we can look at the tapestry we have created and ask ourselves, 'Am I happy with the picture?' If not, our freewill enables us to change it. However, first we must begin to understand ourselves and why we act and react in the way that we do. This is why the knowledge provided by the Enneagram is so fundamental if we are to successfully create the life that we truly desire.

**We can unpick the parts of our canvas that
we are not pleased with and reweave a new,
more beautiful and complete picture**

By gaining true self-understanding, the nature of the life we have created begins to make sense; moreover, the Enneagram has the potential to equip us with the tools we need to bring about changes within ourselves and, consequently, in our lives. Quite literally, we can unpick the parts of our 'canvas' that we are not pleased with and reweave a new, more beautiful and complete picture, a picture that comes from who we really are.

Letting Your Light Shine

Throughout this book, the word *personality* will be used to describe what you may have heard referred to before as the ego. The word *ego* is a term that has, unfortunately, gained many negative connotations because it is attributed to the negative behaviour we observe in others. We might say someone has a big ego or is egotistical, inferring that they are displaying undesirable personality traits. This so often evokes only negative overtones and judgement, rather than the complete truth about human nature and the important place of the ego within it.

As humans, we need the ego. It is fundamental to our being and we would not be who we are today without it. Were it not for the ego, there would be no vehicle to drive your soul's essence through the physical world. There would be no means with which to process your physical environment and no means by which to bring the gifts of your Divine Essence to the world. Rather than 'rising above' or 'letting go' of the ego, the real purpose of personal growth is to transcend the limitations of the personality.

The positive aspects of your personality are who you really are

Through the knowledge and understanding the Enneagram brings to us, criticism and judgement, of both ourselves and others, are replaced by understanding, acceptance and compassion. The less-than-positive aspects of your personality have been a necessary part of your life experience; they were all part of your soul's original design to facilitate your growth. Hiding beneath this negative behaviour is a bright and brilliant shining light. This light is the positive aspect of your personality. It is who you really are.

As you work with the Enneagram, you will come to know and accept the strengths and positive qualities that are already part of your personality. These are the specific gifts of your personality type, and it is through bringing these gifts to fruition in the physical world that your true light can shine. These gifts are already within you; you chose to have them when you (as your soul) chose your personality type. It is through the gifts of your personality type that you intended your light to shine on the world in this life.

Because of the growth that your soul desired to experience, you also chose to take on some of the negative traits of your type; these have led you to develop all manner of limiting beliefs about who you are. Like lampshades, these negative aspects have acted to obscure the true brilliance of your shining light. In fact, some people have so many 'lampshades' that they do not even realise that there is still a light underneath!

It is only through first understanding, and then transcending, the constraints of the negative aspects of the personality that you can begin to remove the 'lampshades' one by one; in so doing, you come to know your True Self which is expressed through the positive aspects of your personality. Although there are many paths towards growth, only the Enneagram offers real, deep self-understanding. It brings awareness of all the different facets of your personality, both positive and negative, in such a way that self-esteem increases as you accept and work with them. Then, real personal and spiritual growth becomes not only possible but inevitable, and the magnificence of your light can really begin to shine!

CHAPTER 2

The Enneagram

What Is the Enneagram?

The Enneagram (pronounced 'any-a-gram') is the map of consciousness that underpins all aspects of your life. It illuminates the nine ways of being in the world and gives deep insight into nine fundamentally different personality types, each with their own way of seeing the world, their own attitudes and ways of thinking, reacting and behaving.

Just as oxygen supports the body, the Enneagram supports the soul. It is integral to us as human beings. The fact that many of us have been unaware of the Enneagram does nothing to alter its influence. Our soul's expansion is inexorably bound to the Enneagram; it governs our cycles of growth and underpins all aspects of life. It is the way our consciousness comes into form.

The Enneagram is the Blueprint of Life

Many people believe that the Enneagram is a modern-day system invented to make sense of human behaviour. Not only is it not modern, the Enneagram was not invented by man at all. It is, in fact, infinitely ancient and is part of the unfoldment and expansion of the universe; it always has been and always will be, for it underpins the cycles of *all* life, on *all* planets, on *all* dimensions. By using the Enneagram, the entire landscape of human consciousness can be mapped and charted; for each individual, the three functioning levels of their mind – the *conscious*, the *subconscious*, and the *higher conscious* or *superconscious* – can be explained and understood. So it is truly the Blueprint of Life.

In ancient civilisations, the Enneagram was considered an essential part of young people's education. The knowledge was taught extensively in order to give people a deep understanding of themselves and others so that they could value and embrace their positive, intrinsic gifts, have carefree, harmonious relationships, and feel really good about themselves.

It unravels all aspects of human behaviour in profound ways that psychology cannot. Whereas psychology often describes what is wrong with you, the Enneagram clarifies what is wonderful and amazing about you and shows you your own personal route to raising your vibration so that life becomes easier, happier, and more contented.

The Enneagram Symbol

Figure 1:
The Enneagram symbol

The Enneagram symbol is an ancient sacred shape that unlocks the secrets of the Enneagram so that we can understand and apply them to our everyday existence. Although here it is drawn in two-dimensional form, it is, in fact, a multidimensional symbol – the representation of the patterns that occur when consciousness expresses itself in form, patterns of thought, attitude and behaviour, and much, much more.

In the Enneagram of Personality, the nine numbers around the circle refer to the nine personality types. Each of us has chosen to come into life via the vibration of one of these nine numbers, and this is what we call the 'personality' – the translation of one of nine types of energy into human characteristics. Each type has its own way of being and patterns of behaviour, and each experiences a different motivation or need that drives those patterns.

Each of the numbers offers us different experiences for life in human form. By coming into life through each of the nine numbers, many, many times, the soul has the opportunity to experience all aspects of being human with the accompanying opportunities for growth and expansion.

Nine Numbers

So why are there nine personality types? Why not seven, ten, or twelve? The Enneagram is all about numbers, so this must be an important question to answer.

'And why numbers?' you may wonder. 'Why not letters?' Well, numbers are truly the building blocks of the universe. Everything that scientists learn about the universe is understood via the medium of mathematics, and the foundation of mathematics is number. The secrets of the universe are being unravelled by observing patterns and using numbers to make sense of them; within human behaviour, there are also patterns and the patterns we find are directly related to the qualities of the number of the personality type.

Numbers are much more fundamental to our lives than most people think. At school, we were taught that numbers begin at the number one and continue along a 'number line' to infinity. That is how we were taught to count, add and subtract. But in truth, numbers do not exist on a line, and although we could 'count' to infinity, there are actually only nine fundamental numbers, as we can see below.

Numbers are cyclical in nature. The number 9 represents the end of a complete cycle. The next number, which we call 10, is the first of a new cycle, or we could say it is 9 + 1. This actually means that 10 embodies the same fundamental numeric energy as 1. (You could compare this to the fact that the musical note C is still C in the next octave.)

So, for example:

10 = (one cycle of 9) + 1 or if we add the digits of 10, we see that 1 + 0 = 1 so 10 is equivalent to the number 1.

11 = (one cycle of 9) + 2 or if we add the digits of 11, we see that 1 +1 = 2 so 11 is equivalent to the number 2.

23 = (two cycles of 9) + 5 or if we add the digits of 23, we see that 2 + 3 = 5 so 23 is equivalent to the number 5.

137 = (15 cycles of 9) + 2 or if we add the digits of 137, we see that 1 + 3 +7 = 11. By adding the digits again, 1 + 1 = 2 so 137 is equivalent to the number 2.

So any number, no matter how large, has the same energy pattern of one of the nine fundamental numbers, and we discover which by adding the digits until we have a single number.

Everything within the universe can be understood via these nine numbers, including the human personality

The ancients knew that numerical cycles held the key to unlocking the secrets of the Universe. They based their numerological divination on the premise that there were only nine numbers and that all others were derived from these. It was their understanding that all of the nine numbers had a special significance and that they had characteristics and behaviours that bestow each number with a personality all of its own.

The Enneagram is all about Nine. The number Nine is about completion, the pinnacle, the all. It is the fundamental number of the universe. People of ancient civilisations knew this and had great reverence for the number Nine.

We still find echoes of the ancient knowledge of the meaning of Nine in our everyday life. It is deeply integrated into our language, and its essential qualities are expressed through common sayings. When people exclaim that they are on 'cloud *nine*' they are professing their highest feelings of joy, love and enthusiasm; to 'go the whole *nine* yards' is to dedicate yourself to the completion of a task; to 'be dressed to the *nines*' refers to being dressed faultlessly with no forgotten detail.

These and many other references to number remain within our language today as a legacy from the ancient civilisations of our planet. For ancient peoples, numbers and their attributes played a far greater role in their culture than they do in our modern-day society, and more than any other number, Nine was held sacred.

Discovering the Enneagram

Until we discover the Enneagram, most of us have been going through life unaware of the behavioural patterns that have been negatively affecting the way we live. We act in habitual ways, reacting to other people and life circumstances as we always have, without any awareness that it might be possible to be different. Perhaps we even say, 'I've always been this way. It's just the way I am.'

Many people try to improve self-worth and bring more balance and ease into their lives by using a variety of methods, such as healings, crystals, workshops, courses, and affirmations. All of these are of value and many help for a while; however, most people discover that life soon resumes the usual pattern and they slip back into their old ways without having gained any real understanding of their deeper selves.

The truth is that the way we experience life is a direct reflection of our inner world, so if we want life to change, we have to change our inner world. However, it is hard to make lasting personal change if you have no real understanding of why you are the way you are. Working with the Enneagram gives us, however, the opportunity to facilitate rapid and permanent spiritual growth. This is because, unlike those other methods that work from the 'outside in' - resulting in little lasting change - the Enneagram works from the 'inside out'. By studying the self-defeating patterns of our personality type and becoming aware of the ways in which our patterns limit us, we can finally begin to change our inner world and experience real and lasting improvement in our experience of life.

For most people, discovering the Enneagram for the first time is a revelation, an exciting time filled with new horizons of understanding about ourselves and others. Suddenly, our own inner world starts to make sense as we discover why we are the way we are, and we find ourselves looking for the patterns of the other personality types in everyone we meet. And as we continue to work with the Enneagram knowledge, we gain further insights into our own behaviour patterns whilst those of others also become clearer – with the result that, instead of seeming complex, other people become easier to understand and to live with.

Even more exciting is the realisation that we have finally found the key to positive change, both within ourselves and our lives. As the Enneagram reveals truths about ourselves that we never knew, we begin to recognise how much of our lives have been run by the negative patterns of our personality; moreover, we realise that, rather than remaining stuck where we are, imprisoned by these apparently unavoidable patterns, we have discovered the way out into expansive freedom and limitless potential. Instead of reacting to life as we always have, we finally realise that we now have a choice about the way we react to our world. In other words, we can start coming off 'autopilot' and start living life as our true selves.

The Enneagram is the key to positive change

Having discovered the Enneagram, it becomes difficult to imagine how we ever lived our lives without it. Our previously familiar world now seems like an exciting new place that needs to be explored and rediscovered. Rather than stumbling aimlessly in the dark, we walk through life feeling as if our eyes are truly open for the first time, our world illuminated with understanding and insight. If persevered with, and used in a positive and proactive manner, the wisdom of the Enneagram stretches deep into the inner workings of the conscious, subconscious and higher-conscious states of being, unlocking all the secrets of that (apparently) complex inner world.

The knowledge that is contained within the Enneagram is powerful and universal, but as with all forms of power, its ability to bring about change is limited to the way in which it is taught, understood, and applied. Merely being aware of what the Enneagram teaches us about the personality is not necessarily sufficient to initiate personal growth. Knowledge only becomes wisdom when it is applied. If approached in a superficial manner, or with a closed mind, the Enneagram can be used to justify negative behaviour. People have been known to say, 'Well, of course, I behave like that. What else can you expect? After all, I *am* a One ... Two ... Three ...' or whatever type they are. This is the sort of approach that will just keep us stuck in patterns that do not serve us by reinforcing previously held paradigms and bias and can reduce the Enneagram to just another method of boxing human behaviour.

If, however, the Enneagram is approached with personal honesty and compassion for self, with real openness and willingness to change negative patterns of thinking and behaving, then the amazing knowledge and wisdom provided by the Enneagram offers unlimited potential for growth, expansion and contentment. This enables each of us to embrace all that life offers with high self-esteem and ease within our relationships.

YOUR INNER WORLD

CHAPTER 3

Unravelling Your Inner World

Going Deeper

O ur consciousness is like a fathomless ocean that stretches out to the boundaries of our awareness. As we move through our lives, most of the time we only concern ourselves with that which appears on the surface of this ocean – our emotions and behaviour. But this only represents a very tiny portion of the immense body of our consciousness. If we are ever to understand ourselves and know the true nature of the constantly moving ocean of pure essence that we are, we must go beyond just observing the waves and ripples that occur on its surface. These surface disturbances do not define the nature of the ocean; they are an indication of the presence of something else below the surface, and the only way to discover the cause of what is visible is to embark upon a voyage of self-exploration; to go beneath the surface and examine our inner world.

As humans beings, we are all aware of the behaviour patterns – both our own and those of others – that seem to dominate our lives. The preoccupation and over identification with these patterns leads us to the belief that what lays on the surface of our consciousness is who we are, and we accept without question the version of the world that these patterns provide us with as 'reality'.

However, these external behaviour patterns are just the waves upon our ocean of consciousness, not the true nature of our being, and are only supported and sustained by undercurrents just below the surface (our internal thought patterns). Although interesting to explore, neither our behaviour patterns nor our thoughts are a true expression of our Divine nature; they are, however, an indication of what is hidden deeper down towards the core of our inner being. It is from this core that we can identify a driving force that is the origin of the 'waves and currents' that spiral upwards and results in our behaviour patterns at the surface. This is the place that defines our true nature, not the thoughts and behaviour that we find ourselves preoccupied with in the physical world.

The Enneagram provides a complete picture of the inner world of each the nine types

By examining what the Enneagram shows us about inner world of each type, we can begin to understand why the patterns of behaviour that we observe continue to occur. Sixes, for example, can be overcautious and indecisive; Eights can be pushy and controlling; Sevens can be scattered and irresponsible. Instead of merely observing this behaviour and reacting to it or judging it, we are now able to gain insight into the bigger picture, the inner truth of each type. With the deeper understanding this gives, where there had been criticism, judgement, or condemnation of either ourselves or others, we begin to have greater understanding, acceptance and compassion. The inevitable outcome of this change is that we experience much more peace and harmony in our relationship with others and, even more importantly, our relationship with ourselves.

Choices

The soul (higher self, divine Essence, inner wisdom, bigger self, or whatever you call the eternal part of you) desires knowledge of itself, growth and expansion. In order to achieve this expansion, part of the soul comes into physical form so that every aspect of essence may be explored. Only in this way can it discover everything about its true nature and come to know itself fully as it truly is – part of the Source.

It would be impossible for the soul to experience all aspects of its true nature in the seventy or eighty short years of one lifetime, so it is necessary to continue to come back again and again, experiencing many, many journeys through physical life. In fact, for the soul to fulfil its ultimate purpose of full self-expression and understanding, it takes hundreds and hundreds of lifetimes, each one providing the soul with the opportunity to learn and grow in a uniquely different way.

Before embarking upon each new journey, the soul must reflect upon the lives that have already been experienced, evaluate the growth it was able to achieve during those lifetimes, and then make the decision about which part of divine essence it wishes to experience next. Of necessity, when the human experience is embarked upon once more, there remains little awareness of the true nature of the soul, nor is there memory of the many lives already lived. Therefore, decisions need to be made that will shape the overall pattern of the forthcoming life and the potential for growth that will be available. Although the progression and outcome of the forthcoming life are in no way set in stone (because we, as humans, have free will), certain key choices are made so that there will be no escape from the patterns of life that the soul has chosen to experience. Each of us made these choices before we came here this time.

Having decided which aspect of essence would be explored in this life, specific life circumstances needed to be in place in order that this life would offer the best opportunity for the desired growth work. So before you came into life, your soul selected the circumstances of your birth: the time and date (and consequently the position of the planets), the geographical location and the nature of the nurturing environment you would be born into. You also chose the major relationships that would form the foundation of this life – your parents, your siblings, your lovers, your friends, even your enemies – since it is through relationships that we as humans achieve most of our growth. Although all of these choices were pivotal in tailoring your human experience, the most important choice, the one that has had the greatest impact on who you are, and therefore, holds the key to your pattern of growth, was your choice of Enneagram personality.

Your personality type provides the
key to your pattern of growth

More specifically, since the root or foundation of each of the nine personality types is one of the nine fundamental numbers, you chose the specific vibration of one of these nine numbers to become your soul's *vehicle of consciousness* in this life. This numeric vibration translates directly into human consciousness as a unique sensitivity that is particular to that personality type. Moreover, because the vibration of each of the nine numbers is very different, the inner world of each of the nine types is very different. Each of the personality types *perceives* their world in a manner that is unique to that type so each has a different sort of experience of life to the other eight types. Predictably, they then *react* to their life circumstances and the other people in their world in ways that are specific to that type. It is in this way that each of the nine personality types provides the soul with different opportunities for growth.

Each type has different deep, and often unconscious, needs from which develop different core emotional issues. It is these issues that get in our way and drive the self-defeating patterns of behaviour that must be understood and truly let go of in order that real growth can be achieved. By understanding the choice of Enneagram personality that was made, we get to understand all the patterns of our own reactions and behaviour, especially those aspects of ourselves that have seemed difficult to make sense of and even more difficult to let go of.

However, if all you were to do with this book was recognise your own behaviour patterns within the descriptions of your type and say, 'Oh yes, I do that. That's me,' you would make little progress towards achieving growth. In fact, gaining only superficial knowledge about the types can lead to mistyping and staying stuck. However, by studying what drives each of the types – what is the underlying need that drives the thought patterns, the behaviour and the reactions – we begin to understand how these patterns originated in the first place and what erroneous beliefs are in place.

Each of the types develops both positive and negative patterns, and it is the negative patterns that we run that cause us all the pain and problems we experience in our lives. These negative patterns of behaviour are what cause almost all the conflict in relationships, including the relationship we have with ourselves. When you understand these patterns, you finally get to understand why *you* react like 'this' when he or she says 'that' and why *they* behave in those ways that drive *you* so crazy!

The Early Years

There exists at the core level of each of the nine types a single fundamental need. It is this one primary need that silently drives the behaviour patterns of each type, shaping the intricacies of the personality from behind the veil of the unconscious. All of the familiar behaviour traits that are so typical of each of the nine personality types arose from this deep, underlying, driving need. Once we know the *fundamental unconscious need* for each of the types – and how each of these needs came into being – it becomes easy to get a clear picture of the true origin of the patterns exhibited by each of the nine types. And once we know *why* we do something, it is much, much easier to change for the better!

The 'Lost' Quality of Essence

Before your soul chose to experience separateness from Source and incarnate into physical life as a newborn child, you selected which aspects of Essence you wished to explore, experience, and grow through in this lifetime. The desire for these specific experiences determined which of the nine numbers was to become the vehicle for your consciousness – the means through which the higher part of you could experience the world.

The nine numeric vibrations all exist independent of each other, embodying and expressing different aspects of the All That Is (just as the individual colours of a rainbow can be seen as individual colours yet they are all part of full spectrum white light). Therefore, because none of these energies can contain *all* of the aspects of the All That Is, the way the world is experienced through the vibration of the number chosen by your soul is a subjective and slightly distorted one. By selecting this number as your vehicle of consciousness, you chose to experience the world through a selective *filter*. This filter gave you the impression that an important quality of Essence was absent from the world.

A Unique View of the World

Each of the nine types has a different filter – a different aspect of essence that seems to be missing from their world – and because of this, each type experiences the world in a slightly different way from the other eight types. (In actual truth, there is nothing missing; this is the distorted perception of the world that was intended by the soul in order to give the intended opportunities for growth.)

When you were born, this filter was already in place; therefore, it never occurred to you to think that your perception of this new environment was incomplete. Naturally, you accepted your version of the world as real, without being aware that your 'reality' was in fact very different from the 'reality' experienced by people of a different personality type.

The Fundamental Unconscious Need

Although in truth we can never actually be separated from any aspect of our Divine Essence, this was the illusion created by the vibration of the number chosen as your vehicle of consciousness. So convincing and overwhelming was this illusion that, as each of us began a new life in a strange and unfamiliar world, it brought about a sense of loss at the core of our physical being. It was this deep feeling of loss that created the unique sensitivity that your type has to the environment. Moreover, it was this sensitivity that brought about the first spark of human individuality as you experienced your first deepest need – the need to reconnect to, or reacquire, the quality of Essence you felt you had lost or become separated from.

This fundamental unconscious need is the origin of the personality and the core driving force behind *all* subsequent behaviour patterns, both positive and negative.

Core Erroneous Beliefs

As we each continued to experience and process our 'reality' through this illusory filter, that fundamental, unconscious need gradually began to give rise to core basic belief patterns that became embedded into the subconscious. These beliefs were not truths; they were conclusions about the nature of the world that we drew when we were very young, and these then became embedded within us as erroneous beliefs. Gradually, driven by these erroneous beliefs, patterns of behaviour began to spiral outwards as a means of coping with what we perceived to be our 'reality.' As we grew, these internal and external patterns of behaviour became increasingly complex and elaborate, creating a strong sense of personal individuality. It is these ripples on the surface of your ocean of consciousness that have come to be labelled your *personality*, or your *ego*.

The Deepest Fear

Irrespective of any other need that arises from our unique sensitivity, all small children fundamentally need love. Although most of us understand love to be a human emotion, in truth the feeling of love is the experience of being reconnected to your Source. This is why love is the emotion that holds relationships together and why, when we experience love, we feel so complete and at peace. Essentially, when you truly love someone, you are experiencing, through them, deep aspects of your Divine Essence, a sensation that feels warm and nurturing. So for a small infant, receiving expressions of love (through the parenting they receive) enables them to experience a continued flow of their own Source. This gives them support and spiritual nourishment as they learn to cope with their new unfamiliar surroundings – much like a small child learns to ride a bicycle with stabilisers to begin with!

Whenever you feel fearful or afraid, what you are actually experiencing is the absence of love (in other words, disconnection from 'who you really are'). Therefore, because each of the personality types experiences disconnection from an aspect of Essence (the true nature of which is pure love), a single basic fear naturally arises within each type.

This deep, unconscious fear remains unresolved within us as children, and in adult years, it continues to colour our experience of life. Moreover, it drives most of the negative emotions, reactions and behaviour that we display in our adult lives and brings us nothing but difficulty and pain. Most of us have never really identified this fear because it has always been there and is so much a part of us. It is only when we become *consciously aware* of the existence of, and reasons for, this fundamental fear that we can do the work that is necessary to transcend its effects and come into awareness of the real truth – that we can never be disconnected from any aspect of our Essence, so there is truly nothing to fear.

CHAPTER 4

The Shaping of the Personality

Your Blueprint

The specific choices made at soul level before you began this life's journey created the **Blueprint** for the coming life. Your number determined the ways in which you were likely to react to the environment and life circumstances you found yourself in; this was the reason why your soul chose your specific personality type for your journey, and not one of the other eight. As we shall see, the filter provided by our number – and hence the sensitivity, the deep, unconscious need, and the fundamental fear – determines the way we react to our life circumstances giving rise to the beliefs, thought patterns, and behaviour that make up the personality. The blueprint chosen by your soul gives you specific opportunities to make significant growth in this life, but of course, the way your life circumstances have affected you is directly related to the way you perceive them, and another personality type would have reacted very differently to the same set of experiences.

Each of us came into life with the positive gifts of our personality type already in place. These intrinsic gifts are the way in which you intended your light to shine on the world this time, and they provide you with your positive aspects, traits that you cannot help but display when you are being your best self. They are the wonderful qualities you possess naturally that you have not had to learn, nor did you need to read a book or go on a course in order to develop them. When you are functioning through the positive of your type, you feel at peace, alive, and inspired; your inner light is shining.

The positive aspects of your personality are *who you really are*

Most of us are not sufficiently aware of what is great about ourselves. In fact, we find it easier to focus on our less-than-positive aspects, our negative stuff – if you were to make a list of your best points and a list of your worst points, which would you find easier? Which might be the longest? Most of us identify much more with our negative traits than with the positive, to the extent that it becomes easy to believe that these negative aspects are who we are. But they are not. They are just coping strategies, patterns that developed as we tried to cope with a world full of challenges.

This negative 'stuff' – our negative attitudes, thinking, or behaviour – is not who we are. It is just stuff that gets triggered by difficult or challenging circumstances, and it prevents our light from really shining. This 'stuff' acts like a lampshade dulling the true radiance of our light. Some people have so many lampshades that it is hard to see their light at all, but it is always there just as the sun is always shining behind the clouds.

Although your positive traits were in place at birth, it was never intended that you would live a life composed only of positive experiences. Many people who have had very difficult times in their lives would perhaps wish it were so; however, our greatest opportunities for growth come about from experiencing the more negative aspects of our personality, and then growing sufficiently so that we are able to rise above them. The soul desires growth and expansion in each earthly existence, but little growth would be achieved if you had only experienced the easy route in life.

Imagine you were a tennis player who wished to improve your game. Would you choose to only play against people that you could easily beat so that you could take it easy in every game, or would you seek out tough opponents who would stretch and push you to your limits? Which sort of game would help you improve?

Your blueprint was intended to offer life challenges that resulted in the development and expression of not just the positive side of your type but also the negative. The fullness of your personality patterns only really began to take shape as your awareness of the world expanded during your early years, up to about the age of ten or twelve, the time when you were learning to cope with the world as a separate being from your parents. Because of the sensitivity and the basic fear that are fundamental to the patterns of your type, you began to adopt core negative beliefs and display signs of the negative personality traits associated with your personality type. As these combined with those shining, positive traits of your type, your individual personality pattern was created.

The Origin of Our Negative Patterns

All young children need to be loved and made to feel safe and secure in their world as they grow up. However, even with the best efforts of those that create the nurturing environment, it is simply not possible to have these basic needs fulfilled perfectly all of the time. No matter how much our parents loved us and looked after us, they themselves were trying to deal with *their* world – and its accompanying problems – from the perspective of *their* personality type and *their* own past. So, even with the best will in the world, there were times when our parents were not able to meet our needs; as a result, as small children, we sometimes experienced life as difficult, confusing, or painful.

During this time, many of the hurtful or painful emotions that accompanied such experiences were not expressed or fully let go of. There are many reasons why children cannot express their emotions. Perhaps the child did not have the necessary verbal ability or the opportunity was never given. Maybe the child believed that expressing these negative feelings would result in less love or attention. Or perhaps, being aware of a difficult, emotive situation going on within the family, the child believed that if their hurt or anger was given expression it might make the situation worse. Whatever the reasons, a great many of the painful emotions experienced in our young years were not given expression – and maybe not even acknowledged. Because emotions arise within the body, there are actually physical and chemical responses in the body when we experience any emotion, and these unexpressed emotions became trapped within your body cells.

Attached to these negative emotions by invisible, connective strands are the beliefs that you took on regarding the situations that caused you problems and pain in those early years. From these new, erroneous beliefs (for they were not truths) about the world, a complex myriad of desires began to form. Essentially, these desires were further expressions and extrapolations of our fundamental unconscious need, designed to (a) get our needs met and (b) avoid our basic fear. Born out of our fundamental unconscious need, these desires were the immediate driving force behind all of our patterns of thinking, reacting and behaving during our young years. Some of those patterns were definitely positive, but plenty of them were negative.

As adults, we now find ourselves going through our lives still seeing the world through the eyes of the children we once were, unconsciously adopting the negative, limited view of the world (a view that is determined by the 'filter' of our type) that is particular to our personality type. Although the accompanying beliefs are not actually true, and we no longer need the coping strategies that we did as children, we are still driven by those unconscious beliefs and still follow the same habitual patterns of behaviour, because we always have – even though they do not get us our needs met and actually keep us stuck in negative emotional patterns.

As we go through adult life, the painful emotions that were stored deep within our cellular memory during those early years get triggered by situations or people that we have to deal with; it is as if there are invisible 'buttons' that external circumstances 'push', triggering these long-held emotions so that we experience them again and again.

Much of this occurs as a result of the interaction with those closest to us, those souls who have agreed to help us experience certain aspects of ourselves. Have you noticed how it is those closest to you that make you feel your worst, most painful feelings? Well, actually, it's their job to reveal to you where you are not whole and healthy – emotionally, mentally and spiritually – and you both signed up for this!

So whenever you have a less-than-good feeling in response to your life circumstances, or to the people you interact with – in other words, you feel negative, you feel uncomfortable, something in you shuts down, or you feel hurt –you are reacting once again as your 'little self'. Deep in your inner world, there remains a three-year-old self or an eight-year-old self (or however old you were when you took on these negative beliefs about the world) that has been emotionally frozen in time, and comes to life, still hurting, when that sensitive spot in your personality pattern gets prodded!

The Self-Defeating Pattern

Each of the nine types takes on a different (and distorted) perspective of the world as a young child; as a result, each of us came to believe that we needed to behave in certain ways in order to cope with what we experienced in the nurturing environment and to get our needs met. The most fundamental of these needs is the need to reconnect with, or reacquire, the aspect of Source that appears to be lacking or missing from the world.

Our patterns of behaviour, then, are our (misguided) way of trying to get the outside world to provide us with what we experience as missing so that we might feel complete again. However, the fact that our patterns of negative behaviour continue year after year, habitually and largely ineffectually, is testament to the fact that we are going about this search in completely the wrong way!

We will not find what we are looking for in the outside world because the aspect of Divine Essence that we feel disconnected from is present within our inner world, waiting for us to discover it.

And even crazier than this, it is precisely the behaviour patterns that we use to try to get what is 'missing' that trip us up, cause us problems and pain, and ultimately bring upon us our greatest fear! This habitual, counterproductive cycle is what we refer to as the *self-defeating pattern*. Each of the nine types has their own unique way of 'chasing their tails', which continues to cause them problems and pain, and ultimately holds them back from reaching their full potential.

If we are ever to find peace in our lives and achieve the growth for which we came here, we must learn to recognise that our current behaviour patterns are not getting us what we really want but are actually pushing it farther away. We must see through this illusion of lack in our world and, rather than try to get what we perceive as being missing, we must come to realise that it was never actually missing in the first place. What we have been experiencing is an illusion crafted by the higher part of us, with the sole (soul) intention of stimulating personal expansion within our lifetime. That is why self-awareness, honesty and self-examination are the keys to finding true peace, and all of the types must undertake this if they are to complete the unique passage of growth available to them.

Ultimately, as we come into awareness about our continuing cycles of self-defeating behaviour, we can finally act to break the habitual patterns that make life less than good and thus come into the truth about our world, which is that we are all complete and whole just as we are, and can never be truly separate from any aspect of Divine Essence.

Growing towards Your Potential

Experiencing difficulties and pain, and finding the inner strength to overcome them, is what brings about real, meaningful growth. So in order to achieve growth, the young you needed to adopt many of the negative traits of your personality type, something that would not have been possible were it not for your specific life circumstances. Your life circumstances provided you with the opportunity to experience specific painful episodes, while your sensitivity to the world provided the fertile, internal environment for negative emotions and beliefs to become attached to these experiences.

It becomes clear then, that if we harbour any desire to understand human behaviour and make significant strides in our own growth, we must become clear about the *needs and desires* that continue to drive the external patterns of behaviour. In order to fully understand what lies beneath these desires, we must first examine the *core erroneous beliefs*. To comprehend why these beliefs were put in place, we must look at the *fundamental unconscious need* and the *unique view of the world*. And ultimately, if a complete picture is to be formed, we must understand how our initial sensitivity to the world was born out of *feelings of separation from a certain aspect of Divine Essence* – a circumstance that the soul chose because of the potential it would provide for personal expansion and growth in this life.

This seed of pure potentiality was the first spark of your individual consciousness, and like a plant in the springtime, your personality grew outwards from this central point before blooming into the person you are today. But what is the nature of your bloom? Is it shining, vibrant and colourful or dull, washed-out and dispirited? Is it big, bold and impressive or small, fearful and insignificant?

Your bloom has the potential to express unspeakable beauty and love. However, in order for its true magnificence to unfold, you must first free yourself from the stuff that is holding you back and stifling your growth – the habitual patterns of negative thoughts, beliefs and behaviour that are clouding its perfection.

CHAPTER 5

The Inner World of the Nine Types

This is an overview of the development of the personality for each of the nine types. Each table shows the way separation from Source is experienced. This is **the aspect of essence** that is perceived by the small child as being absent or unavailable which results in a particular **way of seeing the world**. From this arises a **deep, unconscious need** to reacquire or reconnect to that 'absent' aspect of essence. The need to get this deep need met feels like a survival issue for the child so conclusions are drawn, not only about the nature of this world, but especially about what the child needs to do, be or have in order to survive here in the physical world.

These unconscious conclusions become entrenched within the developing personality as unconscious and **erroneous beliefs**, beliefs that also result in the type's **deep, unconscious fear**.

Driven by the unconscious beliefs and the desire to avoid what the type most fears, predictable attitudes and behaviour patterns develop. These are the child's way of coping with the demands of the world they find themselves in. Many of these coping strategies are actually **self-defeating patterns** in that they ultimately bring about the **deepest fear**.

The One

The Inner World of the One

Aspect of Essence lost sight of:	The Perfection of ALL Things
View of the World:	The world is imperfect and needs improvement
Fundamental unconscious need:	For perfection
Erroneous Beliefs:	I must be perfect and do everything right in order to be loved. I am only perfect if I am always good. If I am wrong I am not perfect
Deepest Fear:	Being imperfect, wrong or bad

The Self–Defeating Pattern

Striving to Avoid:	Being imperfect, wrong or bad…

CREATED THE DRIVING DESIRE...

Driving Desires:	To be perfect; to be good; to improve themselves, others and the world; to avoid and correct 'mistakes'; to be above reproach or criticism; to maintain control of themselves and their environment; to be ethical; to uphold principles and morals; to have integrity; to be fair and balanced; to strive for their ideals…

THE CONSEQUENCES OF WHICH ARE THAT...

Behaviour Patterns:	Ones set themselves impossibly high standard for 'personal perfection' and continually move the goal posts of what they believe is 'good enough'. There is a basic conflict between what they would like to do and what their ideals say they must do. As they follow the dictates of their self-imposed ideals, their inner critic tells them they are not good enough and castigates them for having less than noble desires, inevitably…

THIS ULTIMATELY BRINGS ABOUT THEIR DEEPEST FEAR...

Deepest Fear:	Of being imperfect, wrong or bad.

The Two

The Inner World of the Two

Aspect of Essence lost sight of:	The Eternal Presence of Unconditional Love
View of the World:	Love is not freely available in the world
Fundamental unconscious need:	To be loved and wanted
Erroneous Beliefs:	I am not intrinsically lovable or valuable. Love is only available through relationships. I must earn love by meeting others' needs.
Deepest Fear:	Of being unloved, unvalued and unwanted.

The Self–Defeating Pattern

Striving to Avoid:	Being unloved, unvalued and unwanted…

CREATED THE DRIVING DESIRE…

Driving Desires:	To be loved; to be needed; to help people; to avoid being alone and separated from others and their love; to be appreciated and valued; to be important and necessary to others; to keep close contact with others; to get others to need and want them; to feel worthy by being needed…

THE CONSEQUENCES OF WHICH ARE THAT…

Behaviour Patterns:	Twos confuse being needed with being loved. They try to get love by fulfilling others needs through 'unselfish' giving, but fail to express their own needs for fear of being 'selfish'. When others do not appreciate their giving, or fulfil their needs, they become resentful and hurt. This prevents them from giving unconditionally. When feeling unappreciated or unwanted, they become manipulative, intrusive and controlling often inducing guilt or acting as the martyr. This begins to drive others away from them…

THIS ULTIMATELY BRINGS ABOUT THEIR DEEPEST FEAR…

Deepest Fear:	Of being unloved, unvalued and unwanted.

The Three

The Inner World of the Three

Aspect of Essence lost sight of:	The Value of 'Being'
View of the World:	The world does not value 'Just Being'
Fundamental unconscious need:	To have value by being a success
Erroneous Beliefs:	The world rewards us for what we 'do', not who we are. If I am anything less than the best I will not get love and appreciation. I do not have intrinsic value as myself.
Deepest Fear:	Of being worthless, without intrinsic value; of being a failure.

The Self–Defeating Pattern

Striving to Avoid:	Failure, being worthless, without intrinsic value…

CREATED THE DRIVING DESIRE...

Driving Desires:	To 'be' a somebody that is valued by the world; to be successful; to avoid failure; to distinguish themselves; to improve and develop themselves; to get attention and admiration; to be accepted and desirable; to create a favourable impression; to be liked and accepted...

THE CONSEQUENCES OF WHICH ARE THAT...

Behaviour Patterns:	Threes are striving for accomplishment, success, and image over all things in life. Rather than being authentic they constantly adapt themselves in order to be liked and accepted by others. They can never show others their true self, which they believe is worthless, for fear of rejection. They constantly need to achieve so put focus on tasks and goals with no time for feelings. The heart energy shuts down, creating inner emptiness and even less good feelings about self...

THIS ULTIMATELY BRINGS ABOUT THEIR DEEPEST FEAR...

Deepest Fear:	Of being worthless, without intrinsic value.

The Four

The Inner World of the Four

Aspect of Essence lost sight of:	Undivided Completeness
View of the World:	The world abandoned me
Fundamental unconscious need:	To discover personal truth, be authentic to it and find what seems missing that would make them complete.
Erroneous Beliefs:	I do not fit in. I was abandoned because I am flawed. Others have what is missing from within me. I will only be loved and belong if I can be special or unique.
Deepest Fear:	Of having no significance, not belonging, being rejected

The Self–Defeating Pattern

Striving to Avoid:	Having no personal significance and being rejected…

CREATED THE DRIVING DESIRE…

Driving Desires:	To find what is missing that would make them complete; to discover and express inner truth; to be authentic and loved for themselves; to have a deep heart connection; to avoid being ordinary and be appreciated for their uniqueness…

THE CONSEQUENCES OF WHICH ARE THAT…

Behaviour Patterns:	Longing for what is 'missing' creates self-absorption and envy. Being 'special' increases separation and feelings of not belonging. Searching feelings for inner truth results in withdrawal and emotional inner dramas in which slights and hurts are turned over and over, creating resentment and hostility towards others and thus further separation. Greater separation creates feelings of even less significance. Hatred of the 'flawed' self, combined with envy of others who seem happier, causes touchiness, until eventually their negativity and storminess drives others away…

THIS ULTIMATELY BRINGS ABOUT THEIR DEEPEST FEAR…

Deepest Fear:	Of not belonging, having little personal significance and being rejected

The Five

The Inner World of the Five

Aspect of Essence lost sight of:	Omniscience - The ALL Knowing
View of the World:	The world is overwhelming and demanding.
Fundamental unconscious need:	To feel capable of dealing with the world and its demands.
Erroneous Beliefs:	The world demands too much and gives too little. I must gain all knowledge and understand everything if I am to survive and be safe.
Deepest Fear:	Of being helpless and incapable of dealing adequately with the world

The Self–Defeating Pattern

Striving to Avoid:	Being helpless and incapable of dealing adequately with the world…

CREATED THE DRIVING DESIRE…

Driving Desires:	To gain knowledge and information; to master something in order to feel competent to deal with life's challenges; to avoid being intruded upon; to hold on to that which is necessary for survival - knowledge, time, space, privacy etc; to be self-sufficient and independent of others…

THE CONSEQUENCES OF WHICH ARE THAT…

Behaviour Patterns:	Fives seek privacy to protect themselves from intrusion and demands, and they focus their attention on thoughts and ideas rather than feelings. By detaching from emotions and people they isolate themselves. They think they can deal with their world by observing it and studying it in depth, but without engaging in it. By remaining in this 'preparation mode' they become disconnected from the world, often failing to develop social skills, neglecting physical needs and even appearance. This further isolates them and they feel even less confident in the outside world…

THIS ULTIMATELY BRINGS ABOUT THEIR DEEPEST FEAR…

Deepest Fear:	Of being helpless and incapable of dealing adequately with the world.

The Six

The Inner World of the Six

Aspect of Essence lost sight of:	Knowing (experienced as lack of Inner Knowing)
View of the World:	The world is dangerous and threatening
Fundamental unconscious need:	Need for safety and security
Erroneous Beliefs:	Nothing and nobody in this world can be trusted. To be safe and survive, I must seek security and be vigilant for threats to my security. Finding a way to belong will make me safe.
Deepest Fear:	Of being unsafe, without security, support or guidance.

The Self–Defeating Pattern

Striving to Avoid:	Being unsafe, without security, support or guidance…

CREATED THE DRIVING DESIRE…

Driving Desires:	To be safe and secure; to have support and guidance; to check for danger; to gain approval; to test others attitudes to them; to avoid punishment and disapproval; to overcome their fears; to gain reassurance that they belong and are secure; to know what is the right action; to be seen to be competent…

THE CONSEQUENCES OF WHICH ARE THAT…

Behaviour Patterns:	Sixes become questioning, doubting and suspicious, projecting negatively into the future for what can go wrong and how to deal with it. Seeking certainty in an uncertain, changing world leads to continual anxiety. With anxiety centred in the gut Sixes cannot hear their inner guidance so answers are sought from the mind and outside sources. The answers received are inconsistent, causing uncertainty and indecision, leading to more anxiety. Nothing feels solid and trustworthy and …

THIS ULTIMATELY BRINGS ABOUT THEIR DEEPEST FEAR…

Deepest Fear:	Of being unsafe, without security, support or guidance.

The Seven

The Inner World of the Seven

Aspect of Essence lost sight of:	Causeless Joy
View of the World:	The world does not have enough joy, happiness and fun
Fundamental unconscious need:	To have complete freedom without limitation.
Erroneous Beliefs:	I have to provide my own happiness and fulfilment. It is somewhere 'out there'. If I experience everything I will find what I need to make me happy and joyous.
Deepest Fear:	Of being unable to avoid pain and deprivation.

The Self–Defeating Pattern

Striving to Avoid:	Being trapped and experiencing pain and deprivation…

CREATED THE DRIVING DESIRE...

Driving Desires:	To avoid limitations and maintain their freedom; be satisfied and have their needs fulfilled; to avoid emotional pain; to have fun; to avoid missing out on anything; to keep moving; to stay stimulated or occupied; to get whatever they want; to keep things 'up'…

THE CONSEQUENCES OF WHICH ARE THAT...

Behaviour Patterns:	Endless activity and distractions are used to avoid their negative inner feelings. The need to stay free and avoid negativity results in neglected personal relationships. Sevens jump impulsively from one experience to another 'consuming' their experiences but getting little satisfaction, so they need 'more'. There is endless planning with the belief that something better is just around the corner, so no experiences makes them content. Not finding what will make them fulfilled and happy, they get increasingly frustrated and dissatisfied, unfulfilled and lonely …

THIS ULTIMATELY BRINGS ABOUT THEIR DEEPEST FEAR...

Deepest Fear:	Of being unable to avoid pain and deprivation.

The Eight

The Inner World of the Eight

Aspect of Essence lost sight of:	Omnipotence
View of the World:	This is a hard and unjust world and only the strong survive.
Fundamental unconscious need:	To be invulnerable by gaining power and control.
Erroneous Beliefs:	The powerful take advantage of the weak and innocent, and betray them. I have to be tough and invulnerable in order to survive. I must gain power in order to prevail.
Deepest Fear:	Of being vulnerable and being harmed or controlled.

The Self–Defeating Pattern

Striving to Avoid:	Being vulnerable and being harmed or controlled…

CREATED THE DRIVING DESIRE...

Driving Desires:	To be strong and dominant; to be invulnerable; to gain power; to protect themselves and their own; to assert their strength over others; to be the decision maker; to dominate their environment; to get others to submit; to challenge themselves; to avoid weakness; …

THE CONSEQUENCES OF WHICH ARE THAT...

Behaviour Patterns:	They want closeness and love but equate that with being vulnerable, so they build a fortress around their heart, becoming strong and forceful and using power and control to protect their soft inner core. Confrontation is necessary to defend their position, leading to retaliation by others, and so even more aggression is required to protect self. This forces others away, leading to even less emotional freedom and further isolation, so they are now 'controlled' by their self-imposed fortress, from which they cannot escape for fear of being taken advantage of…

THIS ULTIMATELY BRINGS ABOUT THEIR DEEPEST FEAR...

Deepest Fear:	Of being vulnerable, harmed or controlled.

The Nine

The Inner World of the Nine

Aspect of Essence lost sight of:	Omnipresence
View of the World:	There is conflict here in this world that will damage my harmony and connection with others.
Fundamental unconscious need:	To have and maintain peace and harmony.
Erroneous Beliefs:	In order to survive, anger and conflict must be avoided. To maintain my connection with others things must be kept peaceful and I must not assert myself…
Deepest Fear:	Of disconnection, separation and loss (i.e. opposite to

The Self–Defeating Pattern

Striving to Avoid:	Disconnection, separation and loss…

CREATED THE DRIVING DESIRE...

Driving Desires:	To avoid anger and conflict; to have peace and harmony; to avoid 'rocking the boat'; to have inner equilibrium; to go with the flow; to maintain peaceable connection with others; to bring people together; to keep things as they are; to avoid allowing potential problems to disturb inner peace…

THE CONSEQUENCES OF WHICH ARE THAT...

Behaviour Patterns:	Nines avoid any situation or emotion that disturbs their 'inner peace', especially those with potential for conflict. Anger is feared and therefore suppressed. Emotions cannot be selectively suppressed; positive emotions are lost too so their world becomes grey and bland, making them feel disconnected to life. They become passively immovable when asked to act against their pursuit of 'pseudo' peace; others get angry causing further separation. Isolated from others in a greyscale world…

THIS ULTIMATELY BRINGS ABOUT THEIR DEEPEST FEAR...

Deepest Fear:	Of disconnection, separation and loss (i.e. opposite to oneness).

CHAPTER 6

Your Uniqueness

Nine Ways of Being

With only limited knowledge of the Enneagram, some people might dismiss the idea of there being only nine fundamental personality types, considering it as overly simplistic and rejecting what they view as 'labelling' or being 'put in a box'. And certainly, it is true there are already too many ways in which we label ourselves or others in our attempts to make sense of the world.

However, the Enneagram is certainly not one of these. It does not take away your own uniqueness or threaten your individuality by placing you in a box that can be categorised or easily referenced; in fact, the truth is quite the reverse. Each of us has unconsciously put ourselves in a 'box' of limiting thoughts, erroneous beliefs, and negative behaviour patterns that are both predictable and normal for our personality type. When the wisdom of the Enneagram is understood fully, it shows you the way to *get you out of the box that you have always been in* and guides you towards freedom.

No Labels

Those with only a little knowledge about the Enneagram can perceive it as restrictively one-dimensional and just another excuse to attach labels to human behaviour. When its knowledge is applied within such narrow parameters, we are, indeed, in danger of labelling both ourselves and others. But when understood properly, and used with compassion and discernment, far from placing us in boxes or assigning labels that limit our identity, the Enneagram frees us from the our own unconsciously self-imposed limitations and false identities.

Although the Enneagram teaches us about nine personality types, this does not mean that every other person who is the same number as you is just like you. If that were true, it would be like living in a world painted from a palette limited to only nine colours, which would make for a very bland and uninteresting place to live! However, it is true to say there are only *nine ways of being,* even though the expression of the personality and the resultant life experiences are unique to each individual.

Individuality is fundamental to the nature of human experience. Like individual, beautiful flowers, not one of us is the same as another; we are all unique – similar in many ways but different in so many others. This uniqueness is your bloom, yet it is not random because, like all flowers, your bloom originated from a single seed. This 'seed' is the numerical energy pattern your soul chose as its vehicle of consciousness in this life, and it determines how you see the world and how you react to it.

The Enneagram shows us that there are nine basic 'seeds' – nine core driving motivations. Your uniqueness was born out of one of these nine 'seeds,' but the way your flower has grown and the uniqueness expressed by your bloom is dependent on many other variables.

Unique ... but the Same

The choices made that determine life circumstances influence the way in which the individual nature of the personality type develops, and although we each have available to us every personality aspect of our type, we have not necessarily chosen to embody them all. Certain aspects of your personality type have come into being so that you had the resultant opportunities for growth, while other aspects may not have developed because they were not needed for the work to be done in this lifetime. The overall constituents of your personality, therefore, may not be exactly the same as those of another person of the same type; thus, their overall personality would show slight differences.

Imagine, for the sake of simplicity, that there were one hundred identifiable aspects or patterns typical of your type; we may see only ninety of these as the constituents of your personality. We may also see only ninety in another person of your type, but it is quite likely that they would not display the *same* ninety. Therefore, in some respects, you would seem to be quite different even though you are, in fact, the same core personality type. For example, if you were to compare twenty Ones, each would be their own unique selves, not quite like any other person in the world, and yet there would be core drives, needs and reactive behaviour that they all had in common.

Of course, no two people of the same type experience the same life. The way in which they were parented, for example, would be affected by the personality type of their parents/caretakers. For instance, a Five parent offers a very different sort of parenting from that offered by a One. For each individual, the environment of their young years provided them with unique challenges, as did the personality patterns of siblings and other close family members, the choices made in adulthood, the souls with whom relationships were shared – all of these and more influence the overall patterns of the personality.

Each of us is a mixture of positive and negative traits and that mix is largely a result of these many factors. The way our personality has developed is unique to us and the way we express the predictable patterns of our type is also unique; we are not at all identical to any other person of the same type as ourselves. However, no matter how different two people of the same type and their respective lives might appear on the surface, when examined more closely, we find that their attitudes to life are much the same, they experience the same sort of challenges, what they seek in life at a fundamental level is much the same, their reactions to challenging circumstances follow the same sort of patterns, what drives them both positively and negatively is the same, their emotional make-up is similar, and they have the same sort of problems in relationships. Each is very different from others of the same type but also the same.

Gender

The combination of gender and personality is also part of your uniqueness. Personality type affects the ways in which typical male or female behaviour might be expressed, and your gender affects the way your personality is expressed.

Men and women were never meant to have the same attributes or qualities; they were designed to complement each other, to form two distinct halves of a whole. Most of us have a fair understanding that there are certain qualities and behaviours identifiable as inherently masculine and others that are typically feminine. Masculine energy is naturally more assertive, strong and independent; it is also very often action oriented, single-minded and rational. Feminine energy, on the other hand, is emotionally open and sensitive; it is naturally more intuitive, receptive and nurturing of others.

When we come to study the patterns of behaviour commonly exhibited by each of the nine types, it quickly becomes clear that some types show an overriding bias towards what we understand as 'masculine behaviour' while others show more 'feminine behaviour'. As such, the male and the female of each of the types will express their personality patterns in differing ways. For example, the combination of masculine gender and a type that has strong, masculine energy might intensify the strong independent nature of that type, while the choice of a feminine gender may neutralise or soften the same energy, making its characteristics less extreme. (More about the differences between the male and female of each type will be explained in a later book.)

Interestingly, this combination of personality type and gender can also affect the expression of gender. For example, a woman with a personality type that has a more masculine type of energy (such as Eight) could be seen by others as 'unladylike' because her personality type hardens her soft femininity. Equally, a man with a personality type that has a softer, more emotionally sensitive energy to it (such as Two or Four) may be judged 'unmanly' because he is more sensitive and in touch with his emotions.

The Astrological Picture

Before you came into this life, your soul chose the position of the planets at the time of your birth to ensure that you would have certain specific personal characteristics. These astrological influences add to the individuality of your unique self by affecting the way in which you express your personality type and, although probably the most subtle personality variant, in some cases, this will have a noticeable effect on the 'flavour' of your personality. For example, being born under the sign of Pisces would soften some of the more abrasive aspects of the Eight personality and give greater sensitivity to others' feelings. In contrast, an Eight born as an Aries would be more forceful and pushy.

Nationality

National cultures can mould the personality in different ways. A British Six and a Chinese Six, for example, may appear to be very different because of the way in which their respective cultural society has affected the growth of their personality. Despite what might seem like differing external patterns of behaviour, however, the personality of both individuals has manifested out of the energy of the *number* six.

As bulbs emerge from their winter hibernation in springtime, the type of flower that appears is dictated by what type of bulb it has grown from, but the way it develops is dictated by its environment. The type of soil that it puts it roots into, the amount of sunlight and water it receives, the air temperature and wind speeds to which it is exposed – these are all factors in determining how the plant will grow and flower, but they do not dictate the *variety* of flower that will appear. Just like plants, the environmental factors of our world will dictate how we grow and develop but cannot affect the truth of our inner world. There are only nine types of 'bulb' but there are many ways that we develop and 'flower', and no two are ever identical.

The Swings of Behaviour

Every one of us has available to us all of the positive traits of our type. These are what allow our light to shine into the world; they are gifts that we have chosen to bring to the world. However, none of us is living solely through our positive traits –or as the Collective has said, 'Humans do not attain what humans would see as perfection.' – and just as our moods fluctuate, so does our behaviour.

From day to day, moment to moment, week to week, the way in which we react to our world and deal with the people in it – and the consequent behaviour that we display – can vary enormously. Within each personality type, there is a broad spectrum of behavioural traits, thinking patterns and reactions that may be displayed or experienced. These range from the very positive (the true gifts of that type) to the extremely negative (the low point of that type), and each of us will find ourselves fluctuating across this range, depending upon what we are faced with in each moment.

When we feel joyous, fulfilled, and at peace with ourselves, our vibration is high, our best qualities become available to us, and we function from a high level through our more positive traits. When we are upset or stressed, we react negatively to people or circumstances, some of our less-than-positive traits come to the fore, and our behaviour swings across the range to function at a lower level.

This swing of potential behaviour has such a big effect on the individual expression of personality type that, without proper understanding about this factor, we can often wonder how someone else whom we know to be the same type as ourselves can behave in ways so dissimilar from the ways in which we do. Perhaps they display positive behaviour that we never would, react badly to situations that we are able to deal with quite peacefully, or embark upon projects that we would never consider. Similarly, because of the fluctuations in our own behaviour, we can also appear to others as being a completely different person from day to day or even hour to hour!

Even though we can all fluctuate between our positive and negative traits, each of us essentially has a *centre of gravity* – a point on the behavioural scale of our personality type around which our behavioural swing is centred. The level at which this point sits is an expression of our 'normal' everyday state of being. Most people have a centre of gravity in the average personality range, making them feel OK – not really great but not really bad either. Some people, especially those who have done a great deal of personal development work, have a higher than average centre of gravity. Overall, their day-to-day existence will be less negative and more pleasurable than those who have more negative issues that have never been let go of and, in consequence, a lower than average centre of gravity.

An individual at the *high-functioning* level deals with their world from a place of peace and equanimity. They have a strong, confident centre, are very balanced and clear about who they are, and know what they need to be doing in order to fulfil their true purpose. Being free from old issues, they have few 'buttons' that can be pushed and live most of the time without negative emotional reactions. Should a situation upset their inner balance, they understand their own reactions, take responsibility for why they feel this way, and move back into a balanced state relatively quickly.

At the opposite end of the spectrum, someone at the *low-functioning* level experiences a great deal of negativity. They feel blocked, cheated out of the good things in life, or experience really bad feelings about themselves and others. They respond to people and events in their world mostly from the negative traits of their type. Not being able to accept responsibility for their problems they will look outside of themselves for solutions, often blaming others, or life itself, for the way that they feel. Low-functioning types are usually unaware of their positive qualities and their potential, but even if they have this awareness, they feel unable to function happily.

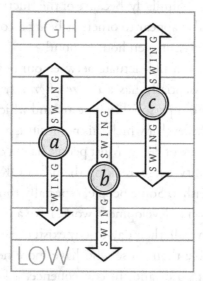

Figure 2: The swings of behaviour

Figure 2 shows the centre of gravity of three different people of the same type along the scale of *high functioning* to *low functioning*.

(a) This person is fairly average and, although not sufficiently high functioning to be able to access all of the positive traits of their type, does not drop into the most negative patterns of their type when life is difficult.

(b) This person will be unable to access all of the positive traits of their type and will go deeper into negativity when life circumstances are difficult. Much of the time, this person will be displaying behaviour that comes from the negative traits of their type.

(c) This person is functioning at a fairly high level so will be displaying mostly the positive traits of their type. When life is difficult, they will not sink very far into the negative traits of their type.

Quite clearly then, not everyone of the same type will be displaying the same range of behaviour. In fact, because the behaviour patterns are so different at the high-functioning and low-functioning levels of each of the types, two people of the same type can appear to be so dissimilar that someone without full understanding of the Enneagram would probably never make the connection that they were the same personality type! For example, high-functioning Threes display openness and authenticity and use their gifts to help and inspire others to be the best they can be. At the lower-functioning levels, however, Threes are self-serving and calculating in their pursuit of achievement and success, and they present a changeable, disingenuous image to others rather than being their true selves.

The purpose of the growth we achieve in life is to raise the frequency of our vibration to a higher level, so that our centre of gravity does not remain static throughout our lives. Those who embark on spiritual or personal growth work – and are able to *truly* let go of their past 'stuff' – will shift their centre of gravity up to a higher level and decrease the extent to which they swing back into their negative traits.

Some people of your type are functioning at a lower level than you are; some are functioning at a higher level; and you can be sure that you have not always been functioning at the same level throughout your life. You may become aware, as you read the description of your type, that you were at a lower-functioning level in your younger years and have since let go of some of the worst of your negative traits. Most of us make some progress to higher levels as we go through life, but anyone can, at times of great challenge, slip into the low point of their type for a while.

Wings

The circle of the Enneagram symbol represents the never-ending cycle of all things. The nine numbers are arranged evenly around this circle, providing each type with two neighbouring types, one on either side. Circles have no beginning and no end, no definitive points or corners, and no divisions or boundaries. So although we can refer to nine discrete or separate types located at definite points around the symbol (each of which has certain predictable patterns of thinking, feeling and behaving), there are, in fact, no definite boundaries where one type ends and the next one begins. *Trying to differentiate boundaries would be like attempting to establish where the air in one room ends and the air in the room next door begins!*

The Enneagram symbol should never be seen as rigid or static; the nine numbers are alive and are constantly interacting with each other. So a more accurate definition might be to describe the symbol as a ceaseless continuum of personality, with each of the nine numbers unavoidably affected by the energy that radiates from its two neighbours.

Although the 'edges' of your type are blurred, your core type *is* your fundamental blueprint; this was the 'filter' your soul chose for this lifetime, and it is clearly identifiable by the fundamental driving need which arose from it. However, the personality that has formed as a result of this driving need will have within its make-up some aspects of each of the two personality types located either side of it. So a One will show some aspects of both Nine and Two; a Four will show some aspects of both Three and Five, and so on. These neighbouring numbers are your *wings*, and the extent to which they influence the expression of your core type plays a key role in establishing your own uniqueness.

There is no such thing as a 'pure' personality type because the wings affect the overall pattern of behaviour of each person, adding an extra 'flavour' to the basic type. We all have access to both wings, but their impact on the personality will vary enormously between people of the same type.

When exploring the effect of your wings, consider the following points:

- Each wing may be almost all positive or almost all negative, or any variation in between.
- A wing may be quite large and have an enormous effect on the way the core personality traits are expressed, or it may be so small as to have little apparent effect.
- The effects of each wing are likely to fluctuate throughout your life. So you might find, for instance, that one of your wings was more to the fore in your younger years but now the other has become more dominant.
- The traits of a wing could be exhibited primarily within one arena of your life (e.g. at work) and barely at all in others (e.g. the family environment).

So there are clearly many ways that our wings affect the way we express our 'typeness'. Every Six, for example, will recognise a little of themselves in the type Five and the type Seven, but the amount of either positive or negative behaviour they are able to identify from those types will indicate which wing is more active during this phase of their life.

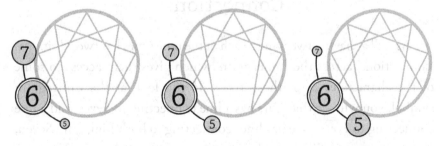

Figure 3: The wings of the Six

Figure 3 shows three states of 'Sixness,' any of which might be expressed by a Six at different times or in different areas of their life. Five is a private, withdrawal type, whereas Seven is an outgoing, interactive type, so a strong Five wing in the Six (c) will give a very different flavour from Sixness than a strong Seven wing (a). It might be that one Six was 'in Seven' (a) a lot of the time during their twenties and hence engaged in fun, outgoing activities, but now he or she spends more time 'in Five' (c), perhaps living a quieter, less social life engaged more often in reading or learning pursuits. A different Six might have always had both wings active but notices that she or he brings to the fore some of the traits of Five (a) at work, and is more 'in Seven' socially (c).

This mix of core type and wings is an essential part of the uniqueness of the individual and part of what makes us all our special selves.

An Important Note
The fundamental need of the core type influences the way a wing is expressed. In our example, even when the Six is expressing aspects of the Seven wing or Five wing, this behaviour will be driven by the fundamental need of their core type (the need for safety and security). The Six who has to make an important presentation at work might spend long hours researching information relating to the subject matter (a Five pattern). A Five would probably enjoy the research for the sake of the accumulation of knowledge, whereas the Six would do the research in order to feel more secure and less anxious about the presentation.

Connections

As well as having two wings, each of the nine types has two additional 'connections' across the Enneagram, which gives them access to some of the characteristics of those types. If you look at the Enneagram symbol, you will see that One has a line connecting to Seven and a line connecting to Four, Five has lines connecting to both Eight and Seven, Nine connects to Six and Three, and so on for each type. The part these connections play in the overall quality of the personality is quite different from the part the wings have. The wing is always present; it is a fundamental part of how we bring our personality type into the world, but the connecting points are places on the Enneagram wheel that we connect to only sometimes, and only in certain ways.

Making this connection is not a choice we make; we cannot choose to embody characteristics from our connecting points just because we want to. Nor is it of any value to try to imitate the attitudes or behaviour of those types in order to bring about growth and advancement in ourselves. True growth involves letting go of our negative traits rather than taking on extra traits, and in fact, moving to our connecting points just happens naturally as a response to the highs and the lows of our emotional state.

When we are feeling stressed or unhappy, we will often find ourselves 'going to' one or other of these points and reacting to our circumstances from some of the lower functioning traits of that type. Conversely, when we are feeling happy and at peace, the connection available to us is positive, and so we may 'go to' our connecting points, but this time display higher-functioning traits of those types.

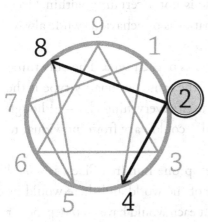

Figure 4:
The Connections of the Two

For example, figure 4 shows the Two's connections to both Four and Eight. When at peace and unstressed, the Two might 'go to Four' to gain access to artistic or creative qualities for leisure pursuits, or perhaps tap into the highly sensitive, empathic qualities of high-functioning Four for his/her work. When Twos are feeling hurt or unhappy, they may 'go to Four' negatively, feeling that no one understands their plight so they feel hard done by and very sorry for themselves.

The positive connection to Eight gives personal power to a Two and, quite possibly, there might also be a desire to help other people to empower themselves. Twos are likely to 'go to Eight' negatively when there is some injustice around them – either injustice towards themselves (especially with regard to feeling misjudged or unappreciated by others) or towards someone they care about – and as a result, they can easily become defensive and aggressively angry.

The Same ... but Different

Your view of the world and the subsequent sensitivities that are present within you are unique to your type and produce certain underlying perceptions of your world. All external behaviour flows from this core energy, spiralling upwards until it becomes detectable to others, but there are no rigid absolutes in behaviour. Each of the types has personality patterns in common, but it does not mean that all Fives, for example, will follow exactly the same pattern and display the same specific behavioural characteristics. If too much emphasis is placed on these external behaviour patterns, then the Enneagram loses its power to bring about change. To suggest that all Fives are withdrawn eccentrics because of their need to hoard what they see as being scarce, is to miss the mark completely. Many Fives will exhibit an exaggerated form of detachment, but this behaviour alone is not a certainty within Fives. Others will follow slightly different patterns of behaviour while always retaining their need to acquire knowledge.

There are no absolutes to the patterns of each type. The only thing that remains constant in all people of the same personality type is the underlying vibration of the number itself; everything else – although likely to follow the patterns described – could vary from individual to individual.

If, for example, you were to line up one hundred Sixes, it would be clear that each had a similar view of the world and there would be obvious parallels in their behaviour. Yet each would have an independent identity and a unique way of expressing their inner need for safety and security. Equally, if you heard a group of Nines talking about their lives, it would soon become evident that they had each formed similar limiting belief patterns; in fact, their lives may even have taken similar paths, but no of two of them would be identical.

DISCOVERING
YOUR NUMBER

CHAPTER 7

What Type Am I?

Take Time to Find Your Type

When people begin to take an interest in the Enneagram, the first thing they usually want to know is 'What type am I?' So perhaps this is the first section that you have turned to and may be hoping for a quick route to finding your type. You may be hoping that reading all the types will not be necessary, so you find yourself tempted to flick through the information about the types looking for something that looks familiar.

It can be tempting to read a little, focus on some small detail, and immediately say, 'I do that. This must be my type', and then go on to read only that type and ignore the rest. The important point to be aware of is that *similar patterns of behaviour can be observed in more than one type.* However, unless the unconscious needs and belief patterns that are driving the behaviour are understood, making a decision about type based only on outwardly displayed behaviour can cause confusion at best and lead to mistyping at worst.

There are many examples of the same or similar behaviour being displayed by more than one type. Here are just a few:

- Ones and Sixes both get anxious and tense.
- Fours and Nines can both be dreamers.

- Threes and Eights are often very successful in what they do.
- Twos and Fours care a great deal what others think about them.
- Fives and Eights are quite independent of the good opinion of others.
- Ones, Fives, Sevens and Eights are all independent types.
- Threes, Fives and Sevens all detach from their emotions.

In each case, the behaviour can appear to be much the same; however, we can see from the table below that what is underneath, driving the behaviour, is quite different. Each of the types has a deep, unconscious need that acts as the inner drive behind *all* their negative behaviour patterns.[1]

What Drives the Nine Types?

The patterns of the One are driven by the need for perfection.
The patterns of the Two are driven by the need to be loved and wanted.
The patterns of the Three are driven by the need to be successful.
The patterns of the Four are driven by the need to know and be their true selves.
The patterns of the Five are driven by the need to acquire knowledge.
The patterns of the Six are driven by the need for security.
The patterns of the Seven are driven by the need for freedom.
The patterns of the Eight are driven by the need to be invulnerable.
The patterns of the Nine are driven by the need for peace and harmony.

From this, we can now distinguish between types that appear to behave in the same way. For example, we can see that the worry and anxiety experienced by a Six is driven by the fears they experience because of their need for security, whereas when a One gets anxious, their worries will be concerned with getting things right or doing a job perfectly. Both are worriers, but the reasons for the worrying are different because what drives their reactions is different.

---

[1] See Chapter 3 'Unravelling Your Inner World' for more detail.

Similarly, both Threes and Eights can be real achievers in business and make a lot of money, but the underlying drive is different. To the Three, the possession of material wealth indicates success to the world, yet for the Eight, the amassing of wealth is not about having money and the associated material possessions; it is about gaining sufficient power so that they can feel invulnerable.

If you believe you already know your type, stay open to the possibility that you could just be another type. It is not uncommon for people to believe for years that they are one type only to discover, with deeper, more accurate information, that they are, in fact, a different type. Even if you are sure, do consider the basis upon which you have determined your type, for some methods are beset with potential for mistyping. Perhaps you used a questionnaire? Incorrect results are obtained by at least 30 per cent of those who use questionnaires. (In fact, Veronica is a Two but mostly comes out as a Seven or an Eight from questionnaires.) Or perhaps someone else determined your type? The truth is no one else can truly know your type, even people who know you well, because only *you* know your inner world and deepest needs. You are the only person who can accurately assess your type.

The best way of being sure of your type is to experience the Enneagram in action via an in-depth course that teaches a three-dimensional sense of the energy and expression of each personality and their underlying needs. This facilitates accurate typing; however, a detailed treatise, such as you find in this book, gives the flavour of each type, albeit a two-dimensional one, from which you will almost certainly find your type. Read all of the types and get the *complete* picture before you make up your mind.

The Complete Picture

A very important reason for studying the information about *all* of the types is that knowing your core type does not give the complete picture. Each of the types has connections to four other types – these are the two wings and the two connections across the circle – and as a result, each will display some of the traits of these other types. For example, a Five has some traits of the Four as well as the Six – the wings of the Five – and at times will also display some traits of the Eight and the Seven – the Five's connections across the circle.

One of the best ways of being sure that you have typed yourself correctly is to get clear about your wings *and* your connections, and then check that the whole number 'jigsaw' fits together to form the complete picture of your personality.

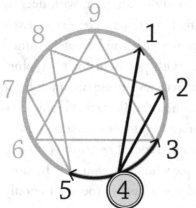

Figure 5: The Four jigsaw

Let us look at an example. Suppose you decide you are a personality type Four. As a Four, you will have both a Three wing and a Five wing. (Remember your wings can be a small or large part of your overall make-up and can be positive or negative.) You will also 'go to' both One and Two at times. So your 'personality jigsaw' will be composed of primarily type Four characteristics combined with some Three and some Five aspects, and sometimes you will display some aspects of both the One and the Two personality. (See figure 5.)

Suppose, however, that you type yourself as a Four but then realise that you do not seem to have all the pieces for this particular jigsaw. Perhaps you seem to have quite a lot of One in you but no Five or Three. However, you recognise some traits of Nine, and you also recognise aspects of Seven appearing within your behaviour patterns. If so, it is likely that you have mistyped and mistaken a strong connection for your core type. With these parts to your jigsaw, you might be a One. (See figure 6.)

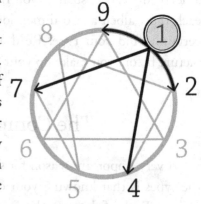

Figure 6: The One jigsaw

The Enneagram has the potential to radically alter the way your life unfolds. However, mistyping renders the Enneagram of no value at all. For this reason, if you are not absolutely sure, be patient rather than make a quick decision about your type. Take your time until the complete picture emerges. When all the pieces fall into place, you will find *all* aspects of yourself within your Enneagram jigsaw.

Points to Remember When Looking for Your Type

- **Remain mindful, open and patient,** resisting the temptation to 'land' on a type too soon. Make sure you look at each type as a whole without focusing on just a few traits. Remember that behaviour alone does not determine type.
- **Stay open.** Even if you already know your type, be open to the possibility that you might be another type. Some people can be convinced for years that they know their type, yet when they get the complete picture that comes with a proper understanding of the Enneagram, they realise they have been mistaken.
- **You only have one 'core' type and this remains the same throughout all of your life,** although you will find a little of yourself in more than one type (because each type has two wings and two connections).
- **Consider yourself when you were younger.** If you have done quite a lot of personal development work or are aware that you have changed and grown a lot as you have grown older, you will probably find it easier to type yourself if you think about the way you were when you were younger, especially in your early twenties.
- **Do not expect the whole of the description of your type to apply to you.** You are unique in the way you have developed and in the way your personality is expressed. However, if you have accurately found your type, you should expect to find that most of what you read rings true. And even if you have never displayed some of the extremes of negative behaviour described,

being perfectly honest with yourself, you may recognise the potential within you for such patterns to be present, if you were in a much lower functioning state.

- **The negative patterns of our own type are often difficult to accept.** In fact, if you read material that makes you feel uncomfortable, you are almost certainly reading about either your own type or about a strong wing! The most consistent sign that you have 'found yourself' is to experience what we refer to as the 'squirm factor' or have the 'Oh my God!' realisations as you read. In fact, if you can read what you think might be your type with only a detached interest and no uncomfortable feelings, you may have misidentified your type, and it is probably best to start again!

- **None of the types is better than the others**. All have wonderful positive qualities and strengths as well as negativities and weaknesses. Therefore, be brutally honest with yourself and be aware of the temptation to type yourself based on behaviour that you deem 'desirable' or 'acceptable'. You cannot become another type just because you think it would be better in some way to be that type.

- **It can be easier to type yourself from the negative aspects of type** - we always seem to know our worst points better than we know our best points! However, when you are clear about your own type, it is essential that you focus regularly on the positive points of your type, for this is *who you really are*.

Points to Remember When You Have Found Your Type

- **Focus on the positive.** It is important that you use what you read to reinforce the positive qualities that you already possess. Each type has a huge number of these positive qualities; they are already in place, waiting to be expressed and experienced. You do not have to become a different person in order to be joyous and fulfilled; all that is needed is to uncover the positivity that has always been there within your inner world and begin to do the growth work that will remove the 'lampshades' that obscure your light.

- **It is essential to understand that the negative patterns of your type are normal.** All of us are a mix of positive and negative traits, and as you identify the negative patterns you are running, you need to realise that these are normal for your type, that there is nothing wrong with you, and you do not need fixing. Certainly, growth work is needed for you to come into a better place, but there is nothing wrong with you.

- **Nothing is gained by focusing exclusively upon the negative aspects of your type**, except increased self-criticism and decreased self-worth, neither of which will facilitate effective growth into the positive. By truly acknowledging your positive aspects – and reading about your type's negative stuff with a light and optimistic heart (perhaps even laughing at some of it!) – you will give yourself the greatest opportunity to become the shining light that you are really are.

- **Do not fall into the trap of using your number as an excuse.** As you begin to recognise the negative patterns of your type, it can be tempting to use the Enneagram to justify your less-than-positive behaviour. Words or thoughts, such as 'Of course, I'm nitpicking and critical. I'm a One' or 'You better watch out. I'm an Eight, and that means I'm in charge', will just result in remaining stuck in low-functioning behaviour. Consider what words of a similar ilk (for your own type) you might have spoken as a justification for behaviour that is holding you back.

An Important Note about the Limitations of Language

The Enneagram, which is the matrix of consciousness and a vortex of pure energy, unravels and explains the complex fabric of emotions and behaviour patterns that make up the characteristics of the nine types. As authors, we are, of necessity, bound by the limitations of words with which to describe them. However, words can never do justice to the intricacies of human experience, nor can they fully describe the complexities of our patterns of behaviour. Therefore, it is important to be aware that the descriptions of the personality types that are offered here may not conjure up or define the exact picture that exists within every person of a given type. Moreover, the reader's interpretation of what is written can be biased by their own 'stuff' and their subjective understanding of the words used.

So we ask that the descriptions of the types be treated as a loose framework within which an overall picture can be formed, rather than being considered as rigid or definitive.

What the Types Say about Themselves

In order to give you a starting point to find your type, you may find it helpful to read the following. Remember not to make up your mind too quickly. Even if one of these descriptions sounds like you, only use that as an *indication*, not a definitive assessment of your type.

The One says,
'I am self-disciplined, hardworking, and organised. In whatever I am doing, I am dedicated to doing the most perfect job I can. I have a hard time leaving things as they are. If I'm doing something, I'm never really satisfied and keep on and on trying to make it even better.'

'Because I have very high standards and am highly responsible, the burden of responsibility to get things done right often falls on my shoulders. I can get really frustrated about the lax standards and irresponsibility displayed by so many other people.'

'I am honest to a fault, believe in justice and fairness, and am a person of strong conscience, although sometimes I know I can be overly strict and moralistic. I am inclined to give other people the benefit of my advice. After all, it's for their own good!'

'I tend to be a bit too serious and often get worried, uptight and stressed. For me, work usually comes before play and it's hard to relax if the job I'm doing isn't perfect. Most of the time, I am hard on myself and think that what I do is not good enough.'

'There seems to be a judge inside my head that constantly berates me about doing things better. I need to get everything right, and this can hold me back from launching myself into something new.'

'Although I can have fun, it's often difficult for me to be spontaneous, and I can feel resentful towards others for being so able to enjoy themselves in a light-hearted way that I can't.'

'I tend to be highly organised and like to maintain my own space in an orderly way. Being an extremely thorough person who makes sure things get done properly, I always try to bring some organisation and order to where it's needed.'

The Two says,
'I am an optimistic, caring sort of person and enjoy lots of interaction with all sorts of people. I tend to see the best in people, and I know that helping them see their good points enables them feel better about themselves.'

'I have a naturally trusting nature, and this, coupled with my tendency to see the good in people, can easily result in me being taken advantage of – emotionally, energetically, and even financially.'

'People often reveal deeply personal thoughts and feelings to me. I guess they feel accepted and understood around me. It often happens that they come to me with their emotional problems, and being a person who is easily moved to tears, I do not get uncomfortable when other people cry.'

'I am good at anticipating other people's needs and will happily go out of my way to do everything I can to help. However, although I try to hide it, I can feel very resentful if the time and effort I put in doing things for someone is not appreciated or valued enough.'

'I believe love is the most important part of life, and my closeness to people I care about is what makes my life feel good. I love doing things for people I care about; in fact, I enjoy being needed. However, my natural desire to be helpful is not always understood, which makes me feel hurt and rejected.'

'Because of my concern for others, I frequently get really involved with their lives. People or animals in distress affect me strongly and I tend to be a bit of a rescuer, yet asking another person to help *me* makes me feel awful – pathetic even.'

The Three says,
'I'm a busy sort of person and happiest when I have a goal in focus. I'm a self-starter and know how to motivate myself better than most people do. I feel adrift if I'm not working towards something. In fact, I have a

workaholic streak. There's rarely any space in my diary, and even my leisure time needs to be scheduled.'

'I'm pretty adaptable and know how to get on with people. If things aren't working with the people around me, I know how to mould myself, to change my behaviour in order to get them to respond positively.'

'I'm willing to do whatever it takes to be the best, and I have been willing to do whatever it takes to be seen to be doing well, even if it means bending the truth or cutting corners a little in order to achieve my goals.'

'I like the kudos and status I get from being seen to be successful and tend to identify myself with my achievements. Failure is difficult for me, even just being overshadowed by others; it makes me feel bad about myself.'

'I hate anything that prevents me from meeting my goals or targets. My feelings tend to get in the way of getting the job done, and I am adept at putting emotional stuff aside so that it does not slow me down. Unfortunately, life is so busy there is rarely time for reflection about my real feelings. I can, however, give a good demonstration of appropriate feelings if the situation calls for it.'

'When I am insecure, I can be rather aloof and cool with people. The truth is I am good at covering up my insecurities because it's important to me that I appear as if I have it all together. However, inwardly, I sometimes feel empty.'

The Four says,

'I am a sensitive, introspective person who feels things more than most people, and it often seems as if no one really understands me. Inwardly, I've secretly wanted people to notice my uniqueness, my sensitivity, the profound depth of my feelings.'

'I examine my inner feelings in depth, and the huge depth of feeling I experience helps me to be authentic. Finding myself and being true to my emotional needs have been extremely important motivations for me.'

'During most of my life, I've been a highly emotional person with strong changes of mood or volatile feelings. Negative feelings can easily overwhelm me, yet there have been times when I've secretively enjoyed being the melancholy one. For me, feelings are the reality of life.'

'My creativity and appreciation of beauty encourage me to want to surround myself with what I need to intensify my mood and reflect my feelings. Mood is actually very important to me. I have to be in the right mood to do things, and if I'm not, sometimes I just can't cope.'

'I often long for what's missing in my life. I want to find the ideal love or perfect circumstance that will make me feel complete in the future. It is difficult to live in the 'here and now,' which can seem so mundane.'

'Although I have always wanted to fit in, I like to appear unique and interesting. In fact, if I'm honest, I would hate to be ordinary like most people are.'

'I have often felt an exquisite melancholy that makes me appreciate both the light and dark sides of life and often withdraw into my own private world. However, there are times when I just long for someone to rescue me, to take me away from all of the dreary mess of life.'

The Five says,
'I am an extremely private person and don't let many people know what I'm thinking and feeling. Few people know the real me. I prefer to be self-reliant and demand little from others.'

'I've tended to be absorbed in my own world and hate too many demands and intrusions; in fact, I find it difficult if I do not have sufficient time alone to recharge my batteries. Although I have been accused of being aloof, I am actually just thoughtful, dependable, and respectful.'

'I tend to watch and observe before I get involved or participate in things, and often, I just think about it rather than do it. Socially, I'm not good at small talk, but I can more than hold my own on any of the many subjects that I am knowledgeable about.'

'I am more knowledgeable than most people realise; in fact, sometimes I find myself looking down on others less intelligent than me. My mind is so intense and busy that it feels like it's working at a million miles a minute. However, I keep most of it to myself. Other people would think I was crazy if they knew what I was really thinking most of the time.'

'I am extremely curious and enjoy investigating why things are the way they are – even obvious things are not really so obvious when you really look at them. I know a lot about a lot of things, and in a few areas, I consider myself to be an expert.'

'When it comes to social situations, I like to know in advance what's expected of me and plan in my mind how it will go. After the event, I unpack and relive the interaction and the emotions from which I had detached from at the time.'

The Six says,
'I am a person that others can rely on to do a good job. Knowing I am responsible and dependable, it's important to me that others see me this way. Most important, I need to know I've done a good job and the right thing. I'm not at ease if I'm in the spotlight so I tend to be happier working away in the background.'

'Anxiety seems to be my middle name. I tend to worry about the outcome of most things, although I can be very clear thinking and level-headed in a crisis. Then I know just what practical sort of help is needed and just get on with it.'

'Making decisions can be fraught with questioning and worrying for me, so I often avoid making the decision and wait to see what turns up. When I do make up my mind, I often question my own decision. However, decision making may be agonising, but I certainly don't want anyone else making important decisions for me!'

'I seem to have an inbuilt detector for problems and am aware of potential problems that others just don't think about. I tend to suss out all the different outcomes of a situation in order to work out how to deal with the worst thing that could happen. It just makes sense to me because you never know what might happen. My tendency to take precautions does mean I am sometimes overly cautious, but 'better safe than sorry' is definitely true for me.'

'I think rules are necessary and important to maintain stability in life, although I don't always follow them!'

'I can be really sceptical, even cynical, about all kinds of things, including people. Other people need to prove themselves to me before I trust them, and I find myself suspicious of others' motives and intentions.'

The Seven says,
'I am an optimistic person and I love life to be stimulating and upbeat. Life is an adventure, and I believe things should be fun. My attention focuses on what is interesting, new, or pleasurable. I tend to spend more money than I should, but isn't life meant to be fun?'

'Coming up with new ideas and getting people excited about them has been one of my major strengths. I am always imagining positive, future possibilities. In fact, planning can often be more enjoyable than the actual doing.'

'It is important to me to have lots of variety in my life; routine and a quiet life bore me stiff. I don't want life passing me by. I hate having my options limited, and people who try to put limits on me can make me angry.'

'I hate being on my own with nothing to do, and when I'm with others I'm often the life and soul of the party. Being unable to slow down has been one of my major problems. When I do have to slow down, I tend to need distractions to stop me feeling restless and bored.'

'People who are depressed, unhappy or stuck bring me down so I try to avoid them. I want to keep things up and happy, so when other people start getting down or emotionally demanding, either I have to escape or I suggest fun things to do that will cheer them up. I can put a positive spin on almost everything, even painful situations.'

'I seem to have great vision for things and I am highly imaginative. I'm good at the big picture – not so much the little details. It's more enjoyable for me to brainstorm a lot of new ideas than to get involved with implementing them.'

'One of my main problems is that I am easily distracted and can get too scattered because my mind is always busy and chattering. It often seems as if I'm thinking of ten things at once.'

The Eight says,
'I am an independent, self-assertive sort of person, and I tend to hit life head on. Other people sometimes find me too direct, but I believe you should tell it how it is and you can't make a difference if you pussyfoot around. I think I can be intimidating sometimes, but really, I'm just a softie underneath.'

'I love a challenge and enjoy beating the odds. I feel most alive doing what others think is impossible. My energy often rubs off on others and challenges them to do more than they think they can, but some people just see me as too pushy and powerful.'

'I believe you can overcome most things with strength of will. Being a decisive, courageous person, I tend to have little patience with indecisiveness or weakness. You have to be tough to survive in this world. Weakness just invites trouble. This is a tough world we live in.'

'My sense of humour can be rather earthy, although I think most people are too prissy and thin-skinned. I don't believe in pulling punches. I say it like it is; people need to hear the truth, not the bullshit.'

'I like to take charge in most situations. I don't follow anyone else's rules, and no one is going to tell me what to do. I expect those around me to be loyal and to treat me with respect. Those who betray me had better watch out.'

'When my anger comes up, I can get in a towering rage and it can flatten most people if they are in the way. I don't really understand why so many people have a problem with anger. It clears the air and fires me up to get on with the next thing.'

The Nine says,
'I am an accepting sort of person and others generally see me as good company and easy to be around. People tend to appreciate my ability to see many different sides of an issue; things are rarely black and white to me. I am a good listener and tend to have a calming effect on others due to my inherent laid-back nature.'

'Most people get themselves worked up too easily; I'm much more even keeled. When troubles start getting to me, I usually tune them out. No matter how bad things get, I tend to maintain a sense of inner calm. You've got to take what life brings. There's not much you can do about it anyway, and most things sort themselves out in the end.'

'My accommodating and easygoing nature does mean that my needs and desires often get ignored or overlooked. Mostly I'm OK with this; however, sometimes it makes me annoyed and frustrated inside, although I rarely show it.'

'I value a peaceful and harmonious lifestyle and like to keep things steady. It helps me to have structures and routines that stay predictable and familiar. If I get pressured to be more decisive or to change, I just dig my heels in and get on my way. I can be quite stubborn if, rather than asking, someone tries to tell me what to do.'

'I would rather give someone their way than create a scene. It's my opinion that confrontation doesn't generally solve anything; it just creates pain and discomfort. I rarely get openly angry; if anger comes up, it gets pushed down again.'

'I don't seem to get the real highs and lows that others have. I've tried to keep my inner and outer world peaceful, stable and steady, but I do wonder if there shouldn't be more 'juice' in life.'

THE NINE TYPES

CHAPTER 8

The One

At their best, Ones are

----

*responsible discerning conscientious hard-working
orderly honourable objective principled consistent tolerant
reforming ethical idealistic productive fair wise honest
self-disciplined appropriate crusading*

Ones are the world's natural organisers, people who try to bring order where they see chaos and improve what they feel is not good enough. Highly industrious and reliable, Ones always give of their best and work hard at whatever they do. At work, the One is likely to be the first one in the office and the last one to leave at night, and is someone who makes sure everything is done right and things are finished. At home, Ones are diligent and dutiful in the carrying out of household tasks, creating order and cleanliness. They tend to live by the philosophy of 'There's a place for everything and everything should be in its place' and make a point of keeping their possessions in good order.

They are great list makers who plan carefully, check everything, and always make sure everything on the list is finished. Other people frequently end up relying on Ones, because they are extremely responsible and trustworthy people who have a great eye for detail and notice things that need doing which others have missed. Ones can always be relied

THE ENNEAGRAM: PATHWAYS TO HAPPINESS

upon to do a proper job; in fact, if you want something done properly, it's usually best to ask the One in your life!

There is often a tidy, scrubbed-clean quality about the physical appearance of Ones as well as in their living environment. Many Ones can appear overly serious and find it hard to let their hair down, yet this is just because they are sincerely trying to do the right thing. They think things out carefully before acting so they seem to be in their heads a great deal, but contrary to appearances, they are, in fact, people of strong instincts and great passion.

Being highly principled people of strong convictions, Ones really want to make a difference – to you, to their environment, even to the world. Many get involved in good works, and their idealism can lead them to fight strongly for causes they believe in; in fact, a great many Ones feel as if they have a mission to put the world to rights, with the result that reform movements are frequently led by Ones. They are the improvers and crusaders of the Enneagram who will do whatever is necessary for the greater good and may even make great personal sacrifices for their belief in what is right. Throughout history, there have been many highly principled Ones who have sacrificed easy, comfortable lives for what they feel is a higher calling and gone on to achieve amazing things. For example, Mahatma Gandhi left behind his family and a successful career as a lawyer to fight for social change in India. His idealism inspired millions, resulting in independence for India and movements for civil rights and freedom across the world.

Even Ones living ordinary lives will generally be leaders not followers, people who are prepared to stand alone, against others where necessary, and to follow their own beliefs and consciences.

Ones are enthusiastic communicators who enjoy imparting their wisdom to those that will listen and greatly desire to help other people improve their lives. Their honest and ethical natures lead them to always try to be fair in their dealing with others, and they are great believers in justice. There are many Ones in the field of law; they make very effective advocates and high-functioning Ones make excellent judges, being fair, balanced and wise as well as believing in the dispensing of appropriate punishment or proper reward.

THE ENNEAGRAM: PATHWAYS TO HAPPINESS

High principles, orderliness and self-discipline are a fundamental part of the make-up of all Ones and give them extraordinary abilities to organise themselves and others. Yet these virtuous qualities are the very traits that cause all but the most highly functioning Ones difficulty, conflict and pain. They view themselves and their world from self-imposed, impossibly high standards, standards that are so high that nothing and no one, least of all themselves, can ever attain them. Hence, they become overly controlled and controlling, perfectionist, critical and judgemental.

The One in Childhood

When the soul 'separates' itself from the All That Is and comes into life as a One, the quality of Divine Essence from which the young child experiences a deep loss of connection is **The Perfection of All Things.**[2] This creates the intrinsic sensitivity of the One, and it is through the filter of this sensitivity that the young child then experiences the world and develops ways of coping with what is experienced.Each small child seeks to find and attain that which seems to be unavailable to them in order that they might survive and get their needs met. The young One therefore seeks perfection within themselves as well as in the world. Drawing the conclusion that they themselves must be 'imperfect,' and therefore not intrinsically acceptable and loveable as they are, the young One then begins to take on these childhood beliefs:

'I must earn love by being good and perfect.'
'If I am wrong, I am imperfect; therefore, I must strive to be right.'
'There is imperfection and chaos all around
me, so I must strive to create order.'

---

[2]   See chapter 3, 'Unravelling Your Inner World: The Early Years.'

The resultant behaviour patterns that spiral out of these untrue beliefs are unconsciously designed to try to avoid being wrong or defective in any way.

Children generally learn about what is right or wrong and what is good or bad, from the discipline imposed by one or both parents, commonly the father figure. The sensitivity that is part of the inherent Oneness of this child caused him or her to feel insufficiently parented with regard to standards and discipline. (There may, in fact, have actually been an ineffectual or absent father figure.)[3]

Believing that they are not good or perfect enough to be really worthy of unconditional love, Ones need to find a standard of good and perfect behaviour to look to and follow. With this apparently not available, young Ones unconsciously decide to 'parent' themselves, to set their own high standards, and to 'punish' themselves when they do not meet these standards.

They always feel they have to surpass these standards so that they will not be punished and will therefore be worthy of love. As a result, young Ones find it impossibly hard to experience the fun and freedom of childhood because they have to continually restrain and police themselves in order to follow these self-imposed rules. Consequently, most young Ones feel that childhood is short; they grow up early, becoming serious and earnest, and frequently take on a role of responsibility within the family at a very young age.

The Uncompromising Perfectionist One

Most of the negative behaviour displayed by adult Ones comes about because they are still unconsciously striving to be the 'good boy' or 'good girl' in order to earn the reward of being accepted and loved, and to avoid punishment. That means they have to always be good and perfect; everything they do and everything about themselves is judged

---

[3]   The childhood circumstances do not create the personality; they were chosen by the soul so that the One personality patterns would fully develop.

by their own high standards, and anything that is judged to be less than perfect is viewed as bad or wrong.

But who makes the judgement? They do. Or rather, their inner critic does. All of us sometimes experience an inner voice telling us that what we are doing is wrong or what we are about to embark on is a bad idea, but the One lives every minute with a relentless inner critic that punishes them for anything that falls short of their self-imposed standards of perfection. Of course, the only way the One can escape the punishment of being harshly criticised by that inner judge is to strive to be perfect and to create or seek perfection in the world around them. So Ones are the perfectionists of the world, people who desire to put right what is wrong, to correct what they see as imperfection, and to create order where they see disorder.

This is a very admirable quality that leads the One towards very high standards in all that they do, but the sad thing is they can *never* reach the required standards of perfection because these standards are so impossibly high. The One's continual inner critic tells them that nothing about themselves, or anything that they do, is good enough, which results in most Ones having problems with guilt and low self-worth.

For Ones to consider:
- *How many times in a twenty-four-hour period do you feel you have not reached the standard of perfection that you should?*
- *What standards are you measuring yourself against?*
- *How often does your inner critic tell you what you ought to, must or should do?*
- *How do you feel if you then fail to do it?*

Control and Anger

Ones are 'should ought must' people. They are continually striving to appease that inner judge and critic, telling themselves that they *should* to be that sort of person, that they *ought* to eat that particular food, that they *shouldn't* feel that way, that they *must* do this better, that they *ought* to get up earlier, on and on endlessly. And since Ones inevitably fall short of perfection, they experience an enormous amount of frustration and anger.

In order to have internal order and consistency (i.e. 'perfection'), the One feels it necessary to maintain control over their own behaviour and their strong emotions, and it is especially essential to the One to maintain control of unacceptable emotions like anger. An angry person is not a 'good' person, so the One is even more self-critical as a result of having these 'bad' feelings and tries to contain the anger. This containment sets up a great deal of tension within the One; there is consequently an air of rigidity about most Ones and they commonly display tension habits, such as foot tapping, hair twiddling, or hand wringing.

As a result of this controlling aspect, the average One can come over as too serious, rigid, or prissy, even as cold and unfeeling or uptight socially. In fact, other people often get the feeling that they would like to see the One in their lives lighten up, have more fun, and be more of the playful child instead of the serious adult! Most people are just not aware of the internal conflict going on inside Ones, but the truth is they are a smouldering cauldron of strong passions and instincts, great desires and powerful feelings, all of which are judged and contained as the One tries to be 'good' or 'correct.' However, the containment can only work up to a point, so the anger can appear in sudden, aggressive outbursts, directed sometimes at themselves, often directed at inanimate objects or other people, but then just as suddenly, the One gets back control and it is contained again.

Anger is not the only strong feeling that the One tries to control. Ones rigorously scrutinise all of their natural impulses or instinctual desires because they fear that there is part of themselves that may, at any moment, go wildly out of control and be bad. Consequently, they feel it necessary to carefully weigh up the consequences of all their actions, unnecessarily denying themselves many of the harmless pleasures of life and resulting in a general lack of spontaneity. They often find it hard to relax socially and come over to others as self-conscious, buttoned-up people full of serious intensity.

For Ones to consider:
- *How do you judge yourself for experiencing anger?*
- *How does your anger come out? How does that then make you feel?*
- *How much does your control of self affect your spontaneity?*
- *What pleasures do you deny yourself?*

Inner Turmoil

Ones are prey to a whole host of emotions even though they rarely show their inner turmoil to the world at large. There is an internal war going on, with the 'good' part always battling with the 'bad' part, and because of those impossibly high standards, the One constantly feels as if this internal battle is being lost. As a consequence, Ones experience a great deal of guilt. There is the guilt about not being a good enough person, the guilt about not having achieved a higher enough standard in what they do, guilt about having bad emotions, guilt about losing control, guilt about their bodies, guilt about not eating the right food or getting enough exercise, guilt for taking time out for themselves, and on and on. This causes the One much pain and constantly eats away at their self-worth.

Anxiety is another emotion prevalent in the One. Because Ones get anxious a great deal, they can easily mistake themselves for Sixes, but the causes of the anxiety are rather different. The One's anxiety may be centred around whether they have remembered everything that they need to do so they are usually inveterate list makers. Decision making is also an anxious and, consequently, a stressful thing for a One, and they can get anxious when making choices about almost anything: which film to watch, which holiday to chose, which garment to wear for a night out, or even what to have for dinner. This sort of anxiety comes about because they fear that the choice made might not bring them the perfect experience and another choice might have been more perfect.

There is also a lot of anxiety in the One when they are considering tackling a new activity. Because of the need to be perfect, they often fear that they may not be able to do this new thing to a high enough standard, and when Ones feel like this, it is quite likely that they will hold themselves back from participating. Then, because this procrastination has led to a missed opportunity, they experience even more turmoil as they get angry with themselves for having missed out.

Another cause of inner turmoil is the difficulty in completing anything because it has to be perfect. And when there is a deadline to be adhered to, this is likely to be a particular problem. Whatever the One is doing, they are never satisfied with what they have done, so it never feels finished. There is always the feeling that, if a little more time was spent on it, it would be perfect. But it never is, so now, not only is the One dissatisfied, or frustrated and angry with themselves, but starts to get worried that this will not be completed in time and the deadline will be missed. And of course, if it is missed, there will be the guilt ... you get the picture.

For Ones to consider:
- *What things about yourself make you feel guilty?*
- *How hard is it to complete any task to your standards of perfection?*
- *How has your need to do things perfectly stopped you from going ahead and attempting things you were unsure of?*
- *How have you felt about yourself afterwards, when you realised what you consequently missed?*

Interaction with the One

The One's drive to create order applies to their outer as well as their inner world, and from their high standards, what they seem to see around them is sloppy, disorganised and irresponsible. And that includes you and me! Their shoulds, oughts and musts are just as rigorously applied to other people as they are to themselves and can be expressed as nitpicking instruction or scolding criticism. The One will be free with their advice, and you ought to listen because it's for your own benefit; they always believe they are right. Ones always have to be 'right' (for if they were not right, how could they ever be perfect?) The infuriating thing is that they so often are right! There is great wisdom in the One, and even when they are at their most infuriating, it is always worth listening to their advice.

They are people who are honest to a fault and will tell you the truth even if it hurts. The One is likely to instruct other people in any arena of life, from their appearance to how they should drive; from the correct way to write a report to the food that they should eat. Unfortunately, Ones see themselves as responsible adults surrounded by irresponsible children so their speaking style is often experienced by others as critical, patronising or arrogant. Yet, from the One's perspective, all this is well intentioned, designed to improve others, to make them better people, or to improve their lives. The One sincerely wishes to improve you for your own benefit and is simply offering sensible, logical advice! However, their frustration often causes them to come over with irritation and impatience and they frequently find it difficult to put over their point of view in a calm, kind way that others find acceptable. So even though average Ones might be full of very wise, sensible ideas, they can get other people's backs up so easily that their suggestions often fall on stony ground.

What average Ones fail to realise is that their way is not necessarily the only way and there are as many right ways as there are people. Their belief that they are right not only makes them inflexible, but they miss out on the perfection in each and every moment because they are always inclined to view the world and the people in it as less than perfect.

Being naturally responsible people who need to have order around them *and* feeling nothing is acceptable unless it's done perfectly results in Ones frequently feeling burdened by responsibility. From their perspective, other people just don't pull their weight, and even when they do get around to doing those jobs, they fail to do things properly. So as far as the One is concerned, they might just as well do it themselves.

This would be fine if it was all done with good grace, but Ones actually get fed up with being the 'only responsible adult' around and then, failing to realise that most of this is of their own making, end up feeling weighed down and resentful. The One then makes sure you know how they are feeling; there might be pursed lips and pointed sighs accompanied by muttered comments, such as 'Why can't anyone else put things away properly?' or outright complaints expressed with critical irritability. Again, the One needs to realise that other people are entitled to have different standards, and that, in fact, not everyone wants the books arranged alphabetically!

For Ones to consider:

- *How often do you speak to those around you with a 'parent-to-child' attitude? (Perhaps you should ask them!)*
- *Do others respond positively to you when you speak in this way? Is it, perhaps, a counterproductive way of communicating?*
- *When you feel it incumbent upon you to make up for the irresponsibility or sloppiness of others, how does it make you feel towards them?*
- *When you are critical of others, does that really make you feel good? Or irritated and/or resentful?*
- *If you were to focus on, and even to verbalise, what is good or positive about those around you, how different might you feel? And how might that make them feel?*

Body Awareness

Striving all the time for absolute perfection, self-control and self-discipline, an important self-improvement project for many Ones is the state of their health and their bodies. Regular exercise is often part of the One's normal routine and they tend to very aware of exactly what they are putting into their bodies; most Ones, in fact, routinely monitor how balanced each day's eating has been. Many follow strict regimes of vitamin supplements or take up 'super healthy' diets, such as macrobiotics, vegetarian, or vegan, and in more rigid Ones, it's not uncommon to find fasting or purging used as a 'punishment' should the One's diet fall by the wayside.

They can become quite obsessed with health matters and will often lecture others about exercise or how to look after their diet, becoming frustrated and perhaps judgemental or sharply dismissive if their advice is not heeded. After all, as far as the One is concerned, sticking to a healthy regime is just a matter of self-discipline, so why doesn't everyone do it?

Always being scrupulously clean, of course, is an absolute must for perfectionist Ones, and showers more than once a day are not uncommon. You just won't come cross a One with body odour, and clothes are likely to be promptly changed should even the slightest mark appear.

Sadly, a great many Ones have grown up with negative issues about their bodies and their bodily functions. Because of the need for perfection and absolute cleanliness, for these Ones the body is viewed as a messy affair, something to be ashamed of. This shows itself in some Ones as an extreme modesty, while in others, it may manifest as sexual prudery.

Time, Work and Play

Ones are practical, action-orientated people who work hard to live a good life and who want to do something worthwhile and useful with their time. They feel as if the time available to them is limited so every minute has to be used to improve themselves or their lives and should not be wasted. Many Ones regularly time how long they take to do things and try to find ways to use less time in completing that activity; for example, Ones might time how long the journey to work takes and then try out all the different possible routes, timed down to the minute, in order to select the most time efficient one. Another timing obsession common to most Ones is regarding the amount of sleep they get. When getting into bed, they work out how many hours of sleep is possible, and when they wake, they check out how many they have actually had.

Finding it difficult to relax anyway, Ones just compound this tendency by feeling the need to justify having time off from purposeful activity. For Ones, work must come before play and time to relax has to be earned, so they will monitor themselves regarding how much they have achieved in a day, in order to decide whether or not they deserve relaxation time. Having fun for fun's sake feels not only frivolous but also purposeless to average Ones, so holidays with a One can be busy, tiring, or just plain stressful! The time away must be justified and will generally be considered worthwhile only if it involves activities that bring self-improvement in some way, perhaps improving their fitness, their minds, or their breadth of experience.

Taking the Moral High Ground

The need to do the right thing and to be 'good' gives Ones an inherent honesty and morality, and they judge themselves harshly for anything in their own behaviour that does not come up to these high standards.

However, as with all the types, the best traits of the One become some of the worst at the lower-functioning levels. At these very negative levels, the inner critic of the One can be so punishing that a way of escaping some of the consequent pain needs to be found. Lower-functioning Ones may need to find some escape valve, a way of letting go of the intense self-control, some aberrant behaviour that they can rationalise or justify to themselves. For example, the pillar of the community may secretly abuse his wife or the upstanding churchgoer might develop a gambling addiction.

Sinking even farther into their self-imposed dark place, it can become much too painful to focus on their multiple 'defects,' so the low-functioning One's critical anger and judgement can become almost wholly outwardly directed, becoming extremely judgemental and punishing. No longer able to look at their own behaviour, they view themselves as the good, moral, or right one and complain about the bad behaviour of others, particularly condemning behaviour displayed by others that they have repressed within themselves. For example, an elderly lady who has always been inhibited about her body might watch young people swimming in very skimpy costumes and condemn them vociferously for being loose and immoral, whilst secretly wishing she had been able to be so uninhibited.

For Ones to consider:
- *What do 'right' and 'wrong' mean?*
- *Where do these right/wrong standards come from?*

Sadly, this degree of moral rigidity and condemnation is not uncommon in church circles. Even though Jesus Christ's teachings came totally from the loving, compassionate energy of Two, most organised religions have taken his teachings and turned them into doctrines that demonstrate much of the aspects of negative Oneness: the controlling, rigid rules regarding behaviour coupled with the threat of punishment or damnation.

If you have a One in your life

In order to facilitate improved interactions and feelings of compassion, it can be helpful to keep in mind what can be hard for the One:

- being endlessly at the mercy of the harshest of inner critics
- experiencing lack of self-worth and anger at self for not being good enough
- obsessing about what should be done and how it should be done, or what shouldn't be done
- beating self up for what has been done and what hasn't been done
- getting frustrated and angry because others aren't doing things properly
- feeling overburdened by too much responsibility
- feeling upset when others fail to appreciate how much effort has been made

- never being able to say 'enough is enough' and be satisfied with the way things are
- being tense, anxious, and taking things too seriously
- missing out on doing new things for fear of not being able to do them perfectly the first time

When not at their best, Ones can be

---

perfectionist judgmental inflexible controlling stubborn tense self-righteous nit-picking critical of self and others impersonal uncompromising overly serious opinionated resentful moralistic rigid condemning dogmatic

---

CHAPTER 9

The Two

At their best, Twos are

----

loving   warm   caring   nurturing   adaptable
generous-spirited   friendly   appreciative   perceptive   light-hearted
feisty   expressive   demonstrative   enthusiastic   encouraging
attentive   empathic   compassionate   joyous

Twos are the most people-orientated of all the types, for whom the main focuses of life are loving closeness with family and friends, helping others, and doing good. They are nurturing, home-loving types who enjoy creating a warm, inviting environment in which they can be surrounded by those they love. For the Two, loving and being loved is what happiness is about, and going out of their way to help others warms their hearts and makes life feel worthwhile. At the high-functioning level, Twos value and appreciate everything that is good in life with a light-hearted freshness that can have an almost childlike quality.

They are sociable, often extrovert people who naturally connect with everyone from the postman to the boss, readily striking up conversations with anyone they meet. For most people, being with average to high-functioning Twos is generally uplifting because they are expressive, fun-loving types who readily smile and laugh, and they have a wonderful way of making each person with whom they come into contact feel good. Being naturally interested in other people, and having a very thoughtful side to their nature, Twos will often notice, and be appreciative of, little positive things about people that others miss, readily offering compliments and enjoying giving others encouragement to see the best in themselves. In fact, with their positive outlook on life, Twos can usually find something good to say about the most difficult people and the most challenging of situations. They rarely hold grudges, and even when things get them down, it's not for long. They quickly bounce back, optimistically looking forward rather than back.

The warm, compassionate nature of the Two tends to draw people to them as bees around a honey pot. Many people feel the need for more love and attention than they generally receive, and the warm, inviting presence of the Two leads many to open up and become self-revealing; Twos give openly of themselves, and their willingness to show their own vulnerability encourages those they surround themselves with to do the same. Even those who are inclined to be private or closed can find themselves sharing their hopes, fears and vulnerabilities with a Two.

All Twos naturally reach out emotionally to others and are able to empathically divine what the other is feeling. They will readily drop everything to help those in need, responding with great compassion and empathy to other people's distress, often at the expense of their own needs. They have tender hearts and, being the world's natural rescuers, cannot refuse to give help where it is needed; many Twos end up surrounded by people or animals that they have rescued. Yet the caring nature of the Two is practical as well as compassionate. They are doers as well as carers, people who will work to make good things happen for other people, and should they themselves be unable to give the required help, they will almost certainly help find someone who can.

Beneath the kind, warm nature of the Two, however, is a feistiness that surprises many people who have only ever seen the softer side. They are much tougher than most people imagine, for there is a rod of steel in the back of the Two that gives them great courage in the face of adversity, an inner strength that enables them to push through problems and come out the other side with their natural optimism to the fore. And despite their desire to please others, if they are being pushed around or told what to do, this determined quality can become rebelliousness resulting in headstrong and wilful behaviour.

The tendency of the Two to be open and giving means that most are inclined to wear their hearts on their sleeves. They tend to be very trusting, even naïve, and because they are inclined to see only the best in other people, they mostly assume that other people will treat them with the openness, honesty and fairness that they always try to give to others. As a result, they can easily lack discernment in their interaction with people, and in their desire to be helpful, many Twos end up finding themselves taken advantage of emotionally, financially, or professionally.

The Two in Childhood

When the soul 'separates' itself from the All That Is and comes into life as a Two, the quality of Divine Essence from which the young child experiences a deep loss of connection is **The Eternal Presence of Unconditional Love.**[4] This creates the intrinsic sensitivity of the Two, and it is through the filter of this sensitivity that the young child then experiences the world and develops ways of coping with what is experienced.

Each small child seeks to find and attain that which seems to be unavailable to them in order that they might survive and get their needs met. The young Two draws the conclusion that love is not freely available within the world and they themselves are not intrinsically acceptable and loveable as they are. They also conclude that if they are to survive, they must seek love and be the sort of person who deserves love. The young Two then begins to take on these childhood beliefs:

'I am not worthy of love so love has to be earned.'
'If I help others and they need me I will be loved and wanted.'
'Good and worthy people do not have their own needs.'

---

4   See chapter 3, 'Unravelling Your Inner World: The Early Years.'

Twos grow up believing that they will not be loved just for being themselves, so the resultant behaviour patterns that spiral out of these untrue beliefs are unconsciously designed to get the love for which they hunger. They come to believe that being themselves is not enough, but if they can be the sort of good, helpful child that would deserve love, if they can do enough for others so that they are needed and valued, then maybe they will be loved. As a result, many young Twos find themselves establishing a nurturing and attentive role for themselves within the family, perhaps helping with household jobs or caring for siblings, ailing parents, or grandparents.[5]

As the young Two grows up believing that she or he is unlovable, negative feelings about self begin to develop. 'If I was good enough,' reasons the Two, 'love would be available to me. Therefore, I am not good enough; I'm not OK as I am.' So within the personality of the Two is not only an inner core of neediness driven by the deep hunger for love but also low self-worth. Their low sense of true worth means that Twos care enormously about what others think of them, and they try to boost their feelings about themselves by being someone that others perceive as a good and worthy person. Consequently, they go through their lives trying to find ways of 'earning' love, by being helpful and doing things to make other people happy so that others will want them and think well of them.

The Selfless, Self-Sacrificing Two

All Twos are natural givers and helpers. This is what warms their hearts and makes life feel worthwhile for them. But only those Twos who are really high functioning and have truly high self-esteem can give of themselves unconditionally, with no need to receive thanks or anything in return. The less-than-high-functioning Two is secretly, and sometimes unconsciously, looking for appreciation, for thanks for

---

[5] The childhood circumstances do not create the personality; they were chosen by the soul so that the Two personality patterns would fully develop.

their good deeds and their selfless giving. To Twos, your recognition and appreciation of all that they do, the praise and attention they receive because of their giving, is evidence that you like them, love them, and want them. Of course, we all like to be thanked for what we do, but Twos *need* it. The way other people respond to them is what defines them, and their sense of self-worth is so inextricably linked to the appreciation, approval and attention they get for what they do that, without a positive, appreciative response, they are likely to feel unwanted, hurt and unloved.

> **If you are a Two,** you may find this an extremely difficult aspect of yourself to acknowledge. Many Twos will vehemently deny this 'giving to get' behaviour at first, because they see themselves as the selfless giver who asks nothing. Be really honest and examine the way you react to others when you feel unacknowledged, unappreciated, or undervalued for what you have done. You may not have been consciously aware that you wanted anything back for yourself, yet how often have you felt hurt or unloved when appreciation was not forthcoming?

Most of the negative behaviour displayed in adult Twos is driven by their inner neediness, yet even though they give so much of themselves to fulfil other people's needs, most Twos find it hard to acknowledge that they have any needs. Most do not admit their needs to themselves let alone feel able to express them openly to others.

The core belief system taken on in the Two's young years is that other people's needs take priority over one's own and that a truly worthy person asks nothing, just gives. Consequently, the self-image of the average Two is that of the selfless giver, the one who does not ask anything for themselves. To ask for one's own needs to be met, or to even acknowledge that there are such needs, would be 'selfish', therefore the Two rarely acknowledges or expresses their own needs. They unconsciously hope that, by putting their own needs aside yet doing all they can to fulfil other people's (often unspoken) needs they will be liked, valued and loved for what they do. In other words, *their* own (unspoken) needs will be met.

Dependency

Because the sense of self of the Two is validated only if others want them, need them, and rely upon them, they must find ways to make important roles for themselves within other people's lives. Basically, Twos need to be needed!

The Two's tendency to equate being needed with being wanted and loved frequently results in codependent relationships. They will try to anticipate your needs, priding themselves on meeting your needs without you having to ask, and even providing things to meet needs you didn't know you had! This pattern can be seen in both personal and work relationships.

The Two who always cooks the evening meal, sets the table beautifully, and has the meal ready just as his wife walks in the door after work is likely to pride himself on always being there for her and on being the only one who knows how to cook certain dishes just as she likes them. He will 'know' he is loved because she cannot do without him. ('If she needs me, she must want and love me.')

Within work situations, Twos take great pride in being the one on whom everyone relies and who knows personal details about everyone in the office. Being needed gives them feelings of self-importance that bolster their self-esteem, and they may work hard to be indispensible to those in important positions. This might mean creating an invaluable role for themselves by arriving extra early, being the one who can immediately lay a hand on the item the boss most needs, or always being the one who picks up the phone before it can interfere with the meeting.

The need to be needed can also result in Twos collecting needy people around them as 'projects' that they believe only they themselves can help. Experiencing what can be an unhealthy sense of self-importance in always 'being there' when this person needs them, the (apparently selfless) Two sacrifices their time and energy and sometimes even their health fulfilling their role of 'fixer'.

However, when Twos create a need in others by having others rely on them and by being indispensable, they usually fail to recognise that they themselves are entirely dependent on the other. Since the Two's sense of self and their self-worth depends on the other person's appreciation of their good deeds, by creating this sort of dependency they are putting their happiness squarely in the hands of another person. And of course, if they are actually successful in 'fixing' the other person the Two can find themselves left with another hole in their lives as the newly strong person moves on.

For Twos to consider:
- *In what ways do you try to be indispensable?*
- *How much do you take pride in, or get satisfaction from, being needed?*

What about Me?

The desire of the average to lower-functioning Two to be all things to all people means they can easily spread themselves too thin, to the detriment of their own personal relationships and their own well-being. When the Two feels unacknowledged for all that they do or for the help they are trying to give, not only do they feel hurt and unappreciated but the underlying resentments that build as they exhaust themselves further begin to lead to a desire to be free of the burden of being needed. Clearly, experiencing these 'bad' feelings does not fit at all with the image they have of themselves of being the patient, selfless one; so now, they not only feel unvalued and unloved but their already low self-esteem plummets even farther because 'only a bad person could have these feelings'.

The resentment and anger felt by the Two is not likely to be expressed openly unless plenty of personal growth work has been done. Instead, the average to lower-functioning Two is likely to go on and on giving more, wearing themselves out despite feeling put upon. Inside, there are thoughts of *What about me?* most likely accompanied by behavioural displays typical of the hard done by martyr: pursed lips, sighing, complaining about all they have to do and how tired it makes them. These are all common signs that a Two is feeling unappreciated. Eventually, the 'selfless' Two, who is not the soft pushover that other people think, begins to want some freedom from all the demands involved in endlessly supporting and giving to everyone. Finally, when it all becomes too much, something snaps, the Two shoots straight to Eight (see 'Connections' in Chapter 6) and – *whoosh!* – all the hurt feelings are finally expressed in an outpouring of what can be quite aggressive, even hysterical anger.

Anger, however, rarely lasts long with a Two, and when it fades away, the Two is likely to experience bad feelings about his/herself for the outburst. It is all-important to Twos that they keep their connection with others open smooth and loving, for if they do not, they might no longer be wanted, needed, or loved. As a consequence, they very quickly seek to put things right when there has been any sort of upset with other people and are quite likely to resort to obsequious apologies, flattery, or present giving in order to smooth things over.

What Twos fail to realise is that, by not speaking up about what they want, other people are not even aware of their unspoken needs, so how could they possibly fulfil them? But from the perspective of the Two, they look for and try to fulfil other people's unspoken as well as spoken needs, so why can't others reciprocate? And when their needs are not fulfilled by others, which they frequently are not, not only is their sense of neediness increased but they draw quite erroneous conclusions – that the other party does not value, like, or love them enough to care about, or even notice, what they need. All of this brings about even lower self-esteem. Of course, the Two reasons, this must be because I am just not good enough and am therefore unworthy of the other's love and attention.

Many Twos find it extremely difficult to acknowledge their own needs to themselves let alone to others; asking for something for themselves feels like selfishness – they must give but not receive. Despite the fact that they will immediately drop everything and rush to give help to other people who are in need, Twos find it extremely difficult to ask for any help from other people. Should they find themselves in a situation where they have to accept help, their dependency on others feels very uncomfortable because it dissolves the Two's self-image of being the strong one that others depend on. Instead of recognising that others might also enjoy being helpful, the Two is most likely to tearfully apologise for being such a nuisance whilst silently berating herself/himself for being useless and helpless.

Lower-functioning Twos may continue to overextend themselves physically (and sometimes financially) for years, depleting themselves and neglecting their health, with illness being the sad result. Interestingly, from the perspective of the Two, their ill health and suffering then becomes 'proof' of all they have done for others and how virtuous and selfless they are, proof that they really have worn themselves out doing for others, just as they have always claimed they did. For some Twos, getting sick when they have taken on too much can become their unconscious way of both validating themselves *and* getting a rest, and can consequently become a persistent pattern.

For Twos to consider:
- *What needs do you really have that are unmet – by yourself or by others?*
- *Do you get adequate rest?*
- *How much time do you give to nurturing yourself?*
- *What unspoken desires do you hold inside? Take some time now and acknowledge what you really need and want.*

Manipulating Behaviour

In order to get their needs met, Twos frequently use people-pleasing techniques as an indirect way of getting attention and getting others to like them. All Twos are naturally appreciative of and attentive to others. Yet when the average to lower-functioning Two focuses on you by buying you flowers, asking you how you are feeling, doing something nice for you, giving you compliments, etc., it is quite likely that within the giving is a need to get back exactly what you are receiving from them.

Some Twos are well aware of their ability to affect the way other people behave towards them; for other Twos, the image they have of themselves as the unselfish and giving person blinds them to the fact that they are actually trying to manipulate the other person into giving them the 'strokes' that *they* need. Although many people are flattered and enjoy the attention, very needy Twos can embarrass others by gushing with their compliments and by giving too much too frequently – behaviour that is likely to drive people away instead of drawing them in.

For Twos to consider:
- *What do you do to get other people to notice you and like you?*
- *What do you do to control or manipulate the way others behave towards you?*

Guilt-tripping others is another common ploy used by attention-seeking Twos. If jobs done in the home or at work are going unnoticed, the Two may wait until someone is watching before tackling something for which they want appreciation. For example, a female Two may be feeling hard done by because her husband never comments on the efforts she makes ironing all his shirts. She might, therefore, wait until he is just walking through the door before starting to iron and then make heavy weather of the job, sighing histrionically or moaning about how hard she's been working or how she has more shirts to iron than her friend. Or she might resort to behaving like the hard-done-by martyr by starting the job just as he is going out and then flinging comments at him, such as 'You just go out and enjoy yourself. I'll stay at home doing the ironing like I always do.'

For Twos to consider:

- *How do you behave when you feel unappreciated for what you have done?*
- *Do you sometimes slip into 'martyr'?*
- *How do you go about trying to induce guilt in others?*
- *How does this behaviour make them feel? (Ask them!)*

Interaction with the Two

Twos love to be involved in the lives of those they care about, but many well-intended Twos have difficulty recognising appropriate boundaries between themselves and others. Their energy naturally reaches out towards other people quite strongly, and for some of the more private types, it is just too much.

The desire to be closely connected to others can make Twos lose sight of what is acceptable interest and what is actually nosiness. Extremely personal questions may be asked of anyone, even someone they only know slightly, questions about financial matters or health, even questions about people's sex lives. With average Twos, it may stop there; however, at the lower-functioning levels, there are Twos who go on to indulge in gossiping. They get feelings of self-importance (and hence feel wanted and valued) by being the one in the know and might share secrets with one or two people (or dozens!) in order to impress others about the special role they have in the lives of those whose secrets they are privy to. Their self-deception about their own motives can reach such levels that they justify their behaviour in the guise of caring for those whose secrets they are revealing. 'Poor Jill suspects her husband is having another affair. I don't know how she stays so strong'.

All Twos are very expressive and demonstrative people who desire plenty of physical contact, so their relationships inevitably tend to involve much touching, hugging and kissing. There are many people who enjoy this, and those in emotional distress will often welcome a warm, caring hug; however, the boundary issues of less-than-high-functioning Twos can make them insensitive to the feelings of less demonstrative types.

Instead of stopping and considering whether others actually want what they themselves desire (which is demonstrative affection), they can easily end up making some people feel intruded upon or embarrassed. Moreover, the sort of 'touchy-feely' behaviour that a Two typically displays can be misconstrued in both the workplace and social settings as implying sexual interest on the part of the naïve Two.

Being naturally inclined towards helping others *and* having no real clarity about boundaries means that most Twos are generally very free about giving unsolicited advice. This can very easily be interpreted by others as interfering, yet the Two would just say, 'I'm only trying to help.' Believing they know better than you do about what you need or what you should be doing, they can become much too pushy with their advice and helpfulness. Average to lower-functioning Twos just don't know when to back off. Often, they will not take no for an answer; in fact, they are quite likely to redouble their efforts to convince you – after all, the helpful ideas or advice *are* for your own well-being and greater happiness! 'Go on, have another helping of potato. I know you really want it.' 'You must put on a warmer coat to go out. That one is much too thin.'

Of course, when those that the Two is trying to help are fully grown, responsible adults who are quite capable of deciding things for themselves, this pushiness is likely to be experienced as overly controlling and bossy, with the result that their 'help' often gets rejected. To the average Two, this rejection is interpreted as a rejection of self, and the consequent hurt feelings of being unwanted and unloved will quite possibly lead to an angry and aggressive, even hysterical, outburst.

For Twos to consider:
- *How often do you offer help before it is asked for?*
- *Might some of the 'helpful' advice you offer be unnecessary?*
- *Do you act as if you know what others need better than they do themselves?*
- *How often do you keep pushing with your ideas about what is needed, even though the other party may have said no?*
- *How does the other party feel when you do this? (Ask them!)*

Need for Love and Attention

Although at higher-functioning levels Twos speak little about their own problems, the need for attention of the average to low-functioning Two can lead to them being quite undiscerning about whom they talk to about what. Other people's interest and concern makes the needy Two feel wanted and valued and frequently results in Twos talking to people indiscriminately about their own personal problems or health scares: the shop assistant, a person they meet in the street, anyone who will listen might be privy to the most private details of the Two's life. Moreover, the nature of problems is frequently exaggerated in a bid for concerned interest and sympathy.

This sort of exaggerating behaviour can be noticeably displayed when complaining about their well-being and health to work colleagues or family; Twos may regularly exaggerate minor headaches or illnesses in order to get caring concern and attention from others or complain frequently about how exhausted they are because of all they have done. This pattern of exaggeration can become so habitual in very needy Twos that hypochondria is not uncommon at lower-functioning levels.

When a very needy Two begins to receive positive attention from someone they admire or are attracted to, they can get hooked on the attention and start adapting their behaviour in order to continue to get the attention so that they to feel wanted and needed. They are then highly likely to suppress any sort of negative expression and, in order to please the other person, may behave in ways that are quite out of character, even to the point of sacrificing their integrity. This can be especially true in the sexual arena where any flattering sexual attention may be encouraged because it appears to the Two to be evidence that they are wanted and needed. The natural ability of the Two to connect with others means that they can be very adept at flirting and may go out of their way to be sexually provocative through their dress or gestures, in order to attract just this sort of attention. A Two who feels neglected within their relationship may display sexually provocative behaviour like this in public situations, causing embarrassment to their companions and then much greater embarrassment to themselves when they later come to their senses and realise how badly they have behaved.

Despite the need to be in a relationship, many Twos are not at ease with sex itself and sexually provocative behaviour rarely indicates a desire for sexual gratification; in fact, it is usually just the insecure Two's way of seeking affirmation of their desirability in order to boost their self-esteem. However, the need for love and attention can be so great in those Twos with very low self-esteem that they can begin to equate sex with love. As a consequence, many female Twos, especially in their younger adult years, can end up being taken advantage of sexually, giving of their bodies in the hope of love in return. If the Two is sufficiently aware of their negative patterns, this behaviour is likely to evoke very bad feelings about themselves afterwards, causing their self-esteem to drop even lower than it was before.

Seeking value and love by doing for others, or adapting themselves to fit in with what the other desires, means that Twos rarely ever feel loved for themselves. Using their sexuality to connect with others in order to feel wanted and loved inevitably leads to unsatisfying relationships; thus, there is a strong pattern within the life of a great many Twos of being perpetually unfulfilled romantically.

The deep hunger for love that resides at the core of less-than-high-functioning Twos can manifest itself in the form of addictions to alcohol, shopping, sex, and very commonly, food. Overeating, especially overindulgence in sweet things like chocolate, can be a Two's way of trying to fill the needy space inside. As a result, a lot of Twos have weight problems, with dramatic weight swings being common. (Using sugary foods as a substitute for love is a pattern that may have begun in childhood. Many parents proffer sweets to keep their children quiet or as a substitute for loving attention.) Unfortunately, instead of this behaviour bringing emotional solace, it just leads to a downward spiral of weight problems, even lower self-esteem, and then depression, all of which makes it extremely hard for the Two to go on and find happiness within other relationships.

Overindulgence in alcohol can result in dramatic changes in the behaviour of some Twos. Where there are strong, suppressed feelings of being unappreciated and undervalued for all the hard work and good deeds that are being done, too much drink can cause all the suppressed resentments to be unleashed, shocking those who are used to the sweeter nature of the Two. The gentle, compliant person who can't do enough for others can suddenly become the hysterical and aggressively angry martyr as all their grievances are dramatically unleashed. 'Look at all I have done for you. You never appreciate all the sacrifices I have made or how I have worn my fingers to the bone for you.'

If you have a Two in your life

In order to facilitate improved interactions and feelings of compassion, it can be helpful to keep in mind what can be hard for the Two:

- feeling needy in relationships
- finding it hard not to give at the expense of their own well-being when others are in need
- feeling not good enough
- feeling drained from overdoing for others
- not doing things they really like to do for themselves for fear of being selfish
- criticism of self for not feeling as loving as they should be
- feeling upset and resentful when others don't appreciate all that is done for them
- feeling unwanted or unloved when helpfulness or advice is rejected
- working so hard to be kind and considerate that real feelings get suppressed
- feeling hurt and misunderstood when the desire to be helpful is viewed as controlling

When not at their best, Twos can be

----

*needy indirect controlling exaggerating insincere
martyred clingy manipulative intrusive effusive prideful
guilt-inducing pushy gushy hypochondriacal hysterical
histrionic suffocating possessive*

CHAPTER 10

The Three

At their best, Threes are

---

*accomplished   outstanding   charming   genuine
inspiring   motivating   sociable   successful   self-accepting
focused   productive   pragmatic   admirable
self-motivating   flexible   adaptable   competent*

Threes are highly sociable people of great charisma and charm who are determined to make the best of themselves and get somewhere in the world. Within a crowd of people, you are likely to recognise the Threes quite easily for they are often the attractive, well-groomed ones who happily chat with all types of people. They are highly adaptable types who can walk into a room, immediately read the situation, and know just how to interact with each person. Having the ability to tune into what each person is looking for, they can tailor their approach appropriately so that each person feels like an individual even when part of a group.

These are high-energy, self-motivated people who make things happen in their lives. Being generally very competent and efficient, as well as prepared to work hard to get things done, they can be highly productive. When they are clear about what they want and have the goal in front of them, they refuse to allow extraneous concerns deflect them from the objective they have set for themselves; they just focus on where they are going and what they want to achieve. Whatever they are involved in they want to make a success of it, and frequently do.

Their attitude towards life is a forward-looking one. Even when things get difficult, the outlook of the Three is that there is always another way, another possibility, another opportunity to keep moving towards a better future. Not being the sort of people to let the grass grow under their feet, if things aren't moving forward in their lives, they will reassess where they are going and alter course. All Threes want to make the best of themselves and achieve something, and many change tack within their working lives more than once, moving on to new careers in the pursuit of fulfilling their own potential. Most Threes are fast learners and throughout their varied careers will work hard to be the best they can be, happily adapting to many different types of work. High-functioning Threes generally achieve great success in whatever they turn their attention to and usually master many life skills. They are self-assured and inner-directed people who believe they will be successful at whatever they turn their hand to and who wish to contribute something to society.

Other people are often drawn to the charm and charisma of the Three, and high-functioning Threes frequently become the role models for aspiring people. Because they are so often successful within their field, others admire and look up to them, seeing the high-achieving Three as the paragon of all that they themselves wish to be. They have a brightness and magnetism that draw others towards them to listen and be inspired, inspired to achieve more than they ever thought they could. Threes believe in themselves and have a strong conviction that whatever they tackle will be successful. Being highly motivated to develop themselves and to make the best of their own abilities, high-functioning Threes often enjoy using their excellent communication skills to help others to believe in themselves. As a result, they can be great motivators of other people; they have developed their own abilities to the full and enjoy motivating others to do the same, so they make talented teachers of whatever skills they have mastered.

Despite an apparent shallowness that is evident in many Threes, there is, in fact, huge depth at the heart of Three, depth that average to lower-functioning Threes have not stopped long enough to discover. Those Threes that do slow down their drive to achieve, and look inward, are able to delve into the depths of their spiritual selves, and when this aspect of them is combined with their practicality and industriousness, they can become great spiritual teachers.

The Three in Childhood

When the soul 'separates' itself from the All That Is and comes into life as a Three, the quality of Divine Essence from which the young child experiences a deep loss of connection is **Beingness.**[6] This creates the intrinsic sensitivity of the Three, and it is through the filter of this sensitivity that the young child experiences the world and develops ways of coping with what is experienced.

Each small child seeks to find and attain that which seems to be unavailable to them in order that they might survive and get their needs met. To the young Three, it seems that 'just being' is not enough and therefore they must have no intrinsic value just as they are. They conclude that if they are to survive and get the love that they need, they will have to earn it by doing and achieving something that gives them value. The Three then begins to take on these childhood beliefs:

'The world rewards us for what we 'do', not who we 'are'.
'I must be successful and admirable in order
to have value within the family.'
'I will get love and appreciation only if I am the best.'

Most Threes grew up to feel that theirs was a special role within the family and that great things were expected of them. Perhaps they were the eldest child who was expected to follow in father's footsteps or,

---

6   See chapter 3, 'Unravelling Your Inner World: The Early Years.'

commonly, they were the only child and only grandchild in the family, with the result that parents and grandparents doted on them. Whatever their place within the family, every little achievement of the developing child was admired and applauded so that the child felt it incumbent upon them to continue to be admirable and to get recognition by achieving. As they grew, only those achievements where they came first or got top marks were applauded; anything less was discounted no matter how hard they had tried. This served to reinforce the erroneous conclusions that they had already drawn about the true nature of love and value, so their experience, or their 'truth', became that they were loved for their achievements not for themselves.[7]

At the other extreme, some Threes come from a family where one or both parents were very dysfunctional and no matter what the child did, nothing got them acceptance or approval within the family. These young Threes strongly absorbed the message that "I am not OK" and so they went on to strive to achieve something big that would get them approval in the eyes of the world.

The Driven Three

The deep erroneous belief that they have no intrinsic value as themselves, confers on the average Three not only lack of true worth, but a feeling that 'who they really' are is as nothing. In their unconscious attempt to reconnect with the lost sense of Beingness, Threes grow up trying to shape themselves into a person that has value here in the world. Having discovered that value can only come from what they achieve and the position they have. Firstly, within the family, and later within the wider sphere of their lives, such as the school they attended, they become a human *doing* instead of a human *being*. From the perspective of the Three, doing and achieving gets recognition; being gets you nothing. And having assumed the role of 'The Golden One' in their young years,

---

[7]   The childhood circumstances do not create the personality; they were chosen by the soul so that the Three personality patterns would fully develop.

as they move into adulthood, Threes only feel confident when they are interacting with others through this role. They fear being themselves, because that would not get them the validation and admiration they need; thus, they must be a success and avoid being anything less than the best, the number one.

What is considered 'success' will depend upon the society or culture within which the Three lives, but however it is defined within their sphere, they cannot be a nobody. They must strive to achieve high status and will be dissatisfied with being anything less than the number one. Success for many means material wealth and its trappings. But for others, it means being the best in their field. As a professional musician, the Three must play the lead or the most valued solo pieces. Threes who enter holy orders have to present themselves as the most pious. The Three athlete must be the winner. (Have you heard the story about the Three at the Olympic Games who stands on the podium to receive the silver medal and thinks, *This is not the colour I came for* ?) Winning, being the best, being out in front of the competition enables the Three to shore themselves up against their desperately low feelings of worth and value, but failure on any scale, especially being overshadowed by others, will trigger their deep insecurities and must be avoided at all costs. To the average Three, failure is death and they must drive themselves mercilessly in order to achieve success.

They can be so driven that they neglect sleep and healthy eating, driving themselves on even at the expense of their health or their personal relationships. The behaviour patterns of the average to lower-functioning Three are that of the classic workaholic (although this does not mean that overworking is the sole domain of the Three, just that workaholism is a typical pattern seen in a high proportion of Threes). It is often very difficult for the very driven Three to have any unstructured downtime because 'not doing' means losing their sense of value and meaning. When they do take a holiday from work, the plane trip and the hotel will probably be viewed as networking opportunities and, even on the beach, you are quite likely to find them on their mobile phones doing deals or maintaining their links with important connections rather than just soaking up the sun.

Experiencing physical fatigue or emotional stress is not viewed by the Three as sufficient reason to stop their relentless pursuit of success, and they find real physical illness threatening. They fear that taking a few days off might ruin everything they have achieved with regard to material stability or status within their organisation. It is as if the Three feels that they have to create their own universe and if they fail to continue to generate and maintain their lives, everything will fall apart and become as nothing. In the world of the Three, everything is up to you, so you have to be constantly doing and achieving, relentlessly pushing forward.

For Threes to consider:
- *What does success mean to you?*
- *What aspects of your life get neglected in the pursuit of success?*
- *What do you fear might happen if you were to relax and take a real break for a while?*

The Three's sense of value relies not only on how successful they are but also on how efficient and productive they are, and they judge others by the same criteria. Three bosses often give out orders to other people assuming they will be just as happy as they are to work all hours and have few breaks in order to achieve goals. When there are complaints, the perplexed and angry Three cannot understand why other people can't just get their act together and achieve something; after all, Threes will keep pushing themselves and will continue to function no matter how tough things get, so why can't others? Though they might appear hostile in response to complaints, underneath they might actually feel hurt because for the Three, *what they do is who they are,* and should anyone criticise any activity they are engaged in, to the Three, that is in effect saying that their own existence is not worthwhile.

In truth though, feeling that they have to be masters of their own destiny, workaholic Threes often find it hard to delegate and end up doing everything themselves. This can very quickly lead to the pressured Three feeling hard done by and unappreciated. In other words, they begin to display the negative aspects of one or both of their wings (Two and Four). These feelings will probably only be displayed at home – at work the Three cannot allow others to notice that they are anything less than on top of the job – so that the little time spent with their families can be ruined not only be exhaustion but by irritability and touchiness as well.

Image

Not all Threes are actually successful, but they all strive to be. They devote almost all of their time to the pursuit of success or, at least, to giving the impression that they are successful. Those Threes that have not yet achieved success decide that if they can deceive the world into believing that they are a success, they will avoid the shame of being seen as a failure. Consequently, to the less-than-high-functioning Three, the way in which they package themselves, what the world is allowed to see, the outer image that is presented for the rest of us to admire is what comes to matter most.

There is a great need in Threes of both sexes to be perceived as desirable and admirable. After all, reasons the Three, if other people notice you, watch you with interest, envy the way you look, that must surely mean that you are better than the rest. Consequently, you will often notice an appearance of youth and body beautiful about Threes, with many of the men displaying a boyish charm and a well-muscled body, and the women being stick thin or displaying the cuteness of the ingénue. Their demeanour is almost unfailingly bright-eyed, cheerful and optimistic. Yet this is not a reflection of true confidence or happiness. Rather, it is present in order to make sure that you buy into the image of success, for if they weren't the success they made out, how could they be this buoyant person who is full of bonhomie?

There are many ways in which Threes present their image so that they will get recognition and give the impression of success and status. But what they mostly focus on are a perfect physical appearance, material wealth and possessions, where they live, or what high-level social connections they have, because in our society, these are the things that are valued by a great many people. They are generally extremely well groomed, and status symbols are frequently paraded in front of the world. These might be anything from the designer watch to the big house in the most expensive area. It might be the Gucci handbag, the flashy car that spells 'expensive', the Armani suit, designer labels prominently displayed on clothing, shoes and bags, etc. There are many ways of saying success. Or it might be that status comes from being able to brag about the spouse who is famous or has an outstanding job, or about clever children who out-achieve all the others.

What is displayed in order to get standing or kudos will vary from Three to Three and from culture to culture. A Three in the academic world, for instance, is unlikely to seek material wealth or possessions but will very prominently display their award certificates, make sure that pupils and fellow staff alike know how many awards and degrees they have, and will almost certainly seek status within the college.

And Threes are not just concerned with their own personal image but also with the impression other people have of those who are close to them. Believing that the way their friends and family look and behave reflects directly on their own reputation and standing, Threes are quite likely to require their families to dress well, their children to be clever and attractive, and even their pets to be beautiful or admirable!

Busyness vs. Happiness

Presentation of a successful and flawless image is more important for the average Three than what lies behind it – and then the image can become an end unto itself. Some Threes even convince themselves that they *are* this image, that what they present *is* who they are. However, inside they feel empty and hollow, perhaps even sad and lonely, but the world cannot be allowed to see the truth of them for fear of rejection, so they go through life like a highly polished shell with nothing of substance inside.

Most lower-functioning Threes identify so much with the role they are playing that they have difficulty knowing how to just be themselves and they lose touch with what really makes them happy. Their endless round of doing, doing, doing means that Threes have no time to look at the scenery on their relentlessly busy journey through life. The sad consequence is that, no matter what they achieve, who they impress, or how much they acquire, they experience very little real quality of life.

There is a great deal of Threeness in modern culture. We want more of everything and we want it faster and better, and we sacrifice the quality of the journey through life for the speed or efficiency we think we want. Then we wonder why we are not really fulfilled and content, but instead of seeking happiness within, we keep hoping that something we acquire or achieve will be the answer. This is the pattern of the Three, although few stop and check with themselves whether all this is bringing real happiness. They get little lasting joy or satisfaction from their achievements. It is, after all, the image that achieved the goal, not the real self (whoever that is). And yes, initially, it feels great to have beaten their opponents, got the car, etc. But as the good feelings fade, there is a restlessness, a joyless quality to the success, and then comes the need to acquire or achieve more. The inner hollowness, the feelings of lack inside prevail and the Three goes on, endlessly performing twenty-four hours a day, often with little distinction between their personal and working lives. There is no let up for Threes; they feel they have to always be 'on', be impressive, display their best, just as if they were at a perpetual interview. How exhausting is that!

If you ask the average Three, 'What makes you happy? What do you really enjoy doing?' they may be quite taken aback by the questions. Not only has the question probably not come up for them before, but when they ask it of themselves, they find they really do not know. Throughout their young years, they got their strokes for what they achieved rather than for who they were so they have never really stopped to investigate who they really are or what would bring them happiness. It is quite common for Threes (especially those who are the eldest child) to choose a career that fits in with the expectation their family has of them. If asked why they chose this particular career path, many, certainly in their younger adult years, may realise that they don't really know, but it makes the family proud.

Also, many Threes find themselves pursuing activities that they don't really enjoy much at all. Because they are always looking outside of themselves for validation rather than focusing on and developing their real talents and genuine interests, average to lower-functioning Threes frequently take up activities that impress other people and further their chances of success rather than for the fun of the activity itself. For example, if the boss plays squash or golf, the Three might decide to take up the same sport and get private lessons in order to impress him or her. But having to make sure that they avoid defeat (which instantly spells failure) *and* always having to be 'on show' means there can be little fun or relaxation in this for the Three.

For Threes to consider:
- *What activities have you engaged in specifically to further your career or improve your standing in other people's eyes?*
- *What do you really enjoy doing?*
- *What has been the true cost to you of not following your heart?*

Comparison and Competition

The image the Three creates – how they look, what they have, what they achieve, etc. – is not based on their own personal values or ideals (as it is for the One), but on those of their family, and the culture or society within which they live or work, so everything for the Three is relative to other people. Their sense of self-worth is inextricably determined by what other people think, and as a result, they live and die by others' opinion. Their overriding concern is about the impact they have on others, and if average Threes discover that someone has a negative impression of them, they find it intolerable and will go to great lengths to put this right even if they have to use deception to do it.

Comparison with others is how they measure themselves, and because they need to be the number one, the result of their comparisons is competition. When comparison shows them to be anything short of the best, the resultant competition they enter into is generally of a silent nature, for if their deficiency were revealed to others, they would be shown up as the failure, so it causes them to push themselves even harder. 'John is looking really fit and tanned. I'd better get down to more workouts at the gym and book a course of sunbeds.' 'Julie's sales are heading towards being higher than mine this month, so I will work my weekends in order to beat her.'

For Threes to consider

- *Consider the ways in which you compare yourself with others. How does the element of comparison and competition in your life affect the way you behave or what you do?*
- *How does this comparison affect your self-worth?*
- *What are you missing out on by always trying to come out on top?*

However, in their endless quest for superiority, many Threes bring a verbalised element of comparison and competition into their interaction with almost everyone: Who is making the most money? Who has the cleverest children? Who is best at sport? Who has the busiest diary? Who went to the smartest holiday resort? And so on, so that interacting with Threes can end up being all about them. Telling them about a success you had at work will prompt them to counter with something bigger they have achieved; your child's success in maths at school will be eclipsed by a story of how their child did even better in English; your plans for your holiday will pale in comparison to the holiday they are planning. They create the competition and they have to win it! All this appears to others as narcissistic and arrogant, yet the underlying drive for this behaviour is the exact opposite. Inside, they feel like a nothing, an empty shell.

The Nature of Truth

Although Threes regularly bend the truth in order to have value in other people's eyes, they do not see themselves as liars. For them, 'truth' has many meanings. Having a pragmatic approach to everything they do, truth is whatever works and, because they are so much playing a role as an actor would, they can get to the point where they begin to believe their own propaganda and forget that this is actually a role they are playing. They believe they are being true – not to Truth but to the role they are playing – and may even come to believe that what they are saying is actually true.

Some of their untruths are just exaggerations or omissions; certain aspects of a situation may be conveniently forgotten and others highlighted or embellished upon in order to distort the truth so that they can create a particular picture without actually lying. Then there are the white lies that are intended to get others to like them. 'You look really great in that tie.' And there are white lies of avoidance. 'I didn't ring you because I never got your message.' There are the bigger lies that are designed to impress about the jobs they have had, where they have been for holidays, what car they are going to buy, etc. And then there are the lies about why the report was late, why that task is not finished, or why they were late for work so that they do not appear inefficient or negligent.

For Threes to consider:
- *In what ways do you bend the truth to serve your own ends?*
- *How often do you exaggerate?*
- *What outright lies have you told in order to impress?*

And at the really lower-functioning level, desperate Threes may tell major lies about their family background in order to avoid the appearance of having come from lowly beginnings, or lies about their qualifications or accomplishments in order to get into the job they want result of this can be that these Threes can find themselves out of their depth and on a relentless downward spiral of having to use charm and continual deception in order to keep their head above water in the job.) At this level, they can be manipulative and ruthless in the pursuit of their goals, not caring what corners they cut or who they make use of in their determination to get to keep their job and get to the top. They can be calculating and unfeeling towards anyone who is in their way and will use cutthroat methods of sidelining the opposition. If they feel it necessary to compromise their personal values in order to succeed, they will be able to convince themselves that that is the right course of action. It's not that these Threes are really unkind or malicious; it's that their inner world, the heart area where their integrity resides, has become unavailable to them, so that they can completely lose sight of ethics and morals.

Feelings

Because of the lack of inner connection, being true to their authentic feelings is often a foreign concept for the Three. Feelings are like speed bumps getting in the way of forward movement, efficiency and success. Threes deal with their world in a pragmatic, cool and matter-of-fact way that is not complicated by unwanted emotional reactions so that they can move expediently forwards and deal with the challenges they meet in pursuance of their goals. So they have to suppress emotions that might involve unpleasantness or conflict; being a success means that others have to like you and expression of complaints or anger may slow down your progress to the top.

Whatever situation they find themselves in, the chameleon-like Three assumes the most appropriate role to put themselves in the best light, and the arena of feelings is no exception. When working with ruthless businessmen, Threes will behave in tough, calculating ways; with members of the nursing profession, they will display tenderness and concern for others; at fun or wild social events that involve colleagues or networking opportunities, they will be the life and soul of the party, even though they may not be having fun at all. Rather than being their authentic selves, like actors on the stage of life, they can detach from what they really feel and give the *appearance* of feeling whatever emotion seems to be appropriate.

Interaction with the Three

The lack of emotionality present in average Threes gives them a sense of cool, untouchability such that others experience them as having 'got it all together'. They present to the world a perfectly polished, exterior coat of shiny varnish that belies their vulnerability and deceives others into believing the mask. But as a result of always having to be switched on, unable to let their guard down for a moment less they be seen in an unfavourable light, the demeanour of the Three often lacks spontaneity and openness.

It can be very hard to discern who they really are because they become whatever sort of person they need to be in order to achieve the result they seek. They change the qualities that they display depending on who they are with, so different people can have very different experiences of the same person. Consequently, there is no permanent substance to the persona of most Threes, which is why they are often thought of as lacking authenticity. Very often when you are interacting with a Three, they are not relating personally to you but to the way you are responding to the image that they are displaying.

For Threes to consider:
- *How differently do you behave with different people?*
- *What are you trying to achieve by not being your true self?*
- *What do you fear might happen if you were to just be yourself?*

In most interactions, Threes reveal little about themselves to others unless they believe it would be to their advantage, yet they fail to realise that most other people would prefer them to be their authentic selves. When with someone they trust and care about, Threes would greatly benefit from letting their guard down and allowing the other person to know about their anxieties and vulnerabilities. To share insecurities and worries would help the Three to open into their real feelings and have more heart-felt connection with others.

Getting the chance to spend time with your Three friends can be amazingly difficult; they are such busy people – or at least, they will make sure that you think they are. Some Threes rarely answer the phone (busy people are always in meetings!) so that you always have to leave a message, or they will tell you how busy their diary is. 'I haven't a free day for weeks,' says the impressive Three, 'but maybe, with some juggling, we could meet up two weeks on Tuesday.'

In social situations, average Threes spend plenty of their time looking for networking opportunities or seeking to turn those around them into an audience whom they can impress. They will let those that they can persuade to listen know how busy they are, what amazing deals they have in the pipeline, or what they have achieved. For many Threes, a regular conversation topic might be name-dropping; letting it be known that they associate with people of wealth or importance gives them, by association, standing in the eyes of others. The frequency and the degree to which they talk themselves up or recount stories involving relationships with such people is, of course, directly related to how low their self-worth really is. Higher-functioning Threes are delightful and interesting company; they are people who spend more time listening to others than talking about themselves and are genuinely glad to hear of other people's achievements without feeling the need to compete.

However, at the other end of the spectrum, there can be a shallow and embarrassing quality to the friendship offered by some lower-functioning Threes. Because they continually have an eye on the main chance, they may proffer apparent friendship because it suits the project they are involved in, and then, seeing another great opportunity, they can very quickly change tack, taking up with new contacts and dropping some people who are no longer useful, of whom you may be one!

If you have a Three in your life

In order to facilitate improved interactions and feelings of compassion, it can be helpful to keep in mind what can be hard for the Three:

- always having to be switched on
- feeling that their true selves are unacceptable
- comparing themselves to people who have more, or are more, successful
- continually putting on the façade of success in order to impress people

- endless fear of failing or of being overshadowed by others who are better
- struggling to hang on to success
- never really feeling able to let up and take things easy
- feeling that in other people's eyes they are only as good as their last success
- feeling empty and dead inside
- losing touch with what would really make them happy
- having superficial, instead of 'real,' friendships and relationships that bring little contentment

When not at their best, Threes can be

---

*image-conscious superficial pretentious untruthful
selfish competitive sycophantic self-deceptive false empty
attention-seeking slick narcissistic devious
self-aggrandising exploitative emotionally cold Machiavellian*

CHAPTER 11

The Four

At their best, Fours are

---

*warm supportive compassionate empathic refined
stylish expressive imaginative inspired intuitive romantic
individualistic perceptive creative self-contented gentle
witty interpersonal self-deprecating*

Fours are warm, gentle people of great emotional sensitivity and depth, people who can connect deeply with others and the world around them. More than any other personality type, Fours process their world through their feelings and, being strongly attuned to their own inner state, are highly perceptive and intuitive, able to read the subtle nuances of a situation that other types might miss.

The smallest, subtlest detail within their world affects them strongly: the beauty of the tiniest flower, a bird song, or the sound of the violins in a piece of music. Many things can move them so deeply that they may be at a loss as to how to verbalise their feelings to others. Yet the need to express the extremes of the light and the dark that they experience means that nearly all Fours need to find creative outlets through which they can express the depths they find within themselves. The way in which they do this may be through the writing of a journal or via a hobby, such as painting or gardening, but many Fours need more than this; as a result, a great many Fours are found in artistic or creative fields, such as design, fashion, or the creative arts.

Were it not for Fours, this world would be a bland and expressionless place. Most of the music we enjoy, especially the pieces that move us, comes from the inner depth of the Four; moreover, fashion, interior decor, fabric design, and art are the realm of the Four.

Although not the only type to be creative, the creativity of Fours is highly personal in its expression, and very often what is produced is a reflection of the way in which their life experiences have affected them. And because the creative works they produce come from the heart, Fours are able to evoke a strong emotional response in others, which helps them to open their own hearts. A great many of the greatest painters, sculptors, writers, poets and musicians have been Fours who were ready to dive deeply into the depths of their own souls and in subtle and beautiful ways communicate profound truths about the nature of human existence.

Although the outer expression of the complex inner world of the Four often takes the form of conventional artistic expression, such as music, art, or writing, Fours also tend to use other forms of self-expression. Having refined tastes and a great appreciation of beauty, most feel the need to use specific colours, lighting, fabrics, fragrance, or music in order to create a living environment that reflects their deepest selves and evokes just the right ambience for their varying moods.

Many Fours express themselves by adopting a unique hairstyle or wearing unusual clothing, others by living an unconventional lifestyle; some, especially in their younger years, may venture into the arena of body piercing or tattoos. However they express themselves, all Fours desire to find their own way of expressing their uniqueness and many people of this type challenge long-held paradigms of society through their ability to break through the barriers of rigid or traditional thinking.

Within all Fours is a great desire to really know and understand themselves and, being seekers of truth, many develop a strong interest in personal growth fields or spiritual matters. These are generally complex, emotional people who can be inclined to be overly serious and intense. Higher-functioning Fours, however, do not take themselves too seriously at all, for they have a refreshingly candid way of being self-revealing and, having an ironic sense of humour and a sharp wit, are ready to light-heartedly poke fun at their own quirks and foibles.

The emotional sensitivity of the Four is both a gift and a curse. It enables them to experience life on a very deep, emotional level and, feeling things so deeply themselves, they are able also to connect with and relate to other people's emotions as no other type can. This is the true empath. The innate sensitivity of the Four means that they don't just pick up on others' feelings as the Two can but they actually feel them within their own bodies. This can even affect some Fours so profoundly that being in a room with a lot of people can be very unsettling.

They are naturally gentle and supportive people and, when in a positive space, are especially willing to listen with great compassion and empathy to someone else's problems. As a result, Fours make very good counsellors and therapists, for they really do know how other people feel! However, their emotionality also confers onto them an endless roller coaster of intense feeling. Everyone experiences the ups and downs of emotion as they go through life, but for the Four, the heights are higher, the depths are deeper, and the vulnerability experienced because of this super sensitivity means that the average Four experiences much pain where other types might be hardly affected at all.

The Four in Childhood

When the soul 'separates' itself from the All That Is and comes into life as a Four, the quality of Divine Essence from which the young child experiences a deep loss of connection is **Undivided Completeness.**[8] This creates the intrinsic sensitivity of the Four, and it is through the filter of this sensitivity that the young child experiences the world and develops ways of coping with what is experienced.

---

[8] See chapter 3, 'Unravelling Your Inner World: The Early Years.'

Each small child seeks to find and attain that which seems to be unavailable to them in order that they might survive and get their needs met. The small Four begins to conclude that they themselves are somehow incomplete and that, because of this something that is missing, not only are they intrinsically acceptable as they are, but they have no real significance in the eyes of their parents. The young Four then begins to take on these childhood beliefs:

'I am incomplete; therefore, I am flawed.'
'There is something essentially missing in life.'
'In order to get love, I need to be special so that I
will have significance in the eyes of others.'

Disconnection from Source is experienced by the young Four as if he or she has been personally rejected and abandoned. In terms of the family they were born into, this translates into a feeling of not really fitting in as a proper part of the family. The Four does not experience any sense of identifying with the family unit but only perceives how unlike the other members of their family they are; in fact, as children, a great many Fours felt they did not really belong in this family, as if Mother brought the wrong child home from the hospital.

The resultant behaviour patterns of the Four child that spiral out of these untrue beliefs are unconsciously designed to discover who they really are and what they need to be in order to have a true place within the world.

The sense of having been rejected and abandoned is projected onto the nurturing parent, usually the mother figure, by whom the Four child feels deeply misunderstood.[9] Feeling unseen and unacknowledged for his or her true self by this 'uncaring and rejecting' parent *and* being unable to identify with their family results in the Four child experiencing confusion about personal identity and their place in the world. 'I cannot see myself in my parents, so who am I? What am I doing here?'

---

[9]   The childhood circumstances do not create the personality; they were chosen by the soul so that the Four personality patterns would fully develop.

The Yearning Romantic Four

The feelings of abandonment experienced by the Four in childhood bring about a deep longing to reconnect, a longing that all Fours feel but which most do not understand. This longing is experienced as a yearning for what they do not have. It is a sad, crying, inner neediness such that no one and nothing can ever successfully fill the sense of lack. It is as though something of their essential self is missing. They feel different somehow; they don't quite seem to fit in like other people do, and real happiness always seems just out of reach.

The outcome of this for all but higher-functioning Fours is that they can go through life without any real direction or sense of belonging, experiencing cycles of tumultuous feelings of lack and loss. Like a boat loosed from its moorings, many Fours experience themselves as drifting through the sea of life, tossed and turned by waves of emotion, with no sense of orientation or direction.

Not having what they need to feel complete and content is so much a part of the sense of 'being' for average to lower-functioning Fours that the experience of longing and not having feels much more familiar than getting. Consequently, a change in life circumstances or a suggestion from another person that seems to offer something positive can be rejected in favour of the continuance of negativity, loss and lack. The sad outcome of this is that, many Fours remain perpetually discontented, endlessly searching and yearning.

The fantasies of the Four are often about being rescued from their 'plight' by their saviour, about finally finding the perfect relationship. *Someday*, thinks the Four, *my knight in shining armour will ride up on his white charger and sweep me away from all the dross of life.* And many Fours fantasise about the day when their true talents will be discovered. *If only things were different*, thinks the Four with a sigh. *If only the world would recognise my true talents.* The fantasy world of the Four can be endlessly unrealistic and, sadly, may keep them longing and yearning instead of getting on with life. *If only I were more like that ... If only there was less of this ... If only I had more of that in life ... If only that perfect love was mine ... Then maybe, just maybe, I could be happy.*

The yearning for what is missing means that Fours are inclined to be incurable romantics, and this, in is its positive sense, can be a true gift, both to the Four and to the world. These are highly imaginative people, and the romance in the soul of a Four is frequently the original source of inspiration for our most evocative music, the storylines of opera, inspirational art, moving poetry, romantic novels, and much, much more.

For Fours to consider:
- *How much of your time do you spend longing for what you do not have?*
- *How often do you value the good things you already have?*
- *Make a list of what you are glad you have in your life right now – even the small things.*
- *How often – or how rarely – do you spend time appreciating these things?*
- *How might this pattern of longing be undermining your happiness?*

The Grass Is Always Greener

There are several types that can have a tendency to experience a degree of low self-esteem, but for average to lower-functioning Fours, it goes much deeper than that. In the young years, Fours come to believe that the estrangement and disconnection they experienced came about because there was something wrong with them and that they were deficient in some way. Then, as the young Four develops into adulthood, these bad feelings about self can spiral out into self-hatred and self-rejection. Because of the deeply held belief that they are somehow fundamentally flawed, even broken, and that something is missing, many Fours fail to see the positives within themselves and their lives. Appreciating their own positive qualities or getting any real joy from the good things that are already in their lives can be very hard for the Four who feels that life did not deliver what they needed to be happy.

Looking inside and negating themselves, these Fours then look outwards and see others enjoying all that they have been denied. Endless comparisons are made and, in the eyes of the Four, other people possess the personal qualities the Four does not have: the looks, the confidence, the talents, the social ease and acceptance, the ability to fit in, and so on and so on. Everyone else seems to have the secret to the happiness that continually evades them, and in the eyes of the Four, that could be the relationship or the looks, the money or the possessions, the job or the lifestyle.

There are Fours who experience themselves as existing on the periphery of life in comparison to others, feeling alone and estranged, unable to be understood or reached by other people; always 'on the outside' and unable to discover the secret of belonging or of being contented. It is as if everything that is positive exists outside of themselves, which inevitably creates endless discontent with self and envy of others.

There is a deep need within the Four to discover and to receive what they do not have, and with this comes a sense of entitlement. They feel that because they have been so deprived and they have suffered so much, the world owes it to them to give them what they desire. However, seeking what they desire *outside* of themselves never really brings them the happiness they are looking for, because their feelings of need and deprivation are not really related to physical needs at all but to their essential loss of connection to the Source. Consequently, when they get what they think they want, the satisfaction or happiness it brings is short-lived and that which was longed for quickly begins to lose its appeal. To the discontented Four, it now seems that there is something wrong with that long-desired object or person, or they convince themselves that this wasn't really what they wanted at all. Their attention then turns to something or someone else and the longing begins again, longing for what is unavailable or not quite within reach. In truth, they do not actually want the things others have, even though they may say they do. It is more that the happiness and contentedness of others reminds them of their own discontent and unhappiness and the things that create the feelings of envy are actually symbols of what might bring fulfilment.

The envy experienced by so many Fours makes many of them feel resentful towards those that seem to have what they have not, yet it's not uncommon for their envy to be hidden behind a veneer of disinterest or denial, or perhaps even an attitude of disdain or disapproval. They may show complete disinterest in a friend's new car, profess to be completely happy with their rather tatty kitchen, or express critical disapproval of another's lifestyle or appearance while secretly harbouring envious and even malicious thoughts. ('If I see another blonde with long legs, I'll kill her.')

At the lower-functioning levels, the Four's envy may turn to hate and spiteful behaviour. Because of all the deprivation and suffering they believe life has dealt out to them, they might feel quite justified in deliberately creating problems or doing someone down in order to bring them down a peg or two. 'After all,' reasons the Four, 'it's just not fair for them to have all the good things in life. If I'm miserable, why shouldn't they be?'

For Fours to consider:
- *How often you make comparisons – between yourself and others or between what you have in your life and what they have in theirs?*
- *How does that undermine any good feelings you have about yourself and your life?*

Who Am I?

In personal growth fields, much is spoken of 'finding oneself', and there is no other personality type who desires more deeply to find themselves than the Four. Fours are the truth seekers of the Enneagram, and the desire to discover the truth of who they are leads many Fours to attend courses and workshops that promise self-knowledge. They deeply wish to be true to themselves, express this authentic self, and have the world acknowledge and accept it.

Fours are complex and individualistic people and often display a unique sense of style or hold opinions that shake up other people's ideas. At the higher-functioning levels, Fours are happy to be different; they enjoy their uniqueness and do not concern themselves with other people's opinion of them.

However, the average Four, who cares enormously about what others think (even though they rarely admit it) desires to fit in and be like the people around them. (After all, they seem happy, don't they?) Yet at the same time, they want to be true to their authentic selves and be acknowledged as the unique and special person they are.

Having spent their young years feeling like a misfit within the family, many Fours 'try on' various different identities in their teen and young adult years. Lacking in any clear direction, they can swing between wanting to fit in and be like those around them, and wanting to be significantly different from anyone else so that they will not get overlooked. When they want to fit in, they may copy whatever they find attractive or admirable in others – hairstyle, dress sense, social or political opinions, musical taste, etc. – whereas, when they are determined to be different, they might embrace extremes, such as gothic dress, crazy hairstyles, body piercing, or tattoos.

The outcome of feeling like the outsider who is separate and does not belong is that many Fours adopt a self-image of how *unlike* other people they are. This creates even more negativity within these Fours because it is an identity that is based mostly on negative comparison. Sadly, this negative identity is often expressed in a disdainful or critical way. ('I could never work in an office like he does'; 'Parties are just not me'; 'I would never wear an outfit like that.') And, of course, when their negativity is expressed in this sort of way, it often ends up alienating other people. This inevitably creates more distance between the Four and others so that the Four can end up feeling even more separate and isolated.

The Special One

Despite the Four's professed desire for belonging and true happiness, longing and despair are at the heart of the average Four's sense of self, and the truth is that many Fours have unconsciously built their whole identity around this. To be the one who searches for real meaning and connection actually *gives* them meaning and connection. To be the one who is never really happy, the one who has it worse than the rest, the one who is uniquely different – all of this gives them identity. And having an identity, even a negative one, is very important to most Fours because it goes towards answering that question 'Who am I?'

Even though they secretly wish they could fit in like other people with ease and confidence, appearing to be ordinary is an anathema to average Fours. In order to have significance in the eyes of others, they *need* to be seen as different from the rest, someone who is unique, someone who is special in some way. This specialness may be developed deliberately. Some Fours express their uniqueness by adopting an unusual, one-of-a-kind style of dress. Or it may come about as a result of unconsciously drawing negativity and suffering into their lives. Either way, this sort of specialness gets attention from others; these Fours *do not* fade into the background as one of the ordinary people.

One very common way in which Fours display 'specialness' is in having specific dietary needs. There is a heightened sensitivity in Fours that renders them more sensitive than other types – to their emotions and their surroundings as well as to sounds, smells, fabrics, and much more. Many are also aware that certain foods do not make them feel good and need to respect the sensitivities of their digestive system. However, what might be a slight sensitivity in some Fours, in others it becomes a real allergy.

Whilst this is, of course, very real for the afflicted Four, at the same time, she or he would do well to consider that this allergy might have come about because of the need to be different. We each create our reality by what we think and believe; most Fours already believe they are different so they can unconsciously create ways of actually *being* different. Those that believe that their suffering goes deeper than it does for others are quite likely, therefore, to unconsciously create a life which has more than the average amount of physical or emotional problems.

Food sensitivities and allergies set the Four apart from others. 'I can't possibly eat that.' It makes them different from the rest and thereby makes them a special case. Of course, it is not only Fours that have allergies, but it is certainly true that more allergies are found in more Fours than in any other type.

For Fours to consider:
- *What special needs or problems do you have that set you apart from others?*
- *Be absolutely honest with yourself. What secret satisfaction do you get from being special?*
- *What would it feel like to just be ordinary?*

For the Four, feeling different from others is both a curse and a gift. It is a curse because it seems to make the simple happiness that others enjoy unavailable to them, and it is a gift because it sets them apart from those they view as less refined or aesthetic than they are – the shallow, common, or uncouth people with whom they do not wish to be identified. This elitist attitude, which is present in many Fours, means that they can manage to feel superior towards others whilst also harbouring secret feelings of envy towards them. Many actually find it painful to be around people who have less depth than they do yet somehow manage to be happier than they are. The complaints expressed by the Four can even appear to have a subtle quality of superiority or boasting. 'No one else suffers as I do, and you just don't have the deeper sensitivities that I have that would enable you to understand.'

Many Fours experience impatience with the ordinary and mundane, with the mediocrity of everyday life. There are those that are so determined to maintain their elitist identity that they withdraw from 'ordinary' life, insisting that they must do things alone, only on their own terms (which only serves to separate them farther from others). Some can end up seeing themselves as above the rules and conventions of normal society, and may come to believe that what can be expected from the rest of the population just does not apply to them. As a result, there are Fours who feel that they deserve special consideration because of their great suffering and their special needs, that they should not be expected to work for a living but be free to do things only as and when the mood takes them. The end result can be that these Fours are likely to waste the talents they do have and squander much of their lives achieving little – waiting until it feels right to do something practical or until they have the right talents, or just waiting to be rescued from the dreariness of life.

For Fours to consider:
- *In what ways do you disdain, even subtly, what you consider to be the ordinary or mundane?*
- *When you are with people, how often do you focus on the ways in which you are different from them?*
- *How might that be contributing to your feelings of disconnectedness from others?*
- *If you were to focus on the ways in which you are similar to them, might you feel a greater sense of belonging?*

Rejection, Denial and Blame

The desire to be authentic and true to themselves is very strong within Fours. However, even though they believe themselves to be in their own truth, a great many Fours continually deny and reject the truth about themselves and their world. In fact, the Four personality exhibits more patterns around rejection than any other type. It is as if the Four spends much time looking at both themselves and their world through a negative filter, dwelling on the negative and rejecting the positive. This can lead to downward spirals of negativity that are hard for the Four to escape from.

A great deal that exists in the present is rejected by Fours, with their attention going much more towards either the past or the future. They spend much time questioning and judging the quality of the experience of the present moment, both the events that are actually occurring and the emotions they are experiencing. In the desire to establish their inner truth and to be their authentic selves, the pattern of the Four is to explore their emotions in depth; some of these emotions are acceptable or familiar and are therefore viewed as being 'me' whereas others may feel unacceptable and are rejected as being 'not me'.

It is quite common for them to reject many of their day-to-day experiences because they do not appear to bring happiness, preferring instead to dream about how life will be when all that they desire is theirs, even though much of this might actually be impossible to attain. In their fantasy world, the fantasy self has all the longed-for material things and all the physical attributes they admire in others: the perfect nose, the amazing legs, or the honed body with rippling muscles. They may weave elaborate fantasies about life with their one and only love, even though the one they long for may be quite unavailable or not even exist. They may dream of being the famous concert pianist yet never sit down at the piano to practice.

Having grown up feeling separate and different from other family members, Fours frequently reject many of their own positive qualities (both of character and appearance) simply because those parts of themselves indicate that they are actually like members of their own family. Furthermore, there are Fours who have rejected much of their childhood. Some are quite unable to recognise that there was anything good about the parenting they received and may speak disparagingly of their parents and what they represent. Others experience shame about where they were brought up or what the family did not have.

Almost all remember the ways in which they were hurt in their younger years. Even when much older, Fours can still blame their parents for the state of their lives today. 'If only my parents had treated me with greater sensitivity ... If only I hadn't been sent to that school ... If only my musical talents had been nurtured ... If only, if only ...' And all the while, they are denying any personal responsibility for all the dreams that never came to fruition. By clinging to memories of hurtful things that were said, of having felt unacknowledged for their true selves, or of having felt abandoned or rejected, they continue to experience themselves as the one who has suffered, even though it is now all history.

Fours can focus so much on past hurts that they fail to even recognise that there are good things in their lives now; they reject the present in favour of holding onto the grievances from the past. All of the past history is repeatedly re-examined, year after year, with the bitter thoughts of the aggrieved Four continually fuelling the held onto hurts. These are highly unlikely to be spoken of openly, for in the eyes of the Four, it's up to those who inflicted these hurts to acknowledge what they have done and to apologise. So instead of taking responsibility for initiating what might be a healing interchange, these aggrieved Fours continue to hold onto blame, not realising that it is only themselves that is being damaged by this self-destructive behaviour. Over the years, the resentment and blame fester and build into hate and anger, until the day when it might finally spill out in a venomous, vicious attack on the unsuspecting recipient.

For Fours to consider:
- *By continuing to hold onto past grievances and projecting blame, who are you really hurting: those that hurt you in the past or yourself?*
- *In what ways is holding onto resentment and blame controlling your ability to experience happiness?*
- *What are you denying yourself by continuing to blame?*
- *We cannot change the past, but we can change our attitude to it. Instead of holding onto the past and allowing feelings of resentment or blame to control your life, what one thing could you do now to begin to free yourself and move on?*

Interaction with the Four

As we have seen, Fours process their world and their experiences in terms of their feelings and, when in a good space, are extremely aware of other people's feelings and are *sensitive* to the way they themselves affect others. They are concerned and deeply compassionate about what others are experiencing and unselfish in the amount of time they will give to those with problems.

However, when Fours drop into a lower-functioning place, they connect with little that is outside of their intense inner world. As a result, they can be very self-absorbed and highly *insensitive* to others, giving most of their attention to their own needs and feelings and little to other people's. This is particularly noticeable when in conversation with many Fours. Either you might find that most of what is discussed is about them or their lives or, if they themselves are not the primary topic of the conversation, they may lose interest and appear bored or rapidly turn the conversation around to themselves. When Fours are in this space, they expect you to listen to all they have to say about *their* lives, *their* problems, and *their* dreams or to take time to attend to *their* emotional needs and give support. Yet they give little attention to your concerns or problems – except when they themselves are directly affected by them.

In social situations, the self-consciousness of the average Four makes it hard for them to be light-hearted or have fun, yet they long to do so. Fours often see others being all that they wish they were – spontaneous, confident, and socially at ease – whereas they themselves often feel ill at ease and self-conscious. Being able to control and shape what happens as they interact with the outside world helps self-conscious Fours to feel more confident so, rather than reach out towards others, they may well withdraw and stay separate, hoping that by appearing interesting or enigmatic they will be able to entice other people to enter their world.

Unfortunately, this behaviour can result in others viewing them as aloof or standoffish, even superior. Yet the Four who behaves this way is probably longing to be noticed and included, secretly hoping that someone will seek them out and rescue them from their plight. Of course, rather than bringing them the connection and inclusion that they desire, this behaviour from the Four is more likely to bring about exactly the opposite to that which they desire: greater separation and even more isolation.

For Fours to consider:

- *How often have you withdrawn from engaging with people or getting involved in social events?*
- *What negative emotions have been present that make you feel you have to withdraw: envy, old hurts from the past, fear of rejection?*
- *What are you trying to avoid by not interacting?*
- *How much does this behaviour contribute to your feelings of being separate and not fitting in?*

Although it is quite common for Fours to seem withdrawn or separate, and have difficulty interacting with ease, other Fours present an optimistic, exuberant face to the world. (Here there is almost certainly a strong Three wing.) These Fours will not run the more typical, woeful pattern of Four but will instead try to convince you that life is full and satisfying and that they have all that they want. However, unless this is a higher-functioning Four (in which case they will be genuinely self-contented, confident, and at ease with life), the upbeat exterior is likely to be a façade hiding the true feelings beneath – the longing that they cannot let anyone see, the despair that life will ever bring the true happiness they seek, and the deep hatred of themselves.

Fours long to be understood and valued for who they really are, yet the complex and difficult behaviour of the lower-functioning Four frequently pushes others away. Despite their deep desire for connection and attention from others, they often find it hard to reach out beyond themselves to accept help or support when it *is* offered. When in this space, they will probably respond with denial or distain to suggestions about ways in which they could help themselves, and should it be suggested that they take responsibility for the way their life is instead of complaining or blaming others, the outcome is likely to be anger and hurt feelings. The problem is always perceived as being outside of themselves. 'No one really understands,' complains the woeful Four. Sadly, people eventually lose interest in the endless negativity. The self-absorption and complaints can drive even close friends and family away, with the result that, despite the desire for deep connection and a sense of belonging, many lower-functioning Fours end up lonely and isolated.

Moods, Melodrama and Melancholy

The emotional life of the Four always seems to be one of intensity. Sadness is not just unhappiness; it is the deepest despair. Happiness must be the ultimate in order to qualify. Fours are the drama queens and kings of the Enneagram, and in their eyes, no one experiences things as they do and no one understands what it is to be them. (In truth, no one but a Four *can* really understand because other types do not experience such emotional extremes.) Their roller coaster of emotions is highly unpredictable and their extreme mood swings may go from elation to despair and back again in so many minutes.

Every comment from others, every aspect of a situation, may be examined and turned over and over in the inner world of the sensitive Four. The tiniest thing can be exaggerated internally until what began as little or nothing becomes a full-blown internal drama. Yet, even though Fours may complain that they would just like to experience some inner peace, they often secretly enjoy their emotional states and inner dramas and will find ways of holding onto and even exacerbating their moods. Certain pieces of music may be played in order to intensify a sad, melancholy state or an intensely emotional love film might be watched so that the emotions the Four is experiencing within a relationship may be felt even more deeply.

Mood can be all-important to many Fours before they feel ready to interact with the world, especially when faced with a challenging situation, such as a first date, an important business meeting, or a party, and quite often, the right mood is created or enhanced with the use of fantasy. However, because the fantasy self created by the Four does not match reality, a carefully woven mood can all too easily be shattered – the taxi is late, someone makes the wrong comment, the Four's clothes don't feel just right for the occasion – and then the Four may feel quite unable to deal with the event. ('I'm just not up to this. I must leave.')

Being around a lower-functioning Four can be just like walking on eggshells. They are frequently touchy and volatile because little is accepted at face value or of the moment. Almost everything is interpreted as having wider, more dramatic ramifications, and hidden meanings are frequently perceived where there are none. A certain expression on a friend's face may be wildly misinterpreted, giving rise to misunderstanding and even loss of the friendship; a loved one's inattention at a social event must mean that love has died; harmless compliments to another are perceived as veiled insults to the Four, setting off a major emotional reaction. 'Your brother looks really great since losing weight' means 'You look lousy' to the oversensitive Four.

All of this just serves to intensify the Four's feelings of rejection, hurt and separation. However, instead of checking out the truth of the situation or asking what was really meant, many a Four will withdraw in order to avoid risking further hurt or rejection, turning inward into inner dramas of hurt and misunderstood feelings. Inevitably, this very behaviour makes it almost impossible to get the reality checks that are so badly needed; consequently, these Fours experience a great deal of unnecessary pain. Periods of depression are not uncommon, and these can last a day, a week, or much longer.

Higher-functioning Fours, however, are unlikely to get overwhelmed by negativity. They view their changing moods more as a benefit than a problem. All Fours experience fluctuating moods, yet the extremes experienced by the Four – the exquisiteness and drabness of life, the light and the dark, the joy and the despair – are often expressed in the art and music that come from emotional Fours. Those who are not Fours do not have such powerfully fluctuating emotions, yet the drama of such pieces can evoke emotional responses within us, bringing richness and depth to our emotional lives.

If you have a Four in your life

In order to facilitate improved interactions and feelings of compassion, it can be helpful to keep in mind what can be hard for the Four:

- endlessly longing for what they do not have
- being dissatisfied with what they do have

- experiencing dark moods of emptiness and despair
- feelings of self-hatred and loathing
- continually comparing self negatively to others
- feeling like the misfit who lives on the 'outside' whilst others are on the 'inside'
- feeling misunderstood and alone
- obsessing over every little thing from both the present and the past
- expecting too much from life
- experiencing inner turmoil and resentments

When not at their best, Fours can be

----

temperamental self-absorbed hypersensitive woeful needy withdrawn volatile envious socially ill-at-ease dramatising depressive snobbish morbid self-pitying self-inhibiting despairing self-destructive

----

CHAPTER 12

The Five

At their best, Fives are

---

objective   focused   wise   profound   gentle   kind   open-minded
perceptive   keeper of confidences   curious   level-headed
insightful   knowledgeable   innovative   calm in crises   self-sufficient

---

Fives are very private people who greatly value their own personal space. Wherever they live, they will find a quiet secluded place that becomes their sanctuary, their private castle where they can raise the drawbridge and not be disturbed. They tend to resent intrusion by others, and this sanctuary will be a place where the needs of the world will not impinge upon them and where they can recharge. Being happy with their own company, the Five will often spend long hours, days, or even weeks in solitude, with just themselves and their interests for company. They are independent people who greatly value self-sufficiency and autonomy, asking little from others, and unless high-functioning, often giving too little as well.

They are the true voyagers within the realm of thought and have minds that are intensely active; in fact, many Fives say that it seems as if their mind is going at 'a million miles a minute'. Although not all are truly cerebral, Fives generally have acutely searching minds and enjoy delving deeply into the subjects that interest them. Acquiring knowledge excites them, and a day without learning or acquiring new information is a day without sustenance for many Fives, just like a day without food might be for the rest of us!

Having a deep understanding of something, acquiring a large bank of facts, or accumulating collections makes the Five feel more confident and capable, more able to take charge of life. Although they may be interested in a variety of different things, many Fives choose to apply their laser-like focus to just one or two fields of interest. As a result, they often become very knowledgeable or even an expert within their chosen field. This may be anything that they are able to master – classical music, science-fiction movies, computers, the works of William Shakespeare, tin soldiers, the private world of the antelope – whatever captures their interest. In fact, many Fives would be the perfect candidate for the specialist subject part of Mastermind!

Many fives are very successful in what they do but they tend to get there by their ideas rather than what they physically achieve. 'Being the expert' is never about getting the accolades; it is about feeling in control, being the one who knows, and it's about finding their place in the world, their own niche.

The independent nature of the Five means that they are also independent thinkers. They are less likely than most to accept other people's opinions or go along with accepted doctrines, preferring to find things out for themselves and draw their own conclusions. Their thinking is often open-ended and far-reaching, pushing back the boundaries of what is known or thought to be possible; thus, a high proportion of scientists, inventors and science-fiction writers are Fives. Whereas the Six thinks *What if?* from a negative perspective (considering all of the worst possible scenarios and how to deal with them), the Five's curious and enquiring mind leads them to think *What if?* from a positive perspective, expanding their ideas into all realms of possibilities. *What if this were true? What if that were possible?*

There have been many high-functioning, inspired Fives who have refused to accept established or conventional ideas, their highly enquiring minds leading them to original, innovative ideas that overthrew accepted views. History is full of genius, iconoclastic Fives, such as Leonardo da Vinci, Isaac Newton, Charles Darwin, Marie Curie, and Albert Einstein. And, in the present day, we have the genius of Stephen Hawking, who has expanded the boundaries of the way we view the Universe.

Fives are gentle, kind people that others find unassuming and nonthreatening. Having the ability to perceive life on an expansive scale, the observations they make about people or situations are usually perceptive and accurate. They are usually patient and kind-hearted, and most will display an equal mixture of detachment and compassion regarding another's problems. They are able to listen unemotionally to the problem and are then likely to bring wise, perceptive views to the matter without getting personally involved with the outcome. This quality of detachment is fundamental to the make-up of Fives and gives them the ability to be objective, calm and clear thinking in situations that may send other types into turmoil. However, it also makes it hard for them to fully engage with life, and many Fives are loners.

The Five in Childhood

When the soul 'separates' itself from the All That Is and comes into life as a Five, the quality of Divine Essence from which the young child experiences a deep loss of connection is **Omniscience** – the All Knowing.[10] This creates the intrinsic sensitivity of the Five, and it is through the filter of this sensitivity that the young child then experiences the world and develops ways of coping with what is experienced.

Each small child seeks to find and attain that which seems to be unavailable to them in order that they might survive and get their needs met. Feeling small and helpless in a world that seems confusing, demanding, and overwhelming, the young Five feels inadequately equipped to cope with their experiences. They come to the unconscious conclusion that if they can acquire sufficient information and knowledge so that they could understand how everything in the world works, they

---

[10] See chapter 3, 'Unravelling Your Inner World: The Early Years.'

would be able to deal with the demands of the world and survive. The young Five then begins to take on these childhood beliefs:

> 'I do not have enough resources to
> cope with the demands of the world.'
> 'Knowledge is the key to survival.'
> 'If I gain knowledge and understand
> everything, I will be safe and loved.'

The resultant behaviour patterns that spiral out of these untrue beliefs are unconsciously designed to enable the Five to avoid being overwhelmed by the world and the people in it, and to acquire or hang onto whatever they need to make them feel more confident and capable.

Young Fives decide that they will no longer feel helpless or inadequate if they can just get to understand what makes the world the way it is and where they fit into it; it seems, therefore, a logical step to decide (subconsciously) that knowledge must be the key to survival in a world that threatens to overwhelm or engulf them. At an early age, the Five discovers that the mind seems to be a safe place to retreat to. After all, no one can follow you into the inner sanctum of your mind, and you do not have to reveal your thoughts unless you choose to.[11] Retreating physically also makes them feel safe, and consequently, Fives begin to develop solitary pursuits, being happy with their own company from a young age. They have highly developed imaginations, and many teenage Fives spend much time alone creating fantasy worlds in which they are strong and in control rather than engaging with reality. In fact, it is extremely common for young Fives to get told by their families that they should get out more!

---

[11]   The childhood circumstances do not create the personality; they were chosen by the soul so that the personality patterns of the Five would fully develop.

The Detached Observer

The Five is often referred to as 'The Observer' of the Enneagram. They have learned that it is safer to withdraw and watch, to take mental notes or accumulate facts, and to stay uninvolved as much as possible. Consequently, they see the world around them with startling clarity, analysing things that the rest of us just don't notice, and drawing highly perceptive conclusions from what they observe.

However, withdrawing and taking mental notes is not the same as doing, and average Fives tend to live much of life 'in preparation mode' rather than fully engaging with life. They use their minds rather like scouts sent ahead to gather information that is used to decide whether it will be safe enough to enter the unknown territory. Unfortunately, all too often, they go on and on gathering more information, practicing a technique, or working things out in theory yet not moving on to take action. For example, learning to dance clearly involves dancing, yet a Five may watch people dancing on a video, take notes, and learn the steps in theory but never actually set foot on a dance floor.

This state of continual analysis and preparation can hold Fives back from reaching their potential for a long time, sometimes for a lifetime. Sadly, they may wake up one day and realise that knowing about life is not the same as living it, that they have not really been living life but preparing for a life that never really happened.

For Fives to consider:
- *In what areas of your life do you tend to be in preparation mode, thinking about situations and analysing possibilities rather than actually doing?*
- *How will you know when you have enough knowledge or information?*
- *How will you know when you are ready to take action?*
- *What are you missing out on by holding back instead of just doing it?*

Managing Space and Energy

There is a real need for average to low-functioning Fives to just be left alone much of the time to pursue their own interests, without intrusion or demands from others. Feeling that they do not have sufficient resources within themselves to deal with their world adequately, they easily feel drained and depleted by other people, so they need to regularly withdraw and shut out the world in order to recharge batteries. Being very private people, they are happy with their own company and rarely experience loneliness. Many Fives are real loners and most accept this as their lot – it's just the way it is. Any feelings of loneliness are easily detached from or repressed by focusing on pursuits that involve mind activity.

The need for privacy can, however, become isolation when the Five has withdrawn from others so much that it begins to feel impossible to reach out. Then, the ivory tower that made them feel safe and at ease begins to feel like a prison. To come out would involve reaching out to others to initiate contact or to ask for help, and this leaves the Five trapped because, as a withdrawal type, they are not going to make the first move and the Five rarely asks anyone for help.

Fives are often accused of being non-giving, and it is true that they tend to withhold sharing many aspects of themselves. They feel that they have to hold onto whatever they have – whether that is energy, thoughts, time, emotions, or even information – for there is within them the fear that if they put themselves out there in the world too much they will be depleted by what is demanded of them.

One of the big concerns of the Five is to manage their own energy around other people, especially when their space has been invaded by close relationships or when they have been around a lot of other people. Then they need time alone to refresh their energy. Often, they avoid sharing their plans with others because it gives them a sense of freedom to know that the people in their life do not know what they are intending to do, or when. This makes it possible to just take off without reference to others or to do unpredictable things.

They often seem to operate on a need-to-know basis, and if challenged about the lack of information offered, are very likely to say, 'I didn't tell you because you didn't ask'. However, the lack of disclosure displayed by Fives has its plus points – if you tell a Five something in confidence, it will go with them to the grave! They expect others to respect their great desire for privacy, and they give equal respect to your privacy. Should they entrust you with some confidential information, never tell other people. It is devastating to a Five if a confidence is disclosed to others; they feel very let down and can get very angry about what they feel is real betrayal.

Unless you have earned the trust of the Five in your life, you will never get to know all about them. They rarely offer details and facts about their lives to friends and acquaintances and, even when directly asked a question about themselves, are quite likely to avoid a direct answer.

Another way that average Fives maintain their privacy is by compartmentalising different areas of their lives. Fives often have many different spheres of interest and may belong to groups or societies where they come in contact with lots of different people; however, friends from one area of interest are quite likely to not be introduced to those of another group. By withholding one group from another in this way, the Five avoids being depleted. Each group gets a little of you; none get it all.

For Fives to consider:
- *How does it feel when there seems to be excessive claims or demands upon your time and energy?*
- *How do you react when you feel intruded upon?*
- *Do you contract into yourself?*
- *What do you do to protect your boundaries?*

Autonomy and Independence

The philosophy of the average Five is 'I'll ask nothing of you, and then you won't ask anything from me.' Fearing that others may expect more from them than they can deliver, they avoid being indebted to others by asking for nothing; they rarely seek help or input from anyone. By not asking from others, they avoid putting themselves in a position of obligation to give back. Many view the Five as non-giving, but that's only true up to a point. It's not that they won't do things for others. In fact, if their help is requested with regard to their sphere of knowledge, they are only too willing to give others the benefit of their often superior knowledge. It's just that their desire for autonomy means that they would prefer to keep themselves to themselves. That way, they can control how much is given and when; thus, they avoid feeling depleted.

For Fives to consider:
- *What, if anything, do you ask for from others?*
- *What does it feel like to ask for help from others?*
- *If others ask for help, are you willing to give it?*

Fives are not influenced by other people's opinion and are not in any way afraid of going out on a limb where their opinion about something differs from the accepted norm. Seeking social acceptance is just not part of the make-up of a Five, and most are generally quite happy to be viewed by others as different or even geeky ('They either like me or they don't.'). Acquiring unusual facts, and having knowledge and understanding of things most other people know little about, gives the average Five a feeling of confidence. They enjoy being the one who 'knows' and when other people say, 'You know what you are talking about,' it strengthens their self-esteem.

Mind and Body

The questioning, searching nature of the Five's mind, combined with a highly perceptive intelligence, results in many higher-functioning Fives exploring the more profound questions of life, looking for deeper meaning even within the mundane. They have the potential for gnosis – the ability to just know Universal and Spiritual truths without knowing how they know. When they access this knowledge and integrate it with what they know about the physical world, then there is the potential for astonishing and groundbreaking insights and ideas.

Whatever Fives focus their curious minds on will be deeply probed, with facts and figures analysed and stored away in the recesses of their minds. The desire to relentlessly pursue their area of specialised knowledge is more prevalent in male Fives than females, and can result in them 'focusing on the trees and missing the forest'. They can find themselves so driven by their field of interest and the intensity of their thoughts that they can be highly strung, overly intense, and absent-minded. With their minds entirely focused on cerebral activity, they may continually lose important notes, forget appointments, or mislay their glasses and car keys. Completely lost in their inner world, they can lose touch with reality and neglect other areas of life, including interacting with their families.

They are continually trying to avoid the world invading their space. They feel that if they let the world in, it will overwhelm them, so they live within the fortress of their minds. They feel secure in the fortress where they can be in control, they can see everything that is going on around them and the world can't get them, and it can take a huge amount of effort to go outside of it. The world of thought is much more interesting than the world of action; what goes on in their heads is what is important, the body being just the vehicle in which 'I' – the mind – is carried around and Fives are inclined to neglect the vehicle. So as they become increasingly detached from the physical world, there can also be a detachment from the basic needs of the physical body, such as the need to eat or sleep; they might work all night, forgetting to eat or surviving on just crisps and Coke and then the next day forget to shower or change their clothes. They can, quite literally, become the 'disembodied mind'.

For Fives to consider:
- *Which areas of your life do you put your attention intently into?*
- *Which areas of your life get neglected?*
- *How often do your physical needs – food, sleep, physical appearance, etc. – get neglected when you are involved in mind activity?*

- *Looking back at the last twenty-four hours, how many hours did you spend in your mind fantasising, theorising, or in intellectual pursuits?*
- *How many hours did you spend interacting with the world or the people in it? Does the balance between these two ways of spending your time need readdressing?*

Being more at ease in the realm of the mind than the physical world, Fives are often ungrounded and many have poor coordination. Most Fives, male Fives in particular, are inclined to avoid much physical activity, and this, combined perhaps with a poor diet, may lead to quite an unhealthy lifestyle. However, higher-functioning Fives who frequently 'go to 7' (one of their connections across the Enneagram) may get involved with all sorts of physical activity because, when emotionally secure, physical sensation makes a welcome change from the endless cerebral activity. The type of activities these Five might engage in will, however, generally have a solitary aspect to them, rather than being team sports. Activities, such as fell-walking or swimming, for instance, allow the Five to retain their autonomy without others having expectations of them.

Irrespective of their body type, many Fives feel themselves to be weak and insubstantial. They experience themselves as being unable to adequately defend themselves physically, as the one who is likely to get picked on or get sand kicked in the face on the beach. Even those who have large strong bodies view themselves as somehow vulnerable and unable to defend themselves adequately.

Fives are the least materialistic of all the types and they can be quite satisfied with the bare necessities of life. They often have fewer clothes and other possessions than other people and do not see the need for more. After all, physical comforts are less valuable and interesting when you live more in the mind than the body. Even when they are in need financially or physically, average Fives will do without rather than ask for help in order to maintain their independence, because getting help from others may involve personal entanglements or the need to return the favour.

For Fives to consider:

- *How do you minimise your wants and desires (especially compared to others)?*
- *Are you even aware of having needs or desires?*

Emotions

Fives only allow their emotions to be felt in private; in public, they will always maintain emotional control. Consequently, to those who do not know this private aspect of the Five, they can appear withdrawn and coldly detached, yet they are actually very sensitive and feel deeply about many things. They have the ability, however, to detach from their emotions and retreat into their minds, where they feel safer and can observe themselves and their reactions from a distance. This way, the Five reasons, a logical course of action can be decided upon or an emotional problem can be solved rationally without the actual emotion getting in the way. Then later, time alone is needed to reflect and assimilate, to allow their feelings to finally emerge privately and to assess and understand what they have been experiencing.

For Fives to consider:

- *What sorts of situations cause you to withdraw emotionally into the safety of your mind?*
- *What are you escaping from?*
- *Next time you are with people in situations like that, see if you can catch yourself withdrawing and stay connected instead. What does that feel like?*

The truth is, much of the time, Fives do not experience their emotions in real time; the exception to this is when something really throws them off balance for being out of control emotionally and making them feel vulnerable. They fear that, if their emotions get the better of them, they might reveal something they do not wish to, that some part of their protected inner self might be exposed. Consequently,

Fives will mostly steer clear of that level of intensity. However, should they experience something that feels really uncomfortable, they will withdraw – physically if possible – or if they cannot absent themselves, they will mentally bring up the drawbridge. Withdrawing into the fortress of the mind gives some much needed time – may only be a few minutes – in order to come up with a response or reaction that enables them to stay in control.

Having this ability to separate emotions from thoughts and memories, the Five is able to remember, or mentally relive, painful situations without actually re-experiencing the emotions that were connected to the actual event. So for example, when a Five is telling you about a childhood trauma or some relationship that ended painfully, it can feel as if the event is being told by a reporter or by someone who was never there but who had heard the details. From the point of view of the Five, it just makes sense to remain objective about things. After all, look what damage over emotionalism causes in the world!

Interaction with the Five

Many Fives come across as self-sufficient loners who have few or even no friends. All Fives are people who resent intrusion and desire plenty of time alone, yet they may secretly feel lonely sometimes and would welcome some interesting person to knock on their door. However, the continual need of the average Five to withdraw and remain detached often results in them having poor social skills; they just don't get the opportunity to practice them! They do not even have to be alone to avoid real interaction. They can be with a group of people but remain detached and unaffected emotionally from what is going on. Even when actually talking, the sense of detachment can result in the Five feeling as if they are outside of themselves, watching themselves, observing their own words and the way they are interacting, without really being involved.

In truth, many Fives find conversation quite a strain, except when communicating from their field of knowledge. They are just not interested in average social gatherings, where they find the small talk pointless or trivial, and lower-functioning Fives can be scathing and derogatory about the pointlessness of talking with 'stupid' people.

However, some Fives can be quite sociable, but as a rule, this will only be with groups of like-minded people – clubs and societies that concern themselves with serious or intellectual pursuits, such as music societies, gardening clubs, yoga groups, and book clubs – or other groups where they might particularly enjoy debating, critiquing, or analysing complex ideas. In situations like these, where the average Five feels at ease because of the knowledge they have, there can be a strong desire to pass on information to others, and they gain confidence when it is well received.

In general conversation, however, most Fives do not contribute very much. It can be tempting for people close to the Five to fill in the gaps and speak for them, a practice greatly resented by the Five. The truth is they have almost certainly formed many ideas and insights about what you are saying, but they often do not bother to share them with you. They may even feel it's not worth the effort because you probably wouldn't understand what they were talking about anyway! If they are encouraged to expand on the little they have said – without the use of probing or demanding questions – they will find their own way to communicate their thoughts, but it has to be on their terms.

Despite appearances to the contrary, Fives have a real desire to connect with the outside world and with other people, and when they feel safe they can be very communicative. But so often, Fives will just sit and listen to conversations going on around them, allowing others to take the initiative while they remain silent. Then, often unexpectedly, they will come out with a highly perceptive observation, a point others have missed, or coolly give some amazing but very relevant factual information that no one else knows. Their perceptive comments can often ruthlessly cut through the 'inconsequential rubbish' (as they see it) expressed by others so that sometimes they can come over to others as tactless or rude. However, Fives rarely care what opinion other people have of them, so they do not fear speaking their minds.

For Fives to consider:

- *Last time you were in a social situation, how much of the time were you mainly watching as an observer rather than interacting?*
- *What is it like for you to interact with others outside of your field of interest or expertise?*

The Five's lack of tact, combined with inadequate social skills, can easily make them appear superior or overbearing even when they are just trying to be helpful with information. However, all Fives like to know something other people do not, and lower-functioning Fives can sometimes be scathing in the way they treat the less knowledgeable. They may even enjoy being deliberately argumentative in order to prove they can run intellectual rings around you.

When expected to be involved in a social situation, Fives like to know in advance what will happen and what might be expected of them, and they generally do not like being expected to reply to questions for which they are unprepared. If the Five feels challenged by a question, it can be difficult to get a straight answer from them because of the fear that the answer may be too revealing, be incomplete, or that it may provoke conflict. Being warned in advance of the nature of demands or questions enables the Five to prepare responses so that there are no emotional shocks or embarrassment to be experienced. Pushing a Five for a response to a question is counterproductive, because when they are not prepared, it can make them feel vulnerable. The response you are most likely to get will be something like 'Tell me what you want to know. I'll think about it and get back to you.' They need to take in the question, integrate it into their inner world, and synthesise any feelings they have about it before they feel prepared (comfortable and safe) to answer it, if at all.

If you have a Five in your life

In order to facilitate improved interactions and feelings of compassion, it can be helpful to keep in mind what can be hard for the Five:

- feeling drained by demands from others
- difficulty with communicating the intricate depth of their knowledge
- finding it hard to get their knowledge and insights out into the world
- being aware that those with better social skills but less intelligence or technical knowledge are often listened to more than they are
- being pressured to be more sociable
- being accused of being unemotional or unfeeling
- feeling defensive when they do not know something
- getting accused of being a know-it-all when, in the desire to make a connection, they offer too much of their knowledge

When not at their best, Fives can be

----

detached anti-social intense withholding withdrawn remote supercilious mean mentally self-absorbed isolated contemptuous mocking cynical antagonistic alienated reclusive nihilistic eccentric

----

CHAPTER 13

The Six

At their best, Sixes are

----

warm-hearted hard-working responsible trouble-shooter
strong bonder authority-upholding reliable vigilant
faithful committed steadfast loyal engaging courageous
co-operative persistent dependable

O ther people generally respond very positively to Sixes because they are warm-hearted, engaging people of personal integrity and strong conscience. They are hardworking and highly responsible individuals who can get very uptight and stressed out, yet when relaxed, they don't take themselves too seriously and can be playful and even funny.

Sixes are people you can rely on. They are people of their word and won't let you down no matter how difficult or challenging a situation they find themselves in. Their persistent determination and amazing endurance mean that they will complete their objectives where less determined types would just give up. No matter how tired they are at the end of a day, if there are duties unfinished, or they have not fulfilled a commitment they have made to someone else, they do not rest until all their tasks are finished. Like Ones, they have the *should, must* orientation, but with a different underlying driving energy.

Although they rarely ask for help from others, Sixes are always willing to give help when there is a need. It is interesting to note that when someone is in crisis, both the Two and the Six will offer help, but each type relates to you in a different way, each offering a different sort of help. The Two will relate to your *feelings* and will want to do something to help you *feel* better emotionally. They are most likely to sit you down and talk with you about what troubles you and how it makes you feel. The Six, however, will relate to your *physical needs* and offer *practical* help to solve your problem but is unlikely to get much involved with your emotional needs. When there are difficulties or problems, and people are in conflict, Sixes will go out of their way to help everyone arrive at a solution where no one loses out, to achieve a win-win situation, but will never look for accolades or seek the best out of the situation for themselves.

You will find few Sixes in positions in life where they get the limelight. They are the 'foot soldiers' of life, rarely the 'generals'. They can be outstanding and committed workers for the common good, serving for the simple joy of being part of a worthwhile purpose without need for recognition; in fact, too much attention is inclined to embarrass them. As long as they know that what they have done has been valued, and that they have done a good job and made a worthwhile contribution, they are satisfied. They get great pleasure from helping other people achieve their goals and will go out on a limb to help, to the point of working until exhausted or even sacrificing themselves financially.

Although Sixes are usually quick movers and people of action, they rarely act on the spur of the moment. They think things out before moving forward on an idea, considering every possible nuance. In fact, you could say that 'Look before you leap' would be their catchphrase. To the Six, this just makes sense; after all, you never know what you might be getting yourself into.

These are the natural troubleshooters of society. They are cautious and vigilant people who check everything out and excel at spotting potential problems. It is as if Sixes have their own personal radar that enables them to notice things that the rest of us miss. They are observant people, as well as being naturally suspicious of everything and everyone. For instance, should they look out of the window at night and see a strange car cruising along the road, they will probably note down the registration number just in case. This suspicious nature means that their minds are perfect for sleuthing, so if you watch a murder mystery with a Six, you can be sure they will spot all the clues and solve the murder before anyone else can!

To the Six, doubting and questioning everything just makes sense. This watchful and suspicious nature is a result of trying to cover all bases in order to create safety and security in an uncertain world and to ensure that everything in the future is going to be OK. Of course, life is unpredictable and nothing is ever really sure about the future; consequently, Sixes experience an enormous amount of worry and anxiety that affects all aspects of their lives. Even when there is nothing particular to worry about, they experience a constant, subtle background of anxiety, so continuous and insidious that many Sixes are hardly aware of it; it just seems normal to them. In fact, many Sixes are surprised to discover that the rest of us do not experience that undercurrent of anxiety all the time!

The Six in Childhood

When the soul 'separates' itself from the All That Is and comes into life as a Six, the quality of Divine Essence from which the young child experiences a deep loss of connection is **Inner Knowing** (beyond trust and faith).[12] This creates the intrinsic sensitivity of the Six, and it is through the filter of this sensitivity that the young child experiences the world and develops ways of coping with what is experienced.

Each small child seeks to find and attain that which seems to be unavailable to them in order that they might survive and get their needs met. Young Sixes sense that their natural inner guidance seems uncertain or absent, and this results in them experiencing their inner world as lacking substance and solidity, as if everything is shifting and nothing can be relied upon. Nor do they seem able to find the surety

---

12   See chapter 3, 'Unravelling Your Inner World: The Early Years.'

and dependability that a young, helpless infant needs to feel safe and secure within their parenting environment. In fact, there is almost always some aspect of the parenting that Sixes receive that is experienced as unpredictable, uncertain, or unreliable.[13] Perhaps one parent had unpredictable moods swings and the quality of nurture and attention varied wildly; perhaps the family circumstances changed suddenly due to divorce, death, or financial hardship; or perhaps the Six was parented by someone who was insecure about handling an infant.

Whatever the circumstances of their young years, the result is that the child comes to the unconscious conclusion that the world is a precarious and frightening place and they are not safe. The childhood beliefs that are consequently taken on are:

'The world is dangerous and threatening and I am not safe.'
'Everything must be checked out because nothing can be trusted.'
'I must seek security and deal with danger, either
by avoiding it or by facing it head on.'

The resultant behaviour patterns that spiral out from the untrue beliefs of the young Six then become all about survival. These beliefs are unconsciously designed to try to create the feelings of safety and security that the Six does not find within this world, a world that is experienced as full of potential dangers. Yet survival answers must be found. Their inner terrain provides little that can be relied upon, so they need to find answers outside of themselves. Everything must be checked out in order to be safe and survive. Nothing and no one can really be trusted; everything must be questioned. Being in this state of perpetual uncertainty and unease means that the Six grows up with a solar plexus that is in a continual turmoil of anxiety and fear. As a result, any gut feeling or intuition that *is* present feels insubstantial and not to be trusted. The outcome is that Sixes grow up out of touch with their own knowing and intuition and with a deep-seated insecurity.

---

[13] The childhood circumstances do not create the personality; they were chosen by the soul so that the Six personality patterns would fully develop.

The Seesaw Six

Most of the negative thinking of the adult Six, as well as their negative behaviour patterns, is driven by this lack of inner security. Finding little within their world that feels secure and trustworthy, and doubting their own feelings and intuitive perceptions, the Six seeks within the mind for answers and solutions to the vagaries of life. However, the nature of the mind is to doubt and judge, creating negativity and fear. It never remains still, constantly shifting and changing, and it cannot be relied upon to give the same answer twice. It goes to and fro, backwards and forwards, this way and that, leading us in one direction in one moment and then, in the next, completely the opposite. Consequently, the Six experiences continual uncertainty, perpetually questioning and checking everything out but always left doubting and unsure.

Sixes are the worriers of the Enneagram and have difficulty being sure of anything – what they feel, what they know, what they want to do, what they believe – and doubt pervades everything. Making decisions is fraught with anxiety, and the longer their indecision continues, the greater their level of stress and anxiety. Their 'inner knowing' is either absent or seems untrustworthy. (The Six finds it hard to distinguish 'gut feelings' from their anxiety because the solar plexus is the body's fear centre and is so close physically to what we would term the gut.) So they seek guidance from people, accepted doctrines, belief systems, or tried and trusted organisations to tell them what to do and how or when to do it. In order to arrive at a decision, they may consult several friends, listen to the opinion of their dentist or the lady working in the library, or read something on the Internet, in a book, or in a newspaper. And if (or more likely *when*) the advice from these different sources conflicts, the Six becomes even more anxious and confused, right back where they started but still not having made a decision that feels comfortable. Sometimes, Sixes will make a sudden decision, any decision, just to relieve their anxiety, but even when a decision has been made, they will often question their own decision, creating further anxiety. Much of the

171

time though, they sit on the fence, unable to go one way or the other, putting off making the decision for fear that they might be making the wrong one.

For Sixes to consider:
- *When you have a decision to make, how do you approach it?*
- *What or who do you rely on to help you make the decision?*
- *What decisions are you putting off?*
- *Are you looking for a safe bet or a guarantee that your decision will be the right one?*

When Sixes find the outside 'authority' that seems to be what they need in order to get the information and answers they are looking for, they become devoted and totally trusting followers. In fact, should this trusted authority come in the shape of a person, the opinion of this person can then become so much valued that he or she can attain guru status in the eyes of the Six. When the Six finds a belief, procedure, or system that they come to trust, they can then find it extremely difficult to change their loyalties or step outside of the established doctrines or rules of the voice of authority that they have come to trust. There is, then, a rigidity and stubbornness in average Sixes that, when combined with their fear, makes it really hard for them to be moved away from what they believe in.

Just as the thinking processes of the Six are constantly oscillating to and fro, swinging this way and that, so are their reactions and behaviour. When we look at the overall picture of Sixness, for every observation made about the Six, it seems as if the opposite is also true. They get anxious and fearful about making decisions yet stubbornly resist others making decisions for them; they avoid being proactive but do not want others to control their lives; they are fearful yet can be courageous; they are both trusting and distrusting; they are thinkers and doers … and so on, and so on.

Inevitably then, the outward display of Six characteristics varies enormously from one Six to another. As a result, identifying a Six as a Six is often quite difficult. Their personalities range from Sixes who can be reserved and hesitant, even timid, to those who can be independent, outspoken and confrontational. So one Six in your life can appear very different from another and, making it even harder to identify or understand them, wherever any Six sits along this continuum, he or she will seem to be a mass of contradictions! In fact, it is the contradictory quality within Sixes that seems to be the very essence of Sixness.

Reliance and Self-Reliance

This contradictory quality of Sixness is found throughout all aspects of the personality and is mirrored by the fact that there often seems to be two different types of Sixes.

The *reliant* Six consults many people when trying to make decisions and thus *relies* upon what others say. In contrast, the *self-reliant* Six does not ask other people (although they will check out their own sources of facts and information written by those that they perceive as experts) and is therefore *self-reliant*, being largely independent of the opinion of others. However, the self-reliant Six actually wants to be the authority that others seek out for guidance; it boosts their confidence to be the 'one who knows' and they will always be willing to offer helpful advice when asked.

In most Sixes, one side of Sixness is predominant; thus, you may recognise yourself as being either the reliant type or the self-reliant type. However, any Six may display *both* types of behaviour at *different* times, in *different* situations, moving backwards and forwards between them.

The Reliant Six

Sixes that are predominantly of the reliant type probably grew up feeling that it was not OK to be strong and that being submissive and malleable was expected. The more insecure the reliant Six is, the more they give away their power and the more likely it is that they will find one particular person that they completely trust to give them guidance.

This person then becomes their anchor, their support, and foundation, giving them some much-needed solidity, and they come to rely on this person as their fountain of knowledge and strength.

Reliant Sixes feel their anxiety and fear acutely and it often overcomes them; it can paralyse them and prevent them from moving forward, just as a rabbit freezes when caught in the headlights of the car. These Sixes are often timid and hesitant in nature and try to stay out of trouble by being compliant to others. They give away their own power to people in their lives that they perceive as stronger or superior (and then may berate themselves for being such a coward!). Although reliant Sixes appears to be an easy pushover, they do have strength, as all Sixes have, but they exert their strength by behaving in passive-aggressive ways. They may say that they will do something, in order to appear compliant and to keep the peace, and then simply not do it. Or perhaps the Six might ask everyone's advice about something and then reject all of it with an inner feeling of rebelliousness. 'I won't be pressured into this.'

The Self-Reliant Six

Sixes that are of the self-reliant type probably grew up having to behave much tougher than they felt and believing that it was not OK to show fear. To others, self-reliant Sixes do not actually appear to experience anxiety or fear, but what they display outwardly is very different from what is going on inside. Their level of anxiety, fear and worry can be just as high as it is for the reliant Six, but judging by appearances, you just wouldn't know. Not only do they not show it externally, but they seek to demonstrate to themselves and others that they are neither insecure nor fearful.

In order to achieve this, some self-reliant Sixes become the rebel, the one who refuses to follow the rules, the one who challenges authority. Most will, at some point in their lives, engage in activities that bring up their fear just so that they can prove to themselves that they can subjugate it. The expression 'Feel the fear and do it anyway' would seem to epitomise the way they approach life! They boost their own confidence and feelings of inner strength and power by engaging in activities that shows their fearlessness. Such challenging activities might include climbing an impossible-looking tree; going hang-gliding, mountain climbing, or daredevil bike riding; snowboarding down a black run within weeks of learning to ski; financially taking huge risks with vast sums of money, and so on.

Reliant	Self-Reliant
Grew up believing it was not OK to be strong	Grew up believing you had to be strong and not show fear
Relies upon others (especially one other) to be the source of information/support	Relies upon self to find out information; does not seek support from others
Feels anxiety and fear acutely; fear freezes and immobilizes	Does not seem to experience anxiety or fear; feels the fear and does it anyway
Appears uncertain, jittery, or lacking in confidence	Displays confident demeanour to the world
Very compliant; gives away own power	Eager to please but maintains personal power
Tries to stay out of trouble	May be a rule breaker
If controlled by others, displays passive-aggressive behaviour; outwardly compliant but experiences inner rebelliousness	Will not be controlled or told what to do
Reacts to being caught making a mistake by becoming nervous and tries even harder to please	Reacts to being caught making a mistake by becoming angry, even aggressive

Anxiety, Fear and Projection

Although Sixes experience many nameless fears, projection into the future shapes much of the Six's world and creates most of their anxiety. They rarely experience true peace of mind because they live in a state of ceaseless guardedness, looking out for the next problem and trying to work out how to deal with it. They just can't seem to help but consider the worst-case scenario, with them continually thinking or saying, 'What if ...' or 'Yes, but ...' If you ask a Six what they worry about, they will probably reply, 'Everything!'

Money matters are a big source of concern for many because money usually means security so Sixes worry about how they will manage if the worst happens (i.e., they end up penniless, homeless, or jobless). Consequently, insurance for everything seems essential for Sixes and most will go for 'belt and braces' and have multiple policies to insure against all possible eventualities.

Planning a trip away can be fraught with worry. 'Have we made the right choice?' 'Will we catch the aeroplane?' 'What will we do if our money gets stolen?' And most Sixes worry about being burgled, so many have multiple locks fitted on their doors. Having the car stolen is a favourite concern, and many Sixes park their car in the most obtrusive place in public car parks and check out the area as they leave in case there are suspicious characters hanging about! Of course, we all need to be careful, but this over cautiousness can go too far, and for a Six in a lower-functioning state, anxiety can turn into panic attacks and caution can become real paranoia, with the Six suspecting everyone and fearing everything.

Continually trying to second-guess how things will turn out is 'just being realistic' as far as Sixes are concerned – "It's better to be safe than sorry" - but to others they can seem to be very negative people. It is unfortunately true that for Sixes, the glass is always half empty. They are naturally pessimists rather than optimists, expecting the worst outcome of every situation before they allow themselves to look at positive possibilities. Of course, they always *hope* things will turn out well, but they don't really *believe* that they will. So even when they are able to convince themselves that everything will be OK, they rarely stay in a positive state of mind for long, and negative thinking soon undermines their hopefulness, which then quickly turns back into doubt.

As a result of all these endless projections into the future and what problems it might hold for them, Sixes are very much more reactive than proactive. After all, from the perspective of Sixness, waiting to see how things turn out and then reacting is much safer than trying to control fate. You know what you're dealing with if you wait to see what life throws at you and then make a decision about how to deal with it. Unfortunately, because Sixes are always trying to make decisions that will make them feel safe and secure, most of these decisions are inevitably based on fear.

For Sixes to consider:
- *What does security mean to you?*
- *Can you ever know absolutely that you are secure and safe?*
- *How many of your 'What if?' projections actually happen? 50 per cent of them? 10 per cent? 5 per cent? 1 per cent? Be honest.*
- *How often do your projections cause you to put off making a decision?*
- *How does indecision affect you emotionally?*

In spite of all the fear they experience, Sixes can become fearless when in situations that would make others afraid. They will dive into dangerous situations for the sake of someone else without a thought for their own safety; they really can be the intrepid hero, which can surprise everyone who knows them, as well as themselves. Afterwards, they may ask themselves how they managed to be so brave. What they may not have realised is that, in this particular situation, action came before thought, so there was no time for the doubting, questioning mind to cut in, whereas under normal circumstances, thought *always* precedes action for the Six, making them think twice about doing something precarious or dangerous.

Although few Sixes would view themselves as courageous, they truly are the bravest of all the Enneagram types. It may seem as if there are other types that are tougher. However, when you begin to understand that average Sixes see landmines at every turn but overcome their fear and just keep going, you realise that just getting through each day must take enormous courage and that Sixes are real *survivors!*

People Pleasing

Although Sixes would like to appear equal to those around them, they think of themselves as being 'less than' – not just one step down from others but more than one. And being people that expect the worst, Sixes have an expectation of being the one who gets it wrong, either in words or in actions.

The need to compensate for what they see as their lack results in Sixes being people pleasers. They feel that if they please others, then those people will have a higher regard for them, which will in turn enable them to have a better regard for themselves. Moreover, they tend to overcompensate for what they see as their deficiencies by putting a great deal of effort into all that they do; the Six can be like a steam engine with no rails to run on. They get themselves such a head of steam that they can wear themselves out unnecessarily. And although they will always be there to help others, they find it extremely difficult to ask for help when they are overburdened or in need.

These are intrinsically good people, but sometimes they are good to their own cost. Sixes are the true martyrs of this world, for they sacrifice their energy and time putting themselves out for others in the desire to please. The unspoken attitude of the Six is 'If those around me are happy, if they think I have done a good job, then everything in my world will be OK and I can be happy.' In truth, the self-worth of the Six relies heavily upon the way in which others perceive them – and they need to be perceived as reliable, trustworthy people who do a good job. Consequently, because the need to be accepted and to belong is strong in the Six, they fear getting into trouble with those they want to please. As a result, Sixes find it difficult to admit mistakes. From their perspective, being seen to be wrong means someone is blaming them. (In fact, nobody blames them worse than themselves, for they judge themselves harshly.) So when they feel they have been caught out in a mistake, they can become very defensive. And when defensive, the self-reliant Six is likely to get angry whereas the reliant Six becomes nervous.

Authority

The tendency of Sixes to view themselves inferior to, or 'one step down' from, others results in most being very respectful or wary of authority. The presence of authority in our lives gives the Six a feeling of safety and solidity in an uncertain world, a sense of protection against potential chaos. Rules give structure, and structure spells safety to the Six. Yet Sixes have an ambivalent attitude towards rules and authority.

On one hand, they believe strongly in the laws and regulations made by those in positions of authority. From the perspective of the Six, without the control exerted by authority, the fabric of society would surely crumble and there would be nothing safe left in the world. Therefore, Sixes generally do all they can to ensure that rules and regulations are upheld. It is not uncommon for Sixes to become highly judgemental or angry about people who break the rules, especially those people whose behaviour flies in the face of what is conventionally deemed acceptable by society. For Sixes, rule breaking threatens security and stability and must be avoided.

Perversely, however, Sixes are also suspicious of authority. Although the Six says other people should follow the rules, they do not want to be personally affected by them. They resist being told what to do and/or they fear getting into trouble. Consequently, when average Sixes come up against a higher authority, they might either rebel against following the rules (the self-reliant Six) or keep their heads down so as not to draw attention to themselves (the reliant Six).

Safe Boundaries

Routine and predictability help Sixes to feel comfortable and secure. Consequently, making changes in their lives is difficult for them because change spells uncertainty. 'How can I know whether this is going to work out? Wouldn't it be much safer to stay with what I know? What if …?' Change also involves choice, and too much choice makes Sixes anxious because choice means making decisions. They are much happier with limited choices that they know and can depend on; the unknown cannot be trusted.

This difficulty with change might show up in many different ways, such as wanting to book the same holiday as last year, always choosing the same dish from the Chinese take-away, taking the same route to work every day, or only feeling happy with one particular colour or make of car. Keeping their world small and secure in this way means that Sixes generally lack spontaneity and, as a consequence, can be perceived by others as stuck or boring. Those involved in the life of the Six can help by giving gentle encouragement to expand beyond their safe boundaries, little by little.

Not feeling comfortable with expanding their boundaries, combined with the procrastination that comes about through indecision, means that Sixes miss many opportunities in life. They find it so hard to just go out and grab life; instead, they wait, hoping that the truly safe option will present itself and that everything will work out without them having to make those hard decisions or tackle the unknown. They are just like a pendulum swinging backwards and forwards but going nowhere. As a result, many Sixes go through life without finding any clear direction or purpose, making endless plans about what they will do when everything feels safe but actually making little or no progress beyond their safe zone.

For Sixes to consider:
- *What opportunities have you missed out on because you were too cautious?*
- *When you have been able to expand your boundaries beyond what felt safe, what did you gain?*

- *In what other parts of your life might you need to break out of the safe zone?*
- *What might be gained if you did?*

Loyalty, Belonging and Duty

Sixes are people for whom loyalty and belonging are very important. They are very family orientated and are deeply loyal to friends, workmates and employers as well as to the groups or organisations in which they belong or work. Belonging gives them feelings of security, something to hang on to; after all, being alone is scary and unsafe and there is safety in numbers. Moreover, familiar situations and being with people they know well reduces the uncertainty and anxiety of the Six; they know what to expect and feel accepted so they can let down their habitual guard and relax. As a result, Sixes are often members of clubs and societies; there are usually one or more Sixes to be found on local committees, and church groups often have many Sixes within their numbers. (It is interesting to note that many Sixes view God as the parent on high who oversees our lives, the one who makes the rules and tells us what to do.)

The loyal nature of the Six is clearly demonstrated in many other areas of life. They display unwavering devotion to ideas, beliefs and information obtained from their trusted sources and can stubbornly refuse to consider other possibilities (to the extent that they can react badly to having their beliefs or information questioned). Also, their attitude to what they perceive as their responsibilities is unfailingly steadfast and dutiful. If a Six makes a commitment to do something, he or she will always do it. They never fail to fulfil their obligations, even at the expense of their own health, and should they be pushed into forsaking their duty, being disloyal or letting someone down, they experience tremendous guilt.

Moreover, in order to maintain the security or sense of belonging that they need, Sixes cannot bear to say no to a request or let anyone down once they have made a promise. If they were to do so, they risk bringing conflict upon themselves, or others might perceive them as unreliable or untrustworthy. As any of this might undermine their sense of belonging and security, they tend to agree to too many different demands in order to keep everyone happy, frequently ending up getting anxious and stressed because they are overextended. Then, feeling taken advantage of, and irritated because everyone expects too much, they become highly reactive – the self-reliant Six becomes angry and rebellious whereas the reliant Six becomes nervous and tries even more to please.

For Sixes to consider:
- *In which areas of your life do you tend to overcommit yourself?*
- *What negative feelings do you have when you know you have overcommitted?*
- *How does that affect your behaviour towards others?*
- *What stops you from saying no? Be honest: what are you afraid of?*

Interaction with the Six

Other types, particularly those that have an optimistic outlook, often find the pessimism and negativity of the Six hard to deal with. For example, when asked what they think about an idea or project, rather than being appreciative or enthusiastic, the Six will immediately offer all the pitfalls or reasons why it might not work. From the perspective of the ever-careful Six, looking at all the potential problems just makes sense; after all, only fools rush in, and the Six knows you wouldn't want to be caught out. However, the other party can quickly feel flattened by this apparently negative response. The Six, though, is a natural troubleshooter and nothing gets past their vigilance, so it may well be worth listening to what they have to say. They think of many things that the rest of us would miss.

Although Sixes are generally warm, friendly people, there is an underlying need within their camaraderie. Their eagerness to please and to be liked is a way of checking in with you. It reassures them that they are wanted and that you like them, and it gives them a much-needed sense of belonging, a surety that they will not be abandoned and are therefore safe. Most Sixes want to be helpful, but they do fear making mistakes in case others turn against them. They are hypersensitive to criticism from others because it makes them feel unacceptable (and consequently at risk of abandonment) and, if caught out in a mistake, their defensiveness can easily cause them to become aggressive towards those they are trying to please. Sixes generally react strongly and quickly but often keep it to themselves. In fact, they feel most comfortable when you don't know what they are thinking.

While Sixes may outwardly appear to be only genial, kind and trusting, the predisposition within all Sixes to expect the worst causes them to view the world as full of untrustworthy people who would as likely do you down as support you. This cynical viewpoint just makes sense to the suspicious Six; after all, how can you deal with what is likely to be thrown at you if you dive innocently in and wait till you are let down? If challenged, Sixes will defend their suspicions by insisting they 'live in the real world', that people can be two-faced, break their promises, tell lies, or undermine you. Consequently, until the Six has seen continual evidence that you really can be counted on and are dependable and steadfast, they watch suspiciously for the other side of you to reveal itself, pessimistically expecting to be let down or rejected. Once you have proven your trustworthiness, your Six will always be there for you, standing at your shoulder or fighting your corner when you are not there; however, if you betray or let down a Six, you are unlikely to ever be given a second chance!

If you have a Six in your life

In order to facilitate improved interactions and feelings of compassion, it can be helpful to keep in mind what can be hard for the Six:

- never being completely at ease
- exhausting self by continual worrying

- having little confidence in self and feeling inferior to others
- experiencing agonies when trying to make decisions
- questioning own decisions even when they have been made
- missing opportunities by waiting for things to happen instead of being proactive
- causing self unnecessary pain by projecting negatively
- experiencing jealousy and fear of abandonment or rejection in relationships
- wishing there was a rule book so they always knew what was the right way forward

When not at their best, Sixes can be

---

over cautious   pessimistic   indecisive   negative

evasive   suspicious   stubborn   inferior feeling

highly reactive   procrastinating   sceptical   contradictory

fearful   overly dependent (or overly independent)   paranoid

---

CHAPTER 14

The Seven

At their best, Sevens are

----

*enthusiastic energetic joyous spontaneous imaginative
optimistic curious quick-minded fun-loving adventurous
gregarious effervescent uplifting humorous
entertaining generous audacious*

Sevens are lively, high-spirited people who often appear to have more energy than other types. Always on the go, pushing forward positively in life and approaching whatever they do with enormous enthusiasm, these friendly and extroverted people have a buoyant freshness to their energy that is infectious. They bring lightness and fun into other people's lives and have the gift of being able to lift others' spirits just by being themselves. It is almost impossible to stay down in the presence of a dynamic Seven; they just make you feel too good!

Ready to get up and go at a moment's notice, Sevens have a bold sense of adventure that has the wide-eyed freshness of a child. They optimistically expect the best outcome of whatever they embark upon, and their outlook on life is one of excited and curious anticipation, just like a child who enters the cake shop and looks around with excited anticipation of all the goodies that are available to them. In fact, Sevens seem to be ever young, whatever their age. They are so upbeat and full of life that, even with advancing years, they have a spring in their step and a youthful, light-hearted attitude to life that renders them ageless. This is the Peter Pan of the Enneagram.

These are people who combine great insight with quick, agile minds that move extremely fast from one idea to the next, making connections others might miss. They enjoy having a rush of ideas, tumbling one upon the other and enjoy figuring out how one thing relates to another, all of which makes them excellent at brainstorming or the synthesis of ideas and plans. Because of the speed at which their minds revolve, almost all Sevens are fast talkers to whom words come easily. Other people find them good company, and being highly sociable and non-judgemental in nature, they tend to have a lot of friends and associates with whom they love to share activities and fun times.

Sevens see the world as a great, big, adventure playground full of exciting things just waiting to be discovered. Consequently, many either travel a great deal, or voraciously consume travel books and programmes. Sevens want lots of new and exciting experiences and, like the child in the cake shop who wants everything available, want to experience everything the world has to offer. (A young Seven, already much travelled at the age of thirty, might well be heard to lament about all the countries he has not yet visited!)

Because they revel in experiencing the new, Sevens often end up as great connoisseurs of all manner of things in life: food and wine, places and people, sports and activities. Whatever they chose to indulge in, they want to experience it all, and probably have! So if you want to know what the food is like at that new place to eat, whether the latest film is worth seeing, or where to go to buy that outfit, ask a Seven! They are likely to be the veritable font of knowledge, having probably been to the restaurant, seen the film, and scoured all the best shops and will delight in excitedly sharing their knowledge, for their own pleasure is greatly enhanced in the sharing of it with others.

Although Sevens are not often true academics, they are usually quick-witted and often very knowledgeable. Having a great appetite for new information as well as generally being exceptionally fast learners, their minds are full of ideas and facts, although they learn practical skills just as easily. They have excellent coordination and manual dexterity, so whatever manual skills are involved in the multitude of activities they indulge in – which could be anything from racquet sports to painting, from learning a musical instrument to driving a car – all the new practical skills needed are easily acquired.

Obviously, this is a great gift, but being able to pick up new skills so fast means that Sevens often do not really value their abilities as much as they would if they'd had to work as hard to acquire them as everyone else does! Also, being so versatile means that less-than-high-functioning Sevens can feel unsure where to put their attention when deciding what activity to give their time to and can end up scattered and unproductive. However, at the high-functioning level, they have an inner sense of their own capability and, being balanced and clear-minded, are able to achieve an enormous amount in a very short time. For example, a highly productive Seven might begin the day with an early morning run, attend a breakfast meeting, make half a dozen phone calls, and work out brand-new ideas on a couple of current projects – all before most people even get into the office!

The Seven in Childhood

When the soul 'separates' itself from the All That Is and comes into life as a Seven, the quality of Divine Essence from which the young child experiences a deep loss of connection is **Causeless Joy.**[14] This creates the intrinsic sensitivity of the Seven, and it is through the filter of this sensitivity that the young child then experiences the world and develops ways of coping with what is experienced.

Each small child seeks to find and attain that which seems unavailable to them in order that they might survive and get their needs met. Young Sevens experience the world they find themselves in as somehow lacking in the essential emotional nurturing that they need in order to feel happy and loved. This does not mean that Sevens were

---

[14]   See chapter 3, 'Unravelling Your Inner World: The Early Years.'

not properly cared for, but it is common for there to have been an early loss of the close, nurturing contact with the mother figure. Perhaps she had to return to work early soon after the birth or was going through a very difficult time emotionally or physically, or perhaps another child came along while the Seven was still very young. Or maybe the Seven was born into a large, busy family where there was little time to give attention.[15] Whatever the truth of the family circumstances, the perception of the Seven child is that the source of nourishing warmth and closeness that brings contented and joyful feelings to a little child is lost or unavailable.

The outcome of this is that young Sevens unconsciously decide that, if they are to survive, they must nurture themselves by taking care of their own needs and making themselves happy. The childhood beliefs that are consequently taken on are

'The world does not provide what I need to be happy.'
'If I am to survive, I have to provide nurturing and happiness for myself.'
'I must keep others happy by being fun even when I feel unhappy.'

Sevens grow up believing that the contentment and happiness that they need is not available within the present moment as life unfolds naturally, so the resultant behaviour patterns that spiral out of these untrue beliefs are unconsciously designed to enable the young Seven to find happiness 'out there' or to create it for themselves.

In order to keep life happy and full up with good things, many Sevens become the funny, playful one within the family so that they can dispel other people's less than happy feelings, and at school, Seven children often get into trouble for being the clown in the classroom. Moreover, for many young Sevens, the family environment is such that they receive attention and approval only when they are happy little souls, whereas their expressions of hurt or unhappiness are met with little interest or empathy by their caretakers. The outcome of this is that

---

15   The childhood circumstances do not create the personality; they were chosen by the soul so that the Seven personality patterns would fully develop.

they learn to suppress what seems unacceptable (their negative feelings) and to remain 'up' in order to get their needs met.

Unfortunately, having taken on the role of the dazzling clown that makes people laugh, Sevens grow up feeling that this is who others expect them to be, whereas their true self is not taken seriously. This can have a detrimental effect on their self-worth in adult years, so that they only feel acceptable when they are being the bubbly, fun one. In fact, deep down in most Sevens is a lack of confidence. Despite appearances to the contrary, they are aware of the superficial nature of their happy demeanour, and they fear that if they stop being bubbly and become just themselves without the happy mask, others might not want them around.

The Effervescent Seven

Having grown up with no real trust in the natural unfolding of life and the belief that joy cannot be found within the present moment, as Sevens move into adulthood, they decide that they can, and must, plan and direct the future rather than allow it to take its natural course. We all desire to direct our lives to some degree; however, for the Seven, it is more than a desire. It is a necessity that enables them to avoid being in the present. The reality of the here and now contains the possibility of re-experiencing the sense of painful deprivation experienced in childhood, whereas envisioning a future utopia where the real juice of life will be discovered seems to contain all the potential for the happiness that they seek.

Energetic and buoyant Sevens appear to always be carefree and happy. In truth, they are not, but they want to create their lives so that it is full of pleasurable and fun things so that they can *become* happy. So for the Seven, pleasure is always in the future, in the planning. They live in a world of busy, busy mind activity that is all about possibilities, positive plans, and idealistic, imaginative futures. They flit from idea to idea, from plan to plan, not staying long with anything, just like the butterfly as it flits from plant to plant – a creature that brings us joy but whose presence in the moment is fleeting. They are always sure that what they are planning, what is just around the corner, will bring them real satisfaction and happiness. The problem is that in their haste to get there, they miss the joy to be experienced on the journey. They 'taste' their experiences yet do not really 'digest' any of them properly, because whatever they are doing, in any moment, their attention is not focused in the present; their minds are full of a multitude of other ideas and plans.

For Sevens to consider:
- *Recall a time recently when you were engaged in something you had been looking forward to. Was your attention completely upon what you were doing?*
- *What other ideas or plans were you thinking about?*
- *What aspects of that moment were you missing out on because you did not take time to savour it?*

Keep Moving and Keep Happy

Sevens live in the fast lane. Because of the need to keep life upbeat and fun, they need to keep moving, both physically and mentally, so they seek the constant stimulation of the new. Getting fresh sensory input from new experiences is exciting; it stimulates their energy and vitality and makes them feel alive. But the planning of interesting and fun activities is also stimulating and exciting, so much of their enjoyment is obtained from making plans. However, when ideas and plans actually become reality, the reality often does not match the fantasy, yet they rarely take the time to acknowledge the disappointment before they move onto something else. It is vitally important to the Seven's avoidance of pain to look at things from a positive vantage point and feel good about everything so the immediate distraction of another idea means that they won't have time to feel anything negative.

Although the reality is that bad as well as good feelings are part of life's normal terrain, for the Seven, embracing the fullness of *all* emotional experience contains the possibility of re-experiencing those desolate feelings that they try to avoid so they just won't entertain the negative side of life. This is especially true of darker emotions, such anger or fear. These powerful emotions seem too scary to acknowledge or express. Either they might alienate other people, and result in separation or lack of loving connection, or they might bring back the painful feelings of distance and lack of nurturing experienced in the young years. Instead, negative feelings such as these are pushed away, with the Seven talking himself or herself out of them or finding a distraction that gives them no time to feel. So if something unpleasant has to be done, the Seven will make sure there are pleasurable plans for later so that they can maintain an optimistic outlook and will mentally revisit those plans many times in order to distract themselves whilst engaged in the tedious or unpleasant activity that couldn't be avoided.

Like the child who fears that they *must* believe in Santa Claus or they will not get what they want for Christmas, the Seven unconsciously believes that they must cling to only the positive parts of their experiences and reframe anything negative so that it has a positive spin. You'll never find them looking for sympathy about their problems, for that would entrap them in their own pain. Instead, they have an amazing capacity to recount stories of their difficult or painful experiences in such a way that the listener is convinced that it wasn't a problem at all but that it was all just 'amazing' or 'incredible'. (Sevens frequently use superlatives when recounting their experiences.) Bits of the real truth are embellished upon and the rest (especially anything negative) is discarded in favour of a positive and upbeat account of the experience. For example, listening to the average Seven telling you about how they broke their leg and ended up being laid up in hospital would sound great fun and just the most brilliant opportunity to get to all those unread books!

The Seven's insatiable appetite for experiences is not just that they want continual stimulation so that they feel upbeat; it is also driven on a deep level by the fact that they have not yet found what they really want. From the Seven's perspective, what they seek might just be around the corner, so they have to try everything so that they don't miss out on nirvana. Therefore, choosing one option out of several is almost impossible for the average Seven. They want all the flavours of ice cream rather than limiting their choice to just one, holidays must include all the excursions so that they don't miss out, and given the choice between a meal out, a visit to the theatre, or a party, they will try to cram all three into one evening just in case!

Being Free

Even though the Seven may speak of all the exciting activities they are planning, it does not mean these things will actually come to pass. For the Seven, being able to think and plan these things makes them feel free and unlimited. It is not so much the *doing* that gives the Seven pleasure as the *knowing* that there are plenty of options that gives them their sense of enjoyment. They want to be free to pick up or put down any amount of interesting plans for future possibilities and free to respond to their impulses as soon as they arise, for one of the most fundamental aspects of the Seven personality is a deep need for *freedom*.

Being able to be spontaneous and free keeps the Seven sunny, but any kind of limitation brings up the dark clouds of childhood deprivation to overshadow the sun. Consequently, Sevens need freedom in every arena of life: freedom of thought, freedom of action, and freedom of possibilities. They resist boundaries or limitations of any kind, including rules and regulations, and in many situations, the Seven is the one who becomes the rebel, the one who actively resists authority. They will not be told what to do, and should you try, they will probably just go the other way to prove how free they are. They find rules irritating and unimportant; they just cannot see the necessity, and anyway, rules just limit the options available to them. And if Sevens feel cornered or hemmed in, they can display sudden flashes of aggressive anger. The anger will be short-lived, but this aggressive behaviour is usually a sign of the Seven beginning to feel panicky about experiencing the pain of deprivation.

The need to keep their options open so that they can be free to pursue pleasure and fun whenever and however it pleases them imbues the average Seven with a self-centred quality. It is not so much that they are deliberately unkind; it is more that, just like the child that they can so much resemble, their needs and desires override their awareness of the needs and concerns of others. However, even though they can appear selfish, it is also true that Sevens usually ask little of others. They will often find it hard to ask a favour because favours generally need returning, and obligations to others may limit or restrict their freedom.

For Sevens to consider:
- *What does freedom mean to you?*
- *How do you behave towards those who try to curtail your spontaneity and freedom?*

Monkey Mind

The mind of the Seven epitomises what Buddhists have termed the 'monkey mind' – a mind that does not reside in the present but jumps from thought to thought just as a monkey jumps from tree to tree above ground. Although having an agile, fast-moving brain is a great gift that endows them with many of their positive qualities, it is also their downfall; it makes them impatient with things that require a lot of time or effort, and impatient with themselves. Sevens want to fly in everything they do in life, not trudge through it, and they are not good at dealing with failure. So although most are multitalented, they are often too impatient to work at developing their natural talents and end up being dissatisfied with, or critical of, their own accomplishments.

Sevens are often the archetypal 'Jack of all trades, master of none', for most know a little about a great many things but fail to master many of them. Certainly, it is true that Sevens learn very quickly, but they are often well-known for being the 'instant expert'. They have a strong penchant for acquiring a small amount of knowledge or skill in a subject and then, impatient to get on with it, they decide that they know all they need to know and are ready to wing it. For example, a Seven on a skiing holiday for the first time might take a few lessons during the first week and by the second week be hurtling down black runs!

For Sevens to consider:
- *How many projects have you given up on before you had truly mastered them?*
- *Why did you give them up?*
- *What might you have achieved if you had persevered?*
- *How many projects have you actually completed and brought to fruition?*
- *Which makes you feel better about yourself – actually achieving completion or moving on to something else?*

The initial excitement of a new project is what entices Sevens, but then, having very limited patience with the tedium of repetitious groundwork or practice, they usually get bored and move on to the next interest. However, there are some Sevens who take the trouble to pursue an interest in depth and become really proficient, yet this would never be their sole interest. Confining their activities to only one field of interest would be limiting their options and leave them without an escape route from boredom if, for some reason, their main activity should become unavailable or impossible. Thus, they need to have many other irons in the fire – interests and activities they can fall back on should it be necessary.

Having a love of ideas, theories and interconnections, and being great conversationalists, Sevens can easily get caught in the trap of talking *about* a subject rather than allowing it to experientially impinge upon them. This is especially true where they might come face-to-face with their personal limitations and fears. For instance, they might spend much time engaging in conversations about astrology or the Enneagram without truly allowing the knowledge to affect the reality of their own path in life. They may spend plenty of time acquiring a lot of information and enjoy theorising and analysing ideas, yet by skirting over the surface, they avoid entering into things with their whole being.

Avoiding Boredom

Sevens have a great appetite for life but never feel full. The distractions they surround themselves with can be as varied as the Sevens themselves. It could be food and drink, perhaps people and places, or clothes and possessions. Perhaps it's high-octane activity that gives an exciting adrenaline rush. However, whatever they are doing, their minds are so full of more plans for the next thing that the experience is rapidly 'consumed' with little proper attention given to the joy of the moment. There is always a back-up plan. For instance, a meal out with friends that sounds like great fun in the planning could just turn out to be pretty boring for the Seven, so 'If things don't work out, I could move on to see that film or get along to that party.'

When sharing time with Sevens, you can never be sure that they are fully engaged with you because much of their attention will be on the back-up plan or may be across the room looking at, or listening to, someone who might just be more interesting. By not really being present to whatever they are involved in, nothing seems to give Sevens any lasting good feelings or satisfaction. So, with real enjoyment and contentment continually evading them, as soon as they begin to feel discontented or unfulfilled again, they need to move on to the next thing.

Average to lower-functioning Sevens are so separated from their real feelings that they are rarely aware that their constant need to fill their lives with endless stimulation and activity is their way of fending off their fears. If you ask a Seven what it is that makes them so busy and active, why they get fidgety and unsettled when they stop, they will tell you that they are just not the sort to sit around doing nothing; they just get bored and restless.

However, the real truth is that, for the Seven, everything they seek in their pursuit of contentment and happiness seems to reside outside of themselves, whereas their inner world seems empty, dark and desolate, a place the Seven does not wish to cease activity long enough to visit. So, although most Sevens avoid admitting this to themselves, when they begin to experience what they call 'boredom', what they are actually beginning to experience is the emergence of feelings of anxiety and agitation as the dark desolation inside begins to filter into their awareness. For example, an evening in without stimulating company or activity must somehow be filled so that the inner anxiety cannot rise up into awareness. So Sevens will not generally be content with just the television to watch. There will probably be a DVD and a good book at the ready in case the TV programme doesn't maintain their interest. And if all else fails, they may well reach for narcotics or alcohol to settle the agitation that begins when the daytime activities have ended and there are no more distractions.

For Sevens to consider:
- *What does boredom feel like in your body?*
- *What other feelings begin to come up if you stay with the boredom instead of distracting yourself?*
- *What would it feel like if you really had no choice but to stop all activities and distractions?*

The Seven's endless planning is also about avoidance of that dark, empty place inside. They unconsciously feel that the reality of the world is that it is a dark, lonely place with little meaning, but if they act as if this is a fun-filled place where everything is fine, then it actually will be. Therefore, they need to create a structure to their future in order to hold their world together and avoid staying in the present moment where they may be sucked into the chaos of their fears. So we see then that for the Seven, the only way they can stay free from the emptiness and despair that threatens to overwhelm them is to keep going and going, not stopping long enough for boredom to set in.

In their determination to always be buoyant and cheerful, and to defend against any possibility of re-experiencing those dark feelings, lower-functioning Sevens become addicted to the adrenaline rush that new and exciting activities give. Each one gives a new high, and as with all addictions, by continuing to pursue the endless highs, they end up needing more and more frequent, and more and more intense, stimulation. Ordinary fun is no longer enough for 'adrenaline junkie' Sevens, so they resort to serious risk-taking in order to get the bigger highs: wild partying and out-of-control hedonism, high-risk sexual activities, physically dangerous exploits such as driving at crazily high speed, or risking huge amounts of money on the stock market are all possibilities. But nothing is ever truly satisfying. Consequently, they have to constantly 'fill up', needing more and more, faster and faster, with many Sevens ending up depleted financially and/or physically.

As Sevens continue to head along this path, addictions tend to be the inevitable outcome – to drugs (both uppers and downers), alcohol, or narcotics – and they can find themselves experiencing cycles of wildly out-of-control behaviour to maintain the highs, alternating with phases of profound self-criticism, debilitating fear, and depression.

Interaction with the Seven

Because Sevens are natural entertainers who love to create a fun and upbeat environment, they generally enjoy being the centre of attention. Within a group of people, you will often find them sitting forward in their seats, bringing their energy strongly into the room and keeping other people's energy up by being entertaining. In so doing, they bring everyone else to life, which is just what they want. After all, reasons the Seven, when everyone else is happy, everything is fine, isn't it? The vibrant, cheerful nature of Sevens is certainly very uplifting, which is why their company is often sought out by others, but sometimes it becomes too much of a good thing. Other types can find that, after a while, it becomes tiring to be bombarded with the super-charged energy of a human dynamo who is so wired and ceaselessly energetic.

Although Sevens can be highly persuasive and are usually able to carry others along with their plans, they often fail to realise that other people just don't have the boundless energy that they have or that what they find fun may not be fun for others. Being adventurous and spontaneous themselves, Sevens also value these qualities in others and often find other types rigid and set in their thinking or behaviour.

When lower functioning, they can be highly impatient about people's foibles and worries, and if others cannot, or will not, keep up with their relentless pace, they can become angry with what they may interpret as rejection. Their attitude can become highly dismissive and acerbic towards those who fail to meet their expectations and can result in them abandoning these 'boring, narrow-minded' people and seeking new friends to share their exuberance with.

Sevens are frequently surrounded by many people, yet they often find other people fascinating without really connecting with them. The interaction can become just an opportunity to collect another experience for distraction or to tell an upbeat story with which the Seven convinces herself or himself that everything in their world is great. There's no doubt Sevens are great storytellers, and they are able to make the most mundane experience sound amazing and exciting in the telling. In fact, listening to your Seven friend tell the tale of some experience you both shared, you may well find yourself wondering whether you were there at all, as the story is told in such exaggerated terms that you hardly recognise it! Their desire for extreme sensory stimulation is so strong that everything they recount needs to take on exaggerated proportions. Something quite ordinary becomes hugely entertaining in the telling when it is described as marvellous, amazing, fantastic, incredible ... Superlatives come easy to the Seven! And as you listen and get carried away with the story, your positive reaction enhances the experience for the Seven who gets excited all over again by their inflated half-truths.

Although Sevens appear to be highly independent people, they do need other people around them to share their experiences with because it enhances the fun. However, there is a downside to this for the Seven, because the very presence of others introduces the possibility of restriction or limitation. Within a group, it is often the Seven who comes up with the new ideas, and of course, Sevens want freedom to do *what* they want *when* they want. Therefore, if another's plan does not fall in with theirs, it's unlikely that the Seven will go along with it. They resist being controlled by other people's needs and limitations and can also be resentful of others' expectations of them. So within any group activity, the Seven will always need to find ways of maintaining their personal freedom, even while enjoying the ambience of being with a group of people.

In their determination to follow their own interests and desires, Sevens can be unreliable and difficult to pin down. Getting them to agree on the details of an arrangement to share some time with you can be difficult because the Seven will want to be sure that they keep their options open. Even when they enthusiastically agree to a plan, you can find yourself let down at the last moment because a better option (one offering more fun) came along. And if the Seven in your life does let you down, don't expect him or her to acknowledge or take responsibility for the upset they may have caused; it's more likely that they will get angry or dismissive with you for having pointed it out or for not having understood that being spontaneous is fun.

For Sevens to consider:
- *What does it feel like when others have expectations of you that do not fall in with your plans?*
- *What do you really think about people who fail to keep up with your pace of life?*
- *Recall a time when you changed your mind about an arrangement you had made with other people and followed your own agenda instead. Did you take the trouble to consider their feelings when you let them down?*
- *What would it be like to take responsibility for the upset that you caused and really apologise?*

In their need to keep things positive and light, Sevens also go out of their way to diffuse any expression of anger or aggression from other people. Getting into angry conflict with others makes them feel trapped and inadequate. There is a 'Teflon' quality to the Seven. They want to glide through life with no resistance or friction so they lubricate life with humour or sweet-talking. If another person gets angry with the Seven, they will make a joke of it or employ beguiling chat to lighten the situation so that the other feels positive feelings towards the Seven once more.

If you have a Seven in your life

In order to facilitate improved interactions and feelings of compassion, it can be helpful to keep in mind what can be hard for the Seven:

- feeling dissatisfied and unfulfilled
- never feeling settled and contented
- getting bored by routine
- not having enough time to experience everything
- too many half-finished projects
- missing out of the joy of the present moment whilst making plans for the next
- not getting sufficiently focused to achieve completion in projects
- having a tendency to be ungrounded
- getting lost in plans and fantasies
- experiencing restriction within intimate relationships

When not at their best, Sevens can be

---

restless dissatisfied easily bored hedonistic flitting hyperactive impulsive excessive sensationalist superficial escapist unreliable rebellious insensitive self-centred self-destructive frantic manic-depressive

---

CHAPTER 15

The Eight

At their best, Eights are

----

*magnanimous   dynamic   forthright   confident   energetic
charismatic   decisive   empowering   servant-leader
determined   protective   generous   enterprising   constructive
supportive   big-hearted   compassionate*

Eights are larger than life characters with a big, dominating kind of energy and a great sense of vitality about them. They are people with enormous drive and vision who are happiest and feel most alive when they can make their presence felt to bring about changes within their environment. And when an Eight makes their formidable presence felt, you know about it!

Taking the initiative and making things happen are as normal as breathing to Eights. They are dynamic and resourceful people with great instincts and enormous willpower who use their practical common sense to great effect and really know how to make sure things get done. They have the ability to look at a difficult situation, make quick decisions, and immediately begin to put a plan into action to solve the problem. Preferring to give orders rather than take them, Eights are natural leaders and decision makers who like to be in charge – definitely cut out to be the general rather than the foot soldier. Whatever their role in life, whether it is chef in a restaurant, mother at home with the family, or business tycoon, the Eight needs to be the boss. Even though they are quite perceptive and well aware of what others think of them, Eights are uninfluenced by the opinion of others, living their lives with an amazing determination and tenacity that can be intimidating to less assertive types. Of all the personality types, they most resist being indebted to anyone, desiring to stand alone, independent and autonomous.

High-functioning Eights really want to make a difference to their world, to leave a legacy as proof that they were here. Their great personal power, drive and charisma encourage others to follow their lead into all kinds of projects, from renovating a derelict property to starting up a company; from waging war to doing battle against injustices at work. There have been many Eight leaders that have helped change the face of the world for the better – powerful Eights, such as Franklin Roosevelt, Winston Churchill, and Mikhail Gorbachev.

The 'can do' attitude of the Eight gets things done *and* empowers others; they challenge and inspire other people to exceed their own expectations and to push themselves beyond the limits they have set for themselves. Whereas many other types view a failure as a real setback, Eights see it as an opportunity to learn something and to push on to greater things. They have the ability to see potential where others only see disaster or hopelessness. For instance, an Eight may look at a shed full of old, dilapidated garden tools as an opportunity to set up a business in gardening antiques *and* inspire the owner to get started on it right away!

Eights have a passion and lust for life such that they always seem to be grabbing life with both hands. There are no half measures with an Eight; they work hard and play hard, engaging with everything they do with huge passion in order to really get the juice out of life. Always looking for a challenge, something they can pit their formidable energy and will at, they enjoy the adrenaline rush that comes with tackling apparently impossible challenges and beating the odds. Some Eights may challenge themselves physically, perhaps engaging in dangerous sports like rock-climbing or pot-holing, whereas other Eights may challenge themselves by taking business or financial risks that others would shy away from.

Being strong characters with both vision and the determination to make their vision a reality, many Eights end up highly successful and financially very secure, yet what drives Eights to make money is never the money itself. To an Eight, money and success mean power, and power gives the ability to build a fortress within which they and their families will be safe and invulnerable. For the Eight desires to be invulnerable because, despite the strong, confident demeanour shown to the world at large, there is an inner core of vulnerability within the Eight that is shielded by the powerful exterior. This inner vulnerability is revealed to only the most trusted people in the Eights life, and for many Eights, it is never revealed at all.

The Eight in Childhood

When the soul 'separates' itself from the All That Is and comes into life as an Eight, the quality of Divine Essence from which the young child experiences a deep loss of connection is **Omnipotence.**[16] This creates the intrinsic sensitivity of the Eight, and it is through the filter of this sensitivity that the young child then experiences the world and develops ways of coping with what is experienced.

Each small child seeks to find and attain that which seems to be unavailable to them in order that they might survive and get their needs met. The young Eight comes to the unconscious conclusion that, in their most vulnerable state, there is nothing and no one available to them that has sufficient power to protect them against the world. They feel that the trust they gave to their caretakers has been betrayed, that they have been let down and their innocent loving selves have been rejected. Drawing the conclusion that the only route to survival is to

---

16   See chapter 3, 'Unravelling Your Inner World: The Early Years.'

be strong and powerful, the young Eight then begins to take on these childhood beliefs:

'I have to look out for myself because no one else will.'
'I have to be tough and invulnerable in order to survive.'
'Power is needed in order to prevail in
this harsh and unjust world.'

Young Eights then experience themselves as alone in a harsh, uncaring world, where only the tough survive and there is no one to protect them from harm. They grow up with a sense of profound injustice or betrayal and vow never to be so weak and vulnerable again. The resultant behaviour patterns that spiral out of the untrue beliefs are unconsciously designed to enable them to survive against the odds, so they feel the need to grow up fast and get tough in order to become impervious to suffering. Feeling that it's 'me against the world', young Eights decide that they have to fight for survival; physical fights with other children are a common childhood pattern, and most get known for being tough little roughnecks.

Although some Eights had loving, caring parents, many had a difficult or violent childhood in which they really did have to stick up for themselves and be tough if they were to survive. Whatever the nature of their childhood environment, because of the sensitivity that is an inherent part of Eightness, even those who had loving parents grew up with a chip on their shoulders and then went on through adult life expecting people to do them down.[17]

The Rock-Like Eight

In order to protect their vulnerability, Eights had to learn to overcome what they perceived as weakness. What laid them open to the hurt of betrayal in the first place was the innocence of childhood – being open,

---

[17]   The childhood circumstances do not create the personality; they were chosen by the soul so that the Eight personality patterns would fully develop.

loving and trusting. So in order to protect themselves from ever feeling that pain again, they have to create a tough, invulnerable outer shell that cannot be penetrated and close down their hearts to 'soft' or 'weak' emotions, such as compassion, innocent joy, sensitivity, tenderness, empathy, and love.

Eights take the Darwinian approach to life – it's a jungle out there and only the strongest survive. And because Eights are fighting for survival, they have come to the (unconscious) conclusion that the price paid for all this protection is worth it. They *will* survive. Their perception of the world and the people in it is that other people are probably out to get you, so you need to be on your guard and get them before they get you. Consequently, Eights push back at life with all the force they can muster.

Because of the essential loss of innocence that occurred in childhood, Eights find themselves unable to come to a new experience, or a first meeting with someone new, from a place of freshness or innocence. They cannot approach anything without expectation of their prejudiced worldview being fulfilled, so no one is trusted until they have proved themselves.

Having mastered their own weaknesses and learned to stand up for themselves and be tough, Eights tend to see themselves as the 'rock' in other people's lives, the strong one, the provider, the defender of the weak. They are the one others depend upon to take the initiative or to make the decisions and then find the right people to implement them. Consequently, Eights seem to radiate a powerful force field around themselves. Some types find this overbearing and intimidating, yet others experience it as a protective shield that energises them and can galvanise them into action.

Being rock-like, however, has its downfalls. They have to defend themselves against their own vulnerability and what they perceive as weakness, so they need to be strong in the face of suffering and just have to get on with it when hurt or loss comes their way. Physical pain is often ignored; after all, only the weak give in to pain and the Eight has to be the strong, invulnerable one. (The high pain threshold of most Eights is legendary!)

Despite appearances to the contrary, within the tough outer shell of the Eight is actually a vulnerable little boy or girl who wants love and closeness but fears, and expects, rejection. Average to lower-functioning Eights are extremely afraid of being hurt emotionally, so the easiest option is to keep others at a safe distance and deny their own vulnerability and needs. Being unable to reach out with love and tenderness to others, and needing to protect themselves from letting any in, the inner world of the lower-functioning Eight becomes empty and lifeless.

For Eights to consider:
- *How do you behave when you fear rejection?*
- *In what way does this contribute to your emotional isolation?*
- *What has been the real cost to you of creating this tough outer shell?*

In order for sensation to penetrate this hard outer crust, Eights try to take in and devour as much as possible from the outside world and need big, lusty, physical experiences. Consequently, Eights tend to be all-or-nothing sort of people who have a tendency towards excess. They want to squeeze all they can out of life so if something is good, they want more – food, fun, sex, power – whatever they want they want it all, and more if possible!

Power and Control

Eights are often large people with a big upper body (which may be considered indicative of the need to protect the heart area), and they have a strong, powerful presence. Even those Eights who are not physically large always seem to take up a lot of room because they actively push their energy forward and at other people around them. Their need to be invulnerable and invincible means that Eights want to dominate their world and the people in it, and to let others know that they are not to be messed with! Consequently, many people find Eights too much to deal with, because their energy is too big – too loud, too pushy, too challenging. Most Eights are not even aware of how strongly they come over to others. As far as they are concerned, it just makes sense to want to be in control in this 'dog-eat-dog' world; after all, why wait till someone else gets the upper hand? Clearly, the philosophy of the Eight is that 'Offence is the best form of defence'.

In order to be dominant, Eights need to be in a position of power and control and refuse to be controlled by others – socially, physically, or sexually. Whatever their sphere of power and influence, much of their energy is involved with trying to make sure that the power they have is sustained or increased. Average Eights who do not have a lot of money, or who are not in a position of power or control, usually have some sort of dream of how they will get the independence, money, or respect that they want in order to be autonomous. Consequently, many Eights are entrepreneurs who work extremely hard to make their projects for success really work. Because of the strong desire to hold onto what they have made their lives about, Eights can be very possessive, viewing their business projects, their possessions, their staff, and even their families as extensions of themselves; you will often hear them speak of 'my people', 'my house', 'my family', 'my business'.

Fear of being controlled means that Eights need to be the one giving the orders rather than taking them, and if necessary, they will browbeat others into submitting to their will and giving in to their authority. To the Eight, any challenge becomes a power struggle, and the Eight has to win the battle. Consequently, going up against the tough, forceful Eight is like pushing against an immovable object. They rarely compromise because compromise feels like capitulation and surrender and they always insist they are right. Being wrong would indicate softness or weakness, but being right makes them in control, strong and invincible.

For Eights to consider:
- *Recall a time when someone tried to use the force of their will to make you do something. Did their behaviour make you feel cooperative?*
- *When you use force to try to make others bend to your will, how do you think they feel?*
- *Does it get the best out of them?*

- *If your forceful methods make others resentful, is the victory really worth having if it is going to make them less cooperative in future?*
- *How much of your energy is involved with getting and maintaining control?*
- *How much control is enough?*
- *Is your determination to be in control really enhancing your life?*

Respect and Loyalty

Eights respect others who are as they perceive themselves to be – honest, loyal and straightforward, with initiative and strength of character – and they expect, even demand, loyalty and respect from those with whom they interact. Many Eights will find ways to test the loyalty of those around them before they give their trust and support. Should you pass muster and prove yourself worthy of the Eight's respect, you may find yourself invited to join the Eight's inner circle, people they really respect and enjoy spending time with. And once they are truly relaxed in the company of people they trust, Eights are often extremely generous with their time and energy and can be truly magnanimous.

Most Eights are honourable people; their word is their bond and if they make a promise, it will be carried out to the utmost of their ability. It takes a lot to earn the respect of an Eight, yet if you do, you will have a steadfast ally and a loyal, hardworking friend who will champion your cause or fight your corner when needed. However, nothing will cause respect to fly out of the window faster than reneging on a promise or a deal without very good reasons that the Eight can accept.

Eights often seek to gain the respect they believe they deserve through the use of power, letting everyone know who is in charge by displays of dominant behaviour (just as dominant males would do in the animal kingdom). This may be achieved in subtle ways that appear helpful and generous but are actually very controlling. 'I know exactly who can help you. *I'll* get them to ring you.' Or in more aggressive ways, such as undermining the other's confidence by means of aggressive threats.

For Eights to consider:
- *If you gain respect by forceful displays of power, how can you distinguish between real respect and fear?*
- *What constitutes real respect?*

A higher-functioning Eight has great respect for strong people with drive and determination to succeed, yet sadly, at the lower-functioning end of the Eight spectrum, we see Eights who feel threatened by people who show strength of character. Having their instructions carried out immediately and without question indicates respect to the Eight. So if someone has the audacity to stand up to their aggressive bossiness or show signs of wanting to take over the Eight's position, they are highly likely to be subject to scathing and intimidating verbal attacks or aggressive, even vengeful behaviour, from the Eight.

Because Eights do not tolerate weakness in themselves, they usually judge others by the standards they set for themselves, and less-than-high-functioning Eights can be very judgemental and intolerant towards what they view as weakness in others. They can often be disparaging and dismissive of those they consider weak or ineffectual, viewing them as unworthy of respect or consideration. Should someone they view as an opponent in business give any outward display of fear, indecisiveness, lack of confidence, or neediness, the Eight may just seize the opportunity to go for the jugular in order to win the deal.

For Eights to consider:
- *How do you respond to vulnerability or signs of weakness in others?*
- *... and in yourself?*

Denial and Blame

Eights do not suffer with lack of confidence or low self-esteem as so many other types do, and their strong feelings of self-belief lead them to always feel justified in the way they behave. In their eyes, they are always innocent of blame. They are just honest and straightforward, realistic and practical, strong and determined. The Eight always believes that their version of the truth is reality and that others are just too 'lily-livered'. What others experience as insensitivity, to the Eight is just being honest; the callous and ruthless way they go about getting what they want is just realistic and practical; their domineering behaviour is just a necessary show of strength in a harsh and tough world.

They deny anything that would bring painful feelings into their consciousness, anything that would make them appear in any way lacking or wrong, because they equate being wrong with being to blame, and the all-powerful person cannot be at fault because that indicates weakness. As a result, they have great difficulty in apologising, because turning the other cheek just invites further damage to be inflicted upon oneself.

For Eights to consider:

- *When have you been insensitive or domineering? (Perhaps you could ask some people you respect to tell you the truth.)*
- *Who have you upset with this behaviour?*
- *Why not go for it and apologise this time? You may be pleasantly surprised at the outcome.*

Eights also deny the truth to themselves about what their physical body tells them. Any physical weakness is ignored and they push themselves at the expense of their own health, pushing on beyond their limits of physical endurance and ignoring pain. It's as if they have a little demon sitting on their shoulders, castigating them for being a wimp or a weakling when they feel tired or ill. Their conviction that illness won't get them, because they are the strong one, means that the early warning signs of life-threatening illness are often just not taken seriously.

Justice and Vengeance

Eights have grown up viewing the world as an unjust place where the rules have to be challenged or sometimes broken, especially to achieve justice and fairness for all. Injustice makes them angry, and when an Eight is angry, they feel compelled to act. As a result, many Eights take up the classic 'shop steward' role, becoming the champion of the underdog and fighting to defend the rights of those weaker, less powerful, or less advantaged than them. They will stand up for what they believe is right and have the courage and determination to take the heat in confrontational situations in a way many other types just couldn't. If someone weaker than them is being harmed or physically picked upon, they are quite likely to wade in with fists flying, without any consideration for their own welfare. And being 'blameless', the Eight will always defend their behaviour by insisting they had no choice, that they were forced to defend the other person.

Having come to believe the whole world is against them, average to lower-functioning Eights expect everyone they deal with to treat them unfairly or betray them. They feel they must protect themselves at all costs so they watch for signs of lack of respect, disloyalty, or underhand behaviour. Then, working out a strategy to regain control or punish, they use all the power they have to wrong foot and undermine the other person in order to exert their authority.

Many Eights can be ruthless when making business decisions, taking the stance that 'You can't make an omelette without breaking a few eggs.' For example, feeling threatened by an employee who shows strong leadership qualities, they would feel entirely justified in dismissing that person even though they had not actually done anything wrong. And not being prepared to allow themselves to wallow in what they view as emotionalism, they rarely feel regret about a course of action, even where their decisions adversely affects other people's lives.

Sadly, in low-functioning Eights, their desire to get back at the world means that the fight for justice becomes a desire for revenge, and their type of revenge is likely to be of the 'eye for an eye and a tooth for a tooth' variety. Whether they have been treated unjustly in business, or hurt on a personal level, the Eight's view is that exacting vengeance is entirely justified and will delight in planning revenge and how it will be implemented. However, this might not be an upfront, 'in your face' type of revenge. It may be taken in a passive-aggressive way, even without the others knowledge, such as withholding useful information to put the other at a disadvantage or destroying the other person's reputation by arranging the spreading of damaging rumour. The idea is to even up the score and have the satisfaction that the other person has suffered at least as much, if not more, than the Eight has.

The Eight and Anger

Anger is a forceful emotion whose true purpose is to bring about change. When it is allowed to come through us and be expressed, it can make us feel powerful, alive and strong – the very way the Eight wants to feel.

So although the Eight fights against or represses other emotions, anger comes easily. When Eights feel threatened, they get angry. When they feel hurt, they get angry. When they feel vulnerable or insecure, they get angry. When they are afraid, they get angry. The anger comes up suddenly and forcefully, yet once expressed, it disappears. What surprises most people is that Eights often actually enjoy their anger; they find it cleansing and it makes them feel alive and powerful. They just can't understand why others have been so badly affected by it when they are ready to pick things up after the anger and carry on as if nothing had happened!

It is very common for less-than-high-functioning Eights to get into situations that end up involving conflict, and because they always believe themselves to be innocent and blameless, they often end up feeling picked on. They so often are unable to realise that their overpowering energy and aggressive attitude gets other peoples backs up and causes offence. To the Eight, it's always the other person who is at fault – he who started it, she who is out to get them, they who treated the Eight unjustly. Underlying their anger are feelings of vulnerability or hurt, and the Eight feels they have a right to be angry because the other person 'forced' the Eight to feel weak, pathetic emotions.

When Eights feel insecure or threatened, they can become highly reactive and explosive. Any minor thing can set them off, such as a favourite shirt not being ironed or a facial expression or tone of voice that does not indicate respect. The low-functioning Eight's anger is unpredictable and frequent, leading easily to violent behaviour and even crimes of passion.

Interaction with the Eight

When in company with people they don't know, Eights will be friendly while remaining watchful, picking up on nonverbal clues, quietly sizing them up in order to determine whether or not they can be trusted, and whether they deserve the Eight's respect and attention. Almost all Eights greatly enjoy social interaction with like-minded people whom they respect, and in such company often enjoy heated debates about controversial topics that many others avoid, such as politics and religion. What to many people would be classed as an argument is to the Eight just a lively discussion. Because they tend to assume that the people around them have the same high energy and stamina to keep going that they have, an evening out with an Eight can end up a test of endurance! There's likely to be plenty of alcohol, plenty of food, and plenty of people. They can be great storytellers and enjoy impressing their listeners with their often exaggerated versions of the truth. No Eights think small, so if the real version wasn't big, they make it big in the telling! Average to lower-functioning Eights, in particular, feel the need to impress so that they appear powerful to others, and their conversation may be full of stories of how they vanquished an enemy or boasts about big plans and achievements.

Eights are straight talkers, and many are extremely direct to the point of being blunt. Their in-your-face way of communicating can be intimidating to many, and it easily gets others' backs up. As far as the Eight is concerned, their way of speaking is just about getting their point home and letting others know where they stand; they seem genuinely confused when they are then met with anger or resistance. They also value directness in others and can be highly suspicious of people that beat about the bush instead of coming to the point. Eights often use coarse or earthy language – nothing else expresses the power they feel behind their words – and 'bullshit' is a word frequently used by Eights when referring to the way some people communicate.

For Eights to consider:

- *How often do you notice the way your big energy negatively impacts on others?*
- *When do people back away or go quiet around you?*
- *When you have been met with resistance or anger from others, could your bluntness or forcefulness have been the cause?*
- *Why is that their fault rather than yours?*

Many Eights do not realise the strength of their powerful energy when interacting with other people and often fail to realise how inconsiderate they can be or the way their brusqueness or bluntness upsets other people. Even when they do realise, they are more likely to tough it out and justify their behaviour than apologise. Lower-functioning Eights can be very contemptuous of what they see as weak, thin-skinned people and can't be bothered with pussyfooting around other people's oversensitivity. They do not seem to be held back by guilt or conscience, feeling that normal social conventions like politeness, courtesy and consideration of others just don't apply to them.

If you have an Eight in your life

In order to facilitate improved interactions and feelings of compassion, it can be helpful to keep in mind what can be hard for the Eight:

- dealing with other types who can't cope with their anger
- having to put up with lack of drive or commitment in other people
- having their honest bluntness misinterpreted as rudeness
- scaring people away unintentionally with their big energy

- not getting the appreciation they deserve for sticking their necks out for others
- never able to forget past injustices or betrayals
- putting too much pressure on self
- finding it hard to let others get close
- denying their softer side in order to maintain the tough exterior

When not at their best, Eights can be

domineering   arrogant   insensitive   inconsiderate   uncompromising
self-righteous   faultfinding   aggressive   unfeeling   combative
boorish   possessive   bulldozing   belligerent   explosive   bullying
ruthless   vengeful   destructive

CHAPTER 16

The Nine

At their best, Nines are

----

*serene egalitarian accepting patient steady centred
level-headed kind gentle supportive wise non-judgemental
receptive unassuming gracious unpretentious mellow
peaceful accommodating*

Nines are easygoing, good-natured people with a positive, mellow outlook on life. Their genial and pleasant natures, combined with their ability to get on with all sorts of people, mean that others generally find them good company and easy to be around; in fact, it is extremely hard to not like a Nine! More than anything, Nines want peace and harmony around them so that their inner world stays comfortable emotionally, and in order to maintain harmonious connections with other people, they tend to adapt themselves so that they fit in almost anywhere and can get on with most people.

At the higher-functioning levels, Nines are truly serene and centred individuals of real humility and they can be great humanitarians, although few become well known for their humanitarian deeds because they are self-effacing people who generally avoid drawing attention to themselves. They will find helping and healing ways of connecting with many people whilst always desiring to stay out of the limelight.

Many Nines are spiritual seekers who find it easy to connect with the higher realms, and these Nines find practices like meditation easier than other types. They yearn to maintain and develop higher connections, and many devote their working lives to spiritual or healing practices, sometimes at the expense of addressing the necessary practical aspects of life in the physical body.

Being non-judgemental and uncritical in nature, Nines tend to see the best in others and maintain an optimistic outlook even in very difficult circumstances. For the Nine, there is always a silver lining where others only see the clouds; they seem to have a deep-seated faith that, no matter how bad things get, everything will work out fine. Other people tend to find the presence of Nines soothing and supportive, especially when there are problems and difficulties. Whilst other people may be losing their heads and getting heated, Nines stay calm and unflustered. They take a level-headed, patient attitude towards problems, and their ability to remain objective and maintain their equanimity in highly emotive situations means that they are extremely good at smoothing things out and calming things down.

They have the ability to merge deeply with others, which gives them an understanding of everyone's point of view. As a result, even though they will personally go out of their way to avoid being involved in arguments, when other people are in conflict, Nines are great mediators. To the Nine, nothing is ever black and white or cut and dried. There is always another option to look at, another perspective from which the issue could be considered, another possible solution. Where two parties cannot agree, the Nine will listen to both sides while staying uninvolved emotionally. Even when loved ones are involved, they rarely take sides but stay balanced and non-judgemental. Their viewpoint, when given, will be wise and without any personal bias, gently and calmly diffusing conflict as they help each party to see the other person's point of view. In fact, Nines are the people others often go to with problems because they are patient listeners who accept other people as they are. They have the wonderful ability of making others feel that they are held in a safe, non-judgemental space while the problem is shared, and moreover, they are able to state difficult truths in ways that somehow don't make others defensive. Where the matter involves deeply emotional issues, the Nine will hold the other person's heart in safe hands whilst compassionately allowing whatever emotional outpouring is necessary.

Those who have Nines in their lives always feel that these are people who can be counted on, because they are dependable types who are almost never erratic or difficult. However, the reason they are able to be so steady and consistent is that they have found ways of not being rocked by the ups and downs of life as the rest of us are. The unconscious strategies that they employ to avoid experiencing the negative aspects of life have caused both their inner and outer worlds to go into soft focus. The outcome of this is that their experience of life becomes somewhat diffused or fuzzy; in fact, many Nines are aware that something is missing but don't really know what it is or why it mostly eludes them.

The Nine in Childhood

When the soul 'separates' itself from the All That Is and comes into life as a Nine, the quality of Divine Essence from which the young child experiences a deep loss of connection is the **Absolute Peace of Oneness**.[18] This creates the intrinsic sensitivity of the Nine, and it is through the filter of this sensitivity that the young child experiences the world and develops ways of coping with what they experience.

Each small child seeks to find and attain that which seems to be unavailable to them in order that they might survive and get their needs met. To the young Nine, it seems that attaining peace and seeking loving connections is the only route to survival.

Drawing the unconscious conclusion that being loved and safe depends on avoiding anything that disturbs or destroys peaceful connections within the family, the Nine decides that blending in and not asserting themselves will achieve the peace they seek and preserve

---

[18] See chapter 3, 'Unravelling Your Inner World: The Early Years.'

harmonious connections with those they love. The young Nine then begins to take on these childhood beliefs:

'To survive and be loved, I must
maintain peace and harmony.'
'Conflict and anger cause problems and
separation; both must be avoided.'
'I must avoid asserting my own will.'

Their subsequent behaviour is then subconsciously designed to try to keep everything in their world as harmonious as possible and to avoid attracting unwelcome attention to themselves. Many young Nines take on the role of peacemaker between family members at a young age. (Perhaps this was the child a couple had to save the marriage, the one who makes things whole.). But others just stay out of the way as much as possible by keeping their heads down and blending in, in order to avoid upsetting or irritating the adults around them.

Anger becomes the big thing to avoid, and there are many possible reasons why they decide this is essential. Some young Nines instinctively sense that any conflict might seriously disrupt the stability of the family unit; others are taught that anger is not considered acceptable within the family. (In this situation, one parent might be a Six or a Nine.) Some experience a great deal of terrifying anger and conflict among family members, whereas others are actually victims themselves of angry and abusive behaviour. Some come to fear the destructive power of their own anger due to some event in their young years where they seriously harmed another child or an animal when overcome by anger. Whatever the circumstances of their young years, the avoidance of anger and conflict feels like a matter of survival to the Nine child.[19]

Most Nine children are quiet, compliant children who don't cause problems, and they are usually viewed by the adults around them as little angels because they rarely ask for much and will happily spend hours amusing themselves. However, this quality has been developed at a high

---

[19]   The childhood circumstances do not create the personality; they were chosen by the soul so that the Nine personality patterns would fully develop.

price. Young Nines end up feeling overlooked or even inconsequential, coming to believe that they are not as important as other members of the family, and most end up with feelings of low self-worth. Even worse, the repression and denial of self that the Nine child employs in order to not draw attention to themselves results in a deadening or numbing of their real feelings and the consequent inability to allow reality to touch them. Certainly, they learn to protect themselves and to maintain a form of inner harmony, but this is achieved at the expense of being able to experience the true richness of life.

The Accommodating Nine

From the perspective of the Nine, confrontation leads to conflict, and conflict leads to feelings that are not comfortable, especially anger. To the adult Nine, anger is an unacceptable emotion that disturbs their peace and harmony and threatens to undermine their union with others. Consequently, all less-than-high-functioning Nines avoid saying or doing anything that may be considered argumentative or confrontational. Asserting yourself means having a clear-cut opinion about something, and that may involve having to defend your position; for the Nine, is it worth the effort? Is it worth the potential conflict involved? Might they alienate those they care about? Why not just go along to get along?

So the Nine goes with the flow in order to keep the peace. It feels like the most comfortable decision and, after all, being able to always see both sides of every question, the Nine reasons that the other point of view may be equally valid. As a result, Nines become overly accommodating people who leave their own wishes and desires out of the picture and give up their own agenda in favour of other people. They find themselves habitually saying 'yes' when they would rather have said 'no'. If, afterwards, they regret saying yes, it's almost impossible for them to backtrack on their decision because that might involve conflict; it's so much easier just to go along with others and put their own wishes aside.

With their attention so much focused outside of themselves, Nines allow external circumstances and the needs of their environment, especially the people within it, to set their agenda and control their responses to life, rather than being aware of and responding to their inner feelings. As a result, they tend to lose proper connection with what they feel, what they really want or need, and even who they really are. Not having their own agenda, and desiring close, harmonious connections, they seem to merge with others, conforming to others' expectation of them and losing sight of their real selves. Most are so used to taking the path of least resistance that they find it easier to know what they *don't* want rather than what they do want. Many drift through life without clear purpose, bending to the will of others and allowing life to pass them by.

Nines can be so self-effacing that they fail to give themselves credit for their abilities, so other people end up taking advantage of them or overlooking them, even where they may have made a significant contribution. Having grown up feeling overlooked by others, in many ways this is only what they have come to expect; however, when Nines get older, this can become a source of great sadness, but it is a sadness they are unlikely to give voice to.

For Nines to consider:
- *What has been the real cost to you of avoiding confrontation and not speaking the truth?*
- *Be honest. How does it really make you feel when your wishes and needs are put aside to accommodate the wishes of others?*
- *What do you really want?*

Avoidance and Pseudo Peace

The easygoing mask of average Nines hides the fact that they are resisting and avoiding a great deal of their lives, both internally and externally. Most Nines do not expect too much from life and satisfy themselves with what they have, drifting through their days content with their daydreams and focusing on the positive in life. They use highly successful strategies to avoid acknowledging the difficult or disturbing aspects of their personal lives, thus minimising the possibility of feeling any unsettling emotions like disappointment, anger, rejection, or hurt.

They refuse to get involved in arguments and will actually walk out of the room rather than engage in confrontation. Where they do stay physically present, they will 'leave' mentally and emotionally, even though that may not be obvious to the other person. Others can do what they like, but they will not react in the face of verbal attack or over emotionalism from others. In stressful situations, Nines consistently use affable light-heartedness or humour to defuse the situation and feel good about doing it; after all, the Nine reasons, everything passes in time, so what's the point in getting worked up about things?

For Nines to consider:
- *How do you deal with conflict directed towards you?*
- *How do you deal with conflict between other people?*

In order to create and maintain the inner stability and harmony that they seek, Nines unconsciously avoid experiencing the difficult emotions that rock most of the other types; should any strong emotions threaten to disturb them, they transcend them or put them to sleep. By numbing out their painful feelings in this way, Nines create for themselves a kind of pseudo peace. They may experience this as a mellow feeling and convince themselves that they have got it all together, that this is the real peace they desire. However, over the years, the things that have been unexpressed or unattended to pile up within the Nine – desires that have not been fully unacknowledged, resentments that have been held onto, painful emotions that have not been properly felt or worked through.

As a consequence, for most Nines, their inner world seems to be a scary and extremely uncomfortable place to enter. They unconsciously fear examining their own feelings because that would force them to face up to the reality of all that has been buried – the multitude of ignored issues and the associated turmoil and pain – which would disrupt the inner tranquillity that they have achieved through avoidance.

Distraction Strategies

So we see that average Nines have unconsciously needed to find ways of distracting themselves from the negative aspects of life. In order to avoid having awareness of what they really feel when something is difficult or hurtful, all Nines can tune out from reality by escaping into daydreams and fantasies, or by 'zoning out'. The avoidance methods used by Nines are as varied as Nines are, but there are common patterns.

Some Nines, especially male, intellectual types, divert their energy away from important matters and their inner world by intellectual pursuits or by accumulating knowledge and information. (This explains why some male Nines can mistype themselves as Fives.)

There are Nines who avoid reality by just staring out of the window or drifting off into a rose-coloured fantasy world in which nothing negative exists and life is working out perfectly. Some become very inactive and zone out using distractions, such as puzzle books, lightweight novels with happy endings, or endless hours of television, perhaps also using comforting food, alcohol, or cigarettes to push down their emotions. Not surprisingly, these individuals are very likely to become the classic couch potato who carries excess weight.

At the other end of the spectrum, there are Nines who achieve avoidance by keeping themselves very busy. Some Nines are highly interactive and manage their energy by expending it in busy socialising or work schedules, leaving them no energy or time to focus on themselves or to deal with issues involving potential conflict.

For Nines with a very busy work or social schedule,
- *have you chosen to do the things that you are doing, or have these activities chosen you?*
- *if you chose to only get involved in activities that would fulfil you, what would they be?*

Other busy Nines lose themselves in trivial, mindless tasks, such as pottering in the garden or tinkering with machinery for endless hours. Female Nines are often very busy on behalf of others, focusing all their attention on household tasks and the needs of their families. (This is why, without full understanding of the patterns of Nine, many female Nines mistake themselves for Twos.) This sort of Nine-style busyness generally involves endless pottering about and getting lost in the minutiae of life, with the result that it can be very hard to be clear about what is really important and what really deserves attention. Then the Nine often ends up focusing on irrelevant details, losing sight of the big picture, or forgetting the original purpose of a task.

For Nines to consider:
- *When you find yourself pottering about doing mindless or trivial tasks, ask yourself what important issues you are avoiding.*
- *When life feels particularly tasteless or dissatisfying, or you are employing endless distractions, this is usually an indication that some deep emotional stuff is trying to emerge. Take some time and connect with your inner world. What is upsetting you? What are you avoiding?*

Anger and the Nine

Nines do not appear to be the type with the most anger, but they are. Many Nines have their anger so pushed down that it is quite likely that they do not even recognise the existence of their anger. Most will tell you they never get angry.

Despite the fact that anger is feared or disapproved of by many people (not just Nines), it is a natural emotion that everyone experiences. It is a powerful emotion that, when channelled positively, can bring about change or stop something that should not be happening. However, to almost all Nines, anger is threatening and damaging. As a consequence, they feel unable to use anger directly or constructively, even in their own defence. They have great difficulty in confronting others, especially about issues that directly affect them, such as not having their wishes considered or not being listened to. Being overlooked in this way would upset other types, but Nines talk themselves out of any hurtful feelings they might have because they don't want to make waves. If Nines are asked why they don't complain or stand up for themselves, you are quite likely to get an answer such as 'It's just not worth it. There's no point in getting angry; anger just causes problems.'

Anger has been suppressed in the Nine for so long that, in truth, it is no longer just anger; it is rage. Within their inner world is a cauldron of suppressed resentment and frustration that has built up and built up until it has become boiling, fiery rage that is ready to explode out if it gets a chance. Although most Nines have this well under control (and most would absolutely deny the existence of this rage), those Nines that have occasionally allowed it expression know how explosive it is. It can be violent and dangerous, and where it has been given expression, it has probably frightened both the Nine and those around her or him, with the consequence that, once experienced, the Nine feels the need to shut it down even more firmly.

The energy of anger often comes up in Nines as a feeling of congestion or heat in the chest or throat, sometimes accompanied by a reddening of the skin or a physical shaking or trembling. And then the Nine pushes it back down and puts it to sleep again or tunes out from it. Being so disconnected from their anger, it is quite common for Nines to come to a realisation that they were actually angry about an incident hours or days after it occurred rather than at the time.

For Nines to consider:
- *What does anger feel like physically within your body?*
- *How far up your body do you allow it before you have to push it back down or put it to sleep?*
- *What might happen if you allow your anger full expression?*

Some Nines will allow their anger to gently leak out by occasionally barking at others or by making nasty, sarcastic comments; others allow it to come out in the form of road rage or as physical aggression towards inanimate objects. However, because the anger of the Nine is not usually expressed directly, it generally comes out in passive-aggressive ways. Although Nines are extremely accommodating and go along with others most of the time, they are actually very stubborn people. If they feel pushed or coerced, they can deliberately slow down or resolutely sit and do nothing whilst tuning out any complaints from others. Without argument or threats, but just by giving you the silent treatment, they can indicate quite clearly that you will not get your way. When you explode in frustration and the Nine says, 'This is all you. I haven't done anything,' you find yourself successfully made out to be the active agent of conflict, leaving you feeling both undermined and helpless.

Lethargy and Inertia

There is tremendous inner strength in Nines that, if well focused, can achieve an enormous amount. However, average to lower-functioning Nines use most of this strength to maintain their internal and external harmony instead of accomplishing personal goals that would move them forward in life.

Continually pushing down strong emotions, especially their anger, also shuts down the Nine's life force and uses a great deal of energy. The result of this is that most Nines experience considerable lethargy or tiredness; a great many Nines need a lot of sleep or frequent naps to get them through the day. There is a tendency towards inertia[20] in the energy of the Nine. Just as it is extremely hard to move a large boulder but, once it is moving, it keeps rolling until something stops it, so it is with the Nine. It often takes an enormous effort for them to get going, but once up and moving, Nines can be highly active and productive. However, once set on a course of action, they have great fervour and can have difficulty changing from the course they have embarked upon, stubbornly persisting with what they are focussed upon.

---

[20] Inertia is defined as 'the tendency to remain at rest or in a state of motion unless an external force is applied.'

Sadly, the pushing down of inner feelings away from conscious awareness cannot be done selectively, so Nines end up numbing out not just their negative feelings but also their best feelings, such as joy. Whereas other types experience the ups and the downs of life, the emotional hills and valleys, for the Nine, all experiences seem to end up as an almost flat terrain. They rarely experience the depths, but they rarely experience the heights either. Life can then be experienced as rather colourless, as shades of grey. With their life force shut down in this way, their ability to experience the real intensity and depth of life is limited so there is a lack of vitality and aliveness in less-than-high-functioning Nines. Although most are not really aware that they are living only half a life, Nines see other people experiencing real aliveness, but somehow it seems to elude them. It's like trying to experience life through cotton wool; they just don't experience the 'juice of life'. For them, life can be like chewing cardboard: it has no flavour.

The deadening of inner awareness and the shifting of attention onto others leads to an internal state of fuzziness where everything can seem rather woolly or muddled. Other people often perceive this as vagueness, indecisiveness, or procrastination on the part of the Nine. Nines themselves may experience the lack of inner clarity as difficulty knowing what action should to be taken. Sometimes, a task seems to be just too much effort and there is no clarity on what would be the first step towards getting it done. If it is clear what needs to be done, there may be difficulty in prioritising tasks, with the Nine getting lost in trivia whilst trying to clear the inner confusion. For example, a Nine who urgently needs to get an extremely important form in the post may spend most of the day clearing out the filing cabinet instead. Sadly, this procrastination and indecisiveness, combined with a lack of inclination for the limelight, can mean that many Nines end up standing on the sidelines of life as other people overlook them or fail to take them seriously.

The Spiritual Trap of Nine

The energy of the number nine is about completion and coming home (see chapter 2, Nine numbers), and when it manifests in the human personality, it imbues the personality type Nine with the ability to easily make connections to the higher realms. Even those Nines who do not actually meditate are aware that they easily 'drift off' to some higher place. Because Nines embody the energy of nine there is a deep desire to return 'home', back to the Source. This is true whether they are aware of it or not, and many Nines who are actively on their spiritual path feel torn between being in the physical body and returning to the realm of spirit.

It seems surprising, then, that many Nines whose lives revolve around spiritual activities or who help other people with their spiritual path sadly neglect their own personal and spiritual growth work. For some, the reason for this self-neglect is that their self-worth is low and they feel they are not important enough to warrant the time and effort involved. However, what stops many spiritual Nines from real growth is that they are already spiritual. They engage with their own growth on a mainly superficial level, convincing themselves that they have done their growth work that they are already 'there'. And some even believe that they are just sticking around in these mundane levels of existence for the benefit of others. This form of spiritual self-importance or superiority holds back many spiritual Nines. Many go from workshop to workshop, from course to course, seeking that which they feel is missing within their lives, yet fail to recognise their own complacency and the consequent self-deception. They may teach about spiritual growth, but avoid their own, and consequently achieve little real advancement.

These spiritual seekers create their pseudo peace by using their ability to connect to higher levels, convincing themselves that they have attained true spiritual enlightenment when, in fact, they are avoiding what needs to done here in the physical world in order to further their own spiritual expansion. They fear that if they put too much of their attention onto their inner world, what might emerge would disrupt the harmony they have created in their lives. Their really strong feelings seem scary and dangerous, so the inward journey that it would be necessary to undertake in order for them to work on their deepest issues is avoided. It is interesting to note that Nines can have such a strong, unconscious need to avoid these feelings that some have even been known to fall asleep during workshops that involve delving into the emotions!

Many spiritual Nines are aware of just wanting to 'go home' and do not want to allow the full impact of being in the body to affect them, yet they would do well to realise that trying to transcend their problems by 'merging with the Divine Light' is not what they are here for. Our relationships with other human beings bring us all problems and challenges for the specific purpose of giving us opportunities for growth. It is the way we deal with those problems, here in the physical world where the problems exist, that determines how much we are able to learn and grow from the difficult experiences we are having. Spending hours in meditation instead of initiating action does not solve real problems, nor does asking the Universe to find a solution for conflict bring about true peace. That can only come from the real expression of each party's own truth. We need to bring both our spiritual selves and our human selves to the problem.

When the Nine avoids the deeper issues brought up by problems, all that is achieved is the flat detachment of pseudo peace accompanied by a deadening of the inner terrain and a lack of vitality. The spiritual Nine needs to recognise that what they are experiencing is not true peace. True peace has a wonderful quality of aliveness in which bodily sensations are heightened, perceptions are sharper, the mind is clearer, and energy levels are enhanced; this only comes from embarking upon real growth work that will bring the Nine into the fullness of *all* their emotions and experiences, negative as well as positive.

Control and Stubbornness

Nines perceive themselves as laid-back, laissez-faire types who let others take the reins. If they are told they are controlling, they are likely to respond with 'No one could be less controlling than me.' Yet when interacting with average Nines, although they seem gentle and easygoing, there is often a sense that somehow you are being controlled. For example, if things start to get heated, the Nine will try to talk you out of the strong emotions you are feeling in order to calm everything down. When they do this, Nines believe that all they are doing is trying to help, but in fact, what they are really doing is trying to shut you down so that your strong feelings are not expressed (which, of course, would disturb their peace). The control of the Nine is often so subtle and covert that other people frequently do not realise that they have been 'handled'; it as if there is a stealth with the control of the Nine.

Nines will not be told what to do. They are much more stubborn than many people realise. Their stubbornness feels very controlling, and it is. If asked to do something they really don't want to do, they often appear to be compliant, saying yes or agreeing with what you say but then they silently dig in their heels and do what they want, which might well be nothing. This is control by procrastination and inertia – gentle and quiet control but control nonetheless. If you go up against a Nine in an argumentative way, he or she is likely to respond with a total shutdown, a complete non-responsiveness, which can be very frustrating, but this is the Nine's way of maintaining control.

Many Nines are creatures of habit and, once having developed a habitual pattern, can be extremely stubborn about changing. This resistance to change is highly likely to be achieved with passive-aggressive methods of control; they are adept at doling out platitudes in order to get other people off their backs, appearing to be pleasant and cooperative by saying things like 'Yes. OK. In a minute' or 'You're right. I do need to do that.' But then quietly and stubbornly they continue to do just what they want to do.

For Nines to consider:
* *What do you do to try to control your external world?*
* *What passive-aggressive methods do you employ to resist being controlled by others?*

Interaction with the Nine

The habitual self-abandonment of the Nine, combined with their tendency to believe themselves to be unimportant in comparison to others, leads to average Nines having great difficulty with having attention focused on themselves. In group situations, they will avoid being in the limelight, tending to blend into the background, often contributing little to general conversation, and rarely expressing their own opinions. Although appearances are to the contrary, in their interaction with others, Nines are the most withdrawn of all the types. Their withdrawal is not obvious, as it is for the Four and the Five, because they are able to still engage with others whilst withdrawn. When anything threatens or potentially threatens their harmony, they are able to withdraw into a private place within their minds where worries and problems cannot intrude, an inner sanctum that is full of positive things, such as happy memories or idealised fantasy. Even when engaged in conversation, they can continue to be smiling and friendly whilst actually being disengaged from the world around them. Having shut out whatever might make them unsettled, upset, or anxious, their minds are now free to focus on something much more pleasant.

They are very kind people and tend to keep any negative thoughts about others to themselves in order to avoid being hurtful or challenging. Where they are required to offer opinions, they are often conciliatory or vague. In fact, Nines are experts in circumlocution: the ability to talk right around a subject but not quite get to the point. When they themselves are challenged about something, they may prevent the other person from making their point by telling their story at great length, bringing in all sorts of trivial details, all the while tuning out the opposition. This subtle but highly effective way of taking control of a conversation can leave the other person confused and frustrated!

Nines are self-effacing people who do their best to fit in with those around them; however, little of their true selves is revealed to most people. Many people think they know their Nine friends, but they will only know the parts of the Nine that have been revealed to them.

Much will have remained hidden, even within long-term friendships, for there is a core of vulnerability within average Nines that they rarely trust people enough to reveal.

Their pattern of not speaking up with their own truth in order to keep the peace can end up being self-defeating for the Nine. In the end, it can cause more problems than it prevents because both parties can end up feeling aggrieved. Misunderstandings are often the real outcome because the Nine can feel upset or hurt that the other party has ridden roughshod over their (unspoken) wishes and feelings. Equally, the other party can end up getting angry when the Nine will not be pinned down to state an opinion or preference about something. So very often, the Nine brings disharmony or conflict upon themselves when these were the very things their behaviour was unconsciously designed to avoid.

If you have an Nine in your life

In order to facilitate improved interactions and feelings of compassion, it can be helpful to keep in mind what can be hard for the Nine:

- not experiencing the fullness of life
- feeling like nobody special
- viewed by others as lightweight and thus not being taken seriously
- finding it hard to put themselves forward and reach their potential
- having their own needs and desires pushed aside by others
- losing a real sense of their true self
- being misunderstood when they are indecisive or lacking in focus
- being unsure about what they really want or what would really make them happy
- lacking in drive, energy and focus

When not at their best, Nines can be

---

*self-effacing   avoiding   resistant   passive-aggressive
stubborn   procrastinating   apathetic   fatalistic   overly complacent
vague   self-forgetful   lethargic   inert   indolent   disengaged
unresponsive   blaming   judgemental   nasty*

CLARIFYING TYPING CONFUSION

CHAPTER 17

Mistyping

Difficulty Finding Type

When studied in its entirety, the Enneagram has the potential to unlock every aspect of the personality, providing insight into areas of life that, up until that point, had remained a mystery. However, some people study the Enneagram and either mistype themselves or fail to identify with any of the nine personality types. There are a number of reasons for this.

There are some who take an interest in the Enneagram who have, until now, lacked self-knowledge and are simply not used to observing their behaviour in the way that the material asks of them. Others may not have sufficient interest in pursuing self-knowledge and growth to take the time to understand the Enneagram properly. The simple truth is that the Enneagram is not for everyone and there are those who are not quite ready for this kind of self-examination. There's no point in forcing the issue prematurely.

Mistyping sometimes occurs when people mistake superficial features of their personalities as indicators of their type. So for instance, a strong-minded Three in a leadership position might mistype as an Eight, an intellectual Nine might mistype as a Five, or a repressed Two seeking freedom from family/household obligations or from endless bad relationships might mistype as a Seven.

When the Enneagram is only superficially studied and hurried assumptions are made based on one or two traits taken out of the context of the whole picture, mistyping can easily occur. For example, a female Nine might incorrectly decide that she is a Two (a fairly common mistyping) when she reads that Twos put their own needs aside for others. Continuing only to study the chapter about the Two, she decides that has 'found herself' without learning anything of the other eight personality types. For a female Nine to believe that she is a Two is of no value at all. Despite some similar, outward expressions of behaviour, the inner world of these two types is very different,[21] so to understand the inner world of a Two will not help the Nine to understand her negative patterns, nor will it facilitate any meaningful growth.

Self-Deception

There are those who recognise their own type deep down but are unwilling to face the negative implications of the descriptions. Many of us find it hard to acknowledge the less acceptable aspects of our personality but do so in the pursuit of growth and understanding. However, those who want to see themselves (or be seen) in a more acceptable or attractive light might acknowledge only the positive traits of their type or delude themselves and others into believing they are another type, because it feels safer or easier than being honest with themselves. For instance, some Sevens might say they are Eights because it feels better to think of themselves as aggressive rather than escapist. Some Fours are so afraid that others would reject them if their 'dark' inner self were revealed that they decide it sounds much more acceptable to be a One, a Two, or perhaps even a Seven.

---

[21]   See chapter 5, 'The Inner World of the Nine Types.'

Behaviour May Not Indicate Type

The important thing to remember when determining type is that *behaviour alone does not indicate type*; it is the deep need or desire that drives the behaviour patterns that determines one's core type so the bottom line has to be 'What do I most want? What drives my patterns?'[22]

Not making a quick decision about type is the best option for all who are starting with the Enneagram but especially for Nines. It is not uncommon for Nines to find a little of themselves in all of the types because they so easily merge with other people, and consequently may have a rather diffuse awareness of themselves and their own desires. As a result, they can experience difficulty recognising their type. Many a Nine will say, 'Surely, all of us display all of these behaviour patterns sometimes,' but that is most definitely not the case. In fact, seeing something of yourself in all the type descriptions is in itself an indication that you may be a Nine, especially if it is the desire for peace that drives your patterns.

Because the female role in most cultures involves nurturing and caretaking of others, women of any of the nine types, especially those who are mothers, are likely to recognise some of the traits of the Two in themselves. In fact, some women can mistype themselves as Twos simply because they love and care for their families. Conversely, because the nurturing energy of Two is generally viewed as feminine in our culture, male Twos commonly mistype as Ones or Threes, which are the wings of type Two. Also, Twos who are not in an obvious helper role in their professional or private lives might mistype themselves, because they may not be aware of their deep, unconscious desire to be of help to others. This can be especially true for male Twos who do not have any children in their lives.

Eights rarely mistype themselves, but other types who seem to be displaying a pattern of angry or aggressive behaviour might mistype themselves as Eights or be mistyped by other people as Eights. It should

---

[22]   See chapter 7, 'What Type Am I? What Drives the Nine Types?'

be remembered that many other types can be aggressively angry when stressed and that this pattern alone does not make someone an Eight. Occasionally, female Eights may mistype themselves because many of the traits typically displayed by Eights have been discouraged in females. This is more likely in those who are in their middle years, whereas younger Eight females, who are generally more at ease with their strength and dominating character, rarely mistype.

The typing of some Sixes can be fraught with uncertainty, but then uncertainty is a quality that we associate with Sixes generally! Sixes have a tendency to question their own decisions, which frequently leads to confusion about their type. 'Am I this ... or am I that?' Moreover, others can find Sixes difficult to type because, not only are they often a mass of contradictions, but the two extremes of 'Sixness' – reliant and self-reliant – can appear so different from others that knowing one Six in your life does not necessarily mean that you can easily type another Six.

These are just some of the typing errors that happen most frequently. Because finding your type is paramount to working with the Enneagram, the following section may be of help in clearing confusion as well as confirming type.

CHAPTER 18

Type Comparisons

In order to facilitate accurate typing, a detailed comparison is given here between each type and all of the other eight types (i.e., between One and Two, One and Three, One and Four, etc.). We describe the (apparent) similarities between each pair that may be the source of uncertainty or mistyping, and clarify the differences that should clear up the confusion. Remember that an understanding of the deepest needs/desires of the types best distinguishes one type from another where external behaviour appears to be the same.

Type Comparison for Ones

One and Two

Confusion between Ones and Twos is most likely where the wing is mistaken for the core type, especially where a female One with a Two wing sees themselves as a Two, or a male Two with a One wing sees themselves as a One.

There are definitely similarities – both types have strong consciences and need to do something worthwhile or be of service – but the confusion can easily be cleared up by looking at their interpersonal styles. Twos seek out very close connection with others. In fact, the closer the integration and sharing with the other, the better (except for a highly functioning Two, who will value more personal space). Ones, however, desire autonomy and resist 'merging' with the other.

Ones exhibit great restraint in the way they give expression of positive feelings, whereas they find it hard not to openly express their negative feelings, especially irritation or dissatisfaction. When they hurt another person by their critical comments, they will probably still persist with the point they have made because they are 'right' or because 'It's for your own good.' Twos are openly appreciative of others, ready to point out other people's good points, but usually find it harder to express negative feelings. The Two with a One wing may be critical like a One but will be very concerned if another is hurt by their comments and will want to resolve the conflict and soothe the other person's feelings.

Both the Two and the One can be pushy with unsolicited advice. Their motives are not quite the same, however. The One desires to improve you, or help you improve your life, whereas the Two desires to help you be happier. If the advice is not accepted, the One is likely to feel frustrated and might even get belligerent. (After all, the One is 'right' and you should listen!) But the Two will take the rejection of the proffered advice as a personal rejection, feeling unappreciated and hurt and probably point out that it was only meant to 'help'.

One and Three

This typing confusion is easy to understand, because there are many superficial similarities between these two types. Both are hardworking, organised and efficient; both are self-motivated and can be highly productive. Both will push themselves hard to get things done and want to make the best of themselves. However, there are great differences when we look at the underlying drives of each type.

Ones are driven by their own internal, high standards to improve and perfect themselves and their surroundings. Threes are driven, not by their own standards but by those of the society within which they live and work, and they strive for success in other people's eyes rather than perfection in their own eyes.

Ones know how they want things to be, and once they have decided on the way to achieve their goals, they are not easily deflected from their course. Their way may not be the fastest, but it will result in the best possible job being done, and moreover, they know theirs is the right way and will defend the path they have chosen even when problems occur. In contrast, Threes look at the goal and work out the most expedient and efficient route to achieving it; quality may be sacrificed for speed (which is never true for the One), but the Three will aim to get there fastest. If difficulties start slowing things up, the pragmatic Three adapts their original plans and may change tack altogether in order to get the job done.

There are many more differences. Threes live and die by the opinion of others. In contrast, although criticism is unbearable to them, the way Ones move forward in life is rarely affected by the opinion of others. Threes desire to be liked and admired by others so are rarely argumentative, whereas Ones can be dogmatic and argumentative when other people disagree with them. Ones are highly moral and ethical and will not compromise their own truth whereas Threes bend the truth for their own ends and, when low functioning, can be ruthless in their behaviour towards anyone getting in their way to the top. Threes must be the best, the number one; Ones strive to be perfect. Threes view themselves in competition with almost anyone; Ones only compete with themselves. Ones want to achieve things to make a difference; Threes want to achieve in order to be a success.

One and Four

These are very different types, yet typing confusion here is not uncommon. Fours will rarely mistype themselves as Ones; however, working in the creative fields may lead some Ones to believe they are Fours. They need to remember that creativity is not solely the arena of the Four, and of course, One has a connection to Four anyway.

The endless pursuit of perfection can lead Ones into periods of melancholy and depression and they can then display much Four behaviour (One 'going to 4' negatively). It is important for Ones to review the whole of their lives when typing themselves at times like these, in order to avoid possible mistyping as Four. However, this typing as a Four would be based almost wholly upon the negative aspects of Four, whereas even lower-functioning Fours will recognise in themselves some of the positive traits of Four, even if their outward behaviour appears to be very negative.

There are some similarities between these types. Both types overreact to perceived criticism, both can feel worthless and experience a lot of anger, and both are full of passions and emotions. However, if we look at the way they deal with feelings, we see a great difference. Fours are emotionally expressive types, whereas Ones are emotionally controlled. Ones are very responsible even when experiencing strong or difficult feelings. They will usually fulfil their responsibilities before they deal with their feelings. In fact, their tendency to not deal with their feelings is a common cause of their depressions. Fours, however, feel the need to understand and work through their feelings first, before they get on with their duties, and may actually neglect doing important things because of what they are going through – and probably feel quite justified in looking after their own needs as a priority. This is the Four's tendency towards self-indulgence, whereas Ones are self-denying. Generally, the control and sense of responsibility that Ones have would mean that they would not allow themselves to indulge in this way for very long; if they did, afterwards, they would be likely to feel very guilty that they have not been doing what ought to be done.

When life presents them with many problems, Ones will look for practical solutions to their difficulties and make plans or lists of what needs to be done. Fours are more likely to withdraw from the reality of tackling life, fantasising about a more perfect life and how they will be rescued from their unhappiness.

Ones experience irritation and frustration over other people's inefficiencies, disorderliness, or lack of responsibility, whereas Fours experience irritation and resentment over another's coarseness or lack of awareness of the Four's sensitivity and depth. When Fours experience resentment or anger, they will usually withdraw emotionally or physically and attempt to punish the other by refusing to communicate (but secretly want to be sought out by the other). Ones do not withdraw when angry but will become increasingly forceful in pressing their point of view on the other, determined that it be acknowledged that they are 'right'.

There is another point to be considered. It is possible a highly functioning Four may mistype as a One where the self-absorption of the average Four has been transcended and the Four is living with purpose beyond the self, as a highly functioning One would. However, the Four is still a Four, having many of the important characteristics of the Four, as well as some aspects of their Three and Five wings. The One will show some traits of Two and Nine, the wings of One.

One and Five

This mistyping is not uncommon, for both types have independent natures and are often intelligent people who enjoy being perceived as the wise or knowledgeable one.

Although Ones often see themselves as thinking types (and it is certainly true that they tend to think a great deal about things, especially before they act), they are primarily people of action, not thought. The thinking of the One leads to practical, purposeful action, whereas Fives allow their thinking to take them along whatever intellectual route that it leads them, without necessarily having an interest in a practical outcome.

They both love to acquire knowledge and information about the world, but for very different reasons. Fives simply want to discover more about the world and accumulate a wealth of facts; Ones want to know things in order to make progress in life so that they may improve themselves or perfect their world.

Both types like being right and can come over as the know-it-all. However, when Ones argue a point, they sincerely believe they are right, whereas Fives may argue a point that is contrary to their real beliefs just because they enjoy using their intellectual capacity and knowledge to debate or philosophise.

Ones are genuinely interested in helping you make your life better and tend to offer you plenty of advice, often becoming quite forceful with it if it does not seem to be accepted. Fives are not interested in giving advice unless it is asked for. If you do ask, they willingly give you the benefit of all they know but will not be bothered if you fail to take their advice. Fives are usually fairly accepting of other people and their behaviour, but average to low-functioning Ones can be very judgemental and moralistic, frequently voicing their opinions about right and wrong.

Because Ones try to keep control of their emotions, they can appear to others as cool and detached, like Fives. However, the One is full of powerful emotions that they cannot detach from. Control is not the same as detachment. The Five can detach from what they are feeling and only allow the emotion to be felt later. The One feels things very strongly in the moment and needs a lot of bodily tension to keep it internalised.

One and Six

Although it is rare for a One to mistype as a Six, the reverse is not uncommon. Both are industrious, conscientious types who a have strong sense of duty and need to complete all tasks or duties before relaxing. There are many other apparent similarities, but as always, it is essential to look at the driving energy behind the behaviour displayed.

Self-reliant Sixes (especially males) can quickly become aggressively reactive and often display angry behaviour; as result, they may confuse this aspect of themselves for the anger of the One. Also, both can be judgemental. Ones get judgemental and angry because you are not doing the right thing according to moral or ethical ideals, because your behaviour is just not 'right' ('Do you realise that carton is recyclable?') or because you still haven't taken notice of what they have already told you. Sixes can become judgemental and angry when someone is 'breaking the rules' or displaying disruptive behaviour that, for the Six, seems to threaten the stability and security that they so need.

Anxiety is part of the make-up of Sixes, but Ones can also experience anxiety. They worry about whether they have done everything that needed to be done, and making decisions can involve quite a lot of worry for the average One, as it can for Sixes. Again, there are different reasons. Ones worry about whether their decision gives them the perfect choice, whereas the Six worries because every decision involves a degree of uncertainty and they need to check out every option, just to be sure.

Another difference is that, although Ones definitely know their own minds and rarely seek another's opinion, the reliant Six may ask several different people. Sixes rely on external sources of information or guidance and come to trust and believe what they have read or been told. Once they have strongly identified with a source of guidance, they can become aggressively angry with anyone who does not appear to give the same credence to this 'authority' or who contradicts their beliefs. In contrast, Ones are their own authority; they seek little external input and are highly likely to be the one others look to as 'the one who knows'.

Doing the right thing or taking the right course of action is important to both types; however, there is significant difference between them. The One knows what the right thing is; the Six is never sure.

The need to do a perfect job when doing things for other people is often displayed by Sixes and can be mistaken for the perfectionism of type One. It is, in fact, a fear of making mistakes and getting into trouble, or not being wanted, which would undermine the Six's security. For the One, it is just about doing a perfect job to satisfy their own high standards.

Neither Ones nor Sixes find it easy to accept criticism and both have difficulty admitting mistakes. For the One, this is because they are already highly self-critical and cannot allow themselves to be less than perfect, whereas on the Six's part, it is because they fear that if you consider them not up to the mark, you may not want them around anymore, which undermines their security and need to belong.

One and Seven

These types are rarely confused by others, although occasionally a very stressed Seven may mistype as a One; under stress, Sevens can 'go to' One negatively and may begin to display some of the lower-functioning traits of the One. When life seems to be spiralling out of control, the Seven's fears may lead them to try to regain control by attempting to create order out of disorder. Then they can engage in activities that are typical of the One, such as list making. Also, when lower functioning, Sevens can become very impatient with their own efforts; they start to judge all that they do as inadequate or lacking in some way, and consequently become highly self-critical, as are Ones. Another possible reason for Sevens deciding they are Ones is that they may mistake their dissatisfaction and impatience with the quality of their experiences for the perfectionism of the One.

However, there are many obvious differences between Sevens and Ones. Sevens are fun-loving, adventurous people who spontaneously follow their desires and impulses. There is an open, uninhibited quality to their energy. When you are around them, you can sense the way their minds are always moving forward, and when they are in the company of a group of people, you frequently see them sitting forward in their chairs, eager to absorb everything. They are curious and open-minded, coming to each of their experiences with the freshness of a child, and they just love input from outside of themselves. In contrast, average Ones have a reluctance to receive input from others so tend to be rigid and opinionated, yet they are very keen to give out information in order to instruct and improve those around them. They find it hard to relax enough to have fun because all their impulses are examined and judged, with the result that they lack spontaneity and are often experienced by others as overly serious or prissy. They tend to be socially uptight and self-conscious, whereas Sevens are unselfconscious and at ease in company.

There are many other differences. Ones are very aware of their strong emotions and experience guilt frequently, whereas Sevens avoid connecting with their negative emotions and rarely experience guilt.

Sevens have a laissez-faire attitude towards others. They want freedom themselves and are happy to let others be who they are without criticism or judgement. By contrast, Ones can be highly critical and judgemental of others. Ones are sticklers for schedules and are always on time, but Sevens like things to be open-ended and can be careless about time keeping. Ones follow the rules and always try to do the right thing, whereas Sevens do not want to conform and are quite likely to rebel against rules and regulations.

Lastly, it is worth noting that high-functioning Ones who transcend their need to control themselves begin to live much of their lives by following their spontaneous impulses and are then able to feel free to have fun. As a result, it is just possible that they may mistype as a Seven. However, the One is still a One whose behaviour patterns are driven by the need to improve both themselves and the world, whereas a Seven's behaviour is driven by the need to be free to find what will make them happy.

One and Eight

These are often confused by others because they are both independent and strong-willed types, people who are hard workers, controlling and bossy. However, these are superficial similarities that often mislead other people, but when we look at the fundamental differences between them, we can see that it is less likely that the two types would mistype themselves. Eights seek to be powerful and autonomous, whereas Ones seek to be perfect and good; Ones are highly self-critical and usually lack self-worth, whereas Eights have an abundance of self-confidence; Ones experience a lot of guilt, yet Eights view themselves as blameless.

Although Eights rarely mistype themselves as Ones – they often see the One's strong conscience and ethical approach to life as weak – Ones may possibly mistype themselves as Eights because they know they have a tendency towards anger. However, Ones try to control their anger, and if it explodes out, they feel guilty. Eights always feel justified in displaying anger and, not only are they highly unlikely to experience any guilt about the way they have behaved, they may be proud of the strength they have shown. The causes of their anger are also quite different. Eights get angry often and for many reasons, especially if someone is disrespectful or makes them feel threatened. The One's anger is usually infrequent and mostly directed at themselves (even though others may well get the brunt of it) for not being good or perfect enough. When it is directed at others, it is likely to be because the One feels overburdened when others are not pulling their weight.

Ones and Eights are both bossy personalities who can be very controlling and are 'always right'. However, Eights tell you what to do because they want to dominate their entire environment, and you are part of it. Ones, however, tell you what to do because it's for your own good, and they want to help you be a better or more efficient person. When they meet resistance from others, although both can be very pushy, their responses feel very different. Because the One sincerely believes you will benefit from their instruction, they will try to convert you to their way of thinking. They use a logical and reasoned out approach, only getting irritated or angry when this fails to convince you. Eights, however, meet resistance with the force of their wills and try to power through your resistance by insisting that you will do it their way, *because* it's their way.

Both types have very strong feelings about justice, but they come from very different standpoints. Ones think a lot about what is right and what is wrong. They want to make the world a better and fairer place because that is the right thing to do and injustice or unfairness is morally wrong. However, the Eight's response to injustices involves little thought; it is more of an instinctual response that brings them rushing to the aid of the defenceless to even up the score in an unjust world. Also, average Eights will fight injustice because they want 'their side' to win and are not interested in ridding the world of corruption or evil.

One and Nine

This mistyping is not common but may occur where a One has a strong Nine wing or a Nine has a strong One wing. There are few similarities between them but many clear differences, especially when we look at their attitude to anger. Both resist their anger but for different reasons. To the Nine, anger is a damaging, even dangerous emotion that must be avoided in order to maintain peace and harmony, whereas Ones resist their anger because it is a 'bad' emotion and their striving for perfection means that they must not allow it.

Nines are easygoing and comfortable to be around. Ones are not easygoing at all; they are nitpicking perfectionists who have strong opinions about many things and generally believe they are right. They will argue their position to the point of getting pushy and even aggressive, because they want to convert you to their point of view. Nines may have strong opinions too but generally cannot see the point in arguing; it's not worth the effort and might bring about the conflict they try to avoid. Apart from that, they can usually see things both ways anyway. Things are never black and white for the Nine, whereas for the One, they always are.

When we look at how the two types handle stress, we see entirely opposite reactions. Initially, Nines tune out and become disengaged from the uncomfortable feelings brought up by the problem, although, should the situation continue for a long time, they may 'go to Six'. Then they become anxious and overly reactive, even angry. When we look at Ones, the pattern is almost the reverse. Initially, they become stressed, driving themselves harder and harder, taking little relaxation or respite, and displaying highly reactive outbursts of anger. In the face of long-term stress, Ones can 'go to Four', as they begin to experience feelings of hopelessness and uselessness and become more and more self-critical. Eventually, they lose confidence to face the world and become depressed and withdrawn.

Type Comparison for Twos

Two and One (see One and Two)

Two and Three

Both of these types are very concerned about the impression others have of them and try to find ways of being liked or desired. They can both be extremely charming and likeable, so it is not uncommon for others to mistype them when their outward behaviour is the only criterion used for the typing. However, they go about getting positive attention from others in different ways; the Two focuses their attention on *others*, whereas the Three's behaviour focuses attention on *themselves*.

Twos desire closeness and emotional intimacy because their relationships are the primary focus of their lives. As a result, they show positive interest in other people's welfare and ask questions to encourage others to share details about themselves. In direct contrast, conversation with average Threes often ends up being about them. They desire to be considered admirable, outstanding, or successful, so they need to 'sell' themselves when interacting with others; they make a point of letting people know how busy they are, what they have achieved, or what they are planning so that others will 'buy' the way they package themselves.

The types themselves may mistype where the wing is confused with the core type. A female Three who devotes most of her time and energy to her role as a mother or homemaker may think she is a Two. However, her feelings about herself as a mother, and perhaps even the way she parents her children, will be coloured by much comparison and competition with other mothers; she will desire to have the best-looking or brightest children, the desirable home, or perhaps an admirable husband in whose success she can experience reflected glory.

Twos working in some business situations may be functioning mostly via their Three wing whilst at work so mistake themselves for Threes. However, there are many differences that can easily clear up the confusion. Although many Twos can be ambitious, few reach the pinnacle of their careers unless their work involves helping others. Rather than desiring to be the best, or the number one as Threes do, Twos are much more likely to desire to become indispensable to the boss, the one without whom nothing would run smoothly. They rarely pursue goals without consideration of others, and often get emotionally involved with other people's problems. Compare the behaviour of the average Three who can be so driven to pursue their goals that they can be selfish and inconsiderate of others feelings; it's the goal that matters for the Three. Emotional concerns just get in the way and too much emotional closeness makes them shy away, whereas it just draws the Two closer.

Two and Four

This mistyping most commonly occurs when a Two is feeling unappreciated or unloved and ends up feeling hard done by (Two 'going to Four' negatively), or where a Four is working in the role of helper, carer, or therapist and is displaying some of the best qualities associated with the Two (Four 'going to Two' positively).

Both have great emotional sensitivity and both tend to be very focused on relationships and to have a romantic nature. However, the Four rejects any relationship that does not fit their ideal fantasy, whereas the average Two will embark upon less-than-ideal relationships out of neediness, even to the point of sacrificing their integrity, convincing themselves that the other loves them, wants them, and will fulfil their needs.

Two is the rescuer; Four is the one who wants to be rescued. Twos want to connect with you and draw you towards them, so their energy reaches out to you; in contrast, Fours want *you* to draw *them* out, so they withdraw their energy in the hope that they can entice you towards them.

When interacting with a Two, the communication tends to be all about you, and they are great listeners. Being more concerned about your needs than their own, so Twos are likely to ask you how you are and what's going on in your life, whereas the self-absorption of the average Four makes them much more interested in their own concerns than yours. Consequently, they rarely listen for very long to what others have to say before turning the conversation back to themselves. As a result, most of the communication is likely to be all about them.

There is also a noticeable difference in the way these two types deal with the painful feelings that they experience as a result of conflict with another person. Both types tend to lack self-esteem and can be easily hurt. Fours internalise their feelings and prolong the problem by going over and over the matter, thereby creating internal dramas. Rather than seeking out the other so that the problem can be aired, they tend to withdraw and sulk, secretly hoping to be sought out by the other. They hang onto grievances and feel justified in their resentments and blaming of the other person because of the hurt they have experienced. In contrast, Twos are most likely to blame themselves for not being what others want, and thereby being the cause of the conflict, and feel guilty if they have resentful feelings. The lack of connection with the other person that results from conflict feels unbearable for Twos so they will always want to talk about the problem and to sort it out quickly. Their anger rarely lasts long, and they do not generally sulk; in fact, they will make a point of seeking out the other person to share how they are feeling and to clear the air.

Two and Five

These types are so different that it highly unlikely that they would be confused. However, with very limited understanding of the types, it is just possible that a Five may be mistaken for a Two with regard to their closest intimate relationships. When Fives form a close emotional bond, they want to keep their partner close by. As a result, they can display controlling and possessive behaviour as a Two might.

In almost every other respect, they are complete opposites. Twos are emotional, people-orientated types who desire closeness with others. Fives are very private and remain emotionally detached; they see emotionality as unnecessary gushiness and withdraw from it, whereas it just draws Twos closer. Fives choose to reveal little of themselves to others, especially their feelings, whereas Twos are often emotionally self-revealing with other people. When interacting with others, Fives will enjoy discussing complex intellectual ideas, whereas Twos are interested in how others are feeling and what is happening in their lives. Twos move towards others energetically, Fives move away, and so on.

Two and Six

Confusion between these types is not uncommon because both are warm, personable people who are helpful and industrious, and Sixes, especially women, can appear to display a lot of the behaviour of the Two, especially care taking of others and meeting others' needs.

They both seek positive input from others in order to feel liked. However, this behaviour in the Two is driven by neediness, whereas the Six wants you to like them so that they have a sense of belonging and to reassure themselves that you will not abandon them. It gives them a sense of security.

Some of the behaviour they display to elicit a response in others is very different. Sixes might be playful, fun, or teasing, whereas Twos will let you know good things about yourself, give you compliments, and offer friendship or love. Both types need approval but for different reasons. Twos wants to reassure themselves that you need them and that they are important to you; however, Sixes want your approval of their good deeds so that they know they have done a good job.

Their emotional response to other people is quite different. If you were experiencing an upsetting situation, the Two would want to engage you emotionally, asking you how you feel about what's going on and supporting you through the emotional upheaval and any accompanying tears. The Six would be unlikely to want to know too much about your emotional state because it would make them feel helpless but would want to do something practical to make things better for you. In relationships, Twos thrive on emotional closeness, the closer the better, whereas, until very confident in the relationship, Sixes tend to back away and avoid eye contact when the intimacy gets too mushy or probing.

Less-than-healthy reliant Sixes, especially females, can easily think they are Twos. However, the reliant Six seeks out stronger characters they trust to help them with their anxiety or indecision. Twos are more likely to be the one that others go to for help, or they will make themselves the authority figure by offering unsolicited advice. Compare this to the self-reliant Six who may well wish to be the one others consult for advice but will rarely offer advice unless it has been asked for.

In many areas, these types are very different. The Two is generally optimistic and does not experience much anxiety; the Six is generally pessimistic in outlook and experiences a level of anxiety most of the time. The Six rarely complains about physical ailments; the Two often complains and wants your sympathy. Two's approach to life is proactive, whereas the Six is reactive.

Two and Seven

This mistyping can easily happen when the outward behaviour displayed by these types is the only criterion used for the typing. Both Twos and Sevens are outgoing, friendly people that others find good company. They are both 'glass-half-full' types who bounce back easily from disappointments and who display a generally optimistic and enthusiastic approach to life. However, the way they interact with others can be seen to be quite different when the whole picture is examined.

Being genuinely interested in other people's happiness and well-being, Twos will take the time to ask about you and your life, and they feel good about fulfilling your needs rather than their own. They want to be emotionally close to others and need to be needed. By contrast, Sevens do not want you to need anything from them because other people's dependency might curtail their freedom and they want to be free to pursue their own needs. Whereas Twos want to hear about your problems and will empathise with your negative feelings, Sevens don't really want to hear about your troubles because your tale of woe might drag them down and they are determined to stay upbeat. Instead of listening to how you are feeling, they will try to talk you out of it by putting a positive spin on your problem or by suggesting something fun to take your mind off it.

Sevens just do not want to get involved in people's lives in the way that Twos do. They enjoy other people's company because having others around enhances the experiences they are having, but they maintain a level of detachment within their many friendships, something that Twos find extremely difficult. Both types can be extremely generous spirited, but the intention behind the generosity is quite different. Twos want to be important to their friends and enjoy being helpful to those in need, because it makes them feel wanted. Compare this to Sevens who might invite a crowd round to dinner or pay for tickets to the theatre for less-well-off friends, not to experience feelings of being needed or wanted but to surround themselves with people with whom to share the event so that they themselves have more fun.

An important distinction between Sevens and Twos is in the arena of emotions. Twos are highly emotional people whose emotional centre dominates their reaction to life. Consequently, their behaviour is more often guided by feelings than logic. In contrast, Sevens avoid connecting with their emotions. Their feeling centre is a place to be avoided, and they achieve this by staying in their minds, making endless plans, and by keeping busy.

When a relationship ends, Sevens may feel sad for a while but are able to easily move on. They do not cling to the past and, because they do not wish to be dependent on others, they certainly do not cling on to the lost partner. Twos, however, find the ending of a relationship extremely difficult, even when it is obvious that it is not working, and can become very clingy and needy if the other person initiates the break-up.

Two and Eight

It is easy to understand why this confusion can occur because these types are both strong-willed, with a tendency to be controlling or dominating and can exhibit similar behaviour at times, although for different reasons.

It is, in fact, unusual for Eights to mistype themselves as Twos, but it might happen when a female Eight has embarked upon a great deal of growth work, especially where this involved learning to overcome what they perceive as their 'unacceptable' tendencies towards anger and aggression. On the other hand, it is quite possible that Twos might mistype as Eights because when stressed, Twos can appear much like Eights. As their behaviour deteriorates, they can become aggressive, pushy and controlling like an average Eight; however, when we look at the underlying reasons for this behaviour, we see that they are quite different.

Eights want to dominate their environment in order to increase or maintain their power, and because you are part of their surroundings, their pushy and controlling ways are designed to dominate. In contrast, Twos try to control your behaviour towards them so that you will give them the appreciation and attention they need, and average Twos with poor boundary awareness can be very pushy and controlling in the name of being helpful. Moreover, Twos tend to become angry and aggressive when they feel hurt and unwanted; Eights will become aggressive when they feel vulnerable.

When Eights are not happy about something, they will have no problem about telling you straight out what and why. They are very direct in all their dealings with others; compare this to Twos who are likely to use indirect means to get you to pay attention to how they are feeling. Both types are prone to exaggeration, but the Two exaggerates problems in order to get attention so that they feel wanted and cared about, whereas Eights exaggerate their stories of conquest in order that you will be impressed by how effective and powerful they are.

Situations involving conflict can affect Twos and Eights very differently. Conflict is very upsetting for Twos because it may be damaging to their warm relationship with you. Twos who lack confidence will redouble their efforts to please you; confident Twos will probably stand up to you and fight their corner and then very quickly want to make everything right with you because they cannot stand the loss of connection that came about because of the conflict. However, Eights are not bothered by conflict and will probably find it energising; they may even pick a fight to challenge you, as a test of your strength or perhaps to liven things up in a relationship. Mostly, Eights are supremely self-confident and care little about the opinion others have of them. However, average Twos care hugely if others view them in a bad light and will go out of their way to make sure they are thought well of.

Two and Nine

Although Twos rarely mistype themselves as Nines, female Nines mistyping as Twos occurs quite frequently, because Twos and Nines display a lot of similar behaviour, most notably, in caring for others and putting others needs before their own. However, when we look at what drives their apparently similar behaviour, we see obvious differences.

Nines put their own desires aside and allow themselves to be swept along by other people's agendas in order to keep the peace. This is quite a different motivation to the Two not acknowledging or expressing their own needs. The Two has very specific needs and deeply wants those needs met, but wanting to be the selfless do-gooder who does not have needs means that those needs cannot be openly expressed. They will often go along with other people in order that these others will want them, appreciate them, or love them, whereas the Nine will go along with other people's agendas in order to avoid conflict.

It is certainly true that Twos also dislike conflict so can appear to be behaving as a Nine would, but their motives are different. Nines avoid conflict because it disturbs their inner harmony; Twos prefer to avoid conflict because it might damage their connection with others, with the result that the Two might feel unwanted or unloved.

We can also see that Nines and Twos have very different ways of dealing with problems that might result in conflict. Average Nines tend to become uncommunicative and show little emotional reaction in the face of conflict with others. If they are treated unjustly, they are much more likely to withdraw than to defend themselves. Twos will openly express angry feelings when they feel it necessary and defend themselves strongly or aggressively, especially when they feel misjudged. They will probably feel justified in being angry – they are not afraid of anger and, after all, they believe they deserve better – whereas Nines, if they actually get angry at all, which they probably won't, fear their own anger and its consequences. To them, it's not worth getting angry; they believe it just causes more problems.

The way in which Twos and Nines react to not getting their needs met is also quite different. The average Two begins to feel resentful and, even though it may be a long while before they become openly resentful or angry, they are very likely to complain about all they have to do, how exhausted they are, or about the shortcomings of the other. In contrast, Nines are used to being overlooked and not having their needs considered so they rarely complain.

Nines are self-effacing types who can give emotional support and love without looking for any return. It rarely occurs to them that lack of response in another means they are not appreciated or loved. They are more likely to give the other the benefit of the doubt and put it down to thoughtlessness or tiredness, or will just accept the other the way they are. However, in the eyes of the Two, a lack of response from others implies that she or he is not wanted, appreciated, or loved. Twos thrive on attention and flattery; Nines do not want too much attention and are often happy to fade into the background. In fact, they can get embarrassed or flustered if given too much appreciative acknowledgement.

There are many other differences between the Nine and the Two. Nines are non-interfering types who allow other people to be who they are; they like to be helpful but do not get bothered when others do not take their advice. Twos, however, find it hard to take no for an answer and often get pushy and controlling with the help and advice they give because they 'know' what the other needs better than the person themselves does. Twos get emotionally involved with others' problems, whereas Nines stay detached, even while being supportive. Twos are emotionally expressive and cry easily, whereas Nines suppress their negative feelings and rarely cry in public. Nines are private and restrained, revealing little of themselves except to very close family, whereas Twos are self-revealing.

Type Comparison for Threes

Three and One (see One and Three)

Three and Two (see Two and Three)

Three and Four

This is unlikely that these types would be confused. However, it can happen where a Three with a strong Four wing is involved with the expressive or creative arts and mistakes themselves for a Four. (Fours almost never mistype themselves as Threes.) With insufficient knowledge of the types, the Three may believe that if you are artistic you must be a Four, but it must be remembered that this arena is not the exclusive field of the Four.

The confusion is easily cleared when we look at the way these types deal with their feelings, which is almost completely opposite. For Threes, it is work first, feelings later, whereas with Fours, dealing with feelings is a top priority. When Fours are experiencing difficult or painful emotions, they always want to stop what they are doing, go into the feelings in order to understand and integrate them, and only when this has been accomplished do they feel able to function effectively again. The way Fours allow themselves to become overwhelmed, controlled even, by their feelings is viewed by the average Three as self-indulgent and unnecessary. Threes will not let their feelings get in the way of the task in hand; to them, feelings just slow you down and make you take your eye off the ball. This cool, detached approach makes perfect sense to the goal-orientated Three but is viewed with disdain by average Fours, who see it as shallow and cold.

Three and Five

Because these two types are very different, confusion between Three and Five is unlikely. However, it may happen when there is an incomplete understanding of the types and this is combined with exposure to mainly negative descriptions of the Three. Where this is the case, some highly intelligent or academic Threes might choose to reject the possibility of being Three and embrace the idea of Five. Fives, however, will almost never mistake themselves for Threes.

The one similarity between these types is that both Threes and Fives detach from their emotions. However, the reasons why they do this are very different. From the perspective of the Three, emotions are like 'speed bumps' that might get in the way of progress towards goals and success, so the usual pattern of the average Three is to suppress any uncomfortable emotion. The Five puts aside the emotions of the present moment so that problems can be dealt with via logic and reason without emotion clouding the issue. Later, in private, the Five revisits the emotions in order to examine and understand them; compare this to the Three, who is usually too busy to examine them at all

Fives enjoy complex concepts and abstract ideas and acquire knowledge for the sake of knowledge itself. Their work does not need to have any obvious purpose or application and frequently allows their thoughts and ideas to take them wherever they go without any particular purpose or goal in mind. Public recognition for their work is not important; in fact, Fives are usually secretive about what they are doing and where their thinking is taking them. In contrast, Threes always want recognition for what they have achieved and working within the academic world is no exception, so they will readily talk about their work in order to impress. Rather than pursuing an idea for its own sake, Threes always have a specific goal in mind for the work they undertake and will readily change tack if success eludes them.

There are many other differences. Threes are friendly, sociable types who care enormously about other people's opinion, whereas Fives, who care little about what others think of them, cannot be bothered with social niceties and may be unsociable, even isolated or reclusive. Also,

Fives care little for their appearance, and neither possessions nor wealth interest them, whereas for Threes, material wealth or possessions are important as status symbols.

Three and Six

This typing confusion is not very common, but it could happen where the types are viewed superficially because they are both hardworking, industrious people who want other people to like and accept them, and who avoid conflict. However, the underlying drive behind their behaviour is very different.

Sixes are warm, friendly people who need to know that others want them around; they need to know that their friendships or their work relationships are secure so that they experience a sense of belonging and security. Clearly, they need to behave in likeable, engaging ways and avoid conflict with others as this might undermine their relationships, and perhaps their job, and hence their security. In contrast, average Threes present their charming, likeable exterior in order that you will buy into the image of success they present. They interact with others with a buoyant, cheerful attitude, letting you know that everything in their lives is working well and that they are achieving all the success they desire. And because it is crucial that they have value in the eyes of others, they will avoid engaging in conflict, as this might undermine the positive opinion you have of them.

Also, what drives Sixes and Threes to work hard is quite different. Average Threes are always working towards creating the image of success and the achievement of goals that will bring about success. Even when working as part of a team, they are really solo players who want to be noticed and admired for all they do, whereas Sixes are team players do not wish to draw too much attention to themselves. From their perspective, those who put their heads above the parapet might get shot down, so they are quite happy to stay out of the limelight. Whereas Threes want to be the best or the number one in the eyes of other people, Sixes are content when others see them as the reliable and competent ones; as long as they know they are doing a good job that others value, they will work away in the background in order to contribute to the team effort.

One other very notable difference between these types is the way they deal with their anxieties and fears. Sixes are highly reactive types who become defensive, nervous, or angry when their worries begin to overwhelm them, whereas Threes, who do plenty of worrying when things aren't going well, keep their fears to themselves and project a cool, controlled image of 'having it altogether' so that their successful image remains intact.

Three and Seven

Confusion between these types is not unusual because both Threes and Sevens are highly sociable people who live busy lives with a full schedule. They both project themselves strongly out into the world, and because others often find them highly inspirational, they can both make good leaders. There are many other apparent similarities which, when viewed only on a superficial level, might cause confusion, but when examined at a deeper level only serve to show the real differences between the Seven and the Three.

Both avoid connecting with their emotions and focus on 'doing' rather than 'being'. However, what drives this behaviour is very different. Sevens are sensation seekers who want to accumulate all the experiences they possibly can and not miss out on anything. The need to keep moving is unconsciously designed to keep them out of touch with their emotions so that they avoid being overwhelmed by the dark, painful feelings inside. Compare this to the way in which the continual busyness of the Three is driven by the need to be successful, or more specifically, to avoid failure. However, there is also a need to be *seen* to be busy, whether or not the diary is full, because for the Three, being busy and in demand gives the impression of success, and the way in which others perceive them is paramount to the Three. Emotions need to be avoided because they just get in the way of the Three's pursuit of goals and success and average Threes generally present a cool, 'got-it-all-together' demeanour, which is usually quite easy to distinguish from the enthusiastic exuberance of the Seven.

There are several other ways in which these two types appear to be exhibiting similar behaviour that can lead to mistyping. Both can be prone to exaggeration, but their reasons for bending the truth are poles apart. Threes embellish the truth with regard to what they have, who they know, or what they have achieved in order to give the impression they are more successful than they really are. On the other hand, Sevens embellish the truth when they tell stories to other people about their experiences. This can be to avoid connecting with any negative aspects of the event, in order to keep themselves in a state of positivity, but often it is so that they get the most juice out of telling the story. Describing an event in terms, such as *amazing, fantastic,* or *incredible* reinforces the sensations they experienced and heightens the fun they have in telling the story.

Another apparent similarity worth noting is that both Threes and Sevens can be highly acquisitive, yet once again, we can see that what drives the desire for material wealth and possessions is very different. For the Three, it is about status and being able to impress the rest of the world with all they have acquired. However, the Seven's desire for material wealth or possessions has nothing to do with what others think of them. On the contrary, it is all about themselves and the excitement and the sensations that these things can make possible. Having money provides them with freedom to engage in every activity that takes their fancy and the accumulation of each possession is another, albeit short-lived, opportunity to experience the buzz of excitement that comes from the acquisition of something new.

Three and Eight

Confusion between Three and Eight is not uncommon, especially within business situations, because there are superficial similarities here. Both are ambitious and competitive types who desire success, and in fact, many wealthy entrepreneurs are one or other of these two types. The apparent similarities are even more apparent at the lower-functioning levels where both can be ruthless in the way they deal with business competitors.

There are, however, many more differences than similarities, the most notable of which is what drives these types to become successful and rise to the top. Eights are natural leaders who want to have a large impact on the world around them or accomplish something lasting that will be a testament that they were here. They need to be the one in control, the one who calls the shots, and in order to do this, they need to rise to the top so that they are in a powerful and commanding position. They strive for material wealth, not for its own sake, and certainly not to impress others, but for the personal power it gives them.

Although Threes are also driven to get to the top, what they seek is prestige in other people's eyes rather than power. They live and die by the opinion of others (compare this to Eights who do not care at all what others think of them) and strive to be seen as admirable and successful. Presenting the image of success is crucial to average Threes, so most strive after wealth and material possessions in order that they can impress other people with all they possess.

They are like chameleons in the way they can adapt their behaviour to give the most positive impression, so what they present to the world depends on the situation and who they are with. Eights are quite the opposite. They are straightforward and upfront types who never put on a show; what you see is what you get, and if you don't like it, well, hard luck. Eights meet conflict head on and will use intimidation and strength of will to overcome opposition, whereas Threes, who need other people's good opinion in order to maintain a positive image, will go out of their way to avoid conflict. When problems or a difference of opinion arise, they will back down, change tack, or use diplomacy to win the other person over.

Another notable difference is the way in which these two types deal with failure. Having huge self-confidence, Eights are not in any way daunted by failure; in fact, it is an opportunity to learn something and to come back bigger and better. However, Threes' sense of personal worth is so inextricably tied to their level of success that failure is like death, a deep humiliation to be avoided at all costs.

Three and Nine

Although this is not a common mistype, it could happen. If Threes experience some disastrous material loss or failure, they can go to the low point of Three and begin to display some of the disengaged, laid-back behaviour of the Nine. Feeling that there is no way out their difficulties, they can become unmotivated and no longer interested in chasing after goals or success. In circumstances such as these, they may mistake themselves for Nines, especially if they begin to realise that they do not have a clear idea of who they are or what really makes them happy. However, the Three would need to look more closely at what has always been their driving force before this difficult time. It has probably been the desire to achieve prestige or material wealth and to be seen by others as admirable or successful, none of which is a core drive for Nines, who want peace and harmony above all else.

Because of the connecting line between Nine and Three, it is just possible some people might mistake a Nine for a Three, although it is highly unlikely that a Nine would make the mistake themselves. Generally, Nines are self-effacing people who talk little about themselves and avoid behaving in ways that get too much attention from others. This is very different from the average Three who seeks to draw attention to themselves by talking themselves up or letting others know what they are doing and what they possess.

Even though the types are not very alike at all, there are some similarities. Both types present a positive face to the world and can avoid dealing with problems. However, the avoidance strategies used are different. Threes become even more focused and bury themselves in work, thereby exhausting themselves so that they have no time or energy left for the problem. Compare the Nine who becomes unfocused and distracted and puts their energy into unimportant tasks and the minutiae of life instead of dealing with the real problem.

Both disassociate themselves from difficult emotions, but again, their reasons for doing so are quite different. Nines want to avoid anything that disturbs their peace and they use a shutdown or numbing-out strategy so that they do not have to experience disharmony. However, the Three avoids associating with their emotions because, to the Three, emotions just get in the way of achieving their goals, so they must be avoided. The bottom line is quite clear here. The Nine seeks peace; the Three seeks achievement and success.

Type Comparison for Fours

Four and One (see One and Four)

Four and Two (see Two and Four)

Four and Three (see Three and Four)

Four and Five

These are both withdrawn types, a fact that tends to be especially noticeable in company. In other people's eyes, they can both appear separate or ill at ease, different, individualistic, or even odd. However, on a personal or emotional level, the two types are very different.

Although Fives are mind types, there are many who are not particularly intellectual or cerebral, and if they easily identify that they have strong emotions, they may mistype themselves as Fours. (This is most likely in Five women where there is a strong Four wing.) However, most Fours are self-revealing, whereas Fives share their deepest selves with very few. Emotional expression does not come easily to Fives. They are happy analysing or intellectualising about what they feel but not comfortable expressing themselves from the actual emotion, and they do not welcome too much emotionalism from others. However, Fours are emotionally expressive, even volatile within their relationships, and need people to respond to them in an emotional way. Fours' thoughts often fuel their feelings; Fives' feelings fuel their thoughts.

In conversation, neither of these types is likely to ask many questions about you, but their conversational styles regarding personal details are quite different. The Five will reveal little or nothing about themselves, whereas Fours tend to talk a great deal about themselves and their own lives. Fives enjoy an exchange of information, and most enjoy debate or mental sparing, whereas Fours get bored when the conversation veers too far away from their immediate concerns.

Being the farthest away from Nine on the Enneagram, both Fours and Fives can sink into a depressed state and experience a blackness or dark void inside. When in this state, Fives tend to focus on their inner emptiness and feelings of meaninglessness or pointlessness, whereas Fours focus on their disappointments in relationships and the blame they feel towards those who inflicted pain upon them in the past, especially childhood.

Both types can be very creative and artistic, but their styles are different. The Fours' creative expression tends to be subjective, portraying their dramatic emotions, their relationships (especially the pain of unrequited love), or their feeling for colour, beauty, and nature. The Fives will try to express where their minds have taken them, perhaps producing art that is abstract, fantastic, or full of unusual concepts. If the artistic Five is creating from their personal darkness, the result may be outlandish, weird, or even bizarre, portraying the pointlessness of life or even the end of the world.

Four and Six

Although Fours and Sixes are very different types, there are some apparent similarities that might lead to mistyping, most notably with regard to negative thinking and self-doubt. Except when high-functioning, both types often seem to approach life with a 'glass-half-empty' attitude. The negativity of the Six is driven by their need for security and is a result of a continual need to check out the future and work out how they will deal with the worst possible outcomes of their situation. However, the negative thinking of the Four revolves mainly around self-loathing and jealousy, leading to internal negative dramas, or it is focused upon their 'suffering' and the blaming of others that they perceive to be responsible for their problems.

Both types can suffer with depression, but the underlying causes are different. When Fours begin to experience real hopelessness that life will ever be what they hope for, they can sink into a state of black depression and self-hatred. Sixes, on the other hand, experience depression when their fears overwhelm them so that they feel unable to cope with life or when they fear that their own behaviour has damaged their security.

Sixes can sometimes mistype as Fours when they have artistic inclinations, but they lack the self-absorption of the Four. Fours are interested in expressing their personal truth and usually create art that has a unique, self-expressive style that is focused around their own personal dramas, whereas Sixes tend to follow traditional styles. (The one exception to this might be the very rebellious self-reliant Six who may deliberately go to extremes in their artistic expression in ways that defy tradition or shock society.) When involved in the performing arts, Sixes are generally happy to perform their part as a contribution to the whole production, but Fours want their individualistic style to be noticed so are more likely to seek special or highly dramatised roles.

In social situations, these types respond very differently. Sixes easily engage with others; they are warm and friendly and make other people like them. Their energy reaches out towards you with the desire to be helpful. In contrast, Fours do not engage with others easily; they are self-conscious and reticent socially, withdrawing their energy and secretly wanting you to come to seek them out.

In the arena of personal relationships, we see very different attitudes between the Four and the Six. Sixes form lasting and steady bonds with those they care about and are loyal to a fault. Their relationships give them a safe, comfortable zone from which they can better deal with the vagaries of their world, and many Sixes hang onto a dead relationship out of the need for security. Fours seek relationships in which they can find themselves, and they dream of that one perfect person who will

THE ENNEAGRAM: PATHWAYS TO HAPPINESS

sweep them away from the mundanities of life. As a result, most find it hard to form lasting relationships, giving up easily when problems arise or when the other person's imperfections get too much to bear.

Four and Seven

It would seem unlikely that Fours and Sevens would be confused with each other because these two types are very different. However, there appear to be several superficial similarities if the types are not properly understood, so it can happen.

Both can be self-indulgent, have expensive tastes, and enjoy fine-quality objects. However, Fours, who love beautiful things for their own sake and for the aesthetic pleasure they bring, may cherish the same possessions for years. Compare this to Sevens, who seek to own expensive or beautiful things because they feel stimulated and excited by the acquisition of something new and frequently lose interest in the desired object quite soon after acquiring it.

Sevens and Fours both tend to be self-focussed and self-centred, yet what drives this behaviour, and the way they display it, is very different. The Seven is driven ever forward to have more and more experiences and, in their desire to keep moving, they rarely stop long enough to consider others' needs. As a result, they are often experienced by other people as self-centred. In their desire to stay upbeat and carefree, they maintain a positive outlook so are unlikely to show much interest in your emotional needs, nor will they express their own, as any attachment to negative feelings just might bring them down. They almost never talk about problems, and whenever anything negative threatens to impinge upon their upbeat, positive outlook, either they find a way to turn it around so that they can focus on the silver lining, or they find a way to distract themselves from connecting with it.

In contrast to the Seven, for the average Four, the glass is half-empty rather than half-full; they focus a great deal on what they do not have, what is wrong in their lives, and on their negative feelings. They create internal dramas about the slightest thing and will talk endlessly about themselves, especially their problems. They take everything to heart and can be moody, prickly and explosive, whereas Sevens take a light-hearted approach to life and want to keep everything happy.

Although it is true that they are both people of extremes, Sevens go to extremes in the outside world, whereas Four go to extremes in their inner world of emotions. Fours are highly self-conscious and extremely in touch with their feelings, whereas Sevens have little self-awareness, being quite out of touch with their inner world and what they truly feel. At the lower-functioning levels, the differences become even more profound; the Four becomes hypersensitive, such that any innocent comment from others upsets them, and certain smells, foods, environments, etc. affect them profoundly. In contrast, Sevens become desensitised, so that their experiences provide them with less and less sensation until, at the lower-functioning level, they are hardly touched by them at all.

It is worth noting another point that can cause confusion between these types. This is that depression is common when they reach their lowest point. However, here again we see distinct differences between the types. Fours are in familiar territory when they feel overwhelmed by negativity; they may even welcome it and wallow in it, melancholy and pain being part of the identity they have created for themselves of being 'the one who suffers so much'. In direct contrast, Sevens will do almost anything to avoid being sucked down into their inner darkness; they are highly likely to indulge in wild, even manic, behaviour in their efforts to avoid their own pain, and should they sink into depression, as a matter of survival, they soon look for positive activities to bring them back out.

Four and Eight

Although these are very different types, confusion can occur. Firstly, because both can be self-centred and insensitive to other people's feelings, and secondly, lower-functioning Fours can occasionally be mistaken for Eights when they are exhibiting the angry and aggressive outbursts that are typical in a Four under stress.

Also, there is a possibility that the types themselves may mistype because both experienced feelings of betrayal and alienation in their young years. However, the way they went on to deal with this as they got older is quite different. Eights decided it was necessary to get over the pain of their childhood and to toughen up so that they could get somewhere in the world and become invulnerable. They got past it and do not want to revisit it. In contrast, Fours refuse to let go of the past. Instead, they hang onto all the memories and the associated grievances, all the pain and the blame, and might well use it to excuse their lack of progress in the world.

There are many other clear differences between the types. Fours are highly sensitive and care deeply what other people think of them; they tend to take even innocent remarks personally. Eights, however, are quite unaffected by others' opinions, and to them, critical comments, even nastiness, are like water off a duck's back. Eights are independent types who are not prepared to ever rely on anyone but themselves; Fours want to maintain their physical independence yet most are ready to rely on another while they find or develop themselves. Emotionally, Fours can be highly reliant on others for support and sympathy and can easily become self-indulgent when they are overwhelmed by their feelings, whereas Eights despise emotional self-indulgence, viewing it as an indication of weakness of character and will not tolerate it of themselves or others.

Four and Nine

The main reason for this typing confusion is that both are withdrawal types. When this fact is coupled with some item of information being focused upon without full knowledge of the two types, mistyping may occur. For example, an artistic Nine may mistake themselves for a Four, or a Four may mistype as a Nine when discovering that Nines can disappear into a fantasy world. However, the distinction between these types becomes clear when we look at the whole picture.

Fours wish to experience their emotions fully and withdraw from other people in order to understand and deal with them, often exacerbating them in the process. Nines do not want to experience any disturbing emotions and will withdraw their attention from others in order to avoid potential conflict. In their withdrawal, Nines may remain physically present and appear to be still fully engaged with other people; when Fours need to withdraw, they usually remove themselves physically from others in order to be alone.

There are many other differences. Nines are not self-revealing. They speak little about themselves, especially their problems, whereas Fours can be very self-absorbed, tend to talk a great deal about themselves, and greatly enjoy having someone listen to all their problems. Fours generally experience huge emotional swings because they feel things so deeply, whereas Nines avoid the emotional highs and lows and try to keep their emotional life as smooth as possible. Fours enjoy being the centre of attention, whereas Nines do not want too much attention and prefer to blend. And so on.

Type Comparison for Fives

Five and One (see One and Five)

Five and Two (see Two and Five)

Five and Three (see Three and Five)

Five and Four (see Four and Five)

Five and Six

It is far more common for a Six to be mistyped as a Five than the other way around. The confusion is most likely to occur where a Six with a strong Five wing enjoys intellectual pursuits and views herself or himself as a thinker, concluding that this makes her or him a Five. In this case, it is essential to examine the way each type thinks.

Both are types with very busy minds, although their thinking patterns and attitudes are very different. The Five is a non-linear, open-ended thinker to whom new and original ideas are far more interesting than the known or accepted, whereas the Six thinks in a much more linear way and is not comfortable with new and untried ideas or processes. Sixes are conventional; they uphold the traditional mores of society and believe in the status quo. Fives are more unconventional; in fact, they are more likely to reject established thinking than accept it.

Fives rarely mistype as Sixes because they know that, although they can sometimes be anxious, it is not often, and they are never at the mercy of their feelings. They are able to detach from uncomfortable feelings and can always escape into some intellectual pursuit as a distraction. They can rationalise and examine the reasons why they are anxious rather than allow the anxiety to control them. Sixes are anxious, to a degree, almost all of the time and find distraction from their anxiety and fears extremely difficult. If they seek distraction, it will be by doing something practical rather than cerebral, whereas most average Fives are not very practical. They are thinkers, not doers.

Sixes are generally much more sociable than Fives, and most are good conversationalists; even the shy or reserved Six enjoys a sociable chat once at ease in company. Fives are not at their ease in social situations, preferring to be left out of conversations unless they choose to contribute something of interest or value. They rarely enjoy what they view as pointless chitchat. Also, Fives are independent loners who do not care about fitting in with others, whereas Sixes are people who need to feel that they fit in and belong.

Five and Seven

Confusion between these types is unlikely, for they are very different. However, there are some apparent similarities, most notably that they are both curious nonconformists, both have very busy, agile minds, and both choose to disconnect from their emotions. Each of these is only a superficial similarity, which becomes very clear upon closer examination.

Both Fives and Sevens are curious about the world they live in and both avoid their emotions by engaging in expansive mind activity; however, what interests and preoccupies them is very different. Although both are in their minds a great deal, Sevens are more *doers* than thinkers whereas Fives would rather *think* than do.

The Five seeks to understand how the world works, and their thinking is highly focussed and analytical; it is cerebral activity that excites Fives, and their exploration of the world occurs within the processes of the mind where possibilities are examined intellectually rather than experienced physically. There is a quiet, withdrawn quality to the energy of a Five, and they are happy in their own company, spending much of their time alone reading, working on their projects, or collecting information.

Compare this to the Seven who seeks to physically explore everything the world has to offer, resulting in ceaseless activity and a busy, humming quality to their energy. In contrast to the type of thought engaged in by Fives, the Seven's thoughts are more about fantasy futures that will provide excitement and fun than about information and analysis, and they cannot sit still for very long without feeling the need to get up and go again. They are very gregarious types who prefer to be in the company of other people, whereas Fives do not want or need social activity.

There are many more differences than similarities. For example, Sevens are highly active; Five tend to be inactive. Sevens are optimists who only want to see the positive side of life; Fives can be drawn to the darker, even macabre side of life and view those who wear rose-coloured spectacles as fools. Sevens are perfectly at ease in company and enjoy talking about all sorts of topics; Fives are socially ill at ease and cannot be bothered with what they consider inconsequential chitchat, engaging others in conversation only when the topic lies within their own sphere of intellectual knowledge and interest.

Five and Eight

It is most unlikely that Fives would type themselves as Eights, or vice versa, but it is possible that other people may confuse the two types because they can show some similarities.

Neither Fives nor Eights care what other people think of them. Both are independent types who can get aggressive in order to hide their vulnerability, but once they have felt threatened and expressed anger, they then continue in very different ways. Eights will keep pushing and not give up until they are convinced that they have exerted their dominating strength sufficiently for you to know who's boss. Fives, however, will display their anger and then disappear into their safe sanctum and not reappear for quite a while.

They can both be very direct and outspoken in the way they communicate, and both can offend other people but do not easily apologise. The Eight doesn't believe in pussyfooting around to protect other people's feelings; they say it how it is and if you are offended, then that's your problem. If Fives appear outspoken and tread on others' finer feelings, it is most likely because of their rather poor social skills. Apologies do not come easily to them for two reasons: firstly, they are often not particularly sensitive to other people's emotions and may not understand why you are upset. And secondly, to apologise to you would involve actively engaging in a difficult communication that could make them feel inadequate or out of their emotional depth.

These types are very different in many ways. Eights have a strong, forceful energy that tends to dominate the room they are in; you cannot help but notice them. Fives are people who withdraw their energy and can easily remain unnoticed in a group until they speak. Eights are assertive pragmatists who deal with life head on, following their instincts and taking practical action when they have problems. Fives are not people who just follow their instincts; they prefer to think around a problem rather than tackle it head on. Eights are big-picture people, whereas Fives focus on the specifics or the finer points of the subject in hand. Eights are very grounded in their bodies and have expansive vision in terms of what is possible in the physical and material world; Fives are not properly grounded (and thus have an ambivalent relationship with their bodies), and they see endless possibilities within their minds.

Five and Nine

Although Fives rarely confuse themselves with Nines, male Nines who are highly educated, intellectual, or who enjoy plenty of time alone in bookish pursuits easily mistype as Fives, especially when they discover that Fives disappear off into their minds to escape their emotions. However, just as creativity is not the sole arena of the Four, being knowledgeable or intellectual does not make someone a Five.

These two types are very opposite in many ways. An intellectually brilliant Nine is likely to be quite self-effacing about their knowledge and may even self-deprecate in order to avoid embarrassing others. By contrast, unless high-functioning, Fives enjoy demonstrating their superior knowledge and being intellectually contentious; they can be scathing about 'stupid' people who do not have their intellectual brilliance, whereas Nines are almost always accepting and kind towards others.

The Nine's thinking tends to be more general than specific and focuses on the overall picture; they tend to seek sweeping, idealistic, and generally optimistic solutions to problems. Once they have come to certain conclusions within their field of interest, they are unlikely to want to expand their thinking further. The Five, however, will focus on the details and specifics rather than the overall picture; they love to take an idea and expand and extrapolate it into endless complex possibilities. Their thinking is highly focused, even laser-like, and they can easily lose themselves in cerebral activity, especially when things are difficult or the world feels overwhelming. By contrast, the thinking of the Nine can be hazy and unfocused and they can have difficulty in maintaining concentration, especially when their relationships with others threaten to be disharmonious.

Both of these types can create fantasy worlds in their imaginations, but whereas the Five's fantasies will veer towards the strange or darker aspects of life, the Nine will fantasise about ideal realities where everything is normal and comforting. The Nine creates happy endings where good always triumphs over evil, but in the fantasy of the Five, evil or chaos rules. Also, Nines look towards an idealised past whereas Fives look towards a threatening future.

Type Comparison for Sixes

Six and One (see One and Six)

Six and Two (see Two and Six)

Six and Three (see Three and Six)

Six and Four (see Four and Six)

Six and Five (see Five and Six)

Six and Seven

Although it may be possible to confuse the Six with the Seven when there is a very strong wing, it is not very likely because these types are not only very different but their outlook on life, the way they view the world and what they want from it, are poles apart.

Sevens are driven by the need for freedom and fun; they have an expansive and excited perspective on life, and the world is viewed as a place full of infinite possibilities, all of which are positive. They are spontaneous people who are ready to go at a moment's notice and want to feel that there are no restrictions or boundaries confining their activities. Contrast this with Sixes who are driven by the need for security with the result that they try to keep their world small and safe. From the perspective of the Six, the world is a threatening place full of dangers that must be thought about and prepared for. They tend to lack spontaneity because they think before acting, whereas the Seven frequently acts before thinking.

The only real similarity between these two types is that neither is fully present in the moment; both are in their minds and project forward into the future. However, the Six is the pessimist who projects into the future negatively and expects the worst, whereas the Seven is the optimist who project into the future positively and anticipates the best.

Further comparison shows many other differences. Although both experience anxiety, Sevens' anxiety propels them into action, whereas Sixes' anxiety prevents them acting or results in procrastination. Sixes are highly responsible, dedicated types, but Sevens can be thoughtless and irresponsible. Sixes are people pleasers who put duty before pleasure, whereas Sevens will let others down or fail to fulfil obligations in their pursuit of fun and excitement. And so on.

It is interesting to note that these types are so different that the Six views the Seven's outlook on life as capricious and irresponsible, whereas to the Seven, the life of the Six seems stuck and lacklustre!

Six and Eight

Although a reliant Six is very unlikely to be confused with an Eight, the self-reliant Six can sometimes be openly angry and aggressive and consequently may be mistyped as an Eight. However, when properly understood, it is clear just how different these two types really are.

Eights have a strong sense of who they are and where they are going. They are decisive and determined people who follow their own convictions without being affected by others' opinions. Conversely, Sixes are unsure of where they are going in life and making decisions is fraught with anxiety and uncertainty. Sixes are reactive; they allow life to happen to them and then react to it. Eights are proactive; they take life by the horns and make things happen.

When we look at the area of conflict, we see very different attitudes. Sixes find both their own anger and other people's disturbing and threatening, and they avoid conflict if they can. When a Six gets angry, they usually regret it afterwards; they fear they may have undermined their security and wish they had taken another course of action. Eights, however, thrive on conflict; they find it invigorating, are not afraid of a good argument, and rarely regret anything afterwards. Both types can get aggressive and combative when in a lower-functioning state, but whereas Eights are likely to get so carried away by the momentum of aggression that they can become utterly ruthless, reason and rationality return to the Six much more easily and their fears about what they have done wipe away their anger.

Both types can be judgemental, but about different things. The Six gets angrily judgemental of people who do not follow rules or who seem to behave in ways that may undermine the stability of society, whereas the judgement of the Eight is directed towards those that they view as weak or vacillating or are not pulling their weight.

Six and Nine

Sixes and Nines have a lot in common and can be easily confused when the types are not fully understood. They are both family-orientated types who resist change, preferring to maintain the status quo and keep things around them steady. Both are kind people that others generally warm to, both tend to underestimate themselves and avoid the limelight, both are more reactive than proactive, and both are liable to display procrastination. However, as with all typing confusions, when we look at what drives their apparently similar behaviour, the differences become obvious.

Sixes resist change because change may undermine their security, whereas Nines resist change because change involves upheaval that may disturb their comfort and inner harmony.

Nines procrastinate because they find it hard to know what action needs to be taken. They look at both sides of the question, see advantages and disadvantages with each course of action, and often end up taking no action at all. Also, making a decision may involve later having to take a stand to defend their position, which might lead to conflict that they avoid. The indecisiveness and consequent lack of action displayed by the Six is not the result of not knowing what action needs to taken, but is a result of them continually doubting the way they are considering implementing it. They take the Devil's advocate stance with their 'what if's', which leads to procrastination.

When upsetting events happen, Nines are able to shut down on their overly strong feelings and can then appear calm and unaffected; in contrast, Sixes get easily rattled and find it hard not to show their feelings. Their agitation makes them fearful or defensive, whereas Nines put on a bland exterior and become mostly unresponsive.

Both Nines and Sixes fear anger, their own as well as other people's, because it may badly affect their relationship with others. However, what drives their fear is different. The Nine seeks peace and connection with others, and anger or conflict potentially threatens both. The Six fears loss of connection with others because feelings of belonging and being wanted give them their sense of security, and if this is undermined, they begin to fear rejection and abandonment.

Type Comparison for Sevens

Seven and One (see One and Seven)

Seven and Two (see Two and Seven)

Seven and Three (see Three and Seven)

Seven and Four (see Four and Seven)

Seven and Five (see Five and Seven)

Seven and Six (see Six and Seven)

Seven and Eight

Although Eights rarely mistype as Sevens, Sevens with a strong Eight wing may mistype as Eights because Sevens are an outward-looking type with a strong tendency to avoid introspection. Also, Sevens and Eights might be confused by others because they both have a strong, even aggressive energy, and both go after what they want; however, what they want and the way in which they go after it are very different. Whereas Eights want power and control in order to be autonomous and invulnerable, Sevens seek variety in their experience; in fact, chasing after power can seem too much effort for the Seven and might restrict their freedom to have fun. Moreover, Eights desire intensity in their experiences, yet for Sevens, although they might seek highs, what they really want is to experience all possibilities and not miss out on anything.

There are several other apparent similarities that can cause confusion. Both Sevens and Eights have high-energy personalities, but the way their energy impacts on their world is quite different. Eights have a physically based energy that is grounded and solid, an energy that gives others the sense that this is a determined, unyielding sort of person. Compare this to the energy of the Seven, which has a quick, restless, mental quality to it. Sevens can be ungrounded, even scattered, and they lack the intensity of focus typical of Eights, who are generally very focussed and practical.

Both types are rule breakers. However, Sevens fight against rules because rules restrict their freedom, and Sevens need to be free, whereas Eights break the rules because they need to dominate their environment, which means they will not be controlled by others.

Another similarity between these types is that both tend to be storytellers and both are prone to exaggeration. However, the storytelling serves different purposes. For the Seven, getting others interested or excited by exaggerated stories full of superlatives enables them to squeeze every last bit of juice from each experience, whereas Eights tell stories which illustrate to others how powerful and important they are and exaggerate or embellish the truth to convince others they are a force to be reckoned with.

There is one very clear difference between Eights and Sevens that helps with typing, and that is their attitude to conflict. Sevens wants to keep things light and positive so they generally avoid conflict, whereas Eights are not only unconcerned about conflict or bruising other people's egos but may deliberately engage another in an argument just to prove they can win the battle.

Seven and Nine

Although this typing confusion seems unlikely because the energy of these two types is so different – Nines generally have a gentle, hazy energy whereas the energy of Seven is bright and breezy – it can happen because there are several apparent similarities.

Both have an optimistic outlook on life and maintain a cheerful countenance. Both prefer to stay away from conflict and look for the silver lining in every experience, reframing the negative to make it appear positive. Both can use busyness to avoid connecting with uncomfortable feelings. However, when we look below the surface, we see considerable differences.

Although both types seek happiness and contentment, what constitutes happiness for the Nine is very different from the Seven. Nines want peace and gentle harmony with others in order to feel good, whereas Sevens want to experience excitement, fun and exhilaration. Moreover, Sevens are generally extroverted, fast-talking people who enjoy taking centre stage, whereas Nines, being more introverted, prefer not to take the limelight; in fact, too much attention embarrasses them.

We see another clear difference when we look at how these types handle change and routine. Nines enjoy routine and steadiness and find change difficult, because it disturbs their equanimity. They prefer to keep things on an even keel, and in fact, even when others around them are highly stimulated, the Nine almost never gets excitable. Sevens, however, get restless when things stay the same. Routine is boring to this type; instead, they seek out lots of change and variety and they want to get a high emotional charge from their activities.

Both Nines and Sevens can experience depression when they slip into a low-functioning state. However, their journey down into this state follows a different path. The Nine becomes steadily more unresponsive and lethargic, whereas the Seven goes through periods of extreme highs and lows, becoming hyperactive, highly charged, and prone to all manner of extremes before withdrawing into a dark place of isolation.

Type Comparison for Eights

Eight and One (see One and Eight)

Eight and Two (see Two and Eight)

Eight and Three (see Three and Eight)

Eight and Four (see Four and Eight)

Eight and Five (see Five and Eight)

Eight and Six (see Six and Eight)

Eight and Seven (see Seven and Eight)

Eight and Nine

It is very unlikely for these two types to be confused because their energy and their behaviour patterns are so very different. Although there are many differences between them, the most obvious one to consider is their way of handling conflict. Eights are assertive and unafraid of conflict; in fact, most positively relish a good argument. They always wish to be in a position of control where they can exert their will and dominate their environment and the people in it. In contrast, Nines are easygoing, accommodating people who go along with others' agenda rather than their own; they avoid their own anger as well as that of other people, so they do not assert themselves and shy away from any possibility of conflict. Where there is a difference of opinion, they give way to others in order to keep the peace, whereas average Eights will continue to argue a point with the specific intention of getting the other person to give in to their will.

Type Comparison for Nines

Nine and One (see One and Nine)

Nine and Two (see Two and Nine)

Nine and Three (see Three and Nine)

Nine and Four (see Four and Nine)

Nine and Five (see Five and Nine)

Nine and Six (see Six and Nine)

Nine and Seven (see Seven and Nine)

Nine and Eight (see Eight and Nine)

PATHWAYS TO BECOMING YOUR BEST SELF

CHAPTER 19

Expanding and Growing with the Enneagram

Coming into Awareness

Each of us as children had to discover our place in the world and get the love and security we needed. We also had to find ways of dealing with life's challenges and defend ourselves against hurt. To achieve all of this, we used what we already had: the qualities we found within ourselves that were an intrinsic part of our developing personality. The coping strategies that we adopted then became our habitual behaviour patterns as we moved into adulthood.

Most of the personality functions automatically and unconsciously; we've always behaved like this; it is who we are or who we believe ourselves to be. However, many of our coping strategies no longer serve us; in fact, they result in self-defeating patterns of behaviour that cause us all the pain and interpersonal problems that we experience. The truth is much of the behaviour that we unconsciously adopted during childhood is simply out of date!

The Enneagram has the power to transform and improve every area of life, freeing us from our painful cycles of negative behaviour and allowing our true self to really blossom. The understanding of our recurring personal patterns it provides is unparalleled; so, too, is its ability to unravel past and present relationship issues, explain life circumstances, and improve personal interactions.

Coming into awareness means becoming aware of your patterns, both positive and negative, and realising how these patterns have created all that is best and worst in your life. No longer blaming the outside world and the people in it for your inner feelings or the state of your outer world, you finally empower yourself to make the changes you want. Moreover, as you move into higher-functioning states, you begin to get your greatest desire. You realise that it was never 'out there' at all; it was always to be found within!

Life no longer feels like a mystery with the Enneagram as our ally because its knowledge imbues us with a deep sense of personal understanding and clarity. Suddenly, dealing with the world and making sense of those that inhabit it seems simple, and we feel sure that we have discovered the route to real growth, happiness and peace.

However, it is not the Enneagram knowledge itself that will break your negative patterns, improve your relationships, and set you free; it is your application of it. Without application, knowledge about the Enneagram has no power to facilitate change and lives as nothing more than printed words on a page. Just as the instruction booklet that came with that new piece of flat-pack furniture will not jump out of the box and build your new bookcase for you, it is you that must do the work to bring about the changes you want.

Knowing about Yourself vs. Knowing Your Self

After the initial excitement and enthusiasm of discovering the Enneagram, the dawning of self-realisation brings with it a lifelong opportunity to steadily grow and evolve towards a higher-functioning self. But for some people, once the initial enthusiasm subsides, the amount of self-examination and personal exploration required to continue to make progress can seem daunting. 'Real life', with its ups and downs, and attendant problems, can get in the way, diverting attention away from the new path. Then, all too easily, the momentum necessary to evoke profound and lasting change seems to be lost, progress stalls, and there can be a falling back into the old patterns.

Don't expect to know yourself completely straightaway. Having read and acknowledged the different aspects of your personality patterns, it can be too easy to believe you have all you need from the Enneagram. However, knowing about yourself is not the same as knowing yourself; true self-understanding is a long-term project that takes continued self-awareness, compassion for yourself, and no small amount of courage.

Be patient too; you will undoubtedly plateau every so often, perhaps even lose your way completely. But don't worry; the signposts will always be there to guide you back on track. Regardless of how frequently we deny our true nature, it will persist in its quest for expansion by gently prodding you. This prodding will usually manifest as a cluster of increasingly unpleasant experiences, likely with a common underlying theme. If we resist these challenging or painful episodes – negating the opportunities for growth they are meant to provide us with – our soul will find bigger, louder, and more disruptive methods of getting our attention, until we finally take notice and address our inner world.

Your personality is your growth pattern; it is the reason the soul chose to come here in the first place. So as much as we try, we cannot escape it. One way or another, we must walk our path. You don't have to understand the Enneagram to progress, but it's so much easier and less painful if you do!

Taking Responsibility

The Enneagram is a dynamic vortex of energy that is constantly in flux. Its cyclical rhythm has the potential to reveal to you increasingly deeper facets of your true nature until the day you die. So once you discover your personality type, the hope is that you keep growing and growing and growing.

However, many people over-identify with their type and become stuck. These people appear to possess insight into themselves but remain trapped by their patterns, reminding themselves of the behaviour they should be trying to curb but not sounding as if they'll ever really bother. Knowing their personality type becomes an excuse for their behaviour rather than a catalyst for change. They might exclaim, 'Don't blame me for being a workaholic! It's what Threes do!' or 'I know I'm always worrying about what might happen, but I am a Six after all!' Rather than stimulate growth, the result of this is a complete reversal of the way in which the Enneagram knowledge should be used.

Real and lasting growth within our personality only comes about from persistent, honest self-observation, compassionate acceptance of the patterns we are running, and a determination to make different choices when next presented with that same scenario. If we are truly honest with ourselves about the negative cycles of behaviour we continue to display and the effect they have upon our day-to-day existence, personal and spiritual growth is inevitable. When we see with clarity what we keep doing to ourselves, there becomes no option but to change; after all, why would we not want to be more at peace and happier in our skin?

The first step in embarking upon any form of personal growth work is to take complete responsibility for who you are and how your life has turned out. However, it is often much easier to adopt a victim mentality and convince ourselves, and those around us, that we are powerless to prevent the negative patterns of our existence – even after discovering about the Enneagram. To point the finger of blame outside of ourselves and relinquish any level of responsibility for how we feel is akin to watching your neighbour mow *his* lawn and being disappointed to discover that the carpets in *your* house are not cleaner as a result!

The thoughts we have, the emotions that accompany them, and the resulting 'negative' behaviour patterns that are typical of our type are all within our ability to change, but we must 'own' them first. Nobody can make us feel anything that is not already present within our inner world. Despite what we might believe, when we have a negative reaction to something or somebody, it was *not* that event or person that caused it.

Think about squeezing an orange. No matter who squeezes the orange or how hard it is squeezed, the nature of what comes out is not affected. What comes out is orange juice, because that was what was already inside. It is the same with our emotional reactions. What we feel and how we respond to people or circumstance is our 'orange juice' and we are the only one responsible for it. The key to benefiting from the knowledge of the Enneagram is to come into awareness about the ways in which the negative aspects of your personality are affecting your life, and to then take control of the grip they have upon you.

Be aware though that taking responsibility for your patterns does *not* mean using them as a stick with which to beat yourself. If you start coming to the conclusion that it is your 'fault' or that you are somehow 'bad' or 'less than' because you slip into these negative patterns of thinking, feeling and behaving, you are going down the route that leads to *lower* self-esteem, not higher. You just need to begin to accept that these patterns are normal for your type yet stay very clear that you *do* have the capacity to change them. This is about acknowledging that the *only* person with the power to change your life is *you*, and having the realisation that no one can make you feel anything that is not already present within your inner world.

As we come to accept all of this, it becomes clear that we can never expect the world 'out there' to fulfil our needs 'in here'. If we want our outer world to change, we must first attend to our own inner world. By taking responsibility for the change we would like to bring about and beginning to shift our inner world into a state of balance, we establish a strong and stable inner core and move towards the higher-functioning levels of our personality type. As this shift in consciousness occurs, almost without realising it, we find our outer reality has aligned to our new, higher vibration and the positive growth that was initiated internally permeates into the world around us.

Catching Yourself in the Act

Catching ourselves in the act – when we are about to go into one of our usual negative reactive states – is one of the first things the Enneagram knowledge teaches us. You realise what you are doing, and why, and perhaps this time you will make a different choice. And even if you didn't catch yourself this time, afterwards you can recognise how your negative patterns contributed to the way things panned out and (hopefully without self-criticism) be more aware next time.

Each time you have moments of self-awareness like this, you take more control of your reaction to life's events and get closer to being more able to function through your positive traits rather than through the negative. Some patterns can be easily let go of once they are understood; some, however, are so deeply interwoven into the fabric of who we think we are that they take longer to break. Be patient with yourself and keep examining your reactions, behaviour and relationships in the light of what you know about your personality type, always remaining open to the fact that, no matter how much growth you have made, there might be more to understand and let go of.

Showing Yourself Compassion

Being courageous enough to take responsibility for your patterns can also bring with it a burden of over seriousness about your negative stuff that must be tempered with compassion. Taking responsibility does not mean judging or criticising yourself when you find yourself following 'negative' patterns you have been trying to change. Often, when we become aware that we are repeating these same negative patterns of behaviour over and over, it is as though we are continually walking up and down the same street, covering the same ground as before without making any real progress. Learn to laugh at yourself (or at least smile!) when you find yourself walking down this familiar street over and over. Turn negatives into positives. 'OK, so I did it again, but next time, it can be different; this is just another opportunity for self-awareness and growth.'

Changing habitual patterns, even though they have caused us so much pain in the past, is not always as easy as we would like it to be. So be kind and gentle with yourself as you tread this path of self-discovery. Congratulate yourself when you find you are on a 'new street', and feel good about the fact that you are finding the strength to change, one by one, these long-held patterns of thinking, feeling, or reacting.

Knowing and understanding your personality type is about accepting and embracing yourself with compassion, tolerance and insight. Regardless of the negative patterns that we may be running, in any one moment each of us is perfect just the way we are. We are an unfinished masterpiece, a 'work in progress'. So learn to love yourself for who you are and the gifts that you bring to the world. Embrace the 'negative', for even these aspects of ourselves are actually positive, for they are a gift from which we can learn and grow. Accept yourself for the things you are *not* as well as the things that you *are*, love yourself for all of it, and know that you have the capacity to move to a higher vibration and live from the more positive qualities of your type whenever you wish.

Remember Who You Truly Are

The negative beliefs that are causing your patterns are just that: beliefs. They are not truths. The truth is you are a shining light of pure Essence. If you do happen to get bogged down in the negative patterns that seem to be consistently repeating themselves, read again about the positive aspects of your type and take time to tell yourself who you really are. Immediately, you will find your mood begin to lift. If you do this repeatedly, you *will* begin to shift the patterns that have been so entrenched within you. Focussing only upon negativity, however, will never bring about such change and only serves to lower your level of vibration further.

All Types Are Equal

The Enneagram teaches us that each of the nine personality types views the world differently and each has different unconscious beliefs that drive their attitudes, negative emotions and behaviour. None of these different ways of dealing with life is better than another; they are just different. No one personality type is 'better' or 'worse' than another. Each type provides the soul with a different perspective of the human experience and another opportunity to grow and learn more about its true nature. So be careful not to compare your personality type to that of others. Feeling inferior or superior to others because of being the personality type that you are will not facilitate your growth; it will only serve to disempower you on your quest for self-knowledge.

Doing the Best That They Can

Finding true peace in who we are, and discovering greater joy in the richness of life, will only truly come about when we learn to be compassionate towards *others* as well as to our selves. One of the great gifts of the Enneagram is that it enables us to accept and embrace the differences between people instead of fighting against them.

Just as we need to have compassion for ourselves and what motivates our own difficult, hurtful, or demanding behaviour, as we work with the knowledge of the other eight personality types, we begin to have compassion for the other people around us whose behaviour we find difficult, hurtful, or demanding. If we judge others for their behaviour, we do not define *them* but define *ourselves* as someone who needs to judge. Forgiveness and compassion for others arise naturally from a deeper understanding of the true motivation behind these people's words or actions, because the truth is:

given the negative constraints of their
personality type and the limited resources they

currently possess to deal with them, *everyone* is doing the best they can in any given moment.

Rather than pointing the finger and telling someone they were wrong to behave in a certain way, seek to understand why they would feel the need to behave like that, which part of their picture is not complete. If we can accept that this person is trying to cope with their world from a limited or distorted picture of it (as we all are), then we can begin to see past their external behaviour and acknowledge the difficulties or pain they must be suffering in their inner world. As we do this, we find that, rather than reacting with judgement, hurt, resentment, or anger towards their behaviour, we can begin to feel genuine compassion for them, for the difficulties they experience, and for the unexpressed pain that they are suffering.

Reframing the Past

This is also true when we begin to examine the characters that have dominated our past. We cannot change the past any more than we can change the colour of our eyes, but we can change our response towards it. As we continue to study the Enneagram and gain real insights into the inner workings of the personality types, we begin to see these 'baddies' from our past with clearer eyes. The natural outcome of this is that we find ourselves reframing past events and no longer blaming these people for acting the way they did. We can even begin to be grateful that we had those experiences because of the opportunities for growth and expansion they afforded us.

Blame is a low frequency emotion, a very slow vibration that damages and disempowers us. It perpetuates our pain. We need to forgive those that have caused us pain in the past if we are to free ourselves from the emotional baggage associated with them. In doing so, we come into a place of peace – a very much higher vibration than blame or resentment.

However, forgiveness is more than just an act of goodwill and compassion. True forgiveness is an act of the heart not of the mind, so if there are people from your past that you struggle to forgive, study the information about their personality type in conjunction with your own. This will help you to understand not only their behaviour but your response to it. And remember that if someone of a different type to your own had experienced the exact same circumstances that you did, they would have had a different sort of response to it. Therefore, your response to that person or those circumstances is a result of you being the type you are. By taking responsibility for your response and accepting it, you can do something about it. While you still blame, you are powerless to change your feelings about it.

CHAPTER 20

Positive Pathways for the One

The Self-Defeating Pattern

The coping strategies adopted in the young years have led to counterproductive cycles of behaviour referred to as the self-defeating pattern. This not only causes problems and pain but actually brings about what the One is trying to avoid.

In the desire to be good and achieve perfection, Ones have created their own internal rules about what is good and what is bad, what is imperfect and what needs correcting. Because these self-imposed standards come from high-minded idealism, and because the One continually moves the goal posts (nothing is *ever* good enough), it is clearly an impossible task to achieve an acceptable standard so the One is destined to be continually critical of their own efforts. And by continually perceiving the world and the people in it as less than perfect, the One misses out on the perfection in each and every moment. The inevitable outcome for the less-than-high-functioning One is to be continually dissatisfied with the way things really are in their outer world, and especially with themselves. So no matter how much effort is made to be 'good', the relentless inner critic constantly berates the One for falling short of perfection.

Feeling the need to improve others and thus help them closer to 'perfection' means that the One sees endless faults in those around them. They truly believe they know what is for the other person's good and that they are doing the right thing when they proffer their advice in their parent-to-child manner, yet to others, it just feels like criticism. This critical attitude towards others undermines their relationships and can eventually drive others away, leaving the One feeling unworthy and wrong. If they are unworthy then, in their reasoning, they must be 'bad,' and if they are wrong, they must be imperfect.

Thus, the negative patterns of the One cannot help but bring upon themselves what they most fear: being imperfect, wrong, or bad.

Self-Observation

Until now, many of your responses to life have been automatic; they were strategies you adopted in childhood in order to deal with your world. Those that do not serve you are no longer needed, but until you can see your own patterns, they control you. As they come fully into your awareness, *you* are able to take control and then to shift to a higher vibrational level.

Considering these self-observation questions will help you to have greater self-awareness and enable you to let go of your negative patterns, little by little. Take the time to go over these questions regularly and perhaps keep a notebook handy to jot down thoughts, insights, or experiences. As you become more aware of how much or how often your negative patterns arise, do not make yourself 'wrong'. **Remember this behaviour has been normal for your personality type and now you are on the road towards change.** Take your self-observation lightly, learn to smile at yourself, and keep rereading your positive traits, for **that** is who you really are!

The One tends to focus a great deal of attention on what is not right or needs improving and to correcting mistakes. Ask yourself:
- ➤ How much does my attention go to what is wrong or needs improving?
- ➤ How much do I focus on what is not good enough?
- ➤ What sensations and feelings do I have in connection with these?

The inner critic of the One is relentless and harsh. There is constant judgement and criticism of both self and actions. Ask yourself:

➤ How constantly present is the voice of judgement?

➤ In what ways do I judge and berate myself for not being good enough?

➤ How does my inner critic make me feel?

➤ What behaviour/emotions/situations do I perceive as 'good/bad' or 'right/wrong'?

➤ Where do these standards come from?

Ones set impossibly high standards for themselves and expect others to conform to the same standard. Therefore, the One tends to judge others and often feels that no one but they can do things properly. Ask yourself:

➤ How often do I judge others?

➤ How do I feel when I am judging others? Do I feel resentful?

➤ How does this make me behave towards those I have judged?

➤ Who says my way is the right way?

➤ How often do I end up feeling overburdened because I believe only I can do it right?

The constant inner critic of the One, combined with resulting low self-worth, means that they themselves often feel judged or criticised. Ask yourself:

➤ In what ways have I felt that I was being judged or criticised?

➤ How often do I perceive criticism within other people's well-meaning suggestions or advice?

➤ How do I react to what I perceive as criticism?

The need for perfection can hold the One back. Ask yourself:

➤ How hard do I find it to be satisfied with tasks I am doing?

➤ How hard is it to let things be and say 'enough is enough'?

➤ How does it feel when I leave a task 'unfinished' (less than perfect in my eyes)?

➤ How has my need to do things perfectly stopped me from going ahead and attempting things I was unsure of?

➤ What have I missed out on as a result?

Taking the New Path

Being human not perfect

Ultimately, you need to remember why your need for perfection came into being in the first place. It was the way you coped with the world as a small child, the way you hoped to get your needs met. As the rational, reasoning adult that you are now, you no longer need to strive to be a 'good boy or girl' in order to find acceptance in anyone's eyes, least of all your own. The self-imposed standards that have been running your life have caused you endless pain and difficulties because they are impossible to reach.

Human beings are not meant to be perfect (that privilege is reserved for the All That Is!), so when you find yourself slipping into self-critical patterns or obsessing about the way something needs to be done in order for it to be perfect, ask yourself, 'Who says everything must be perfect? Will the sky fall in if it is not? What does perfect mean anyway?' Accept that you do not have to be perfect to be 'good'. You just need to be human! This doesn't mean that you won't strive to be your best. It simply means that you accept that there is no such thing as perfection, especially in life. There are many good things and good people in your life that are far from perfect; imperfection is inherent to being human.

Perfection may exist in a moment, but it will not last because change is the natural order of things; trying to create or maintain perfection just causes you frustration and unhappiness. By embracing your own imperfections (as well as those of others), you embrace yourself, and then you can begin to take yourself and life less seriously.

Using your energy and time wisely

You have the ability to see the world very clearly and to know how it should be. Just being angry about the way things are wastes a huge amount of energy, so instead of being angry, stand back a little and accept the way things are. Then, use you innate wisdom and insight to become more aware of when it's worth your time and energy to try to change things. There will be some circumstances when letting things be is the best course of action (or rather, inaction!). Hanging on to anger and resentment is pointless if there's nothing that can be done about it, so you may as well let it go. Be compassionate towards yourself as you do this and don't start telling yourself you are lazy or slovenly; you are just using your time and energy more wisely.

When the list of things to do seems overwhelming, it creates a lot of tension within you and then you do not function well. When you feel overwhelmed like this, your time would be better spent letting go of the need to complete your tasks and do something that relaxes you. As you do this, your thinking will become clearer and it will become apparent which task you can most effectively – and most pleasurably – work on now. And getting pleasure from your industry as often as possible is important because when you are enjoying what you are doing – instead of doing what you 'ought' to be doing – it will flow more easily. When everything feels like pushing a boulder uphill, you achieve less.

Shades of grey

Your inner critic has limited your field of experience and has made it difficult to find satisfaction in what you do and in your relationships. Everything has been viewed in black and white terms. By studying the Enneagram, you cannot help but realise that your way is not necessarily the right way, nor is it the only way. There are no absolutes in life, only variations, differences and exceptions to the rule. Life is full of ambiguity, paradox and change. You cannot know absolutely how something or someone should be; you can only know how you perceive it through the filter of your Oneness.

You need to recognise that, although it seems as if there is only one right way to be or to do things, there are many 'right' ways to be and many 'right' answers. Accept that things don't always go to plan; mistakes and imperfections are the natural order of things and some things just don't get done. What appears right or perfect according to your standards may not necessarily be what is *best* for you, especially when it shuts you down to happiness and joy. By moving away from the single right way to do something and embracing the many right ways to do the same thing, your world will become more expansive and you will experience more fulfilment and inner peace.

Challenge your inner critic

Does your pattern of vicious self-criticism actually help you to improve, or does it just undermine your self-esteem and create doubt and tension within you?

It's time to begin developing some compassion and acceptance for yourself. When you start beating up on yourself, stop a moment and notice how you are judging yourself or your actions and labelling them 'good' or 'bad', 'perfect' or 'imperfect', 'right' or 'wrong'. Recognise how this pattern of self-judgement just leads you into guilt and self-blame and learn to say, 'I am who I am, and things are the way they are,' and keep repeating this until you feel a little lighter. Beginning to accept yourself as you are will include accepting the less 'acceptable' aspects of self, such as your negative feelings, natural desires, and bodily functions. You are not the only one in the world who gets angry, feels guilty, and has unspoken desires or whose body has its messy moments. And does that make all those other 'imperfect' people wrong or bad? (If your first thought in answer to that was 'Yes!' ask yourself, 'Who says so?')

It would be helpful to practice thinking of your inner critic as 'separate' from yourself and to imagine its commanding voice not as your own but just as that silly demon or gremlin that sits on your shoulder making comments. Try to be conscious of your self-criticism and judgements for a single day by observing the flow of your thoughts and making a note of the number of times you find yourself indulging in self-directed criticism. By becoming more aware of the tone of your thoughts, you can challenge and redirect them. When the critical self-talk begins, take it less seriously and say to yourself, 'Here it goes again. This is just my negative One stuff; it's not who I really am.'

As you begin to smile at that inner critic instead of letting it direct your behaviour, it will begin to quieten. Your self-worth may have been completely dictated by it in the past, but now, as you begin to put it in its place, take the time – perhaps in conjunction with a trusted friend – to examine your true worth based on who you really are and what you have already achieved in your life. It will be helpful to go back and reread the positive, best qualities of the One and remind yourself that these qualities are intrinsically who you are.

Your inner critic will never go away completely, but it can become more satisfied with who you are as you become more balanced, and by freeing yourself from self-judgement, you will really begin to flourish.

Let up on yourself

Be aware of how you often push yourself too hard. Sometimes, you just have to say enough is enough and take a break. Taking some time for yourself will not send things into chaos and catastrophe. Fortunately, not everything is up to you and the state of the world is not your sole responsibility!

What you are doing will not suffer from regular breaks. In fact, when refreshed, you are likely to get fresh perspectives on the task in hand. Taking exercise during your breaks is especially beneficial. You tend to hold a lot of anger and tension in your body, so any kind of exercise, such as running, dancing, or yoga, can be extremely effective in releasing the tension. Other types of bodywork such as massage would also be of real value in removing tension and would enhance your emotional and physical well-being as would deep breathing exercises and grounding techniques.

It would also help you to become aware of the ways in which you unconsciously use more tension than is necessary when performing even simple tasks. When doing anything, from writing to driving a car, take a moment to ask yourself, 'Where am I holding tension? Do I really need this tightness in order to do what I am doing?' Breathe more deeply, relax, and allow yourself to get some enjoyment out of the task you are engaged in.

Have some fun

You are inclined to only allow yourself do something you enjoy if you can justify it to yourself: you can watch a film if you have completed your tasks, you can have that cookie if you have only eaten healthy food all day, you can have a day off if you go to the gym, etc. However, you do not need to be afraid of pleasure. Giving yourself some time out and just having some fun will not make your 'bad bits' break out of control. Finding pleasures you can give yourself without feeling guilty is an important step towards taking yourself and life less seriously. Being more in the moment whilst engaging in something pleasurable, such as playing with your dog or walking in the countryside, will enhance the experience. And whilst engaged in this way, avoid focusing on the 'to do' lists or champing at the bit about how much time you are wasting; give yourself up to it, revel in it, and just have the experience without evaluating its benefits.

A great deal of the tension in your body is created controlling your emotions and impulses. By finding ways to relax, you will more easily get in touch with your feelings (both positive and negative) and allow them to flow through you. Certainly, it is true that this requires you to become more at ease with some degree of loss of control, and that may feel uncomfortable at first. Start by letting your positive feelings run you for a while. Instead of reining them in for fear of where exuberance might lead you, express your pleasure, laugh out loud, and have some fun, and you will gradually find you can take each moment a little less seriously.

As you start to let up on yourself, you will more often make choices based on your desires rather than the 'shoulds' and feel more able to follow your natural impulses. So when you find yourself following your gut instincts or acting on impulse, give yourself a pat on the back, for decisions made from gut instinct always lead to success and happiness.

Appreciating the differences

Try to curb your tendency to talk down to people. Your inherent belief that you know best leads you to talk to others as 'parent to child'. Remember, there are many other ideas and ways of being that are just as 'right' as yours. (Not everyone wants their CD collection arranged alphabetically!) Create more space for serenity in your life by seeing errors, mistakes, and imperfections as acceptable *differences* and by appreciating the positive in what others do.

Resist your tendency to instruct others in the right way to do things. One of the hardest lessons for the average One is to allow other people to be who they are and do things in their own way. You may be quite right that your ideas will improve them or their lives, but remember not everyone is ready for self-improvement, and most people do not have the degree of self-discipline that you have. Within you are great wisdom and discernment, so use them. Learn to recognise when something should be said and when it is better to hold back and let others find their own path. And if they ask your advice but fail to act upon it, let it go and accept that now may not be the time for them to take your advice. They have their own path and will make changes when *they* are ready. Also, listen to others when they give *you* advice. Other people can be right too, and by giving them a fair hearing when they have an opinion that is different from yours will make it more likely that they will listen to you.

Having patience

It is far too easy for you to work yourself up about the lack of application or wrongdoings of others. However, whether or not you are right, getting irritated or critical with them will be counterproductive; in fact, you need to realise that you often behave exactly the opposite to the way you intend. When you complain and criticize others, you are not only being less than fair-minded but you are also not being the positive force of change and improvement you intend. They stop listening and you just get more frustrated at what you perceive as their

307

perverse refusal to do the right thing. Your consequent anger is a self-righteous anger that alienates those you are trying to change and does nothing to help them see another way of being. Being more patient and compassionate towards others will achieve far more.

Patience with yourself is also very important. You excel at self-evaluation but avoid evaluating or judging your progress excessively. Accept that you are a work in progress and that there will be times when you slip back into old patterns. After all, these negative patterns of yours have been in place most of your life, so be patient with yourself. Praising yourself when you see small improvements within yourself will achieve far more than berating yourself when you fall short of your own expectations.

Opening up

Try to be more open and honest about your emotional needs and vulnerabilities. You will not become less in other people's eyes if you ask for help or let them see when you are upset; in fact, being more real in this way is a key element in opening up and accepting yourself, as well as being closer to others.

You create much stress for yourself by believing that you are the only one who can do things properly. As a result, far too much falls on your shoulders. Ask others to do their share, explaining – without lecturing or criticising – why you are asking this of them. Let them know what you are struggling with. Then be sure to recognise that, if their way of doing the job is different from yours, yours is not the only way. And make sure you express your appreciation when others do something, even if it was not up to your standard. You are probably known for your candour and truthfulness, so a compliment from you will mean a great deal and can go a long way to improving relationships with those who have felt criticised by you in the past.

Becoming a High-Functioning One

Ones reconnect to their Essential nature by recognising
that everything and everyone is already perfect and that
the Universe is unfolding just as it was meant to do.

The need to be good, and to achieve perfection, has resulted in you reacting to your experiences, and your perception of yourself, by evaluating and judging them as 'good' or 'bad', 'perfect' or 'imperfect'. This has made it hard to learn from your experiences, and consequently, it has blocked your growth.

The true wisdom of the high-functioning One is the awareness that reality 'just is' and no amount of anger or force can change the reality of a situation. As you open to the truth of the perfection within you and around you, you can begin to accept that there are no absolute truths about right and wrong and you discover that there is nothing to fix inside you. You find yourself able to just allow your experiences to touch you and to accept 'what is'.

As those standards of yours soften and relax, you let go of the beliefs about what should be, or shouldn't be, what is acceptable, and what is not. Instead of trying to be something better or different, you can see yourself compassionately and accept your own imperfections. You can embrace the variations and differences between people as being part of the fabric of life. As a result, you find yourself able to accept others' quirks and foibles with compassionate tolerance. Moreover, you find that you can allow yourself to just be the way you really are.

This quality of allowing brings acceptance, and acceptance brings peace and serenity. Your emotions calm down, things no longer ruffle you, and you become more open and non-reactive. As your mind and body relax, you discover that you can achieve far more from a peaceful state than you ever could from a place of tension. Discovering the need for balance in your life, you begin to know when enough is enough, and you allow yourself to move on to rest or play. There is less seriousness in you and you can become more playful, even silly at times! What fun to discover that you can be spontaneous and go with the flow.

Continuing along your path of growth, you begin to know that being wrong about something does not equate with being imperfect or bad. A high-functioning One has true humility and wisdom, and this means allowing yourself to sometimes be the one who does not know or who is happy to be wrong. As you become more accepting – of yourself, others, and life – you will gradually learn to stop pitting yourself against reality. Instead, you will accept whatever arises, both internally and externally, meeting each moment with openness of heart and mind. By letting yourself be touched by whatever is here, without judgement, and with the knowing that there is nothing that needs to be fixed, you will finally gain the serenity that comes with going with the flow. Now that's perfection!

As your inner light shines more, life begins to open up. It becomes richer, more spontaneous, and wondrously unpredictable. A profound inner spaciousness begins to develop within your inner world where the words *good, bad, perfect,* or *imperfect* no longer have any meaning. More and more you find yourself at peace with yourself and your world knowing, at last, the inherent perfection in all things.

The Serenity Prayer

(Perfect for Ones to remember!)

God, grant me the serenity to accept
the things I cannot change,
courage to change the things I can,
and the wisdom to know the difference.

CHAPTER 21

Positive Pathways for the Two

The Self-Defeating Pattern

The coping strategies adopted in the young years have led to counterproductive cycles of behaviour referred to as the self-defeating pattern. This not only causes problems and pain but actually brings about what the Two is trying to avoid.

Less-than-high-functioning Twos are concerned with presenting the image of being the unselfish and truly good person who puts other people's needs before their own. They believe that having needs would be selfish. As a result, the real needs of the Two are rarely expressed openly and calmly, for if they were, that would mean that the Two was not a good and worthy person. However, despite not expressing their needs openly, the Two wants others to not only be aware of their unspoken needs (for that would indicate that the other party cared enough to know) but also to fulfil them. Their hope is that by trying to anticipate and fulfil the needs of other people, those others will, in return, meet the Two's needs.

However, others have little chance of knowing that the Two feels needy, let alone what it is that the Two needs; moreover, by attempting to get their needs met by giving to others, the Two is destined to be unsuccessful. The unfulfilled needs make the Two feel unloved, hurt and resentful ('What about me?'), and this prevents the Two from giving unconditionally. In their attempts to get their needs met, they become more intrusive and controlling, often manipulative, and thereby induce guilt in others ('Look at how I've worn myself out doing all this for you') as well as displaying aggressive and hysterical emotional outbursts. So as their behaviour deteriorates, they start driving others away and end up feeling unwanted and rejected.

Furthermore, in their determination that they know what other people need better than they themselves do, Twos are often much too pushy with their offers of help. Refusing to take no for an answer, they keep pushing and pushing, in the belief that they are just trying to help, which just results in others getting angry or not wanting them around, so rejection is the outcome.

Thus, it is clear that the negative patterns of the Two cannot help but bring upon themselves that which they most fear: being of unwanted and unloved.

Self-Observation

Until now, many of your responses to life have been automatic; they were strategies you adopted in childhood in order to deal with your world. Those that do not serve you are no longer needed, but until you can see your own patterns, they control you. As they come fully into your awareness, *you* are able to take control and then to shift to a higher vibrational level.

Considering these self-observation questions will help you to have greater self-awareness and enable you to let go of your negative patterns, little by little. Take the time to go over these questions regularly and perhaps keep a notebook handy to jot down thoughts, insights or experiences. As you become more aware of how much or how often your negative patterns arise, do not make yourself 'wrong'. **Remember this behaviour has been normal for your personality type and now you are on the road towards change**. Take your self-observation lightly, learn to smile at yourself, and keep rereading your positive traits, for **that** is who you really are!

The Two believes that, by anticipating and fulfilling others' needs, they will be loved and valued. Ask yourself:

➤ How much does my attention and energy go to others' needs?

➤ How much satisfaction do I get from being needed?

➤ In what ways do I act as though I am indispensable?

➤ Do I take pride in knowing they couldn't manage without me?

➤ How much does my self-worth rely on being needed or wanted?

In the need to be needed, the Two can be pushy about what they think is needed. Rejection of their help feels like a rejection of self. Ask yourself:

➤ In what ways might I be overly helpful?

➤ How often do I wait to be asked for help?

➤ Do I often act as if I know what others need better than they themselves do?

➤ How often am I pushy with my ideas about what was needed, even though the other party may have said no?

➤ What effect does this behaviour have on others' attitude towards me?

➤ How do I react when my helpfulness seems to be unwanted?

➤ How does it really make me feel when all that I have done goes unnoticed or unappreciated?

Twos often neglect their own needs and have difficulty receiving from others, because they believe value or worth comes from meeting other people's needs, not from needing from others. Ask yourself:

➤ How have I neglected my own needs and desires or failed to support or nurture myself?

➤ Do I even acknowledge to myself what my own needs are?

➤ How do I feel when I have to ask for real help from another person?

➤ In what ways have I let myself receive from others?

➤ Do I give and receive equally?

➤ How have I felt when my unspoken needs were not acknowledged or met by others?

➤ In what ways have I altered my behaviour or actions to fit what others seemed to want?

The Two's behaviour may deteriorate when their own needs are not met. Ask yourself:

➢ How do I behave when I feel undervalued or unappreciated for what I have done?

➢ How often do I slip into 'martyr'?

➢ What behaviour or words have I used to induce guilt in others in order to manipulate their behaviour towards me?

➢ How do they feel about this? (Ask them!)

Taking the New Path

The most important relationship

Your most important task is to realise how much your personal relationships have been your source of self-worth and value. Being centred upon others, and therefore dependent upon them for your happiness and fulfilment, life has been mostly dominated by the emotional feedback you have derived from your interaction with other people.

The need to be needed, and hence to feel wanted and loved, has made it difficult for you to feel complete without a relationship. As a result, you have almost certainly not spent enough time developing a separate sense of self. The only route to real freedom and happiness for a Two is to discover that great contentment and fulfilment can be experienced by spending time alone, pursuing independent interests, and developing a sense of self separate from others. As a Two, you need to be away from others in order to make significant strides in your growth, because other people's needs are so compelling when you are around them it is hard to focus on yourself.

Even more important is the discovery that you can exist happily without being in a relationship at all. When a relationship ends, the normal pattern of the Two is to immediately seek another. Trying to fulfil your needs through intimate relationships is a strategy doomed to fail because that inner hunger can never be satisfied by another.

What is needed now is connection with yourself, giving to self and love and appreciation of self. Should you find yourself as single rather than part of a couple, realise that this is a very important stage of your life. It is an initiation of empowerment. By learning to live life for yourself rather than for others, you learn to really value and love yourself. This is fundamental to your development, for only then are you ready to attract healthy, balanced relationships - relationships in which you give but also receive.

Meeting your own needs

Giving to others, and being there for them when they are in need, warms the heart of all Twos. However, when the drive to help other people has at its root a deep inner neediness, growth cannot occur. Instead of orientating your attention outward by trying to make people happy and reacting to their needs, it is time to turn your attention inward. Just as you would be there for anyone else in need, so too you need to 'be there' for yourself.

Only when you feel full and complete because your own needs are met are you able to give without wanting anything back; however, it is important for you to realise that there is no one other than *yourself* who can meet many of your needs. You need to redress the balance of your life by transferring some of your concern and attention away from others and focusing on yourself. Consider what would give you pleasure, peace, or joy and start by giving yourself one of these things each day. Take time out of each day just for yourself, alone. Begin to give more attention to the needs of your body before it screams at you. This may seem like a selfish course of action to one who has felt guilt ridden when not there for others, but until you do this, you will not be able to help others in the way you want to: unselfishly.

It is not selfish to make sure you get adequate rest, spend time alone to restore yourself, and give nice things to yourself to make yourself feel good. It just makes sense, because only when your needs have been met can you give unconditionally as you wish to. By giving to yourself as a priority (not just fitting your 'me time' in between your doing for others), everyone will benefit. Not only will you be happier and less needy, but other people will find you easier to be around.

Initially, friends and family may not like the changes in your behaviour; they may feel threatened or confused, but as time goes on, your self-determination will empower them to be less dependent on you. Codependent relationships are not healthy for either party involved, and the most loving thing you can do for those that have depended upon you is to help them not to need you anymore.

Learning to love and value yourself

Having found much of your identity within relationships, your unconscious tendency is to measure your own worth by what others think of you. With your self-esteem dependent upon how others behave towards you and with your core belief that you are not intrinsically loveable, you have needed constant reassurance from others. This leaves you at their mercy, not in control of your own happiness. You now need to look at how much your self-esteem rises or falls with another's approval or lack of it, their desire for your help or their rejection of it, and their expression of love and affection or the withdrawal of it.

It is the pattern of the Two to only feel good about yourself when you are preoccupied with other people's needs or you are receiving 'strokes' for your good deeds, but this is a very fragile sense of worth. When those relationships change or end, self-worth plummets; a sort of identity crisis can occur with the Two thinking, *If I am no longer needed or wanted, what value do I have?*

This is about separating your self-worth from what you do for others, from another's acceptance of what you offer and from what they offer you. Ask those close to you what qualities in you they really value and love. You will probably be surprised. As you begin to realise that others love you for who you are – not for what you do for them – you will gradually come to accept and love yourself more.

Becoming true to yourself

In your natural desire to make strong, supportive connections with people, you tend to 'go over' to the other person energetically in order to be with them emotionally. And in doing so, you unconsciously alter yourself to mirror and match them. This is a great gift that puts others at their ease and makes them feel accepted. Be aware, however, that there are times when you use this gift in order to feel wanted and included; when you do, realise that you are manipulating the other person in order to get your own needs met. Should you find yourself doing this, recognise that it is lack of confidence in the acceptability of your true self that is the cause and that you still have considerable growth work to do in this area.

In going over to the other person energetically and emotionally, you also lose connection with your own feelings; in fact, many Twos do this so habitually that they can lose sight of who they really are and what they really want. Ask yourself this: if there was no one in your life who needed you, who would you be? If this question makes you feel uncomfortable, then it is very important now to develop a much stronger sense of self, separate from those to whom you are regularly giving out. Take up new interests, go places alone, and most essential, practice letting go of feelings outside of yourself and connecting more with your own feelings.

You have almost certainly felt much unexpressed resentment towards those that you have been serving, especially when you have felt unappreciated or your intentions are misconstrued. It is important to acknowledge this now and find a healthy way to express it. And when you feel internal resentment, consider whether you actually need to do this thing. What would happen if you didn't? What have you hoped to receive in return?

As you become kinder towards yourself and you become more accepting of a 'positive' kind of selfishness, you will be more able to disentangle your own feelings from those of others. By becoming more aware of your own feelings and more able to acknowledge and articulate your own needs, you will gain greater awareness of the times when your desire to reach out to others is actually to affirm your sense of worth.

You are not indispensible

Being needed tends to give you a rush of good feelings, and your tender heart can lead you to be too impulsive in your desire to rescue someone in need or to alleviate another's suffering. As a result, you end up taking on too many people as 'projects' that you believe only you can deal with.

Realise that not everything needs to fall upon your shoulders and let go of the need to be indispensable. When you find yourself endlessly 'doing' for others, ask yourself why you are doing it. Being indispensible has given you the feelings of being wanted and needed that you have sought, but as you work on developing high self-esteem, you will become more comfortable with saying no. Learn to give what is needed and no more, and accept that you cannot fix everyone. As you get clearer about what you can achieve and what you can't *and* accept your own limitations – physically, energetically, and emotionally – when you do help others, you will find it much easier to give wholeheartedly without needing anything in return. Remember also that those you love, or are already responsible for, may end up feeling neglected if you spread yourself too thinly, and that your primary commitments should be honoured before you spend time cultivating new connections.

Asking for help

The undercurrent of resentment you can experience when your own needs are not being met by others taints your giving, yet the power to change that lies within your own hands. Twos find it hard to ask directly for anything from others – after all, they are the 'givers and helpers' who appear not to need anything for themselves – so you have tried to get your needs met by indirect means. However, expecting other types to intuit your needs and desires in the way that you can divine theirs is the route to disappointment and resentment. Instead, practice being honest and straightforward in requesting what you want.

Instead of maintaining the image of being the one who needs nothing but is always there for others, acknowledge that there are times when you need another person's help and start asking when you *do* need it. Yes, this may make you uncomfortable at first, but with a little practice, you will learn to receive what is offered without feeling bad about having had to ask. And remember, you are not the only one who enjoys giving help. Other people enjoy being helpful too.

Giving unconditionally

Be more aware of your own hidden motives when giving to others. Each personality type unconsciously gives to others what they most want for themselves; for Twos, it is the giving of love, approval, gifts, flattery, etc., and it may have been hard for you to realise that you frequently give in order to get because you have viewed yourself as the unselfish giver. Be brutally honest with yourself now. When you give out to others, ask yourself this question: 'If I get no thanks or acknowledgement for this, how will I feel?' If the honest answer is 'hurt and resentful,' then the good things you are doing or giving are designed to get you strokes in return. You want someone to like, appreciate, or need you, or you are expecting something similar back from them. Then you are not giving of yourself as you believe you are. Be sure that whatever you give – whether it be your time, a personal gift, or a compliment – is given from the heart and not because you hope the other party will reciprocate in some way. Only when giving is done unconditionally can real love come back to you.

Better boundaries

You are always sensitive to the needs of others, yet there is an aspect of you that can also be insensitive. You often fail to recognise when holding back or moving away would be more appropriate than continuing to offer help or advice or ask questions. For example, Two's ability to know when someone needs sympathy or warm words of approval is a wonderful gift, yet they can be quite oblivious to a more detached person's need to be left alone. It is vital now that you develop better boundaries.

In your desire to be close to others, you have been happiest when the boundaries between you and others become blurred and indistinguishable so that you feel 'at one' with the other person, but sometimes you push too hard to make that connection. There are some things that are your business and some that are not; you need to learn the difference. It is not necessary to know every detail about your friends' or loved ones' lives in order to have a happy and satisfying relationship with them. Twos generally enjoy sharing and comparing intimate details with others because it gives them a feeling of bonding and close connection, but most other personality types like to keep aspects of themselves private, at least some of the time. Consider the appropriateness of your questioning and check in with yourself whether you really need to know these things. Pull back more often and wait for them to tell you; they either will or they won't. Let them be who they really are, which is different from you! Remember, loving unconditionally is about allowing others to be themselves, not what you wish they were.

Apart from your intimate relationships, you should also consider how close you get physically as you interact with others. You probably have a tendency to get too close as you move towards people to communicate. Unless there is an intimate connection between you, a space of about four feet feels comfortable to most people; less than this and the other party may feel that their personal space is being invaded. Use your natural sensitivity and observe the other person's behaviour. If they start backing away, you can be sure they are feeling uncomfortably close to you!

It is also important to realise that other types are not as physically demonstrative as you are. Again, use your ability to intuitively know what others need and learn to recognise that hugs or personal touching just make some people uncomfortable. If you are unsure, ask.

Developing discernment and detachment

You have a propensity for acting immediately on your feelings. This can be very admirable, but it is essential now that you learn more discernment and detachment. By taking time to sit with your feelings about a situation before you act, you will find it easier to bring balance into your life. Although you can intuitively sense what another person needs, consider whether rushing in to try to fulfil those needs is appropriate. Maybe this is not the right time to offer help, or perhaps this person does not even want the sort help you have in mind. Not everyone wants input from others; many prefer to manage alone.

Instead of priding yourself on being the one who knows what is needed by others, start developing the humility to realise that sometimes you do *not* know. It is often better to ask people what they really need instead of being determined that you know what they need better than they do themselves. Lack of humility in Twos causes them to have little real awareness that people like to make up their own minds and that they are adults who actually do know what is good for them. It is essential that you become more willing to take no for an answer. You have identified so strongly with your role as the helper and giver that you can feel deeply hurt when what you offer is rejected, yet if your help or advice is refused, it is simply that they do not want or need what you offer; it is not a rejection of you. By learning to recognise the difference, you will save yourself much pain.

As you become less pushy with your help, your relationships will be better all around. Not only will you stop experiencing so much hurt and rejection but others will find you easier to be around and will want you more. And within your loving relationships, remember that others can express love in many different ways; not everyone is as demonstrative or verbally expressive with their love as you are. Some people may have other ways of showing they care about you. Make the effort to recognise these different approaches to showing love and appreciation and learn to value the differences.

Claiming your personal freedom is an essential part of your movement towards a higher-functioning state, but the paradox for the

Two is that they have the desire to be free but to still be attached. You can, however, have an important role in someone else's life and still sometimes merge without getting lost. You can be attached *and* detached. Having detachment does not mean lacking in compassion for others. It means loving without smothering; it means being interested in another person's life without feeling the need to know every little detail, and it means stepping back sometimes and letting others make their own mistakes and fend for themselves. It means sensing another's feelings and emotions without taking them on yourself and feeling compelled to act upon them, and it means not trying to be indispensible in someone's life but supporting them instead in ways that facilitate their own growth and empowerment.

Becoming a High-Functioning Two

Twos reconnect to their Essential nature by
recognising that love cannot be earned or lost. Love
is what we are; therefore, it is always available.

Seeking love and appreciation from others for the things that you do or the self-sacrificing ways in which you give of yourself has never brought you anything other than problems and pain. As you progress along your path of development, you will come to the realisation that no amount of helping or self-sacrifice will bring you the sustainable love and attention you are looking for and that your self-worth does not depend upon being the one to fulfil others' needs. You discover that there is no relationship with another that can make you feel complete or fulfil your needs, but that the one and only person who can be relied upon to make you feel whole and full inside is yourself.

The nature of your own Essence is Unconditional Love. This is the source of the truly nurturing love that you have been seeking; it is there within your own Essential nature. This love is constant and endlessly available, so it cannot be lost or diminished. It is not a commodity, so it cannot be earned or withheld. It is what you are. It just is. As the awareness of your Essential nature develops, you discover that there is nothing that you need from others, that all you need is within.

As you move into high-functioning Twoness, you truly discover that the search for love and appreciation is finally over, and then you begin to experience a wonderful lightness and freedom. Relationships take on a completely different flavour. As your neediness subsides, your confidence and self-worth increase and you become free to be yourself, with no need to exaggerate or hide your feelings and no need to give endlessly of yourself in order to get the love and the strokes you have so desired. You can begin to allow yourself to be loved for who you are, not for what you do. Your sense of your own identity becomes strong and sure and you discover that not only do you no longer need to lose yourself within another, but you no longer even need to be in a relationship to experience feeling good. In fact, as you move up to a higher-functioning state, and you learn to consider and take care of your own needs, being alone becomes something that you regularly need, a precious joy that refreshes and restores you. Yet when you *do* receive love from another, you realise that this has now become a bonus rather than a need, the icing on the cake of peaceful contentment that comes about from already being full up inside.

With a stronger identity and the newfound confidence that arises from greater awareness, you gain acceptance of yourself, your failings, and your needs and find you can express those needs or say no without concern about loss of love or acceptance. Your appreciation of your own best qualities brings about true humility so that, as you continue to do your good deeds – which you surely will because it is your true nature to help and care for others – you can give unconditionally, without expectation of return or reward. The only reward you need becomes the knowledge that you have made a contribution to someone's life, and the joy and fulfilment that this brings far surpasses any expressions of appreciation or love that you may have sought in the past. Then giving can be done with the pure joy of giving for its own sake freely, unconditionally and lovingly.

The quality of this Unconditional Love is pure, gentle and joyous. It does not draw attention to itself, nor does it demand anything. It lasts because it does not depend on the changing vagaries of the personality. As you begin to experience this, you will find that you can experience the joy of love by being connected to your inner world and by being at one with yourself and everything around you. As you discover the presence of love within you, you also discover the presence of love in others, and you know that you deserve to receive love just by being who you are. Every moment is discovered to be potentially full of joy and love.

CHAPTER 22

Positive Pathways for the Three

The Self-Defeating Pattern

The coping strategies adopted in the young years have led to counterproductive cycles of behaviour referred to as the self-defeating pattern. This not only causes problems and pain but actually brings about what the Three is trying to avoid.

Less-than-high-functioning Threes believe that value and acceptance comes from success and recognition and that failure means humiliation. They become performers and achievers, continually comparing themselves and their achievements with others, even though they may not actually be gaining any personal satisfaction or fulfilment from what they are doing. They even come to believe they *are* the outer image they present and lose sight of who they really are and what they really want out of life.

The constant need to achieve puts all their focus on tasks and goals with no time for feelings. The heart energy shuts down, creating an inner emptiness or deadness. The Three then feels like an empty shell: all surface veneer with nothing of substance or value inside. Believing that their true inner self has no value and would, if revealed, be completely unacceptable to others lowers self-worth even farther.

Consequently, the inner world of the Three is neglected in favour of the outer mask and they have to strive even harder to be successful to prove to the world that they have value.

They can never feel valued for themselves because they are not being themselves. They do not allow others to see the true inner self because they feel that that self is without value. They become so out of touch with their inner self and their true identity that they cannot interact with others from their heart. Whatever admiration they get from others is for the outer image, not for their true selves; therefore, at a heart level, it has no real value and is never sufficient to make them feel good about themselves.

Whatever recognition or fame the Three achieves is only fleeting – more achievements and success will be endlessly needed to maintain value in other people's eyes. Without the heart connection, the successes remain valueless and unfulfilling, bringing about continuing inner emptiness and lack of good feelings about the self. So it is clear that the behaviour patterns adopted by the Three cannot help but bring upon themselves what they most fear: feeling worthless and without real value.

Self-Observation

Until now, many of your responses to life have been automatic; they were strategies you adopted in childhood in order to deal with your world. Those that do not serve you are no longer needed, but until you can see your own patterns, they control you. As they come fully into your awareness, *you* are able to take control and then to shift to a higher vibrational level.

Considering these self-observation questions will help you to have greater self-awareness and enable you to let go of your negative patterns, little by little. Take the time to go over these questions regularly and perhaps keep a notebook handy to jot down thoughts, insights, or experiences. As you become more aware of how much or how often your negative patterns arise, do not make yourself 'wrong'. **Remember, this**

behaviour has been normal for your personality type and now you are on the road towards change. Take your self-observation lightly, learn to smile at yourself, and keep rereading your positive traits, for **that** is who you really are!

The Three wants to be seen as successful; being perceived by others as anything less than number one feels like failure. Ask yourself:
- ➤ What does success mean to me?
- ➤ What does it mean to my peers or my family?
- ➤ How have I been comparing myself to others?
- ➤ How have I dealt with my failures? Have I admitted them or glossed them over?
- ➤ How often do I talk up my projects, my accomplishments, and even myself?

The impression others have of the Three strongly affects their sense of self. They rely on presenting a good image in order to get the positive feedback they need to make them feel good about themselves. Ask yourself:
(Some of these can be quite subtle. You may find it helpful to ask those who know you well.)
- ➤ How much effort do I put in to looking good and creating an acceptable image?
- ➤ In what circumstances do I adjust or match myself to fit in with what I think will be most acceptable to others?
- ➤ In what ways do I attempt to 'sell myself'?
- ➤ What have I done to specifically get recognition?

The Three's main focus of attention is on things to accomplish, since they believe that achievements and success will bring about approval and admiration. Ask yourself:
- ➤ What goals am I currently setting myself?
- ➤ How much of my time and energy are focused on achieving these goals?
- ➤ Do I really enjoy what I am doing, or is much of this activity just about getting a result?

> ➤ Even when there is no major goal in sight, how much of my day is focused on getting things done and keeping active and busy?
> ➤ How often do I allow myself to do nothing?
> ➤ What or who have I neglected because of being so task orientated?

Emotional matters may get in the way of efficiency, accomplishment, and success so the Three tends to put feelings (other people's as well as their own) on the back burner or ignore them all together. Ask yourself:

> ➤ What negative feelings do I try to avoid?
> ➤ When something uncomfortable comes up, what do I do to take my attention away from the feelings?
> ➤ What am I feeling right now?
> ➤ How much attention do I give to others' feelings?
> ➤ How might this be affecting my relationship with others?

Taking the New Path

Life is a journey

Life is a journey. Threes, however, live much of their lives with their sights firmly fixed on the goals, the outcomes, and the destination and, in so doing, miss the journey itself.

Consider this analogy: Suppose you were planning the holiday of a lifetime. You make your plans and then list the places you will visit and the things you wish to do along the way. The reason for going on the trip is to experience everything, to enjoy each day, and to have fun; otherwise, why would you go?

However, if you actually go on this trip with the intention of getting to your destination (i.e., reaching your 'goal') as quickly and efficiently as possible, you would complete each item on your list as speedily as possible (never mind whether you had time to enjoy what you were doing!), tick it off the to-do list, and then move onto the next item, congratulating yourself on your accomplishment. You would do this until you reached your final goal, which is to be back home. But if that was your goal, would there be any point at all in going on the trip? Of course not!

So ask yourself this: have I sacrificed the journey, the experience of my life, on the altar of speed and achievement?

Slowing down

It is essential now that you begin to take life a little slower and give yourself time to smell the flowers along your life's journey. Start by taking regular breaks instead of pushing yourself to exhaustion. Rest periods are not a waste of time. They are important in order to reconnect you with yourself and your real identity. Even a few moments of deep, regular breathing will help to recharge your batteries and bring freshness to the task in hand. Use some of this time to ask yourself whether this task is actually pleasurable and satisfying, or you are simply chasing some end result.

There is great depth within you, but until now, you have rarely stood still long enough to discover it. Looking inward instead of outward now needs to be one of your major 'goals', so perhaps you might consider beginning a regular practice of meditation. Few Threes will take time out to meditate because 'doing nothing' makes little sense to a task-driven person. However, meditating is far from doing nothing. It would be a real achievement for you to learn to just be. After all, you are a human *being*, not a human *doing!*

However, it is important that you do not view meditation as another task to be done or something at which you can excel. You cannot compare your 'success' at meditating with anyone else's, nor can you 'fail'. Each person's experience in meditation is a unique one and each time you meditate your experience may be different. There is no best way to meditate; however, there are techniques you can learn, and being a Three, no doubt you will put them into practice successfully!

Looking inward

Embarking upon personal growth requires us to be honest with ourselves. You have managed the mask you show the world in order to prevent others from looking at the truth of you, but this has also prevented *you* from looking at yourself and your life with honesty. It is time for you to admit the truth – only to yourself initially, not necessarily to others – that the continual performing does not actually make you happy and that there has been little real satisfaction in reaching out into the world for recognition and admiration.

Realise how little attention you have given to your inner world. You have unknowingly sacrificed inner awareness for what can be achieved in the outside world. In doing so, other people's opinions have largely determined your perception of your own value. As a result, you have felt like an empty shell – polished and impressive on the outside but devoid of any really good feelings about yourself. Moreover, with attention focused outside of yourself, you have lost touch with the truth of who you really are, what you really want, or what you really enjoy. Only by beginning to look inward will you find true happiness and fulfilment.

However, looking inward is not an easy task for a Three so begin by asking yourself what you really value in life, what you really love doing, and what you would stop doing if you no longer felt the need to be 'somebody'. Then ask those you love and trust what they really love or value about you. Not what they value about what you *do* but about who you *are*. Initially, you may be inclined to reject what they say for you may not have valued qualities, such as kindness or compassion; after all, they do not seem to speak of success or achievement. But listen to them. Then with their help, consider each of the best qualities of the Three (listed near the beginning of chapter 10) and consider which are applicable to you now and which you aspire to.

Becoming your authentic self

It is important that you begin practicing being your authentic self. A scary proposition perhaps, because this involves dissolving the false image you have presented to the world. Initially, you may experience fear that when the mask drops there will be nothing of value there. 'If I am not this job, this role, this image, then who am I?' But remember what others have said about what they value about you. *This* is who you are, not the things you have done.

At first, there could there be many times when you slip back into the old pattern of presenting the acceptable image. However, be patient with yourself. Perhaps you could ask one or two trusted people to gently let you know when you are not acting or speaking authentically so that you can learn to recognise when you have switched on your image. You may even realise that there are times when you become your image within your close relationships.

It may be helpful to think of yourself as two people – the 'real' you and the 'other' you (i.e., the image you present to others) – and when you find yourself play-acting again, do not feel that you have failed. Instead, congratulate yourself when you *are* your authentic self. What is important is to understand that having awareness of your behaviour patterns gives you choice, and each time you choose to be your authentic self is an important step forward. It will get easier and you will begin to realise that appreciation and love are coming to you because of who you are, not for what you accomplish. Moreover, you will discover that other people actually prefer the real you!

Being true to yourself

A great deal of your growth work is about truth – discovering what your own truths are and becoming your true self. It involves moving away from what you think others will admire and connecting with what really matters to you.

It is essential, therefore, that you reconnect with your own core values, likes, and dislikes. Many Threes are so used to adapting themselves in order to impress others that they lose sight of what they really believe, what they enjoy, and how they really feel about things. Check in with yourself at intervals during the day and ask yourself whether you really believe the opinion that you are offering, whether the stance you are adopting really reflects your own attitude, or whether that activity you are engaged with is something you really get pleasure from. And most importantly, give yourself the gift of doing some things just because you enjoy them, even though they may not further your goals.

Giving to others

You will make enormous strides in your growth by getting involved with projects where the effort you put in is not for your personal advancement but for the good of other people. You might consider voluntary work, or perhaps give some time to community projects (without being the head of the team or the one out in front!). Giving of your time and effort cooperatively instead of competing with others and seeking personal goals can bring enormous rewards, not least of which is an increase in self-value.

You have often been too busy to bother with other people's emotional concerns. Now that you are reassessing your core values, make yourself available to listen to others when they have problems. They will appreciate you taking time out from your busy schedule and you will gain much from being there for someone else.

As you become more aware of what others need, realise that there are times when it is important to take time out of your day to really connect with and appreciate what the other people in your life are doing. Your workaholism has often made you insensitive to the needs and desires of those around you, so try to develop more empathy and understanding; realise that there are eight other personality types and each will have quite different priorities to yours. Make a point of supporting and encouraging others in their efforts, and take the time to appreciate what other people are contributing (including your family members). Verbalise your admiration and appreciation instead of seeking strokes for yourself; others will like you more, you will be more desirable as a friend and colleague, and you will feel better about yourself.

Also important is to find the courage to reveal your concerns and vulnerabilities to people you trust. Contrary to what you might expect, sharing ourselves in this way endears us to others, because they have their vulnerabilities too. Remember your 'can do' attitude to life may be inspirational to many but can be off putting to some. It may well be difficult for you to admit when you have problems or when you have taken on more than you can deal with, but admitting when you are unable to do something, when you have reached your limit of understanding or when you need a break, is not failure; it is honesty.

We are all equal

Threes need to realise that we are all equal – different and unique but equal – and that no achievement, no success, no wonderful image can make us better than others or of more value in the world. Life is not a competition. We are not here in order to be *the best*; we are here to become *our best self*, which means letting go of our negative patterns so that we can live through our positivity.

Reappraise your attitude to failure. In striving for success, you have allowed setbacks and failures to impinge hugely on your self-esteem. As you discover more and more that you have many valuable things to contribute other than your achievements, and that your intrinsic value is in just being who you are not what you accomplish, being less than successful or not being the number one no longer needs to be viewed as a disaster. Accept that everyone makes mistakes and has failures; they are just part of life's journey and can, in fact, be opportunities to grow a great deal. It is inevitable that not everything you undertake will have the successful outcome you hope for, so lighten up on yourself when things go wrong and look for the silver lining within the clouds. There is always something to learn from unsuccessful ventures.

Connecting with your feelings

You may be concerned that if you spend too much time in looking at yourself that your outer goals will not come to fruition. And as your self-assessment has until now been based on your achievements, if you neglect outer activities, you ask yourself, 'How will I know if I am making progress?' The answer is: by the way you feel.

Increasing awareness of your inner world of feelings is essential if you are to know yourself more and to become your authentic self, but you must allow space in your life to make this connection. As you go through your day, slowing your pace sometimes will help you to know what you are actually feeling in the moment.

Connecting with your inner emotions may not be easy at first, so begin with gaining more body awareness. What sorts of things create tightness in your body? Where do you feel that? What does agitation feel like? When you feel relaxed, what changes do you notice in your body? What does it feel like to be centred?

As you become more aware of your bodily sensations, when something is upsetting, you take time to connect with the feelings instead of losing yourself in activity. Ask yourself, 'What is this? Anxiety? Resentment? Guilt? Sadness?' Begin to get used to noticing what patterns of emotions come up and give yourself the gift of finding ways to resolve them rather than ignoring them. When necessary, be honest with those that are evoking these feelings instead of pretending that you've got it all together and everything is just fine.

Your spiritual goals

Finally, a few words of warning. It is possible that you might look for some payoff from your personal development work, in the world of work or within relationships, perhaps in the form of appreciation from others for being so spiritually evolved! It is important to remember that you are working on your own patterns for *yourself*, not to get admiration from the outside world. Removing the mask only to adopt a more 'enlightened' mask that is acceptable to your spiritual sphere is not true growth at all.

Spiritual growth cannot be touched, nor can it be bought; it is not something to be displayed to others for the purpose of recognition, yet the rewards it brings are far greater than any achievement in the physical world. It brings contentment with self and an inner peace, for as you grow, you will enjoy solitude more and find pleasure and satisfaction in small things.

Finally, be aware of your tendency to want quick and measurable results. In the past, your desire to complete tasks and goals has made you inclined to cut corners in order to be the best or to change tack when the current route did not seem to be bringing results fast enough. Now that you have stepped upon your path of growth, you have embarked on a lifetime's journey of transformation that will bring satisfaction and joy. However, resist the temptation to want to hurry the process. Take it a step at a time without expecting too much of yourself at first and remember that you are always going to be unfinished. None of us will get it all 'done' or become 'perfect', but we can enjoy the ride as we travel towards becoming our best self.

Becoming a High-Functioning Three

Threes reconnect to their Essential nature by giving up the mask and discovering that real success and happiness are found by being their true selves.

Your endless activity has been your way of escaping the place inside that felt so empty, escaping the fact that you had lost contact with your real Essence. As you begin climbing to higher-functioning levels of being, you will probably ask, 'If I am not this image, then who am I?' Yet by gaining more understanding of your behaviour, and gaining compassion for yourself, your heart will open and you will discover that what was thought to be emptiness is, in truth, an inner spaciousness where your real happiness and stillness reside.

As a Three, you have the innate awareness that for something to become successful, you need to invest into it time, energy, and perhaps money. So as you progress, you discover that your evolvement towards a high-functioning state is worthy of your effort and investment. By spending more and more time making forages within your inner world, what becomes important now is truth – being fully aware of, and present to, your emotions, pursuing activities that bring you joy, not just recognition, and being true to yourself. Gradually, you begin to feel more substantial and real; you discover that you are not an empty shell but that your inner world has great, untapped depth. You begin to develop a true love and appreciation of self, which is the complete opposite of narcissism.

Once your self-worth stops relying upon the opinion of others (for how can they really know who you are?), the mask you have habitually presented becomes unnecessary. You no longer need to hide behind a false image, for your true self is more than enough, so the mask falls away. Instead of endlessly performing, you become your authentic self – natural, genuine, and at ease with the truth of you.

A high-functioning Three is able to truthfully assess and value their best qualities and talents with simple humility but also accepts their limitations without taking themselves too seriously. Failures are accepted as part of the learning of life; moreover, you find that you can share them with other people with honesty and candour. In so doing, you become an inspiration and a role model as your experiences help them understand and overcome their own difficulties and failures.

As you learn to appreciate yourself as you truly are, gifts and weaknesses alike, you become able now to appreciate and value others more. Other people's achievements and successes are now causes for celebration and congratulation, not competitiveness on your part. People warm to the genuineness of the high-functioning Three, and as you continue on this journey, you begin to experience the joy of knowing that, by living through your truth, you are everything you appear to be. Free from the endless merry-go-round of having to perform and achieve, you discover an amazing freedom and lightness of spirit in just being yourself.

Many high-functioning Threes have become great leaders. They seem to be imbued with an inner light that radiates out, drawing people towards them to be motivated and inspired. They speak their truth from the heart with simplicity, kindness and directness. High-functioning Threes are touchingly genuine, admirable people with deep humility and gratitude for being the capable and talented people they really are.

As the mask drops and the lack of self-worth is healed, where you thought there was nothing but emptiness you discover that you are full and whole inside. You no longer need appreciation or validation from outside of you because, living through your Essence, you know that your worth comes from the very fact that you are here. Living and being in truth and wholeness, you can now become the outstanding person you always wanted to be – just by being you. Finally, you become what you truly are: a human *being* instead of a human *doing!*

CHAPTER 23

Positive Pathways for the Four

The Self-Defeating Pattern

The coping strategies adopted in the young years have led to counterproductive cycles of behaviour referred to as the self-defeating pattern. This not only causes problems and pain but actually brings about what the Four is trying to avoid.

Having their own inner world as their main focus, Fours overuse their imaginations to dramatise their emotions, believing that they will find themselves in their feelings. Most of their negative feelings tend to be centred around hurts from the past, self-rejection and envy, with the consequence that hypersensitive Fours tend to take everything personally, often construing negative meaning where there was none intended. This leads to lower-functioning Fours being touchy, volatile and temperamental, which drives others away, creating rejection and greater separation from others.

Rather than deal with reality, less-than-high-functioning Fours retreat into an imaginary world, where they create fantasies in which they can be anything they want. They make endless comparisons between themselves and others, seeing in others the personal qualities and talents that they desire and rejecting the good points or talents they have. Thus, they can waste much of their lives missing real opportunities while they 'find themselves' and find it difficult to play a role of significance in the world. Their withdrawal from the world to find themselves or deal with the complexities of their inner world sadly results in the Four having even less confidence and feeling even more of a misfit.

As their imagination leads them into a downward spiral of negativity, Fours experience real hatred of themselves and hostility towards those whom they believe are responsible for their pain and difficulties. Withdrawing to protect their inner hurts results in them feeling even more separate and rejected, and their feelings of not belonging and being socially insecure are exacerbated by their lack of involvement with others. Their storminess, self-absorption and negativity ends up alienating those around them, and their 'specialness' and their need for withdrawal further separates them from others.

And so it is clear that the behaviour patterns adopted by the Four cannot help but bring upon themselves what they most fear: being rejected and abandoned with little sense of personal significance in the world.

Self-Observation

Until now, many of your responses to life have been automatic; they were strategies you adopted in childhood in order to deal with your world. Those that do not serve you are no longer needed, but until you can see your own patterns, they control you. As they come fully into your awareness, *you* are able to take control and then to shift to a higher vibrational level.

Considering these self-observation questions will help you to have greater self-awareness and enable you to let go of your negative patterns, little by little. Take the time to go over these questions regularly and perhaps keep a notebook handy to jot down thoughts, insights, or experiences. As you become more aware of how much or how often your negative patterns arise, do not make yourself 'wrong'. **Remember, this behaviour has been normal for your personality type and now you are on the road towards change.** Take your self-observation lightly, learn to smile at yourself, and keep rereading your positive traits, for **that** is who you really are!

Fours feel that they are intrinsically flawed and that something is missing from their lives. Therefore, attention goes to negative comparison and what is 'missing'. Ask yourself:

➤ How often do I compare myself to others?

➤ In what ways do I see myself as flawed?

➤ What does that make me feel about me?

➤ How much is my focus of attention on what seems to be missing in life?

➤ How much does longing and envy for something, or someone, come up?

➤ When have I experienced disappointment in myself or in others?

Fours try to understand their world through their emotions. This makes them susceptible to fluctuating feelings and moods, and for them, their depth of feeling indicates what is true and important. Ask yourself:

➤ What range of feelings might I experience in just one day? In just one minute?

➤ How much do my feelings go to extremes rather than staying appropriate to the situation?

➤ How often do my real feelings get intensified because I go over and over things?

➤ Do my feelings always tell me what is true?

➤ How do my feelings influence my actions negatively?

Fours seek to know themselves and to be special or unique because that gives them an identity that will get others to 'see' them (as their parent/s did not). This often leads to separateness and self-absorption. Ask yourself:

➤ In what ways have I believed myself to be different from others or to have special needs?

➤ In what ways have I put down or disdained (perhaps quite subtly) the ordinary or mundane?

➤ Have I been feeling a pride in my being different?

> ➢ Or have I felt shame in being less than my ideal?
> ➢ How might this be contributing to my sense of separateness or not fitting in?
> ➢ In what ways can I be self-absorbed?
> ➢ How often have I given little attention to others' experiences or feelings but expected them to listen to me?

Fours often experience unnecessary pain because they tend to turn things over and over, creating inner drama and turmoil. Ask yourself:

> ➢ What comments or events have I recently misconstrued or overdramatised?
> ➢ Do I easily allow myself to find negative meaning where there is none?
> ➢ How much pain does this cause me?
> ➢ How might this cause me to react to others?
> ➢ Do I distinguish between what was really meant and what my imagination tells me?
> ➢ How often do I ask what was really meant?

Fours tend to look for someone or something to blame for their circumstances and they hold onto grievances from the past. Ask yourself:

> ➢ What or who have I blamed for the way my life has turned out?
> ➢ How much pain does holding on to blame cause me?
> ➢ How does blaming disempower me?
> ➢ What if I let go of blame and decide to take responsibility for changing my life?

Taking the New Path

Accepting 'what is'

It is paramount that you stop resisting the experiences you are having and accept 'what is' if you are to bring balance into your life. Consider how you have tried to mould or shape life rather than accepting the way it is. The dissatisfaction and longing you often feel is a result of resisting and rejecting what you are actually experiencing, accompanied by the desire for the experience to be different, perfect, or out of the ordinary. This is one of the main reasons why you fall into despair. It is not possible to find the perfect life situation that does not have some difficult challenges; there is no such thing as a perfect relationship, nor can you create beautiful and perfect harmony in your inner and outer world. Only when you accept this will you find satisfaction in the beauty or perfection you *do* find in the world and within yourself.

Notice how much your focus tends to be around the past or the future instead of in the present moment. When you think of the past, it is either about old hurts long held onto or about how things were so much better then than they are now – and the fantasy future seems to contain all that you long for. The past is gone; we cannot change it, nor does the past dictate the future. We can never experience the future moment, and we cannot know what the future holds. The only moment we can experience is now. By living in the past or in some nebulous future, you miss what is amazing about the present. All the power to effect change in our lives is to be found within the present, so if you have felt disempowered or unable to make the changes to your life that you wish for, make an effort to focus on the one moment that is real – the now.

Breaking the pattern of longing

Because Fours seek intensity in their experiences, it is often in the ordinariness of life that they feel a sense of something missing. In order for you to find satisfaction and fulfilment in each day, it is important to work on finding happiness within the ordinary rather than hoping for the extraordinary. Allowing yourself to experience satisfaction in the simple things of life will allow you to begin experiencing fulfilment in many other areas of life.

Every morning, spend a little time focusing on what you appreciate about life – perhaps your home or work, the people or animals in your life, or the miracle of your body or of nature. There is always something to value and appreciate even when things are at their worst. Then, before you retire, focus on things that went well today for which you are grateful. (Even within a really bad day, something will have gone well!) Appreciation and gratitude move us into a more positive, happier frame of mind, so by making this a habit, you will more easily be able to pull yourself out of negativity. It is the change from glass half-empty to glass half-full.

It is especially important to work on breaking the pattern of longing. Fours give the impression that they long for what others have, yet the truth is that it is not the concrete things that they want; it is the happiness and contentment that these things represent. Once they have the longed-for someone or something they are disappointed – the longed-for contentment does not come about so they turn away from what they had wanted and reject it. But then, when it appears no longer available, it looks interesting again and they decide they do want and need it. It is essential that you break this cycle of longing, getting and rejecting if you want life to feel different.

Practice noticing when your attention is moving towards that which is absent, unavailable, or unattainable. Notice how you focus on the positive aspects of the absent whereas you focus on the negative aspects of what you actually have. This leaves you endlessly dissatisfied. This that you long for is not the answer. After all, when you have attained that which you have longed for in the past, dissatisfaction began to set in again fairly soon. The answer is to focus on the *positive* aspects of what is available to you in the *present* moment.

To begin with, try focusing on just one positive aspect of your present situation or relationship, even if this aspect seems quite trivial. Now write down all that you can in appreciation of that one aspect. Feel the essence of the appreciation and the feelings of lightness, satisfaction and even joy it engenders. (You will be most successful initially if you work on finding satisfaction and joy in some part of your life that does not hold an emotional charge for you, such as your flower garden, your book collection, or a favourite possession.) Then do the same in another area of your life and work up to spending some time every day finding things to write about that raise your vibration into a state of appreciation.

Be kinder to yourself

One important task is to accept that all your internal searching has not provided the desired result. It has just fuelled more intense feelings of deficiency and longing.

Your feelings of disconnection have been exacerbated by the rejection of the way things are and the longing for something better, but also by your tendency to compare yourself to others and measure yourself against some unrealistic picture of how you should be. In so doing, you reject and abandon yourself, creating inner feelings of hopelessness and depression. Your self-talk can be vicious and unkind; your harsh judgement of yourself is far worse than anything you would mete out to others.

Be kinder to yourself. Make a list of the things you have done in your life that you are proud of, and then write in a positive vein all you can about each of these. Ask a trusted friend to help you begin to appreciate what is great about you, and do not immediately reject what is said! Ease up on yourself. You deserve better.

Also, understand that problems, disappointments and lack are part of the fabric of life, not an indication of your deficiencies or the unfairness of life. When something goes wrong or a problem crops up, remember this: when a problem presents itself, so does the solution. However, you cannot align with the solution from a place of negativity; only when you begin to feel more positive will the solution appear. So focus on appreciation and gratitude instead of lack.

Letting go of the 'specialness'

While you may feel miserable and profess to long for happiness, it is time to recognise that you actually cling to your suffering because it sets you apart from others and gives you feelings of specialness. In your eyes, no one else suffers as you do and they cannot understand what it is to be you. This painful pattern only serves to set you apart from others and creates your feelings of entitlement; it is only by gaining a real understanding what you have been doing to yourself that your suffering will begin to dissolve.

Your need for specialness needs to be replaced by a recognition and acceptance of your humanness, with all its quirks and frailties. By continually creating impossible pictures of how you want to be, or ought to be, you have left very little room for good feelings about yourself. Recognise that your self-worth does not arise from being special or extraordinary but from just being yourself, and accept your true identity – which is that you are a unique and individual expression of the Divine, inseparable from it and perfect just as you are. By accepting yourself as you are, without needing to be special and unique and by embracing how much alike you are to others (as well as how others also experience pain), you will bring much needed peace into your inner world.

In order to help you accept yourself as you are (and perhaps even get to like yourself!), ask people you trust to write a list of your special qualities and talents as well as the ways in which they value you. Also, ask them to tell you gently and honestly about your shortcomings. Listen to what is said with a little detachment and humour. Everyone has their faults, but having faults does not make you wrong; it just makes you human! Of all the types, Fours are the most prone to take themselves too seriously, and it only causes them pain. So why not lighten up and learn to laugh at yourself with friends!

Feelings are not always truth

Your emotionality is both your gift and your downfall. It gives the richness and depth to your inner world but also leads you into exaggeration, unreality and over dramatisation.

Recognise how you shape and form ordinary reality into painful dramas full of exaggerated emotionality in which everything has ramifications beyond itself. A simple comment from someone else is never just an innocent comment. It is full of not just meaning but layers of meaning. Taking everything personally causes you much unnecessary pain. Remember your feelings are *your* feelings, not necessarily the truth of the situation, and they often mislead you. All they are telling you is what is going on inside you at that particular moment, and no more than that. They certainly do not provide accurate information about the intentions of other people, and believing that they do frequently causes you to read negative meaning into innocent words or actions. Accept the fact that you and your affairs are not the focus of other people's attention; their chief concern is their own lives. Therefore, those remarks that you dwell upon were probably quite innocent and not intended to cause hurt; in fact, it is quite likely that they were not aimed at you at all.

When something said or done by another person sends you into a downward spiral of negativity, take a moment to consider whether you are in need of a reality check. Instead of going over and over it, charging it with more and more negative meaning, check in with that person about what they really meant And remember that even if you do receive an unkind comment, that person's unkindness is a reflection of the low vibration within *their* inner world, not a truth about you.

Let go of the past

One of the most important aspects of personal growth and spiritual transformation is forgiveness; therefore, letting go of real and imagined hurts from the past is vital if you are to move forward into real contentment and happiness. Unless you are willing to let go of the past, with its attendant hurts, old resentments, and blame, you will never make any real progress, nor will you get on with your life. Blaming others for the way you are, the way your life is, for what did or did not happen, simply disempowers you. It puts the power over your future happiness squarely in the hands of those who hurt or wronged you.

Focus on what is positive and real in the present and accept that the past is the past and you cannot alter it. It happened, and no amount of dwelling on it will change the facts. However, you *can* change your response to it. The greater wisdom that comes from studying the

Enneagram will enable you to begin to see the 'baddies' with clearer eyes. Looking at the past behaviour of those who hurt you with eyes wide open to the personality type they are, or were, will make it easier to reframe past events so that you can begin to have compassion for them. In so doing, you will begin to let go of the anger, resentment, or hurt and move towards forgiveness.

Restoring the balance

Beware of using the people close to you as the dumping ground for all your troubles and complaints. Your intense emotional reactions and self-pity can cause you to be self-focused and to demand a great deal of attention from others. This tendency can drive away those who care about you. Remember they have their problems too, yet how often are you prepared to give time to listening to them? Is there balance between how much you give and how much you receive? Make the effort to restore balance by sometimes putting your concerns on the back burner for a while; listen properly whilst someone is telling you about their worries and problems without succumbing to the temptation to turn the conversation around to what is happening in your life.

Getting outside of yourself

It is important for you to realise that you feed your melancholy moods, that *you* are doing this to yourself. When you recognise that you are going into this pattern, do something to start to take yourself out of it, such as going for a walk. You do have choices. There are possibilities other than staying in the misery.

Although it is always good to follow your intuition, there are times when putting things off until you feel sufficiently 'together' or are in the right mood simply serves to isolate you. Try getting on anyway and doing something constructive; you are likely to discover that becoming active and working at something will lift your mood. Only by reconnecting with the world and doing something of value will you gain a real sense of your own worth and thus break the pattern of withdrawal and self-hatred.

Staying connected to the real world and participating in it, especially getting involved with ways of helping others, will take you out of your self-absorption and will bring out the best in you. Also, remember that it is important to work on being consistent in action despite fluctuating and intense feelings. Taking days off and hiding under the duvet will solve nothing, whereas doing something that helps another or improves your local community will bring surprising satisfaction and an increase in your confidence and self-esteem.

Gaining emotional equilibrium

Although you get a certain pleasure from emotionally charged situations, you need to start developing more emotional balance in order to bring equilibrium into your life. It will be helpful if you try to approach each experience without overreacting to it and without dramatising it. Practice stepping outside of yourself and observing what you are experiencing without allowing yourself to be swept away by it. By surrendering to what is actually happening, internally or externally, without judgement, rejection, or dramatisation, you will find it easier to respond to each experience only as much as is truly necessary, and little by little, you will begin to develop the wonderful quality of equanimity.

It will always be your inevitable tendency to move towards depth – because you desire the authentic and because you view life through the filter of your aesthetic nature – so you will still experience complexity and contradiction. But you will become a person who is attuned to the beauty of existence, the perfection of the paradoxes in life, the creative spirit within. You will become a person with a rich inner life who feels very deeply, but that depth is now experienced through the calm clear depths instead of being obscured by the turbulent, stormy waters.

Give up trying to find the pot of gold that would give life satisfaction and meaning and discover the joy of just being on the journey of life, of being present to each unique experience. Then you will have what you have longed for, satisfaction, meaning and fulfilment, living a life that is both fruitful and contented.

Becoming a High-Functioning Four

Fours reclaim their Essential nature by meeting each experience with equanimity and allowing true compassion for both themselves and others to be their guiding principle.

Your natural sensitivity as a Four has led you so easily into being oversensitive and self-rejecting, creating internal dramas that have little substance in truth. This has brought about negative and overly emotional states of mind. Seeking self-understanding and personal identity via a turmoil of emotions that have their root in endless analysis and self-criticism has been destined to bring more dissatisfaction than happiness.

As you begin to understand your reactive patterns more clearly, you can begin to be kinder to yourself and accept yourself for who you are. Gaining self-acceptance enables you to develop real compassion for yourself and brings about a much lighter frame of mind about those things that previously caused you to take life so seriously. In letting go of judgement of yourself, you can now start to recognise and accept your own positive, amazing qualities and, in so doing, begin to acknowledge the real beauty within.

Moreover, in your newfound self-acceptance, you discover that your state of mind is no longer governed by the habitual process of internal analysis and emotionalism. Instead of allowing yourself to be drawn inwards into emotional turmoil and unrealistic melodrama, instead of going into that place where there has existed so much rejection of both yourself and your experiences, you are now able to stay present to the truth of each moment as it exists within yourself and in relationship with others.

Your newfound emotional honesty enables you to accept reality as it is; you find new truths awakening within you and discover that your true identity is being revealed in each and every moment as *you* just being *you*. It is a relief to recognise that, by your very humanness, you are just like others, yet you also embrace the awareness that you are unique and special, not because you are trying to be but because you *are*. There really is only one of you in the Universe!

No longer at the mercy of your own emotional reactions, you find yourself wondrously touched by the ever-changing nature of life and experiencing your internal emotional state with equanimity. This means allowing it to be what it is, without dramatising it, judging it, or being swept away by it. You consequently begin to feel an open spaciousness inside, free and at ease with yourself, able to be spontaneously joyous and confidently self-aware without being self-conscious.

A stronger sense of self is developed by connecting with others and working to contribute something worthwhile to the world in which you live. Instead of getting caught up with your own emotional states, you now find you are more able to fully focus on others instead of yourself. As you take time to listen to them and to empathise with what is happening in their lives, you discover, to your delight, that it is your connection with others that brings so much of the peace and contentment you have long sought.

The state of self-acceptance that you now experience spills over into acceptance of the past. Instead of holding onto blame from the past, you realise that the blaming you have done has only ever hurt you, not those you have blamed. Old resentments are replaced with gratitude for the lessons that came about as a result of those past hurts and the suffering involved. You realise that it is those very experiences that have enabled you to grow into the amazing individual that you are. Moreover, letting go of blame raises your vibration up to a higher level so that you experience much more positivity and even greater inner peace and happiness.

You discover that who you really are is a result of a continual flow of rich and satisfying experiences, which are more amazing and wonderful than anything that your imagination could conjure. The outcome of this realisation is that you become fully alive, joyful and energetic, connected fully to others and to all of life. The amazing truth is that the high-functioning Four is the embodiment and expression of the continual ebb and flow of life, ever changing, endlessly transforming, and creating, endlessly self-renewing. Truly a wondrous expression of the Divine!

CHAPTER 24

Positive Pathways for the Five

The Self-Defeating Pattern

The coping strategies adopted in the young years have led to counterproductive cycles of behaviour referred to as the self-defeating pattern. This not only causes problems and pain but actually brings about what the Five is trying to avoid.

In order to avoid feeling overwhelmed by the world, Fives seek privacy to protect themselves from intrusion and demands; they focus their attention on thoughts and ideas rather than feelings so that others who are looking for emotional engagement often experience the Five as unfeeling. The outcome of this is that average Fives have few intimates with whom to interact. Moreover, by withdrawing from full interaction, they do not develop easy social skills. Many are awkward in company and unaware of normal conventions of social graces; this can result in alienation of others, creating further separation and feelings of inadequacy.

A common pattern with Fives is that they try to gain confidence and feel competent to deal with the demands of the world by pondering on everything in order to understand it and gain insight. They literally think too much – overanalysing, compartmentalising, and attempting to gain knowledge of the smallest detail about whatever has captured their interest. Feeling overwhelmed by the world and the demands of the people in it, Fives tend to withdraw both physically and mentally and can become the detached observer who accumulates and analyses information, forms ideas and theories, but does not fully engage with the world.

Believing it will only be 'safe' to come out and engage with the world when they have acquired enough knowledge, average to low-functioning Fives can stay in 'preparation mode' and thus remain disconnected from fully experiencing what the world offers them. Lack of integration with others and minimum involvement in the world means that the Five continues to experience feelings of poor confidence and incompetence.

The loss of connection with the outside world makes it impossible to develop a full role within society and they can get lost in realms of the mind so that they get more and more out of touch with reality, more and more isolated. By being so focused in their minds, Fives do not fully inhabit their bodies. Consequently, they tend to be ungrounded and out of touch with their own physicality. Poor awareness of their physical body contributes to feelings of powerlessness, which contributes further to their fear of being unable to cope with the world and to feelings of being overwhelmed.

So it is clear that the behaviour patterns adopted by the Five cannot help but bring upon themselves what they most fear: being unable to deal adequately with the world.

Self-Observation

Until now, many of your responses to life have been automatic; they were strategies you adopted in childhood in order to deal with your world. Those that do not serve you are no longer needed, but until you can see your own patterns, they control you. As they come fully into your awareness, *you* are able to take control and then to shift to a higher vibrational level.

Considering these self-observation questions will help you to have greater self-awareness and enable you to let go of your negative patterns, little by little. Take the time to go over these questions regularly and perhaps keep a notebook handy to jot down thoughts, insights, or experiences. As you become more aware of how much or how often your negative patterns arise, do not make yourself 'wrong'. **Remember, this behaviour has been normal for your personality type and now you are on the road towards change.** Take your self-observation lightly, learn to smile at yourself, and keep rereading your positive traits, for **that** is who you really are!

Fives fear that the world they live in and the people in it will want too much and/or give too little. They withdraw and contract their energy to guard against intrusion and to conserve what they feel are limited resources. Ask yourself:

> ➤ In what sorts of situations do I feel that there are excessive demands being made upon my time or energy?
> ➤ How does it make me feel?
> ➤ How do I behave when I feel intruded upon?
> ➤ What do I do to protect my boundaries?
> ➤ When might I withdraw from contact?
> ➤ If I stay physically present, what do I do in order to contract into myself?

Fives detach from their emotions and go into their minds in order to deal with difficult, emotive situations. They often spend more time in their heads than in fully engaging with activities and living. Ask yourself:

> ➤ What sorts of circumstances cause me to disassociate from my feelings and go up into my mind?
> ➤ What am I escaping from?
> ➤ What do I fear will happen if I allow my feelings 'in real time'?
> ➤ How often do I spend time thinking about situations and analysing possibilities rather than actually doing?
> ➤ Am I trying to figure things out in advance in order to gain predictability?

Fives avoid being vulnerable or dependent on others and believe that if you don't want, you won't lack. They ask little from others and often give too little. Ask yourself:

➤ What, if anything, have I been prepared to ask of others?

➤ How hard is it to ask for help?

➤ How much of myself am I prepared to share with those close to me?

➤ What do I withhold?

➤ How do I minimise my wants and desires, especially compared to others?

➤ In what ways do I neglect my physical needs, such as nourishing food, sleep, physical activity, and appearance?

Fives can unintentionally (and sometimes intentionally) make others feel ill at ease. Ask yourself:

➤ How often have I forgotten social niceties because of my involvement with my current projects/interests?

➤ How might my knowledge/intelligence/brilliance have intimidated others?

➤ Have I looked down on others whom I think are less intelligent or less knowledgeable?

➤ How did I behave towards them?

Taking the New Path

Soften the boundaries

Although more emotional types may view the detachment of the Five as a desirable quality, the degree to which you have consistently employed detachment as an unconscious method of self-protection has blocked you from engagement in the fullness of life. Developing non-attachment instead of detachment will allow the energy of life to flow through your body. Non-attachment brings lack of attachment to any particular point of view and the ability to take in exactly what is needed and let everything else go. This necessitates letting go of the need to hold onto anything, including your time, energy and knowledge, but mostly it requires you to let go of the need to stay distanced from yourself and your emotions.

Consider how much you have detached from others and withdrawn from the world in order to prevent having your energy depleted. The fear is that if you open the doors your energy will flow out and nothing will come back, leaving you with an empty cupboard. The result of this habitual stance is that the walls of your inner fortress are probably quite strong and, perhaps, impenetrable.

One of the major areas of growth that you need to embark upon is to soften the boundaries between you and other people – not attempting to demolish them with a pickaxe but to become a little more flexible. You can still have your fortress, but begin to allow other people in so that you can receive the benefits of going out into the world. The challenge is to engage. You don't have to do it all the time; just open the door sometimes and experience what it is like let other people's energy impact upon you. Do this initially with those that understand, those who are not going to push too hard or trample all over you. Perhaps this is a scary prospect, for you cannot help but fear that if you lower the walls that others will come charging in and take too much. So you need to try this with people who can be gentle and respectful of what you allow them to see and what you share with them.

If you take the risk of actually engaging, you will discover that other people's energy can help you, not just invade your space. By becoming more generous with your presence, others will be generous back and there will be a richness of interchange between you. Take it a little at a time and you will discover that there is real joy to be had in letting others come towards you without feeling you have to protect yourself all the time.

Giving and receiving

Experiencing yourself as having few inner reserves, you have tended to give out only little bits of yourself, living unconsciously with the fear that the rest of what you have will be taken from you. This has often led to you being perceived as non-giving or ungenerous. Recognise that there are ample resources and that life's real needs are met by the flow of Universal energy.

Your fear of invasion will gradually diminish as you experiment with being more generous in what you share of yourself with others. Instead of the tiny bits of yourself that you have parcelled out sparingly, allow more of yourself to become visible to others; talk about yourself sometimes. Share what you thought about this, what that was like for you. And it is just as important to find ways of nurturing or supporting other people. Try asking them sometimes, 'How do you feel about …?' or 'What was that like for you?' without being afraid of having to cope with their feelings. You have a wonderful gentleness that only a very privileged few have ever experienced; give others that gift too. By giving to others, you will be nurturing your own growth.

As you begin sharing more of yourself and allowing more people into your protective circle, also begin to take in more support from others. You tend to find it hard to trust people and ask for help or support. Make an effort to reach out to those people you know you can trust when you feel vulnerable or lacking in confidence. Your life will be greatly enriched if you make your needs known and allow others to help you. Family and real friends will not expect anything in return. Let them know when you feel invaded, and ask them to respect this.

Knowing about yourself is not the same as knowing yourself

Your natural tendency to overanalyse and rationalise your experiences takes you out of the immediacy of the moment. You are gifted with extraordinary mental capacities, but they can lead you into the trap of retreating from connection with yourself, as well as with others. This has been a habitual pattern for you, yet in order to make effective steps towards growth, staying connected and present rather than withdrawing is essential.

If you wish to understand and move beyond your self-defeating patterns, then you have to work on maintaining greater connection with your inner world. Introspection comes easily to the Five, but for real growth, this introspection needs to be emotional rather than mental. Real, tangible growth that is truly embodied and lived cannot be achieved solely through the mind. No amount of knowledge about consciousness, the human soul, or the nature of your personality structure can substitute for directly experiencing your inner terrain and allowing each moment to touch you. Such information can be very interesting and helpful in clarifying the journey you need to take, but it is important to recognise that accumulating facts can lead to the temptation to avoid real exploration of your inner self. The journey towards becoming who you really are has to be lived, not just studied from afar.

Many Fives mistake detachment for spiritual growth, but only by moving forward into life and experiencing your feelings in the moment will you come into true Beingness. Let yourself begin to feel your emotions without analysing on a deep level; emotions come and go and often defy logic and reason. Stay connected to your emotional centre and practice becoming more aware of what you are feeling, especially when your thoughts are taking you out of the immediacy of your emotional response. By associating with your feelings and having real experience and connection, you will discover that more life energy becomes naturally available.

Staying present

As you begin to develop a closer relationship with the world, there will initially be a sense of loss of privacy, which may make you inclined to move your emotions back into hiding where they can be kept under control. It is important, however, to become more at ease with a wider range of feelings; allow yourself to experience them in real time and sometimes to verbalise them in the moment.

As you begin to get more used to staying present to strong feelings instead of disconnecting from them and withdrawing into your fortress, you will discover that not only do you not lose anything, but you actually gain an enormous amount. This applies to your good feelings as much as to your uncomfortable feelings. Allowing yourself to be present to, and experience, strong emotions, such as love, joy, or excitement, and expressing them without analysing, rationalising, or holding back, is as important as experiencing and expressing painful emotions. There are things in life that you feel passionate about; communicate this passion to others sometimes. There are people in your life you care about; share your feelings with them in the very moment you feel them in your heart.

Anger is the hardest emotion for Fives to show because it makes them feel out of control. If you allow control to slip, there is the fear that you might be more self-revealing than you intend, yet you have to accept that some conflict in relationships is a fact of life and work it through with the other person instead of withdrawing into isolation.

There will still be times when you will have to withdraw as a matter of self-preservation, but make sure that you discuss your boundary issues with the other party. And in your intimate relationships, consider your partner's feelings when you need to withdraw. Explaining what is going on for you will help prevent misunderstandings.

Rejoin planet earth

You will always be something of an observer of life, but remember not to get lost in this; return to planet earth regularly! Life is not an abstraction just to be studied or over intellectualised; life is to be lived, and you have real presence that matters and can make a difference.

However, in order to become fully engaged with real life, you will need to address the areas where your confidence is low. Instead of getting so involved with fascinating projects, pastimes, or games that do not necessarily support or improve your life situation, take decisive action to reach out into the world. By sharing more of yourself with other people as well as allowing them to truly affect you, you will gain more confidence than you can just by spending your time acquiring more knowledge or exploring obscure ideas.

Start to take note of when you are theorising or analysing too much rather than engaging with others or with real life. You experience an enormous amount of your life in your head and there is a tendency to not communicate thoughts and ideas enough with the result that other people can feel left out of the loop or even shut out. Connecting with others and sharing ideas and insights is essential for Fives in order to get used to bringing themselves into the outside world, but this connection needs to involve real people and not just Internet technology. Sharing your thoughts with those around you can be very rewarding – they might just understand more than you think they would! – and finding groups of like minded people with whom you can verbally exchange ideas will help to keep you grounded here in the real world.

Also, become aware of how much you tend to stay in 'preparation mode' rather than doing. Getting together your facts before you engage in something unknown makes sense; it feels safer and boosts your confidence, but when taken to extremes, this tendency only serves to prevent you from engaging in life. Only by becoming fully present and getting on with living will you acquire the confidence you are seeking. This will enrich your life, not deplete it. You will not lose yourself; you will gain the world.

Balancing mind and body

Many Fives live mainly in the mind and, as a result, their bodily needs become less important. Disconnecting from your body results in imbalance, yet your mind is sharpest when your body is in healthy balance and full of vitality. There is nothing wrong with sedentary activities, such as reading or working on the computer, but it is essential to address the balance between body and mind.

An important first step is to reconnect with your gut instincts when you need to make a decision. Instead of always relying on gaining enough information or analysing the situation, sometimes just go for what feels right and trust the inner knowing that you have instinctively. Your mind does not have all the right answers.

Also important would be to take up some sort of physical activity that will wake up your body – perhaps walking, running or dancing, or even martial arts. If you feel physically weak, consider gym work; if you get too intense or highly strung, try yoga. Also, make a point of taking regular breaks from your intellectual pursuits to check out your bodily needs, such as food, sleep, fresh air, or clean clothes.

Meditation can be a real respite from all the frantic energy going on in your head. You might find it quite hard at first because of self-analysis and theorising, so engage in physical activity with a meditative quality that takes you out of mind into your body. Options include yoga (balance postures are very effective), martial arts, Pilates, and shiatsu – something so engaging that you have to focus on the physical with no space left for conceptualising or analysing, and your mind can reach a place of rest. Even walking can be a meditation as long as you do not use the time to continue your thinking; feeling the movements of your body as you walk is very grounding.

Maintaining distance between you and others feels most comfortable to you, but allowing people to venture closely into your space would help your work on connecting with your inner world. Consider engaging in an activity that involves close one-to-one contact, such as massage or dancing. Both would help ground you in your body and, if accompanied by music that evokes strong emotions, would enable you to connect with feelings in real time.

Interacting with grace

There are times when your normal Five behaviour is helpful, and there are times when it can be working against you. Remember the breadth of your knowledge and your mental acuity can be intimidating to others. Sometimes it is important to ask yourself, 'Is a bit of Fiveness appropriate here, or will I just be blinding them with my knowledge?'

When others react negatively towards you, consider whether you, rather than they, may have inadvertently begun the antagonism. Looking down on those who are less intelligent than you, or behaving in intellectually arrogant ways in order to exert your intellectual muscle, makes others feel uncomfortable and alienated, and contributes towards your separation and isolation.

Try to listen more. You don't have to accept other people's opinions, but don't automatically dismiss their views as worthless either. Remember there are eight other ways of being in this world that are as equally valid as yours, and there *are* other people who know things worth listening to. Your extensive knowledge means that sometimes you feel the need to disagree with others, but instead of being disdainful or abrasive when you disagree, help others expand their vision and knowledge in kind and compassionate ways. And if conflict ensues, use your natural gifts of perception and understanding to consider where others are coming from and be prepared to risk reaching out instead of withdrawing.

Becoming a High-Functioning Five

Fives reclaim their Essential nature by making full connection with their inner world and their outer world and by allowing each experience to touch them emotionally.

Through simultaneous observation, analysis and synthesis, the high-functioning Five has the capacity for true insight, intuition, expanded vision, and understanding. However, in order to reach your true potential, you need to become fully grounded in your body and able to utilise both your mind and your Beingness.

You have unconsciously felt that facts and knowledge are the key to survival here in the physical world. You need to become very clear now that no amount of knowledge about the Five personality structure, or the nature of your own consciousness, can bring about personal or spiritual progress. Such information is very helpful to enable you to understand the way you have dealt with your world up until now, but inner transformation can only come about by allowing your experiences to touch you on a deep level.

All experiences, even those that are difficult or painful, need to be truly moved through and felt. As you connect fully with your inner world and learn to be fully in your feelings and experiences of the moment, you will learn to resist the impulse to detach from, observe, or analyse each inner experience. This will require the courage to willingly connect with yourself in an experiential way, allowing your mind to *follow* your direct inner experience – instead, as has been your habitual stance, of your mind taking the lead and *figuring out* what you are experiencing before you actually contact your bodily and emotional experience.

As you begin to trust this inner process, you will develop the quality of *non-attachment*, which is quite different from detaching. Non-attachment is not emotional repression or disengagement; it is the ability to be open and liberated, free to experience everything, able to move from one viewpoint to another without the need to hang onto any particular one.

From your perspective as a Five, the feeling of having insufficient knowledge has contributed to your experience of being left out of the flow of life, to being an onlooker trying to understand what is going on and how to deal with it. On a fundamental level, this is the experience of disconnection from both Being and Essence. By reconnecting with your inner world, you will reconnect with the aspect of Essence that is related to Fiveness – the source of true insight and Universal Knowledge.

This reconnection brings about the capacity of being able to simultaneously analyse knowledge from memory, or from observation of the physical world, and synthesise it with the knowledge and understanding gained from connection to the universal mind. As a high-functioning Five, you then have the potential of true vision – the ability to understand the interconnectedness of all things, the ability to draw together threads of insight gained from whatever source, and put them together in new ways. This brings about the possibility of bringing all manner of expansive and revolutionary ideas to whatever you focus your interest upon.

By allowing yourself to become more and more touched by, and in contact with, reality, you will gain more and more connection with yourself. You will become increasingly open and spacious yet feel stronger and fuller inside. As this transformation continues, your heart opens and you become free to be deeply touched by all the beauty and depth of each of your experiences. In so doing, you will not only develop your capacity for huge insight but will now combine it with great compassion for others; you find yourself now desiring to not just bring to others the rich tapestry that is your mind but also the warmth of your heart.

CHAPTER 25

Positive Pathways for the Six

The Self-Defeating Pattern

The coping strategies adopted in the young years have led to counterproductive cycles of behaviour referred to as the self-defeating pattern. This not only causes problems and pain but actually brings about what the Six is trying to avoid.

The continual striving to find surety and certainty in an uncertain, ever-changing world means that it is inevitable that the Six will experience endless anxiety. By projecting into the future, mentally checking out all the 'what ifs', the less-than-high-functioning Six is caught up in an endless spiral of negativity, each negative possibility piling on more anxiety and worry. The busy mind questions everything, suspiciously checking everything out. It goes back and forth looking for certainty but finds none and the Six is left in a state of anxiety and indecision. As a result, the solar plexus is continually turning over and over with fear to such an extent that the Six's inner world is experienced as having no stability or solidity.

The ceaseless activity of the solar plexus area means that Sixes cannot connect with their gut instincts, those feelings that come from the voice of their inner guidance. Only from our inner guidance do we experience a certainty about the right course of action, and it is only when we have that certainty are we able to move forward in life without feeling unsure or unsafe. Even when the Six does hear that inner voice, the mind questions, and frequently rejects, what is heard, thus creating uncertainty once again.

In trying to overcome their self-doubt and anxiety, the Six seeks guidance and security from the outside world in the shape of other people, received knowledge, accepted social structures or relationships. Little coherence is found within the information received from these 'authorities', and even when the Six does make a decision and acts, they continually question their own decision so cannot escape the feelings of being unsafe and unsure.

Finding nothing solid, certain, or trustworthy inside or outside, the resultant patterns of the Six cannot help but bring about their deepest fear: being unsafe and without security, support, or guidance.

Self-Observation

Until now, many of your responses to life have been automatic; they were strategies you adopted in childhood in order to deal with your world. Those that do not serve you are no longer needed, but until you can see your own patterns, they control you. As they come fully into your awareness, *you* are able to take control and then to shift to a higher vibrational level.

Considering these self-observation questions will help you to have greater self-awareness and enable you to let go of your negative patterns, little by little. Take the time to go over these questions regularly and perhaps keep a notebook handy to jot down thoughts, insights, or experiences. As you become more aware of how much or how often your negative patterns arise, do not make yourself 'wrong'. **Remember, this behaviour has been normal for your personality type and now you are on the road towards change.** Take your self-observation lightly, learn to smile at yourself, and keep rereading your positive traits, for **that** is who you really are!

The main focus of the Six is what might go wrong or what might threaten their security. To them, the world is a dangerous place and you just can't trust anything or anybody. Ask yourself:

➤ What makes me anxious or fearful?

➤ (For the reliant Six) What have I avoided because it felt threatening or fearful?

➤ (For the self-reliant Six) What have I challenged myself to do even though it felt threatening or I felt fearful about it?

➤ In what ways have I been overcautious or under cautious?

➤ What do I need in order to feel secure?

The anxiety and lack of trust experienced by Sixes naturally leads to worst-case thinking (the 'what ifs'). Ask yourself:

➤ How much does worst-case scenario thinking preoccupy me?

➤ How does this make me feel?

➤ What situations have I gone over recently in my mind as potentially threatening?

➤ Was my fear justified? How much of what I have been worrying about actually came about?

➤ How much unnecessary stress do I cause myself by thinking negatively?

The Six questions, doubts and checks out everything before moving forward. This frequently leads to procrastination and indecision. Ask yourself:

➤ How much are questioning and doubting present in my internal dialogue?

➤ How often am I unsure over a course of action or do I have doubts about trusting another person?

➤ When has putting off making a decision, or doubting a decision I have already made, had negative consequences – emotionally or practically?

➤ How much have doubting and questioning held me back?

The need for security can lead to mistrust of others, especially in close relationships. Ask yourself:

➤ When have I questioned others' motives or assumed they might have a hidden agenda?

➤ How do these negative projections make me feel?

➤ How does this affect my behaviour towards them?

➤ Have I experienced jealousy because of my insecurity?

➤ What behaviour did that cause me to display? Did I withdraw or become fearful and clinging?

➤ Did my behaviour have an adverse effect on the relationship?

➤ In what ways might this undermine my relationship? (Discuss this with him or her.)

Taking the New Path

Growth for average Sixes can often be quite slow, and in many cases, it only comes about in later years. The trouble with most Sixes is that they do not give themselves the time to make progress. They rarely focus on themselves at all but give all their attention to the tasks that they need to fulfil. As a result, Sixes generally do not know themselves well and many feel as if they take two steps forward and then one back – or even one step forward and two back!

Self-enquiry does not come easily to the Six, yet it is essential to connect more with yourself and to look honestly at both your positive and negative aspects if real progress is to be made.

True security

Seeking security by trying to make your outer world secure has brought you endless fears and negativity. True security comes when there is a radical shift from hope and belief into faith and knowing.

It is time to accept that nothing in the world is static and there are no guarantees about the future – except perhaps with toasters! In an ever-changing world, a degree of uncertainty about what will happen is inevitable. You cannot second-guess every eventuality, so why not give up trying? The ultimate task for you is to reclaim trust in yourself, others and the world, and begin to accept that each moment is unfolding exactly as it should. It is possible to live comfortably with uncertainty and move ahead anyway. This means staying with situations requiring courage and accepting that everyone experiences a degree of anxiety. It also means noticing, and resisting, the impulse to move away from fear or to challenge it.

One of your biggest stumbling blocks has been your inability to hear, and trust, your inner intuition. Your mind misleads you. It constantly changes, going to and fro between this path and that path, questioning every decision you do make and creating endless stress and uncertainty. However, your inner authority, that inner knowing that you have, never misleads you, so it is important to practice connecting and trusting it and allowing it to guide your decisions.

When a decision is needed, your intuition often kicks in very quickly, but then you question that decision and unsettle yourself again. Learn to use your body as the barometer to 'tell' you what is the right decision – the instinctual feelings in your body will not mislead you. Try going with that first feeling on matters of little importance first; then, as you learn to trust your inner knowing, it will be easier to allow it to guide you with the big stuff.

Meditation will help you connect with your intuition as well as to gain a direct experience of being in contact with your higher self, your own essence. Be aware, though, that you may, at first, find difficulty with meditative practices that require an empty mind; instead, moving to music, chanting, or focusing on the breath are all good methods for you to try. You may also find it helpful to read spiritual or inspirational literature regularly in order to keep you on your path of growth. You know how easily you can get swept up with the 'real world' and its problems!

Only when you finally know deep down inside that you are not alone, but are safe and connected, will your feelings about life truly change. Then you can come out of survival mode and start to get the peace you seek even within all the change and uncertainties that are part of the natural flow of life. This knowing will create feelings of stability and solidity within your inner world; therefore, nothing is more important than taking time out for yourself and your own emotional and spiritual development.

Quieten your mind

Your overactive imagination has been the source of most of your anxiety – our thoughts generate our emotions and the emotion your negative thoughts generate is anxiety to one degree or another. Therefore, finding ways to quieten your mind is essential for your progress. Focusing on the breath is a time-honoured way of quietening the mind, and this process is especially beneficial for Sixes because most Sixes are shallow breathers.

When we experience anxiety or fear, our natural bodily response is to stop breathing properly; the breathing becomes very shallow or irregular and much tension is created in the shoulders and neck. At its worst, this creates panic attacks.

The following procedure will help you learn to breathe properly.

Lie flat on your back, your left hand on your upper chest and your right hand on your abdomen. If you are breathing too shallowly, you will notice your left hand rising and falling with each breath whilst your right hand mostly remains still. This indicates that you are only breathing into the top part of your lungs, yet your abdomen should also rise and fall with each breath. Make a full, slow out-breath, expelling every bit of air from your lungs, and then begin a full, slow in-breath so that your right hand (abdomen) rises first then your left (chest). This will fully inflate your lungs. Practice this deep breathing often, until you begin to do it automatically. As you practice, focus all your attention on your breathing – perhaps by counting breaths 1 – 10 and then repeating the count. In doing so, your mind will quieten and you will begin to connect more with yourself.

Making stronger contact with your body helps quieten the mind, so consider ways of increasing your body awareness. Massage will focus attention in your body, reduce stress, and relax both body and mind, especially if combined with deep breathing. Taking up new physical activities, especially those that focus on awareness in the body rather than the mind, should be considered; perhaps consider dance, chi gung, tai chi, yoga, or martial arts. You will benefit greatly from contact with nature – walking, swimming, gardening, etc. – as this will ground you, but be sure not to use this time to worry or strategise about your work or other concerns. As you engage in these activities, maintaining your focus on your bodily sensations will help reduce mind activity. For example, focus on the way the wind feels on your face, the water on your body, or the way in which your feet make contact with the ground.

Finding joy in the moment

As a Six, you often do not give yourself time to experience joy as you rush from activity to activity and take little time to savour the pleasure of the moment. Your mind tends to be either in the future or in the past, but by finding pleasure in the 'now', you will begin to experience greater joy. Perhaps you have not always believed that joy is for you; hard work, yes, and the pleasure of rest that provides satisfaction and a gentle happiness. But the uplifting quality of joy is not often experienced.

Your default setting is to look at the negative and thereby miss the joy of living. Practice focusing what is positive about the task in hand, instead of worrying about the future or dwelling on the past. By learning to focus more in the moment, feeling gratitude for what is in your life right now and finding joy in small things as you work, you will move into a more positive frame of mind. It will take practice and you will have to keep reminding yourself not to rush forward or dwell on the past, but it will bring great rewards.

Confidence brings more confidence

Despite your view of yourself, you are not in any way inferior or less than anybody else. Refer back to the best qualities of the Six and discuss them with people you trust. By accepting and owning the positive qualities of your personality, you will develop an essential but realistic positive belief in yourself.

Six are often too busy to notice the small successes in what they do. Take time to savour those moments when you have achieved your objectives, instead of immediately launching into the next job or the next worry. Enjoy and absorb the feeling of competence your achievement brings. Then, when you doubt yourself in the future, remember this moment. Reliving positive feelings is one of the best ways to move out of your negativity and fears.

You also need to realise it is good to tell yourself you have done well when you have succeeded in being positive rather than negative, or when you focused on the moment and allowed the joy of the moment to touch you. Congratulate yourself on the small successes.

Connecting with your strong emotions

You have been mostly outwardly focused – on tasks that need to be done or on pleasing others – but now you need to become more inwardly focused. Your habitual practice is to hide from your strong emotions by engaging in physical activity, but if you are to move into a higher-functioning place, you must be prepared to focus on your inner emotions and really explore them.

It is important to begin to acknowledge and sit with your emotions, especially the uncomfortable ones. In order to begin to know yourself better, you need to find ways of staying still long enough to focus on what you feel and why. This may require courage and patience with yourself, and you may need help in understanding and accepting your inner fears and other strong emotions. As you begin to explore your inner self, you may be surprised how little you know about your inner world of emotions, but it will help to verbalise them or write down what you feel.

Anger is an emotion that has felt threatening to you because of the fear that it might undermine the security and stability of your world, yet it is essential that you connect with and face your own anger as well as that of others. (Be aware that rising feelings of aggression can indicate the presence of fear, so when this emotion comes up, take a moment and ask yourself if there is something you are afraid of.)

Work with someone you can trust and allow your anger full expression when it comes up. Moreover, work at allowing another party to fully express their anger without reacting to it. By allowing the presence of anger and discovering that it does not necessarily undermine your relationships, your inner security and confidence in yourself will increase.

Projection or truth?

It is your natural proclivity to try to cover all bases by projecting into every awful possibility. However, this has only served to increase your level of anxiety and stress, and if you wish to reduce your level of anxiety, you need to curb your tendency towards negative projection. Begin by working at distinguishing fearful projections from real possibilities. In reality, how often do these imagined events actually come to pass? Often? Rarely? Never? Be honest with yourself. In order to help yourself change your thinking, start taking note of how often things turn out well despite your worrying about what might go wrong. Record these positive outcomes and begin to notice that, more often than not, the way things turned out was just fine, even if it was not what you expected.

As a Six, you are a gifted people watcher, often intuitive and insightful, and you quickly make decisions about other people. Although you often come to very accurate conclusions about their intentions or behaviour, it is important to recognise that, with your tendency to distrust as well as to expect the worst, sometimes it may be your own mental processes that are being perceived as belonging to the other. The conclusions you come to can easily be a reaction to your own projection instead of to accurate information. You are inclined to view most people in very black and white ways – as friends or enemies – with little in between, and sometimes you move away from people based upon very little knowledge. Sixes love checking things out, so why not be sure you check out your projections against what is really true before you make a judgement!

Recognise your limits

Your need to please others can easily result in you feeling overstretched or under pressure, and then you are inclined to overreact emotionally – either with anger (self-reliant Sixes) or with greater anxiety and even more need to please (reliant Sixes). These situations are of your own making and the solution lies in your hands; you need to begin to recognise your limits and take control of your own time and energy. It is very empowering to discover that saying 'no' sometimes does not result in the world falling about your ears. Moreover, others will learn to have greater respect and appreciation for you when you do make yourself available to help. Remember, you do not have to keep proving yourself; real friends value you anyway.

Admit mistakes

Although you are a very responsible sort of person, your fear of getting into trouble or being seen as 'less than' means that you have great difficulty in accepting responsibility when you are caught out in a mistake. Instead of justifying your actions or abdicating responsibility, take your courage in both hands, own up, and apologise. It may surprise you to discover that you will rise, not fall, in other people's estimation. (Ask them!) You will actually end up feeling better about yourself.

Expand your boundaries

Sixes are much more inclined to assist others in achieving their goals than to pursue their own. They wish to please others because when others are happy, they can relax and be happy; it makes them feel more confident and brings feelings of security. But in their people pleasing, they very often do not look at what they themselves want, what would bring themselves pleasure.

Discovering what you want is part of you beginning to know yourself more. There may be many things that you have not done in your life, dreams that got swept away in the busyness of your doing, and you have kept your world small in order to feel safe. You need to learn to please yourself, but first you need to ask yourself what you would like to do. You may convince yourself that you are content with your small world, but in order to really grow, you need to begin to expand your boundaries – take a few risks and move out of your comfort zone.

There may be some accompanying anxiety, but you can observe these feelings without reacting to them; accept that some anxiety may be inevitable. Start by trying different foods then seek out new activities. Booking a different sort of holiday or interacting with new people will give you new perspectives so that you learn more about yourself and the world. And embark upon just one small adventure, something that would uplift and excite you, something that you have not done, perhaps something that a long time ago you wished to do but never did, for this will expand your horizons. Each new experience will greatly expand your realm of safety and your base of support, thus increasing your comfortable feelings in the world.

And finally ...

Self-Reliant Six – Let your guard down sometimes and allow your vulnerability, fears and needs to be expressed to those that matter to you. Surprisingly, you will discover that admitting your vulnerabilities will make you stronger.

Reliant Six – Begin to embrace and acknowledge your own courage and personal power. It may be helpful initially to ask the help of a close trusted friend to encourage and support you in your forages towards self-empowerment and to help you appreciate the times when you are courageous (which are, in fact, the times when you are in the worst states of fear yet still take action).

Becoming a High-Functioning Six

Sixes reclaim their Essential nature by making
full connection with their inner world and finding
their support and guidance from within.

Instead of creating the safety and security that you have sought, your identification with thoughts and negative projections has led to your endless feelings of anxiety and fear as well as lack of clear direction. When we identify with guidance from outside of ourselves – from other people, belief systems, or other outer authorities – we feel we have no solid foundation or groundedness. Our mental constructs have to be constantly checked out, shored up, and reinforced in order to uphold our sense of who we are and to discover which way to proceed with our lives. Becoming a high-functioning Six means you connect with, and learn to trust, your intuition, the voice from within that guides you correctly every time if only you will follow it. When you no longer need to second-guess life, and you can let go of the beliefs and positions taken on from society, organisations, or the media, you can begin to discover your own deepest truths and have the confidence to live them.

As you continue to make sustained contact with your inner terrain, you begin to experience a sense of safety and solidness that allows you to relax and develop real confidence in yourself and your own decisions. You can comfortably begin to expand your boundaries without fear, moving into new and uncharted areas of life with the confidence that you know what is right for you just by the way it feels. You develop the courage to let go of anything you have previously held onto for security.

It is always said that the Six is more likely to be a foot soldier rather than a general, yet many high-functioning Sixes display outstanding courage and leadership qualities, leading with a deep understanding and compassion of others' fears and insecurities. Where they display leadership, they do so without ego, knowing that followers may become leaders and leaders may become followers, depending on the circumstances and the abilities and talents needed to complete the job in hand. The high-functioning Six can teach everyone about the benefits of community, commitment and cooperation and the joy of working selflessly for the common good.

One of your best qualities is your commitment to following things through and completing a job once started; now this can be applied to your personal growth. The more you learn to quieten your mind and connect with your inner world, the more solid and safe you feel. The confidence and security you have tried to find outside of yourself by being a believer or a follower steadily become more available to you as you learn to recognise and listen to your inner guidance. As your mind steadily quietens, you hear that inner voice more and more. Learning to trust your inner wisdom allows your anxiety to further subside and your confidence to grow, so the mind chatter quietens even more ... and on and on, in an ever upward spiral of positivity.

Knowing that you are safe, solid and secure, and that your inner guidance is ever present, allows hope to develop into faith and belief into knowing. When you have knowing, you begin to live moment to moment without continually projecting fearfully into the future. Living in the present moment allows life to flow with ease and joy. Being present to yourself and your inner truth brings the real inner peace and security for which you have always searched. As you finally come to realise that you are an integral part of a benevolent Universe that provides all your needs and supports you completely, you discover that who you really are is indestructible and your inner foundation becomes unshakeable.

Finally, you can focus on growing flowers in the garden of your life instead of continually pulling weeds!

CHAPTER 26

Positive Pathways
for the Seven

The Self-Defeating Pattern

The coping strategies adopted in the young years have led to counterproductive cycles of behaviour referred to as the self-defeating pattern. This not only causes problems and pain but actually brings about what the Seven is trying to avoid.

The overall pattern of the Seven is one of busy, humming vibrancy; these are people who are full of busyness and energy. In the attempt to avoid their dark inner terrain, they engage in continuous activity and distractions so that they do not have to experience or deal with the negative feelings within their inner world. By believing that fulfilment is somewhere other than here, that something better is just around the corner and 'the grass is greener', Sevens have to keep on the move, seeking that perfect experience that might finally bring contentment. Happiness and satisfaction are always perceived as being somewhere in the future whereas the here and now has to be avoided, for should they stop, they become 'bored' - in other words, they begin to touch the anxiety, self-doubt, and the 'inner darkness'. Any satisfaction found in the present moment is fleeting as they continually anticipate and live in the future.

Sevens 'consume' their experiences with little or no personal internalisation of them and thus no real satisfaction or joy is experienced, no matter how much they fill their lives with fun and activity. Fearing that they might miss out if they fail to experience everything, they jump impulsively from one experience to another, which gives rise to the need for more and more, faster and faster, never quite getting the fulfilment they seek. Speeding through life and avoiding anything that slows them down or restricts their freedom, they are often neglectful of those who care about them, which can damage relationships and therefore expose them to the very anxiety and pain they seek to avoid.

And so it is clear that the behaviour patterns of the Seven cannot help but result in dissatisfaction and lack of fulfilment, as well as anxiety and pain, thus bringing about their deepest fear: being trapped in pain and deprivation.

Self-Observation

Until now, many of your responses to life have been automatic; they were strategies you adopted in childhood in order to deal with your world. Those that do not serve you are no longer needed, but until you can see your own patterns, they control you. As they come fully into your awareness, *you* are able to take control and then to shift to a higher vibrational level.

Considering these self-observation questions will help you to have greater self-awareness and enable you to let go of your negative patterns, little by little. Take the time to go over these questions regularly and perhaps keep a notebook handy to jot down thoughts, insights, or experiences. As you become more aware of how much or how often your negative patterns arise, do not make yourself 'wrong'. **Remember, this behaviour has been normal for your personality type and now you are on the road towards change.** Take your self-observation lightly, learn to smile at yourself, and keep rereading your positive traits, for **that** is who you really are!

The Seven's thoughts are usually on the next positive or exciting activity, with the result that their attention is distracted from 'now' so that they often miss enjoyment of the present. Ask yourself:

➢ How often does a new, more interesting idea come to mind while I am already involved in doing something?

➢ How much do I find my mind off in the future, away from the present moment?

Consider a time recently when your mind was on the next exciting possibility rather than 'now'. Ask yourself:

➢ Which aspects of the activity with which I was engaged did I not savour as a result of not being fully present?

➢ What did I miss?

Sevens avoid limitations and restrictions because they become uncomfortable or bored. Ask yourself:

➢ In what circumstances have I felt restricted and, as a result, experienced boredom?

➢ What does boredom feel like in my body?

➢ What activities might I engage in to distract myself from being bored?

➢ What would it feel like to have to stop, unable to relieve boredom?

Keeping life up and positive requires the focus to be on one's own plans and desires. Consequently, the Seven's attention goes to themselves rather than to others. Ask yourself:

➢ In what ways and how much does my attention keep going to what I want, feel, or think about things?

➢ Have I tended to forget others' feelings or needs?

➢ How do I respond to blocks to my plans, ideas, or actions?

➢ What emotion does that bring up for me?

➢ How does that affect my behaviour?

➢ What does the emotion feel like if I don't act out but instead stop and let myself really feel it?

Sevens don't allow their attention to go to pain or distress because this would undo their basic strategy of keeping life up and 'boundless.' Ask yourself:

➢ What events might have caused me to experience pain or distress if I hadn't used distraction techniques?

➢ How do I react to negative events, feelings, or feedback?

➢ What do I do so that I do not have to connect with negative emotions?

➢ How do I react when I notice distress or hurt in others?

➢ What do I do in order to avoid addressing this?

➢ How do I behave when I know I have caused another person distress or pain?

Taking the New Path

Being present

Your most important task is to discover what really brings you joy, for you have tried to convince yourself that what you have been reaching out for is what you want, yet you have experienced little satisfaction from those experiences. In your eternal quest to keep stimulated and have fun, you have missed out on many of the simple pleasures of life. Life cannot always be fun – not fun in the sense that you might have defined it in the past, yet great enjoyment and contentment can be found in simple things or even in mundane tasks.

Take a little time out to acknowledge the truth – that your pattern of future-oriented thinking and planning has not actually given you the fulfilment and happiness you have desired. You may have filled life with a multitude of experiences that are playful or adventuresome, but rarely have you been sufficiently present and connected to any of them to gain real satisfaction or joy.

What you think you enjoy is not really what you want. You want contentment and joy, but it is to be found in the small things that already exist in your life. How often do you go through whole days without really tuning in to what surrounds you? It is too easy to have a habit of seeing things without really taking them in, yet there is much pleasure to be found in the ordinary aspects of life. When we are fully present to the moment, each of our experiences can be satisfying and the ordinary is transformed into the extraordinary.

When you step out of your door each morning, pause for a minute and close your eyes long enough to let your senses absorb your surroundings. Listen and breathe deeply until you hear the wind rustling through branches, smell rain on damp grass, or see the sunlight shining on the flowers. Take a walk under the stars or listen to the birds singing; feel the wind on your face; observe the light as it filters through the leaves of a tree or watch the concentric rings a raindrop makes as it plops into a puddle.

Sevens often perceive the future as bleak and depressing if there are no exciting possibilities planned, yet being fully present in the moment requires some of the best qualities you possess as a Seven: being 'on the ball', observant, and spontaneous. Being in the present instead of in a future full of plans does not mean darkness and deprivation but a life full of sensory stimulation, moments of delight and passion. So take your foot off the accelerator pedal and practice being truly present. It is only by learning to put your attention into the very moment you are actually experiencing – and keeping your mind from future projection – that you will discover that the natural flow of life brings far greater rewards than continual planning.

Moment by moment

As a Seven, you have lurched forward in life searching – maybe it's there, maybe it's that – and none of it has really provided what you seek, so you need to change the direction of your searching. If you stop just for a moment and search in the moment for what is good, what makes you feel good inside, you will discover that what you seek is right here. Understand that joy is composed of small moments, not big highs. You have looked for the extreme, the pinnacle of the exciting doing, yet true joy is an inner contentment in a moment that lifts and opens the heart.

It can be found in many, many places, but only for a moment ... and then another moment ... and then another.

Recognising the quality of a moment, and acknowledging to yourself the feeling of that moment, will help you find the next moment that brings joy or satisfaction. But you need to understand the nature of moments. Stopping long enough to find the satisfaction that is found in the moment, just for a moment, makes it easier to find the next satisfying moment, and then the moments become more until the moments will become where your focus is and then you will begin to find what you have been looking for.

Quality not quantity

You can enhance the quality of life's moments by considering what you have right now that you are grateful for and savouring the gifts life has already given you. We live in an age of quantity and speed. The media influences us with the persistent message that larger, faster and more are synonymous with better. We come to believe that we have to have this or do that in order to have a great life, yet it is not how much you live, have, or do but what you make of everything that counts.

A smaller quantity of anything that is high in quality will almost always be more satisfying than a truckload of mediocrity. A single piece of our favourite chocolate can satisfy us more than a whole packet of a product that we don't really enjoy. One amazing interchange with a very special person gives us far more joy than a week spent with people whose company we are indifferent to. Similarly, one fulfilling experience can eclipse many empty ones strung together. It is not the quantity of new things to do that matters but the quality of what you experience during each and every thing you do.

Simplify life and slow down

Until now, you have probably been running too fast for the little pleasures to touch you. As you slow down now and embark upon this new way of being, you also need to reduce your tendency to seek instant gratification and excess. Try simplifying your life and having only what is really needed. Each time you desire something new, instead of just going for it and gratifying your desire *now*, stop and hold back a while. Ask yourself why you want it. What will this give you that your other possessions do not already provide? Do you really need another pair of shoes, a painting, or whatever? Is this just a distraction? What are you seeking to avoid? What would it be like if you didn't have it? As you learn to reduce excess, you will become more discerning about what you bring into your life and more satisfaction will be found in what you already have.

Meditation practices can be very helpful in helping you slow down. However, the average Seven resists meditation, because it seems such a waste of time when they could be out there experiencing something new – and staying with the present moment sounds limiting or boring! Yet as you embark upon this new way of being, it is good to work at meditative practices. The initial problem is that when you begin meditating, the ceaseless chatter of your restless mind is likely to be challenging to the meditation process so trying to empty your mind will be futile. Meditative practices work best for the busy mind if there is something to focus upon, such as concentrating on your breathing or a specific piece of music, or perhaps using a mantra, chanting, or a mandala to focus your mind. Be patient with yourself and begin with only a few minutes at a time; even one minute at a time is a positive beginning.

Also, body-centred exercise, such as yoga or tai chi, would be very beneficial, as they will bring you into your body and away from mind activity. However, it is not just engaging in such practices that will be helpful for you but also your intention when you reach the end of your meditation or yoga. The quality of the quiet mind that you achieve will do little for you if it is confined to those few minutes you have given to yourself, so avoid the temptation to lurch out of your meditative practice looking for action. Come back into normal activity gently and slowly and try to carry your inner quiet with you as you continue with your day.

When the going gets tough

Sevens' proclivity to give up when things get too hard or when the initial enthusiasm has died down can be a problem with regard to making real progress.

It is not unlikely that you might seek what seems the fastest route to growth – perhaps by trying visualisations or affirmations, or by following some other route that promises rapid results with little work, such as transcendence or workshops that offer spiritual highs. Whilst there is some value in any of these methods, there are very good reasons why they do not work for Sevens. The outcome of attending workshops that offer spiritual highs is that, not only is there unlikely to be any substantial change, but also you will inevitably come down again – an unhappy prospect for any Seven. Affirmations and visualisations rely primarily on the use of the mind rather than truly connecting with your inner world – and it has been the desire to avoid connection with your inner world of feelings that has kept you in a place of having to continually stimulate your mind. So any strategies that use the mind will not serve you now. What is needed is to let go of the control of mind and just be with yourself - to just 'be'.

There was a story told by a Sufi about a monkey who puts his hand into the neck of a bottle in order to grasp a delicious-looking cherry. However, he soon discovered that he could not remove his hand without letting go of the cherry. If he continued to hold onto the cherry, the monkey catcher would get him. If he wanted to be free, he had to let go of the cherry.

This story perfectly illustrates that in order to become really free, the Seven needs to let go of all the delicious goodies (experiences) that he has been seeking. (Interestingly, the agile mind of the Seven has been referred to as 'monkey mind.') Your desire to only experience the positive has prevented you being free to experience anything else. Connecting with your inner world means experiencing both your positive *and* your negative feelings, with honesty and without overemphasis.

Embracing all feelings

Slowing down and examining the feelings evoked within you by something really allows you to *be* in the moment. However, having lived mostly in your mind, you may find initially that connecting with your feelings about an experience is foreign territory for you. In fact, when asked what they feel about something, most Sevens will answer, 'I don't know.' The truth is that it can feel quite threatening for Sevens to allow a full range of emotions to touch them because they fear that by casting aside their view that life should be full of fun, they may lose themselves in painful negativity. But always remember that what you fear connecting with – the inner sense of pain and deprivation – is actually the held-onto stuff from your young past. It has already happened and you survived!

It is important to recognise that it is limiting to seek only the positive; the full spectrum of experience and the deeper purpose of life include both sides of life – the up and the down, the light and the dark. Learn to embrace all of your emotional life as it exists in the present moment: boredom and limitation, fear and suffering, as well as pleasure, excitement, and stimulation. Begin to allow pain and uncomfortable emotions to be fully experienced, and have the courage to stay with your negative emotions, explore them, and trust that you will not get lost in them. Let yourself feel your feelings in your body without resorting to distractions to avoid them.

Take time out to explore what each experience feels like, even when it is good. Whenever you are doing something you enjoy, sometimes stop and ask yourself, 'What is good about this? How is it making me feel?' Any time you feel in danger of being 'bored' (such that you desire to find some distraction), stop and look at what you are avoiding. Especially notice if you are upset or anxious about something. And when you find yourself mentally revved up, take a moment, breathe deeply, and think about what is really going on for you. Ask yourself, 'What's up? What am I feeling?' Almost always, you are masking some source of anxiety or fear, so take the time to notice the way in which the speed of your thoughts tends to lead you away from experiencing these feelings.

Connecting with your bodily sensations will help. Where in your body do you feel the sadness, anxiety, etc.? What does it really feel like? And where do you feel eagerness or excitement? Simply identifying a feeling and saying to yourself, 'I feel sad' or 'I feel happy,' is a good beginning, but then have the courage to stop and go on and really feel what it is like. Letting events, even painful ones, touch you deeply will only enrich your experience of life and make the joy you experience more meaningful and real.

Of course, if you allow negative emotions to be felt as they arise, you are likely to have to face up to your fear of being abandoned or unloved if you are not cheerful and 'up'. You need to realise that it is in fact *you* that rejects your less than happy self, not other people, and that all of us sometimes get down or feel depressed. Be honest with yourself and others when you are not feeling good and share with those you trust what you are feeling. Opening up about your negative feelings will help you identify the nature of these feelings and will help those close to you to share more in your experience of life.

Considering others

Your tendency towards the gratification of your own desires has led you to focus on your own needs rather than considering those of others. Now you need to consider the desires and well-being of others in equal proportion to your own as well as making and keeping commitments. Begin to consider how your actions are affecting those you care about. Should you cause hurt to another, own up to it and allow the other person the right to their feelings without wanting to negate or avoid them. When those you care about have worries and concerns, take the time to listen instead of trying to distract them with suggestions of activities.

Also, try to share your feelings of happiness and exuberance with others without pushing or trying to stir up the moment. You are most profound and effective when you are grounded and steady. Anyway, if your joy is real and genuine, it is *your* experience and cannot be diminished or lost if others aren't reacting to it. Watching a tiny bird, feeling the wind on your face, sharing time with a loved animal, enjoying a perfect sunset – these are all perfect experiences in themselves whether or not others are involved.

Having patience

As a Seven, you tend to be impatient with the pace and energy of others but also extremely impatient with yourself. Because you are talented in so many areas, your impatience with yourself and the process of learning or acquiring skills may have resulted in you not having fully developed any of your talents completely. Be on guard for your tendency towards being the 'instant expert'. Sevens hate being referred to as superficial, yet the impatience and desire to move onto the next new thing can cause others to see you this way. Learn to focus more by enjoying the small moments of satisfaction and enjoyment you experience as you develop your talents and perhaps consider how you could focus some of your restless energy in using your skills to contribute something valuable to the world.

It is the journey, not the destination

There are a couple of other pitfalls that Sevens sometimes experience when pursuing real and lasting growth that you would do well to be aware of.

Be aware of the temptation to talk about your path to growth with excited enthusiasm without actually engaging with your feelings. Many

Sevens make the mistake of approaching growth on a purely intellectual level; they will talk about the way their negative feelings affect them without actually allowing the feelings to touch them on an emotional, heart-felt level. And avoid the trap Sevens easily fall into: treating the path towards growth as just another experience to be planned for and get excited about. It can be too easy for a Seven to decide to just have some fun with all of this rather than letting it have any real impact.

Be patient with yourself on this inner journey. Give yourself time and space for your transformation to unfold in its own time without pushing, hurrying, or anticipating. But be prepared to stick with it. Your tendency to rush things or abandon them when they get tough may lead you to turn away from the personal inner work that is needed for your spiritual development. 'Getting there' is not really the goal. The journey, and the experiences that it brings, is the true goal. This is a lifetime's path and there is no quick fix, but it *can* be fun!

Each present moment is completely new, and nothing like it has happened or will ever happen again. As you move through your day, remembering to stay present in each moment, you will begin to find the joy you seek without having to wait for the future, for joy is a celebration of Being, an emotion that happens spontaneously as we open our hearts and find each and every moment a wondrous delight.

Becoming a High-Functioning Seven

*Sevens reclaim their Essential nature by giving up
the search for satisfaction and happiness outside of
themselves and discovering the whole world within.*

When need for the new or exciting comes from the desire to fill an inner emptiness or to run away from inner pain, only dissatisfaction and ultimately depression can result. In your fear of restriction, you have unconsciously *placed* restriction upon yourself by believing that happiness is 'out there' somewhere in the physical world. True contentment cannot come about as a result of going somewhere, doing something, or getting something. It is a state of Being that arises from being fully present in the moment. By living in the future, you have disconnected from your Being.

The real happiness you seek is to be found by reconnecting with your inner world. The more you open your heart and deal with and let go of the inner fears that arise, the more you will discover a whole world within yourself. Now as you learn to stop, reconnect with your inner world, and become fully present, you will discover what you have been missing: the pure pleasure of existence.

As your contact with your inner world deepens, be ready to let go of the picture you had of what your transformation process might be. Let your intuition be your guiding force. It is the voice of your soul, and your soul knows how all this needs to unfold. You are taking the huge leap from planning and directing every area of your life, to attuning yourself to the natural unfoldment and flow of life. By taking quiet moments of contemplation, reflection and meditation, you will learn to listen to that inner voice instead of your mind. You will be gradually finding your inner self. Through this inner journey, you will discover that your spirit is, in fact, whole and needs nothing, that real freedom comes from within rather than being 'out there' somewhere. You will also discover that you can trust that things will turn out perfectly and, even if they don't, that you have the inner resources to deal with them.

As you redefine what you believe to be fun, you can rediscover the joy in the ordinary. Your Sevenness imbues you with the wonderful quality of being able to find joy in every little thing: a child's smile, the sound of the waves on the beach, the wonder of the bubbles on the dishes as you wash up, etc. True joy is a celebration of Being. It arises from being present to the unfolding of every moment. As you let go of the conditions you have placed on what you think might make you happy or be fun, you discover the simple pleasure of existing. You begin to know that fulfilment is not what you thought, but that it is the state of Being that arises when you free yourself from the endless mind talk and planning, and experience the richness and perfection of each moment.

Beginning to see the world with the freshness of a small child will bring you the wondrous experience of causeless joy – the real and lasting joy that arises just because you exist. Moreover, you cannot help but bring hope and cheer to others. Your infectious spirit already draws many people towards you, and now, leading by example, you will find yourself helping others to see that, even though there are problems in this imperfect world, there is much beauty and joy in the smallest thing.

So as you grow into your high-functioning state, you will discover that you can be satisfied with very little. You need much less but have so much more. The pot of gold at the end of that rainbow was always within your grasp. It is the gift of life itself!

CHAPTER 27

Positive Pathways
for the Eight

The Self-Defeating Pattern

The coping strategies adopted in the young years have led to counterproductive cycles of behaviour referred to as the self-defeating pattern. This not only causes problems and pain but actually brings about what the Eight is trying to avoid.

From the perspective of the Eight, this is a world where only the strong survive, where you have to fight for survival because 'they' will get you if you don't get 'them' first. Having overcome and hidden their vulnerability and weaknesses, Eights are determined to protect themselves from ever being vulnerable again. They feel the need to not only survive but to prevail, so their environment and the people within it must be dominated and controlled.

From the perspective of the Eight, attack is the best form of defence. When threatened, Eights hide their vulnerability with aggression and intimidation and try to prevail by means of power and control. However, using power and confrontation inevitably creates counter force from others, which just creates distance between themselves and others. Despite appearances to the contrary, Eights actually want closeness and love. However, they equate having these needs with being vulnerable and weak, which is exactly what they seek to avoid.

The fortress of dominance and aggression they build certainly seems to offer effective protection against threat and makes them feel safe from harm or violation. However, the end result can be emotional restriction and loneliness because the Eight cannot then let their guard down sufficiently to reach out emotionally to others and are unwilling to let others in. So their interaction with others cannot be open, free and easy because they are allowing themselves to be *controlled* by the suit of armour they wear.

In order to protect themselves and maintain their power, they have to always be watchful for any threats to their autonomy, but in doing so, they are actually allowing external circumstances to *control* how they feel. Moreover, by hiding their vulnerabilities, they are always going to be rendered *vulnerable* to the threat of exposure.

And so it is clear that the behaviour patterns adopted by the Eight cannot help but bring upon themselves what they most fear: being vulnerable or controlled.

Self-Observation

Until now, many of your responses to life have been automatic; they were strategies you adopted in childhood in order to deal with your world. Those that do not serve you are no longer needed, but until you can see your own patterns, they control you. As they come fully into your awareness, *you* are able to take control and then to shift to a higher vibrational level.

Considering these self-observation questions will help you to have greater self-awareness and enable you to let go of your negative patterns, little by little. Take the time to go over these questions regularly and perhaps keep a notebook handy to jot down thoughts, insights, or experiences. As you become more aware of how much or how often your negative patterns arise, do not make yourself 'wrong'. **Remember, this behaviour has been normal for your personality type and now you**

are on the road towards change. Take your self-observation lightly, learn to smile at yourself, and keep rereading your positive traits, for **that** is who you really are!

The Eight's need for self-protection prevents them from experiencing or expressing their own vulnerability and softer side. Ask yourself:

➤ How do I respond when I notice any weaknesses or vulnerabilities in myself?

➤ How often do I push myself beyond my physical limits?

➤ What stops me from admitting to those around me that I do not always feel all-powerful and confident?

➤ What do I do to avoid acknowledging my fears and susceptibility to be wounded?

➤ How much am I able to express my real feelings to those I love?

➤ How do I behave when I expect to be rejected?

➤ In what ways has this contributed to my sense of isolation?

The Eight's tendency to perceive softness or indecision as weakness often prevents them from displaying kindness or compassion towards those who appear vulnerable or unsure. Ask yourself:

➤ How do I react to seeing vulnerability or weakness in others?

➤ Am I insensitive or dismissive?

➤ How might my behaviour have made others want to turn away from me?

➤ How much does this contribute to a lack of emotional closeness in my life?

When expressing their big energy, Eights don't readily notice their impact on others. Ask yourself:

➤ What negative impact does my big energy have on others?

➤ Does anyone back away or go quiet when in my presence?

➤ When have I caused resistance or confrontation in others?

➤ Does their reaction really serve me?

➤ Have I driven anyone away?

Taking control is as natural as breathing to Eights. Ask yourself:
- ➤ In what ways do I exert control or power?
- ➤ How much control do I really need?
- ➤ Is my drive for control really enhancing my sense of well-being?

Eights try to gain respect and invulnerability through assertive action. This tends to come out in a very direct or confrontational way, with little restraint. Ask yourself:
- ➤ What circumstances make me confrontational?
- ➤ Am I sometimes too quick to express anger or be confrontational?
- ➤ How often do I just 'go for it' without thinking?
- ➤ Are there times when delaying action and reflecting would be better or wiser than taking direct action?

Taking the New Path

The world is not against you

The unconscious stance that you have taken – of having to dominate those around you, take charge of every situation, or 'get them before they get you' – has resulted in a constant need to be on your guard. The signals you send out when you expect rejection or betrayal cause others to feel alienated and turn away from you or back off from the dominating effect of your powerful energy. Now that you have greater awareness of your own patterns, you can begin to understand that the world is not against you and you can start to soften the suit of armour and lay down your weapons.

Begin to re-establish trust in your world and try to approach each person or situation you encounter with a fresh, unjaundiced eye and positive expectation. By believing others are against you, you have found yourself reacting against them – and their attitude towards you when they become alienated by your defended stance simply confirms your own fears of rejection. It is time to realise that those around you are not getting ready to do you down, so do not prejudge them. When you feel yourself readying for a fight, catch yourself and sometimes try to do the opposite; pull back, connect with your breathing, and centre yourself in your heart.

It is also time to consider how the need to be in defensive mode has implicit within it the belief that you may become a victim if your defences were down. Do you really see yourself as a potential victim? If not, then lay down your sword and be confident in your own ability to work with others as equals without needing to dominate or control.

Letting others in

Work is important and your family or friends do need your support, yet working yourself to death will not get appreciated. Recognise that nurturing intimacy in your life is just as important as work and that those who love and care about you want the whole of you, not just the provider and the protector. Give them some quality time, and lighten up. Consider what would change for the better if you were a little less driven.

A tough, hard exterior is not the same as true inner strength. It takes real courage to let down our defences and own up to our vulnerability and weaknesses, to open our hearts or speak of our love for another, yet this is what you need to do. You need to connect on an emotional level with those you care about so that you can begin to experience the intimacy you desire. Only you know how much you have secretly wanted to be closer to others, but you have to allow your feelings to be seen. You have a big heart full of love and you also have your insecurities, so let your defences down sometimes and show them that you do not always feel all-powerful and confident. You do not always have to be the rock upon which others rely.

Don't presume that others do not want to hear about your hurts or your troubles. This is not to suggest that you bare your soul to all or wear your heart on your sleeve. That would be alien to your nature, but there are probably people in your life that you can really trust. Many people care about you, but when you are in your worst Eight stuff, you do not easily let them in. Letting in the affection that is available does not make you weak; it will actually increase your real strength and bring you the support you often feel you don't get. Talk with them about matters that are really getting to you and allow some of your feelings to be seen. Denying your feelings or lashing out in defence will not bring about a solution, but letting others reach you with their caring and concern will bring great rewards.

Listen to what others say to you in response to your unburdening and be prepared to offer the same hearing to them. Showing you care about their problems will allow them to see your true greatness of heart and will bring about the respect and loyalty you desire far more than any display of power.

Opening your heart

Growth for you is not just about letting your defences down but about opening your heart. You may have avoided a deep connection with others for fear of exposing your own vulnerability, or closed your heart to the emotion of love. This painful state came about as survival strategy adopted as a child in order to protect yourself from hurt.

Hidden beneath your strong demeanour are all the feelings that you have resisted because they have meant weakness to you: need for love and fear of rejection, sadness, and loneliness. By opening your heart and acknowledging your inner truth, you can begin to be touched emotionally again. Embrace and acknowledge your deep desire for loving closeness and be prepared to allow others to get close enough to love you – and work at staying in the presence of their love and intimacy. If it becomes too much and you sense yourself closing down again, close your eyes, breathe deeply, and centre yourself in your heart. Your openness and vulnerability can become your greatest strength.

It will help if you find ways to allow heart-felt emotions to really touch you, perhaps by listening to music that affects you deeply, especially that which moves you to tears. There is a lot of sadness and grief within you that needs release, and tears are nature's way of cleansing our hearts, leaving them open to receive love.

In order to grow into open-heartedness, you need to embrace your connection to Two. The higher-functioning Eight is the true servant-leader who works for a higher order, so begin to ask yourself this question: 'How can I serve?' You might consider giving some of your time to working with those in need or with children. This sort of work will bring you great joy, but do avoid trying to control or dominate the people you work with. A servant-leader knows that serving others means leading from behind instead of being out in front.

Managing your energy

One of your greatest gifts is your huge energy. When this is combined with your ability to take control and act, you really make things happen. However, you are inclined to put too much forceful effort into much of what you do – from opening or closing a door to restructuring an organisation – and even though this behaviour is as normal as breathing to you, sometimes it would benefit you to exert a little self-restraint and pull back from exerting your natural forcefulness.

When you feel challenged, instead of directing your power outwards in a destructive way or into your defences, make an effort to delay immediate action and catch yourself before you engage your intellect and power to demolish the other party with words. Considering what negative impact your forceful immediacy might have will help to you to reduce your assertiveness and intensity.

In order to increase your awareness of the impact your huge instinctual energy can have, you might want to enlist people you trust to let you know when it is excessive. There are many interactions in which you would get better results if you were less challenging, so ask those close to you for input about the ways in which your challenging approach impacts on them, negatively and positively. This way, you can gain awareness of when it is helpful to be challenging and when it is not, and then apply what you learned to your dealings with other people.

401

As you move away from your negative patterns, you can begin to focus your formidable will and your ability to control onto control of *yourself*, and you can learn to redirect much of that instinctual energy. Activities such as martial arts would be a good outlet for your excess of physical energy and to help you to feel more centred so that you can begin to focus inwards into your heart. This will make you feel more whole, more invulnerable, and you won't feel the need to act out as before. It will nourish you and enable you to achieve self-mastery.

Consideration for others

Be aware of your capacity to wound others with words. Sometimes, you focus so strongly on where you are going or what you want you just don't 'see' anyone else. Use your knowledge of the Enneagram to understand others more and start to recognise that all have their frailties and pain. Remember there are eight other ways of being human that are just as valid as yours and none is better than the other, just different.

There are some types that are very sensitive especially to displays of aggression or anger. Respect this more and pull back when you can, and when you can't, help others to understand that your aggressive demeanour is not meant as a personal attack. Your anger mostly comes up when things are starting to feel out of your control, when outside forces are making it hard to stay in the dominant role. Try to explain this to those you are close to and, at least, let them know when your anger is not personal. It will soften it for them.

Be more patient with those who do not have your personal drive or confidence and embrace those that do not demonstrate your strength with your bigness of heart. Having greater compassion for others will connect you more to your heart centre.

Relinquish some of your control

The need for power or control has meant that you are constantly reacting to your environment. This state of being is, however, the opposite to *being* in control because the events and people around you control how you will behave rather than you being free to just be yourself. The truth is, your fear of being controlled has actually controlled *you* all of your life. Real control is about knowing when to surrender control.

Although there will always be people who will rely on you and see you as the rock in their lives, it is time to realise that not everything is down to you and you don't have to carry the weight of the world on your shoulders. You cannot take control of everything, and there are many people in your life that would be willing to take charge of certain tasks. Letting others know that you do not always want to cope on your own, and sometimes asking for help, will not only relieve you of some of the responsibility, but will also help those around you to feel more empowered. And a higher-functioning Eight desires to empower others instead of being the only one who wields the power.

And as you begin to practice ways of letting go of control and allowing others take charge, you could also consider less direct ways of letting up. It would almost certainly help you to engage in bodywork such as massage where you surrender control and let another person's energy take over.

Fallibility is not weakness

In your need to be all-powerful, you know that you sometimes take a stance over unimportant things just to make your point and dominate the argument. There are many moments when there is actually very little at stake; this is when you can yield to others without sacrificing your position or power. Also, recognise that not only are you sometimes wrong, but that you do not always have to appear right in order to maintain a position of power. Instead of always wanting to come out on top, it would serve you much better to aim for a win-win situation whenever you can.

And if you make a mistake, do you own up to it or bluster your way out of it? Refusing to admit your mistakes only diminishes you in other people's eyes; they may be afraid of you, but they will not respect you. Owning up and admitting that you are not infallible will not only be seen as a strength rather than a weakness but will serve to increase your standing in their eyes. Those around you will respect you far more for your authenticity and honesty than for any display of dominance or infallibility.

The true nature of power

Your journey through life as an Eight gives you the opportunity to explore all aspects of power. You know that you are powerful; you have a powerful presence, a powerful mind, and great leadership qualities.

Yet your real potential lies in your ability to uplift and inspire others. You have the power to inspire others to do as you have done – face their own challenges and exceed their own expectations – and you will grow immensely if you use your leadership qualities to further other people's desires, not just your own.

When Eights use their power for a higher purpose than just their self-interest, they can achieve amazing things. You have the potential for great vision and the ability to create opportunities for others so look for ways in which you can begin to act as a benefactor to other people. This is the mark of a higher-functioning Eight. Moreover, by giving a leg up in life to those less able than yourself, you will gain the respect and loyalty of many and your largesse will be remembered long after you have moved on.

Inner work

The more you push against life and the more your energy is 'out there', the less sense you have of your inner being and your true essence. Past experiences may have left you scarred and jaded, but resolving a situation with force or by avenging yourself will not fundamentally improve anything – only your inner work will. You need to see that the problem is not what others have done or might do *to* you but what *your* response is, so begin to re-orientate your attention from the outer world to your inner world.

Becoming more present to the child within you that just wants love and closeness can feel like giving in to weakness for the Eight. It requires a letting go of the defended stance you have habitually adopted, and that is far from easy. Yet it this very defensive strategy that has kept you separate from that which you really desire and needs to be relinquished if you are to make progress. Take it one step at a time. You do not have to lower the defences all at once.

It is important now to take some time out to explore who you really are and discover what you really want. You might consider attending a retreat and just see what comes up or find other ways to restore your inner sense of self. This might sound scary, but the results would be extremely valuable for your growth. Also, quiet, centring practices, such as deep breathing, yoga, or tai chi, can be extremely helpful in reducing your stress and intensity. Be with yourself, enjoy some time in nature, do some of the simple things in life.

Learning how to 'just be' can take a long time, but meditation can be very helpful. In meditation, connect with your body; literally meditate upon each part of your body. Connect with it, breathe into it, feel it, and be present to it. With practice, you will find that not only does this sort of physical focus absorb some of your excess energy, but you will begin to experience calmness and expansiveness, a connection to everything on a vast scale.

Becoming a High-Functioning Eight

Eights reclaim their Essential nature by laying down the
weapons of defence and recognising the true nature of power.

The feelings of hurt and betrayal experienced long ago led to your believe in separateness; that it's 'me against them', that you may be attacked or challenged, and that you have to fight the world every day in order to survive.

Now that you are beginning to feel more powerful within, you no longer feel the need to demonstrate power outside of you by having power and control over others. Eights who demonstrate real strength are those who believe in 'power with' rather than 'power over', those who have discovered the wonderful qualities of *empowerment* rather than the use of *force*. By learning to contain your great energy, you have available the true force of that energy – a power that can inspire and lead others, empowering them to achieve more than they believed they could. This energy can truly create lasting change in the world.

No longer needing to dominate and control your environment, you learn to control and channel your huge power and energy, thereby achieving true mastery. You discover that it is counterproductive to challenge and beat the world every day and that your real freedom and happiness come from having a more relaxed and balanced relationship with the world.

True personal empowerment comes about from the discovery that you are not, in fact, a separate entity for whom survival is a fundamental issue, and that you are not someone who needs the tough, challenging exterior to give protection from something outside the self. Realising that you are part of a world where hurts that we inflict on others only hurt ourselves, you can finally give up your battles and gain real peace.

As you come to fully realise that the impenetrable, outer shell you developed is no longer necessary for your survival, you discover that letting your defences down does not make you weak but, in fact, strong. That tough exterior made it really hard to let love in, but now as you let go of old hurts or the fear of betrayal, you discover that, by being open with others and being prepared to show that you, too, have hurts, frailties and vulnerable parts, you gain the closeness you have always desired.

Becoming a higher-functioning Eight means still looking for respect and honour in others whilst respecting the dignity of all people and creatures in your world. As you move farther into your high-functioning Eightness, your naturally protective nature means that any violation of the rights or needs of others or any form of injustice, feels like a personal hurt to which you have to respond and take action. Courageous, strong and determined yet gentle, humble and compassionate, you cannot help but put yourself on the line to protect the weak and fight for fairness and justice. Really high-functioning Eights can use their strength, power and vision to be a tremendously influential force for good.

As you finally give up your war against the world, you can embrace your role within the balance of a world where all is interrelated, and become an embodiment of true gentle power, helping others to experience the empowering energy of 'I can.'

CHAPTER 28

Positive Pathways for the Nine

The Self-Defeating Pattern

The coping strategies adopted in the young years have led to counterproductive cycles of behaviour referred to as the self-defeating pattern. This not only causes problems and pain but actually brings about what the Nine is trying to avoid.

The need for peace, in both their inner and outer worlds, causes the less-than-high-functioning Nine to avoid conflict at all costs. They believe that putting aside their own agenda in favour of everyone else's will sustain peace and maintain harmonious relationships with others. However, this avoidance of conflict comes at great cost.

Although the Nine appears to be unconcerned at being persistently overlooked and unheard, they actually experience frequent unexpressed niggles of resentment. These little niggles are again and again pushed down and out of the Nine's awareness in order to maintain their fragile inner peace (or what they come to believe is peace). This peace can only be achieved by numbing out their feelings and forgetting themselves, and this in itself causes disconnection from their true selves. Moreover, it creates emotional and mental distance between the Nine and those with whom they want close harmonious connection.

Also, the Nine's apparent compliance hides a stubborn refusal to be coerced into changing or doing what they do not want. By responding to requests with a vague acquiescence and then employing subtle passive-aggressive techniques of refusal, the Nine can put off or not do what is asked of them. This unresponsiveness behaviour, combined with their propensity for being unwilling to deal with the reality of uncomfortable problems, results in those around them getting frustrated and angry, which brings about the very conflict their lack of self-assertion and withdrawal is intended to avoid.

This creates disharmony around the Nine and disrupts their inner and outer comfort. To protect themselves, Nines have to withdraw farther into their inner world of daydreams, numbness, or distraction strategies, thus creating even more separation from people around them and other people get even more frustrated at no longer being able to make connection with the Nine. So it is clear that, in several ways, Nines bring upon themselves their deepest fear: being disconnected and in conflict with those they love.

Self-Observation

Until now, many of your responses to life have been automatic; they were strategies you adopted in childhood in order to deal with your world. Those that do not serve you are no longer needed, but until you can see your own patterns, they control you. As they come fully into your awareness, *you* are able to take control and then to shift to a higher vibrational level.

Considering these self-observation questions will help you to have greater self-awareness and enable you to let go of your negative patterns, little by little. Take the time to go over these questions regularly and perhaps keep a notebook handy to jot down thoughts, insights or experiences. As you become more aware of how much or how often your negative patterns arise, do not make yourself 'wrong'. **Remember, this behaviour has been normal for your personality type and now you are on the road towards change.** Take your self-observation lightly, learn to smile at yourself, and keep rereading your positive traits, for **that** is who you really are!

Nines tend to be overly accommodating, going along with what others want or need and not addressing their own agenda. Ask yourself:

➤ How much do I just go along with other people's agenda?
➤ Considering a time recently when I did this, what might I have liked to be doing instead?
➤ Was I aware of how it really felt not to have my desires taken into account?
➤ What were those feelings that I suppressed?
➤ In what ways have I lost myself by merging into others?
➤ What happened to my real priorities?

Nines avoid anything that might cause conflict, because conflict threatens their peace. Ask yourself:

➤ How important is it to me to keep the peace?
➤ How much am I influenced by wanting things to be comfortable?
➤ How have I resisted others wanting me to change or behave differently?
➤ What behaviour do I engage in in order to resist?
➤ How do I handle conflict directed at me?
➤ How do I handle conflict between others?

Nines resist their strong, negative feelings because the emotions themselves feel disharmonious and threatening. Ask yourself:

➤ How do I respond when something uncomfortable comes up?
➤ In what ways do I 'lose' time (e.g., staring out of the window, watching TV etc.)?
➤ How often do I get sidetracked into doing secondary pursuits, such as chores and familiar or habitual things, rather than addressing something that feels uncomfortable?
➤ What might I have been avoiding feeling?
➤ When have I reframed things in the positive in order to avoid acknowledging the negative?

Nines shut down their anger to sleep or numb it out. This also leads to tiredness and to not experiencing intensity in positive feelings. Ask yourself:

➢ In what sorts of circumstances do I often feel resistance or frustration coming up?

➢ What does it feel like when frustration or anger comes up?

➢ Where in my body does anger come in?

➢ How do I manage to put it to sleep again?

➢ How much weariness do I experience?

➢ Have I been aware of not experiencing the 'juice' of life – aware that other people are really experiencing life's intensity and I am not?

Taking the New Path

Your inner world

It has been your habitual pattern to focus on other people's needs or agenda and to disregard yourself. There has been a year-on-year pile-up of unattained desires, inner feelings that have not been acknowledged or expressed, and problems that have not been worked through to a place of freedom.

As a result of repressing so much, delving into your inner world has almost certainly felt like a scary proposition, something to be avoided for fear of what might be discovered. However, the most important step towards making real progress in your growth now is to transfer your focus from what is happening outside of you to what is going on within. In order to make this radical shift, your desire to know yourself deeply via your inner world must be stronger than your desire to avoid uncomfortable feelings.

The way to freedom

The most important aspect of yourself to look at is your fear of conflict and how much it has shaped your life. It is not important to unravel why you have this fear, although there may be events or people in your younger years that you could pinpoint as being the cause. All Nines fear conflict – it is one of the fundamental patterns of Nine and the real cause is that they have brought into this life a soul memory of some kind of conflict from a previous life. Even though you may have no conscious awareness of this, as a Nine, what is important is to acknowledge and understand your avoidance of anger and conflict so that gradually you can clear it and be free. Now you have the opportunity of doing this with the help of the Enneagram, because by fully knowing yourself as a Nine, you will be able to understand your inner world and learn to deal with conflict and anger in a healthy way.

It is essential now to be completely honest with yourself about the feelings you have experienced and what has been repressed. Most Nines will insist they are not people of anger, and on the surface, they are not, but when they are honest with themselves, they will privately own up that it is not all peaceful and light inside; there are actually specks of darkness in there. For the sake of your own growth, now is the time to acknowledge to yourself that these specks of darkness are, in fact, anger.

You almost certainly have some deep-seated awareness of your repressed anger. Perhaps this awareness has been on an unconscious level or perhaps you do have a conscious awareness of it but have not wanted to acknowledge the existence of it because anger is 'not nice' or because 'anger just causes more problems than it solves'. Maybe you would not call it anger because you never allow it to get that far. However, the 'anger spectrum' of emotions includes many lesser emotions that, if allowed to build up inside, contribute to something much bigger. All those little bits of annoyance, frustration, or resentment that you have suppressed have been pushed down again and again, year after year, into that place inside, until what you have there is huge, and it certainly feels like something to be avoided.

The hugeness of the angry feelings accumulated over the years means that if at any time the lid has blown off your inner cauldron, it is likely that it was an explosive event that you have only allowed a very few times in your life. However, there are many Nines who have never been angry. Is that you? If so, perhaps there has been a time in your life when you have *demonstrated* your rage but demonstrated it in a positive way on behalf of another – not a fierce rage but as rage demonstrated by you being willing to speak up for another person because of the depth of your compassion. If so, you will know the power of it.

Anger: good or bad?

Anger is not the horribly negative emotion it is made out to be. It is a normal emotion experienced by everyone. Even the animals we share our lives with can be angry. The purpose of anger is to stop something happening or to change something that we feel strongly about. It takes us from being overwhelmed or powerless into feeling strong, in control, and empowered. Anger is only really a problem when it is suppressed for a long time so that, when it does emerge, it comes out with force or violence; however, when it is given expression before it builds up, it leaves us in a healthy way.

In the Nine's habitual avoidance of conflict, they give away much of their power, resulting in feelings of constraint, unable to be the self they really wish to be. They feel held back, perhaps overlooked, having lived a life full of lost dreams, wishes, desires, and perhaps unreached potential. On the physical level, repressing their strong feelings, especially the angry ones, commonly causes skin problems, such as rosacea or acne. It contributes to weight gain and a lack of vitality and drive (for pushing down powerful feelings requires much energy and reduces the available life force), and it causes high blood pressure, arthritis, and worse.

Moreover, it is important to realise that it is not possible to be selective in pushing down strong feelings in order to keep the inner domain peaceful and comfortable. *All* intense feelings get suppressed, which includes feelings of joy, with the result that life often feels bland and tasteless for the Nine.

As you begin to understand the patterns of the Nine, you have to ask yourself, 'Am I losing more than I am gaining by avoiding anger and conflict? Is there another way?'

Reclaim your power

Nines generally do not identify with their Eight wing; in fact, most Nines would deny any association with what they see as the forceful aggression of the Eight, an anathema to the peace-loving Nine because it seems dangerous and damaging.

Yet what you need to do in order to make changes within yourself is reconnect with that part of you. Not the negative aspects of Eight, for you will never be an aggressively angry person – that is not in your nature – but to reconnect to your Eight wing *positively,* for therein lies your power. The positive aspects of Eight empower you to take control of life and be all you know you can be.

So what are these positive aspects of Eight? Being unafraid of the consequences of speaking up in defences of your own wishes and preferences, standing up and being counted when your opinion differs from others or when you feel wronged, following your own agenda and being free from constraint. What is needed is not necessarily to *be* angry but to lose your *fear* of anger and conflict so that you will be more prepared to take a stand without the fear of what might ensue.

Breaking the pattern of going along with things in order to keep the peace needs to be tackled in small steps. Start by identifying your own anger in its many forms so that you can use it constructively and appropriately to bring about change or protection of your own agenda. Try speaking up for yourself and taking a stand in small ways first so that you can discover that it is OK to do so. Each time you discover that, not only does speaking up create positive change, but it also causes much less disharmony than you expect; you will gain confidence and a feeling of empowerment. Others in your life may be surprised at the change in you, but they will soon gain new respect for you.

Gradually, as you begin to demonstrate your anger by standing up for yourself and taking control of your own agenda, as you begin stating your own position whether or not it is congruent with the other person's, you will move from being someone with unacknowledged anger to one who has found their source of empowerment and drive.

You will also begin to be more comfortable with normal levels of anger without fearing the consequences of that inner cauldron of rage. Conflict will be discovered to be not only worthwhile but also empowering and energising, even sometimes enjoyable. It infuses life with that spark, that essential something that you have felt was missing. The peace that comes from the resolution of conflict has a satisfying quality to it rather than that numb, stultifying pseudo peace that you experienced before. You will also find that it creates union instead of the separation you have feared.

Embrace the ups and downs of life

Because Nines are so unprepared to disrupt their peace, they shut out the normal ups and downs of life, desiring only to experience what feels comfortable. Yet it is the negative or painful aspects of life that offer each of us the opportunity to expand and develop our spiritual selves. By their very nature, Nines are inherently spiritual, but most are not experiencing the growth that other personalities benefit from through their own ups and downs because of this determination to not experience the down periods.

While you continue to keep things on an even keel, avoiding your negative emotions so that you do not experience the unpleasant aspects of life, you will remain static, stuck and blocked. Your growth depends largely upon you starting to accept discomfort and conflict as part of the normal up and down of life and becoming more aware of, and accepting of, the full range of emotions you experience, both bad and good.

Maintaining momentum

Many Nines can find it hard to maintain momentum along this path of growth. It can be too tempting to let up and give yourself a rest, falling back into the old ways of avoidance.

First, identify your methods of avoidance and then, when you find yourself slipping into your habitual behaviour, ask yourself why you are doing this thing. If your strategy of avoidance has been busyness, ask yourself of each activity whether you have really chosen to do this for yourself or whether you have adopted it because others wished you to. If you find you are 'zoning out' from a person or relationship, ask yourself if you are uncomfortable or angry with them about something; after all, people and events affect you mentally and physically whether you like it or not. (However, do remember that Nines will often only realise their true feelings later.) If you are upset with someone, talking about it rather than avoiding it will help you reconnect with yourself and with them.

Although meditation comes easily to you, it is not a practice that will help your growth at this point; it can too easily be another form of avoidance. Instead, consider taking regular exercise, such as running, cycling, or yoga all of which would enhance your body awareness, allowing you to sense your feelings more easily. In order to make real progress, avoid anything that numbs your feelings, such as ceaseless activity, alcohol, tranquillisers, and TV. Coping unaided with negativity and uncomfortable feelings may be hard at first, but each new beginning will increase your self-awareness and your confidence to stay present to your own negative feelings. And remember, whatever uncomfortable feelings you allow yourself to feel, this too will pass!

Owning your emotions

As you become more familiar with your full range of emotions, it will become less and less threatening to own them. If you feel angry, recognise that it is just another emotion and everyone is entitled to be angry sometimes. It is only through your anger that you will burn through your inertia and reconnect to your own power. Tell people when you are upset with them, and why. Acknowledging and admitting your feelings will sacrifice your peace of mind temporarily but will bring about much more satisfying relationships.

When you begin to realise how much you have resisted your strong emotions and avoided standing up for your own desires and values, you may also experience guilt or grief. If so, do not let these painful feelings send you back into emotional numbness. Remember, you cannot help being who you are – a Nine – with all the attendant ways of dealing with disturbing emotions. This time, allow the feelings to be felt; sit with them and allow them flow over you. Explore the nature of negative feelings; by doing so, you will become more fully alive, more fully connected to yourself.

Once you have conquered this determination to not experience the down periods and are able to let the ripples affect you, you will begin to realise that experiencing the full range of human emotions is what makes us feel alive. Moreover, you will be able to truly unlock the growth that will lead to completion and the return to oneness that you have been seeking.

Establish your own priorities

In their desire for oneness and harmony, Nines lose touch with their inner separate self and their own agenda, merging with others and reacting to events outside of themselves. Start to recognise your own importance and reclaim your separate self. By becoming more fully awake and alive to yourself, you will begin to realise that you are somebody who matters.

Take some time to recognise what *you* want from a situation. Often, you can be so busy taking into account the views of others that you tend to lose sight of your own. Because of this tendency, you may not know what you really want straightaway; if necessary, do not be afraid to ask for a moment to consider the options. It may help to set your own personal agenda by a process of elimination and then to keep a journal of what you discover about yourself. And you are allowed to have wants, so don't be afraid to pursue the option you prefer when you are clear.

Ask those closest to you to help. Let them know what you are trying to do – that is, focusing on yourself and your own desires. Perhaps instead of accepting your accommodating agreement, they could ask you what you really want in the present situation. Initially, you may not even be sure about your own desires, so it is essential to take the time to be with yourself and go within for answers.

Learn the value of the word *no*. It is good not to want to disappoint others, but when you are presented with something that you are not comfortable with, it is better to be truthful at the outset rather than agreeing to it to keep the peace or to be 'nice' and later regretting it and perhaps feeling resentful. Also, others are much more likely to be upset with you if you resist their plans passive-aggressively after you have initially agreed to them. There are soft ways of saying no. Get some useful phrases under your belt, such as 'I would like to do that, but right now I need/I am doing ...' or 'That sounds nice, but I prefer ... if that's OK with you.' It *will* get easier!

Life is for living

You may have felt, as many Nines do, as if your life has been happening to someone else or that you have not really been experiencing the juice and intensity of life that others do. As you begin working to really feel all your emotions and to reclaim your power, be determined to start living each and every moment, both good and bad, and feel the magnitude of being alive. Work on focusing your attention and on becoming more mentally and emotionally engaged in the world around you. Focus on the way your body feels, and work with your body to increase your vitality and level of activity. Exert yourself to do something with each day, especially if you regularly let days go by doing unimportant or trivial tasks. And welcome in these changes for what they are: a new beginning, not a threat to your inner peace.

Becoming a High-Functioning Nine

*Nines reclaim their Essential nature by dealing with
their underlying fear of losing connection and by letting
go of the belief that they are nobody special.*

Your gentle, unassuming nature combined with your habitual avoidance of the negative, especially strong or intense emotions, has led you to lose much of your connection with your true self. You have come to believe that you don't have to stand up and be counted, and that it is better to blend in than to 'show up' in life. What others want has mattered more than what you want.

As you learn to recognise your intrinsic value, you will discover that your personal development is worth the effort, that you really *can* put in the time and energy needed to find and develop your potential. You need to work at putting yourself out into the world and letting people know what you have to offer. You may often have found that doing something good for yourself has led to feelings of heaviness or lethargy, but as you grow into your high-functioning Nineness, you will find your energy and vitality increasing, and with it your personal charisma. Others will seek you out more, will want to listen to what you have to say, and you will find your true self more appreciated than you were as your less-awake self. As *you* become more energised, you will find that others are energised and motivated by you.

Many Nines hope that self-development and transformation will happen without the comfortable and familiar parts of self and life being affected. You need to fully realise that true connection and unity are not achieved by tuning out from reality or by creating fantasy worlds in your imagination. Only by fully engaging in the present moment, allowing your real response to the situation to develop, and staying self-aware while fully engaging with your inner feelings do you become truly alive.

You cannot become *more* by negating or denying aspects of yourself. Embracing all aspects of yourself, negative and positive, is the only successful route to achieving the full potential of your true nature. Accepting the wholeness of life's experiences is what brings about wholeness of life. Detaching from or repressing negative emotions detaches you from the aliveness of being, from the joy of living. Connecting with and confronting your feelings of anger or rage can feel very threatening. But by staying with it, acknowledging that these feelings are really present and that they need an outlet, you will get the real inner peace that you seek instead of the pseudo peace that you have achieved in the past by numbing your feelings or tuning out. Real peace has a quality of aliveness, of scintillating vitality and boundless contentment.

As this real peace develops within you, it will become the core of inner stability and serenity that you return to when strong emotion has been present. You will discover that it feels great to experience the full range of emotions and to experience the ups and the downs of life, that life consists of opposites – pleasure and pain, sadness and joy, union and loss, peace and anxiety – and without the downs, we cannot fully experience the ups. Experiencing and appreciating the value of each experience as it comes, and fully feeling the accompanying emotion, is *truly* going with the flow of life.

By becoming fully present to your inner world and your full range emotions and by having the courage to stand up and be counted, your connection with the outer world will become stronger and more dynamic. The intensity of true reality here in the physical world will finally be yours as you become scintillatingly alive, energetic, alert, dynamic, serene, and joyful. You see, you really *are* worth the effort!

CHAPTER 29

The Route to Happiness

Raising Your Vibration
with the Enneagram

From autopilot to empowerment

If you have correctly identified your Enneagram personality type, it is important for you to have understood how the erroneous beliefs unconsciously taken on by your young self have been driving your habitual patterns of thinking, feeling and acting. These patterns are the 'lampshades' that prevent your inner light from shining with its full brightness into the world.

Before you had any real awareness about these patterns, it is likely that, instead of it being 'who you really are', you were like an automated system reacting to life in habitual ways, following the same route, and feeling like a powerless passenger. Now, with knowledge about your true inherent nature and the reasons why you have often been less than your shining self, you can take back control and steer yourself towards living as a more high-functioning version of yourself, for this is where happiness awaits.

As you do this, you must take responsibility for your self-defeating patterns so that you can move from *powerlessness* to *empowerment*. Of course, 'owning' your patterns does not in any way mean you are to blame for them (and blame is always disempowering), because up until now, you have been doing the best that you could, given the tools available to you.

You now have powerful transformative knowledge – the Enneagram – which, if applied, will navigate you back to your true state of being. It will empower you to make choices that are different from those that have held you back for so long. Finally, you can *consciously* choose the path to happiness and well-being rather than repeat the mistakes of your past. And in so doing, you don't need to change and be like somebody else but just become more of who you *really* are, without the negative patterns of your type holding you back.

Allowing your True Self to unfold by just being

All that your soul ever wished your human self to be is already within you, albeit partially hidden from view behind the clutter of your negative 'stuff'. No amount of forcing, doing, or trying will facilitate your unfoldment or accelerate the process. Becoming a high-functioning expression of your type is a process of *allowing*, a process in which *being* takes the place of the *doing*.

Resisting the magnificent expression of the 'you' that is your natural state has been such hard work that it has caused you all manner of problems and pain. But just as it takes much more effort to dam a river than to let it flow, it takes far more energy to hide your light than to allow it to shine.

Taking small steps

For many people, making the shift from where they are now to a high-functioning state of being – a place where one lives mostly through the positive qualities of one's personality – can seem like an impossible prospect. And it is true that a shift from low vibration to high vibration is huge and cannot be made instantaneously. Reclaiming your personal power is a gradual journey of introducing thoughts, emotions and actions that are of a slightly higher vibration than where you are right now. Trying to make a quantum leap from depression to joy or from fear to inner peace is simply too much of a vibrational gap to bridge at one time; you have to approach it step by step.

Each of the nine personality types has different obstacles that need to be negotiated in order to reach their high-functioning expression, different negative patterns that need to be broken and let go of before their true self can emerge. But despite the differing terrain, the steps required to negotiate it remain largely the same.

Preparing the Ground

Transformation is about creating the right environment for your Divine Self to flourish; this means getting out of your own way and removing the obstacles that are stopping you from moving forward.

Imagine the Enneagram knowledge to be a seed that will not geminate or bear fruit if the ground in which it is planted (i.e., you) is not suitably prepared. If this were the case, despite the fact that you may be aware of your patterns, meaningful strides in your growth can prove very difficult or, at best, painfully slow. If you really want to shift your vibration and become more high-functioning, it is necessary to begin to break down your limiting constructs, the self-imposed practices, and beliefs that render your 'ground' infertile. If this is not done, they will continue to act to negate your progress and serve to keep you in your negative, self-defeating cycles restricting your ability to move to a higher vibration.

Stop making excuses

It is true that the experiences of your past – particularly those of your younger years – have caused you to adopt certain untrue beliefs systems. These beliefs about yourself and the world are what continue to drive your negative patterns of thinking, feeling and behaving.

That said, it is not your past that keeps you from being happy and high functioning; it is the fact that you have bonded yourself to wounds that were sustained during that time. You cannot change the past; you can only change your reaction to it. The only moment of power you truly have is in the present, and using your personal story as an excuse for the way you are, or the way you behave, will never serve to shift your vibration to higher levels.

Excuses immobilise us and hand our personal power to something or somebody else. They transfer our inner power to outside circumstances that we have no control over and keep us tied to our past, stuck within our self-sabotaging patterns. By then hoping that our outer world will change so that we can be contented and happy on the inside, we lose any power to alter our situation. The only route to happiness is to change your inner world.

Despite what you might believe, dysfunctional upbringings are the norm, not the exception. The chances are that whatever you experienced in your past was no worse than that experienced by many, many others. In fact, if you were to examine the past of any of the most inspirational and self-empowered people on the planet today, you would find such things as abandonment, poverty, violence, or worse in their formative years. This was what they had to experience to become the amazing people they are today.

You chose the life circumstances you experienced for very good reasons – because the higher part of you considered these obstacles to be the perfect recipe for facilitating personal expansion and growth. So rather than dragging the weight of your past with you everywhere you go, begin to see it as your greatest gift, without which you would not be who you are today or who you are to become.

Having come into awareness of your negative patterns, you may also have jumped to conclusions about what set of circumstances brought them about. You may be right; you may not be. It is actually not important either way. Without any means to process your past pain, focusing on it just keeps you from moving forwards and stops you reclaiming the power of the present moment. Right now is the only moment you have in which to make the choices that will dictate your future, so don't waste it by making excuses about your past. Sooner or later, you've simply got to get over using yesterday to explain today's behaviour!

Surrounding yourself with vibrations that lift you

Everything that you come into contact with during your waking day has a frequency of vibration. The people that you interact with, the music you listen to, the building you work in, even the movies or television shows you watch all emit a subtle vibration that has the ability to change your own vibration when you become exposed to it. Some of these energies act to raise our vibration and strengthen us; when we are exposed to these energies, we come away feeling uplifted, joyous, carefree, and high with life. Other lower energies weaken our vibration and leave us feeling heavy, depressed, tired, or just generally 'low'.

An important part of initiating meaningful change is creating a life where the vibrations you are exposed to act mainly to raise your vibration – even if only temporarily – rather than lower it. Being selective about the vibration of the things you allow into your life makes it easier to take those small steps forward into a place that feels increasingly more like the real you.

Which people in your life make you feel tired and drained? Wouldn't you rather be with folks that make you feel energised or who make you laugh, smile, and feel good? How often do you read a newspaper or watch the news and feel guilty, annoyed, or upset? Compare that to when you read spiritual literature, poetry, or an inspiring autobiography. Wouldn't you rather feel like that more often? How do you feel walking through a polluted inner city compared to taking a stroll in the park or the countryside?

You and you alone can choose the component parts that make up your life. Where you work and who you work with, who you socialise with, what you listen to, read, or watch – these are all within your power to change. So make choices that make your heart soar rather than sink, and if, for whatever reason, you begin to make excuses about why you can't, examine what erroneous beliefs you have that make you feel powerless to change these aspects of your daily life.

Allowing emotions free expression

All emotions are energy; they have a vibration – positive emotions have a high vibration whereas negative emotions have a low vibration – and it has been said that the word *emotion* can be read as *e-motion*, meaning *energy in motion*.

Ideally, emotions should naturally flow through us. When we allow them to do this without attempting to block, suppress, or control them, they disappear very quickly. However, if we try to interfere with that flow, they remain stuck in our cellular memory and continue to affect us negatively for days, weeks, and even years after the event that triggered them! (Compare this to an electric current trying to flow *through* a conductive substance such as metal. If the conductor resists the flow of electrical energy, the result is heat and it will eventually damage the conductor.)

Many of our modern societies perceive emotionality as weakness, so we are unconsciously taught to control our emotions rather than allow them to control us. Suppressing our emotions or natural desires is a recipe for disaster, both physically and spiritually; you need look no farther than the ever-escalating number of cases of hypertension, heart disease, and cancers to see evidence of that. Your emotions are your body's natural feedback mechanism, indicating how aligned you are in any given moment. Failure to experience them or fully express them is to negate the whisperings of your soul such that, when you suppress emotions, you are, in effect, moving farther away from your True Self and its guiding wisdom.

Of course, it is always important to consider the sensitivities of others when emotions need to be expressed openly. And freely expressing your feelings does not mean that you immediately have to turn into a volatile and unpredictable person who is impossible to be around! There are many non-disruptive ways to healthily express negative emotion:

punching a cushion, going to the gym, playing sport, or yelling your head off in the middle of a field are just a few.

All of these forums can be extremely valuable, but sometimes it is important to get emotional support and encouragement in order to fully process the feelings. In that case, an understanding and compassionate friend, or a loved one who is not involved with the emotion, can be invaluable to use as a sounding board – as long as they are able to allow the emotion to be present in the environment without feeling uncomfortable. There will, of course, be times when emotions need public airing, and those involved with the emotion need to be part of the process of full expression. So it will be necessary to discern when others need to hear you and when they don't.

Your Well-Being

Taking care of your body

If we really want to give ourselves the best opportunity to experience happiness and allow a spiritual transformation to occur in our lives, we must adopt a holistic or 'whole-istic' approach to our existence. Physical well-being (of both the inside and the outside) is an integral part of letting go of our negative personality patterns and establishing spiritual balance, because our biochemistry is directly linked to our emotional states.

Unfortunately, a great number of people have their personal priorities so misaligned that they tend to treat their automobiles better than they do their own bodies! But just watch the problems you get with your car when you neglect its maintenance or put diesel in the tank rather than petrol. Your car simply will not function properly under those conditions, so why should you expect your own physical vehicle to be any different? It too needs to be 'serviced' regularly to be kept healthy and requires the right kinds of 'fuel' to run smoothly and problem free.

By eating the right kinds of food, drinking plenty of fresh water, and taking regular exercise, we tap into a constant flow of vitality that comes from being aligned with one's True Self. Whereas we might have felt sluggish, unbalanced, or slightly fuzzyheaded before, when the vibration of our physical cells shifts, we naturally feel lighter, more alive, and properly present. We also regain a sense of genuine personal stability, which provides us with the inner strength to deal with unsettling emotional upsets and problems in an equable way. Quite literally, we feel like a more whole and balanced person mentally, physically and spiritually.

Eating habits, in particular, are one of the most difficult, unconscious habitual patterns to give up, as they are deeply entrenched within the fabric of our lives. However, if we wish to initiate a transformation in the way that we feel and behave, it is vital that a harmonious physical environment is established. As a starting point, begin by cutting out toxic substances, such as alcohol, caffeine and nicotine, and supplying your body with the balance of nutrients it requires. Regular physical exercise, such as walking, swimming, or yoga, will also begin to release the latent life-force energy that is vital to become a high-functioning person.

The condition of your physical body is the best and most reliable reality check you have available. When there is a problem with your body – with the way it feels or functions – it is a clear message that you are out of balance in some way. Like a radio receiver for listening to the broadcast wisdom of your Higher Self, its subtle sensations provide constant feedback about the present moment – the only moment the physical body can ever experience.

Finding and committing to a personal practice

A devoted personal practice can take many forms, such as writing, painting, meditation, yoga, prayer, reading inspirational literature, dancing, running, or tai chi. Any practice like this begins to disrupt our habitual personality patterns and awaken the Eternal Self that is sleeping within us. We are reminded over and over again that we are not the negative patterns of our personality but the sun behind these temporary clouds whose brightness, warmth and light never ever goes out. Regardless of what practice you choose, it is important that this is a period where you can be with yourself and listen to, and explore, your inner world, becoming more familiar with your true nature. Without a daily practice of some kind, the Enneagram knowledge can easily lose its potency. The great insights into your type need to be combined with a daily commitment to yourself that gives you the opportunity to be alone with your thoughts and emotions; only then will the true effects of this ancient wisdom begin to take hold.

Eventually, a regular and committed practice yields huge benefits on every level of our being. It helps sustain periods when we are fully spiritually awake – those times when our eyes feel completely open to the world and we experience an insight beyond sight. We increase our powers of perception, experiencing more aspects of ourselves and understanding life with greater depth and clarity. Inner resources are cultivated, allowing balance, well-being, and wholeness to re-emerge, and free from condemnation, criticism, or expectation, nothing comes as a surprise.

If you can spend fifteen to twenty minutes a day away from distractions or interruptions, just embracing silence and listening to your inner self, the new insights into your personality patterns will amaze you. Life will become an experience of unfolding wisdom, filled with fresh opportunities to move back into the positive aspects of your personality.

You might feel as though taking time for yourself every day is selfish or that there are too many other things that need to be done for you to fit it in. But it is only by self-centred focus (i.e., a focus centred on self) that genuine spiritual realignment can occur, enabling you to return to your positive state of being. So make your personal practice part of your daily routine and resist the inevitable urge to sacrifice it when life becomes busy, for this will be the time when you will feel its benefits the most.

For each of the types, some practices will act to free them from their negative patterns, while others will merely enable them to continue. When selecting a practice, it is important not to choose one that enables you to continue your negative personality patterns but one that will break your patterns. This should be a time to listen to the silent inner voice of your Higher Self, a forum for personal honesty and not an excuse for escapism, wallowing, or self-criticism. Remember that your chosen practice should bring balance to your imbalanced personality pattern, not enable the imbalance to continue. So ask yourself, 'Does this practice serve to move me into a better place or allow me to stay in my negative cycles?'

Fours, Fives and Nines are inwardly focused by nature and benefit from being brought out of themselves and grounded into their physical bodies. Active practices that get them in touch with their physicality, such as vinyasa yoga, dance, or walking meditations, are ideal for these types. Although it is likely that they would prefer a more sedentary practice, periods of inactivity and silence can very often enable these types to continue their negative personality patterns rather than free them!

Threes, Sevens and Eights are extraverted 'doing' types that have lost connection with their heart centre. Meditation, or practices that allow them to express their emotions, such as painting or writing, can be transformative, as these practices reconnect these types to their inner world. However, they may consider such activities a waste of time and be tempted to adopt a 'doing' practice as a means of distraction!

Ones, Twos and Sixes are 'should, must, ought' types who put duty before their own needs. Slow, deep, contemplative practices such as tai chi or yoga, are ideally suited to quieten the mind of these types and centre their intuition. Their practice should help them learn to relax and receive. (Receiving could be in the form of massage or in receiving guidance from their Higher Self.) However, self-orientated activities may not fit with their strong conscience and sense of duty, so they might consider such time an extravagance!

Allowing the seed to take root

According to *The Yoga Sutras,* written three thousand years ago by the great sage Patanjali, 'Practice becomes firmly grounded when well attended to for a long time, without break and in all earnestness.'[23]

---

[23] Taken from the fourteenth sutra of *The Yoga Sutras of Patanjali,* translation and commentary by Swami Satchidananda (1992).

Unfortunately, all too often, we want results immediately; we lack the patience required to make the progress desired.

When you plant a seed in the ground, you cannot rush its growth; it is a process of trust and allowing. If, having not seen any evidence of growth after a few weeks or even a month, we get impatient and decide to dig up the seed or give up entirely, we negate the growth process completely. The chances are that the seed had begun to put down roots and was sprouting upwards towards the surface when it was dug up – growth was occurring despite the way it appeared on the surface. It is the same with your personal practice. Your new 'seed' must be nurtured in properly prepared ground, with both patience and detachment from the outcome if its benefits are to be experienced. The changes you desire may take a few months; they may take years!

Cultivating Awareness

Making peace with 'What Is'

Habitual patterns of resistance – such as making excuses – only serve to sustain an environment that is not conducive to meaningful spiritual growth. If these patterns of resistance are left to continue, personal transformation can only occur painfully slowly and will likely be beset with persistent obstacles and difficulties. The simple act of paying attention to the physical body as well as committing time and space to self-examination in the form of a personal practice begins to loosen deeply held resistance. This readies the 'ground' to accept fresh perspectives and creates potential for further spiritual growth to occur.

Awakening to our negative personality patterns was the first phase of self-improvement. The next was to shift your mind, body and spirit into a place where real growth can be nurtured. Now the careful cultivation of awareness must begin because whenever awareness is present in a part of our life, that part can improve.

Most of us, on some level, fight against our reality. Instead of *accepting* the circumstances and events that occur in our lives, we push against them with thoughts about what *should* be different. This resistance to our reality sets up a misalignment with our Higher Self and is the source of much unhappiness and pain.

'If only my wife would agree with me …' 'He should be more considerate of me …' 'Why did *this* have to happen today?' 'I should not be feeling like this …' Such thoughts are arguments with the facts of our reality, that this *is* happening and you *are* feeling like this. When we resist in this way, we shift our focus away from what *is* and instead apportion blame to ourselves, others, or outside circumstances. But it doesn't matter how much we argue that this version of reality is not 'right' and want it to be different; reality always wins!

It is important to stress that accepting what *is* does not mean overly focusing on the negatives of your situation, nor does it mean that your desire to feel different or to change your patterns and move into a higher-functioning space should be suppressed. In the future, you will have the opportunity to make different life choices or change your reaction to a situation, but you simply must start with what *is* first and move forward from there.

By bringing greater compassion to your awareness of *who* you are – complete with all your 'stuff' – and accepting *where* you are right now, your symptoms of stress, anxiety, worry, or pain will fade away. Just this act of releasing resistance immediately raises your vibration level and, better still, leaves you with the perfect formula for rapid spiritual change – being comfortable with your reality but taking action to improve your future.

Living in the eternal moment of 'Now'

The internal conflict between what *is* and what we believe should be, which has created so much discomfort and disharmony in our vibration, is a product of the mind. The mind is preoccupied with looking backwards into the past and projecting forwards into the future, the result of which is that most of us experience only a limited awareness of the present moment. Yet this eternal moment of 'now' is the only time we can ever truly *be*. The past exists only in the mind as a collection of former moments of 'now' stored in our memories; the future only exists as mental projections of moments of 'now' still to come.

We cannot step out of our front door and turn right into last September anymore than we can turn left into next July, but we can be so transfixed by the activity of the mind that we function on 'autopilot' and miss the only moment in which we have any power: the 'now'.

The 'now' is the fresh edge of consciousness, the leading frontier of physical life from which all is possible. When we do not have our attention directed on the 'now', our lives are filled with problems and resistance, leaving no room for new growth to occur. It is impossible for you to experience a negative reaction to something when your consciousness is solely in the 'now'.

In the instant you grasp the concept of being fully present, your consciousness will shift from the confines of the mind to explore the essence of your Being. When you are in the 'now', you release expectation of your future and judgement, guilt and blame from your past. Instead, you experience a peaceful stillness free from the resistance that has kept you separate from your higher-functioning self for so long. Freedom from this limited view of reality – that which the mind perceives – allows life to be experienced through your higher senses, those that reinforce your connection to the eternal positivity of Source.

If we had no thoughts, it would only ever be possible to live in the eternal 'now.' Of course, the mind is a key component in the unfoldment of life, so zero mind activity is clearly an impossible goal, even for the most enlightened souls on the planet. However, we *can* temper the amount of control it has over our experience of 'now', the moment that holds the secret to our inner truth.

Notice how often your attention is centred in the past or the future rather than on what is occurring right now. An essential part of revealing inner truth is allowing the background noise of the mind to fall silent.

Your chosen personal practice needs to be a regular period where you take time out to distance yourself from the distractions of the world, switch off your brain, and just *be* with yourself. This practice should be orientated primarily towards facilitating an increased level of personal awareness through periods of self-reflection. At heightened states of awareness, it becomes possible to glimpse high-functioning levels of consciousness, enabling you to see what wonders await if you continue to learn and grow spiritually.

The cessation of mind activity is achieved through singular focus. Practices such as yoga, meditation, or tai chi emphasise singular focus and the stilling of thoughts, but others, which still encourage self-reflection, may be built on different principles. If your personal practice is not geared towards achieving a quiet mind, we suggest you find an additional practice where you can experience the bliss that comes from being free from thought.

Breathing exercises are particularly effective for focusing the mind; so too is the repetition of a mantra or the act of deliberate movement. All activities that have a singular point of focus and encourage deliberate concentration can be called meditations, because they infuse oneself with a sense of inner control. Not all such practices involve sitting still either. You can quieten your mind washing the dishes, painting a fence, or pruning roses. The important factor is that your sense of awareness feels heightened and you feel *more* connected to the present moment, not *less*.

N.B. We can all engage in these kinds of activities as a means of distraction from things we don't want to face and end up disappearing off into daydreams or feeling numb, but that is not the same as mindfulness.

Listening to the calling of your Higher Self

All of the answers we are seeking lie within us. There is no question we can ask of the universe whose answer lies outside of our own inner world, because we all have an inbuilt guidance system that stems from our eternal connection to the infinite wisdom of Source. You may not realise it, but you will have encountered this guidance system when you experience a gut feeling about something, or when a friend rings you at the exact moment they drift into your awareness. This is your inner voice calling you to listen to its guidance.

Present in *every* moment are subtle – and not so subtle – messages from this part of the 'bigger' you, designed for no other purpose than to provide feedback about your current status along the journey of life.

Despite what you may have come to believe, this journey is not supposed to be a struggle. Certain negative experiences are necessary since they allow us to acquire the learning, motivation, or tools needed for further expansion into your True Self. But those states were supposed to be temporary; it was never the plan that you would get stuck there for so long!

The Higher Self sees the broader perspective of you and your life. Again and again, it calls to you to awaken your senses to the bounties that await you beyond the negative patterns of your false self. It watches as you stray temporarily into the darkness and calls you endlessly back towards the light. Most of us, however, have become so adept at resisting our true nature and ignoring its endless guidance that we have come to believe that that struggling is somehow noble. After all, there is never gain without pain, right? No. This is nonsense. Falling asleep to this higher guidance and resisting its whispering has led us to experience unnecessary discomfort in all areas of our lives. We have become entrenched in undesirable life conditions, relationships, emotions, thoughts, and physical problems, but there is a way out.

Remember, when you (as your soul) selected your personality type for this life you chose to bring certain unique gifts to the world. Moreover, the eternal spiritual guidance and support of your Higher Self is trying to help you avoid unnecessary inner turmoil and to express those unique gifts, so that you may become the fullest expression of the beautiful you.

A committed and mindful personal practice will bring you closer to these deep, soulful utterances. As your mind becomes quiet, you will discover the power and wisdom that reside in the stillness. The voice of your inner guidance will speak loudly to you in a voice that is much more profound than the transient thoughts of your mind, which continues to doubt and question. This is the ultimate truth that only comes from unity with your Higher Self.

The wisdom of your Higher Self can erase your erroneous beliefs and establish your life as an experience of grace and joy. So keep looking for the signposts that can guide you back to where you wish to be; they are always there. The guidance could be in the form of negative emotion, feeling unfulfilled in a relationship, or a health issue. Becoming aware of recurring patterns in your life is the first step to acknowledging them for what they are: your Higher Self trying to get your attention. Then once awareness dawns, you can begin to address your undesirable life circumstances head on and move forward towards being higher-functioning.

Letting Your True Self Blossom

Sustained awareness will allow this potentially transformative 'seed' to put down roots and grow in strength and wisdom. Eventually, if mindfulness is practiced for long enough, these roots will bed in so deeply that *they* will become the habitual patterns rather than those pesky negative ones!

Mindfulness is non-judgemental awareness. Any practice that involves a single point of attention to cultivate calmness and stability will encourage mindfulness. It is the ability of the mind to observe whatever arises in the present moment with acceptance, trust and impartiality. In this state, thoughts and feelings are not ignored or suppressed but welcomed without any desire to analyse or judge them; they are just accepted for what they are: sensations that do not define the True Self.

When one begins to approach this state, there are no longer feelings of being trapped or controlled by negative patterns of thinking, feeling and behaving; waking consciousness begins to expand in every direction, and this newfound level of emotional and physical well-being becomes utterly addictive. All of a sudden, regardless of type, life becomes driven by one thing and one thing alone: to expand into higher and more glorious expressions of the eternal, magnificent Self.

Becoming a truth seeker

On your spiritual journey, new and higher versions of yourself will always be lining up to reveal themselves to you. The 'you' with whom you identified yesterday is not the 'you' of today, nor will the 'you' of today be the 'you' of tomorrow. We are ever-expanding beings, and to make the mistake of accepting *this* truth as *the* truth is to negate scope for further self-expansion.

As personal awareness deepens, it is only natural that the quest for truth – especially about one's personality – becomes a major factor in daily life. With increased awareness, that which made it difficult to discern the real truth of self from the falsehood of negative personality traits begins to dissolve. Whilst experiencing this heightened state of consciousness, probably for the first time since childhood, the Shining Self within feels more real than the fogginess that had existed before.

There is a sense of self-acceptance, personal contentment and peace, and a desire to garner greater and more insightful truths with which to continue the stream of well-being already established. Yet it is necessary to avoid becoming too attached to, or identified with, each new truth of self as we uncover it.

Even with the new tools that become available through the knowledge and wisdom provided by the Enneagram, we must make peace with the fact that we are all incomplete. No matter how far we may have come spiritually, what we believe to be true about ourselves and the world around us is still just a stepping-stone on our journey, not the destination itself.

Ask yourself, 'Is what I considered five years ago to be true about myself still true today?' If not, your present 'truth' is unlikely to still be true in a further five years. The key to expansion is to remain unattached and open. Each new truth about the self must be honoured and allowed to catalyse growth, whilst not being held in such reverence that it limits openness towards deeper, broader, and more profound truths for us to expand into.

In the end, ultimate truth is only ever found in those things that never ever change, those that are universal. So seek within your inner world for that which never changes and you will discover the only thing that can ever be considered real and true: your soul.

Enjoying the ride

It is so easy in our fast-paced, modern lives to forget what the human experience is really all about. We zig and zag through life in exhausting and often misguided efforts to go places or get things done, and end up losing sight of the pure pleasure of existing.

The truth is that there is really nothing to *do* and nowhere to *go* in your life; all that is required is for you to just *be*. Even on a spiritual path, we can become so overly attached to the treasures that await us at the end of our new journey that the 'pot of gold' becomes the motivation for continued self-exploration rather than the enjoyment of the process itself.

In its infinite wisdom, your soul chose the unique journey of this human life, not because of the destination that it would eventually arrive at but because of the exhilaration of the ride itself. This higher part of you knew that, by making specific choices about life circumstances prior to birth, certain 'negative' experiences would become an inevitable part of its journey. Unlike your human self, your soul did not label any of these forthcoming experiences 'negative', 'bad' or 'wrong' but was actually excited by the way these experiences would allow continued expansion into new and improved versions of self. *Every* aspect of the journey was seen as an opportunity to explore and enjoy different aspects of self through the magnificent contrast of physical existence.

Making contact with your Higher Self and shifting the vibration of your consciousness to a higher level involves aligning with the enthusiasm of your soul's experience. That means surrendering your resistance to all aspects of your personality and all aspects of your life – both 'positive' and 'negative'.

When we can sit back, relax, and enjoy the ride that life is giving us, cherish the ups and downs that make it so interesting, and just allow the journey to unfold in front of us naturally, life becomes the most pleasurable experience imaginable. We see more beauty in the world, experience joy and appreciation for all of life's wonderful creations, and move into a place of greater self-acceptance and love.

Finding reasons to be grateful

Gratitude is a powerful and transformative act of the heart. More specifically, it is an expression of self-love, recognition of the awesome perfection of the world and your valuable role in allowing it to unfold. When you practice being thankful, even for the smallest of things in your life, it heightens awareness of your gifts and strengthens the relationship you have with the source of all wisdom and abundance in the universe: The All That Is.

Finding reasons to be grateful for every moment of your life is a marvellous way to acknowledge how blessed you already are. A good way to encourage yourself to do this is to take a notebook, perhaps each evening before you go to bed, and list everything that you can be grateful for that day. You may be grateful for the special people in your life, the animals you love, or the sunshine that warms your face; for you, perhaps, it is the intoxicating beauty of a flower, the precious gift of food and shelter, or the wondrous organs of your body.

Expressing true heartfelt thanks is an extremely high-frequency practice and therefore a very simple way to keep your vibration high. However, when you are experiencing troubles or pain and your vibration is low, uncovering positives can be very hard indeed; yet even within the darkest cave is a shaft of light waiting to be found. At the root of all negatives is a positive – a gift for you to discover – because its very existence identifies where you are not yet whole and complete, therefore showing you what you still need to work on to become truly high-functioning. When you recognise that every undesirable experience in your life is, in fact, an opportunity to grow, it becomes much easier to surround these negative aspects with love and thanks.

So if you find yourself slipping into the lower-functioning aspects of your type, give a gentle nod of recognition towards the wisdom of your Higher Self and the perfection of even the unwanted aspects of your life. Notice how much lighter and happier you feel when you're able to stay focussed on the positives in your life, and be grateful that you life is now geared towards finding solutions rather than focusing on the problems.

Laughing at yourself

We all love a good, hearty belly laugh because of the way it makes us feel, but few people realise what a powerful tool for transformation laughter really is. While it might seem clichéd to say that 'laughter is the best medicine', there is significant scientific evidence to suggest that the act of laughing actually activates the body's natural pharmacy, creating a unique environment where healing can take place.

When we laugh, we naturally experience a lovely, euphoric high that seems to temporarily wash away pain and anxiety. This is because the act of laughing causes endorphins (the body's natural painkiller) to be released into the bloodstream. At the same time, levels of cortisol (a hormone released by the adrenal gland when we are stressed) are suppressed, making us feel calm and relaxed. The body's immune system is also fired into action when we laugh; natural killer cells and T-cells, which attack viruses and even some cancer cells, are released throughout the body. Moreover, laughing floods our lungs with oxygen that heightens activity in the brain. This gives us the ability to think clearly and rationally, and our heart is given a workout, leaving it healthier and stronger. And after the laughter fades away, these natural health benefits remain in our system to support it, symptoms of which are the familiar warm and relaxed feelings that accompany episodes of bellyaching laughter.

Laughter also promotes healing and growth on a spiritual level. When we laugh, it releases blocks in the body's energetic field, freeing us to open and expand our awareness beyond the limit of our physical senses. When this occurs, we are able to connect to our environment and those in it on a level of awareness that transcends the associations of the physical plane. When we laugh, the way we experience any situation immediately becomes transformed into one of positive optimism, immediately promoting personal and emotional healing.

Ultimately, if we are to allow the Enneagram to transform our lives into the joyful experience we all desire, laughter must never be far away. It reinforces the spiritual and emotional shift that occurs as our awareness begins to expand, while keeping us connected to our 'truth' throughout the journey.

It can be all too easy when studying the Enneagram to focus on our negative patterns rather than our shining gifts. Even as we discover the truth of our potential, we find that we slip back into our patterns of self-defeating behaviour again and again. When this happens, it is so tempting to berate ourselves for not being the person we believe we should be. When we slip into this form of self-criticism, it lowers our vibration and negates further personal expansion.

Since the purpose of the Enneagram is to facilitate personal transformation and healing, humour and laughter are fantastic natural tools to catalyse this growth work. Life becomes much harder when you take yourself so seriously, so stop it! Human beings are not perfect and never will be. It is simply not possible to achieve perfection while we are here on earth, so learn to be nice to yourself when you slip back into your negative patterns.

Let the recurring patterns of your type become your own private source of amusement. Say to yourself, 'Oh that's interesting. I've slipped into my negative (Twoness, Fiveness, Nineness … or whichever type you are)', and take it lightly instead of beating up on yourself. Smiling or even laughing at yourself lets you know that it's OK to be human, and if you can live with, and laugh at, the remaining 'flaws' of your personality, you'll reduce the stress of not always meeting your own high expectations. And it will be much easier to take a different route next time a situation like that occurs.

Compassion at all times for all people

It is easy for us to find compassion in our hearts for victims of unfortunate circumstances, such as an orphaned child, a hungry kitten, or a terminally ill cancer patient. But just how easy do you find it to be compassionate towards someone who is behaving 'badly'? How easy, for example, would you find it to be understanding or loving towards a rapist or a child murderer? Could you find it within you to send love in response to a person shouting words of hatred, abuse, or criticism at you or your family?

Sending love, forgiveness and compassion towards such negativity is one of the most difficult spiritual principles to practice. It becomes easier, however, when we understand that every individual behaving badly is only doing so because they are suffering serious emotional pain. It may seem ludicrous, but just as you are coping with your world as best you can, so too are they – albeit from a very low-functioning perspective.

Would you castigate a child who is afraid? Would you punish an infant for feeling abandoned and unloved? No, of course, you wouldn't; you would respond with love, support and kindness. Yet inside every adult who is displaying inappropriate behaviour is a child that is screaming from pain.

When you respond to negative behaviour with judgement, intolerance, anger, blame, or revenge, your own negative responses act like an aggressive cancer that eats away at your own vibration, causing vast amounts of unnecessary pain and suffering for you. However, if you are able to be loving, forgiving and compassionate in the face of negativity, your vibration takes a quantum leap; you move yourself closer to the All That Is and you begin to experience life from higher levels of consciousness. (This does not mean that we should condone dreadful acts perpetrated by low-functioning people. It means having compassionate understanding.)

Loving yourself

Loving yourself unconditionally is without doubt the ultimate goal of any meaningful spiritual transformation work. When we shift our consciousness into the genuine self-acceptance that emerges at high-functioning levels of being, we experience an overwhelming and profound sense of *unconditional* love for *all* parts of our human self. This experience of genuine self-love is the gateway to the Higher Self and eternally loving Source – that from whom you were never separated and whose very nature is unconditional love.

Nothing is more important for anyone wishing to improve their life than discovering the truth of their Shining Self and enveloping all aspects of their human self with love. In fact, it was humanity's collective desire to do just that which called forth into consciousness the transformative insights into the human personality that have become available through the Enneagram. Although this work can provide emotional, intellectual and spiritual expansion, its most important purpose is to bring as many people as possible into a state of self-unity, a place where we love ourselves so profoundly that *nothing* and *nobody* can possibly make us feel bad.

It is only when we feel whole and complete just as we are – without the need for *anything* or *anyone* to facilitate it – that our love of self can be termed 'unconditional'. Since the initial feelings of self experienced by all of the nine types in their young years was not wholeness but, in fact, disconnection (from a specific aspect of Essence), this journey back to feelings of completeness is one we have all embarked upon, regardless of our Enneagram personality type.

Every phase of growth that you have experienced in your life has subtly, and in many cases unconsciously, been drawing you towards this one seemingly simple act of self-love. In addition to that, every piece of guidance, clarity and advice offered in this book has been geared towards enabling you to discover new methods of bringing yourself back into alignment with your True Self and experiencing the self-love that is synonymous with it.

Love of self is the truest and highest expression of spirituality. When our interaction with the world, and those in it, evokes within us negative thoughts and feelings, this is only because those experiences have revealed to us aspects of our personality that we have not yet learned to embrace with love. Our resultant reaction, manifesting in the form of our negative thoughts, attitudes, or behaviour, is just an expression of what we hold inside: a disharmonious negative view of self. When all we have within us is love, all we have to give away to others and all we see in the world is love. Negative responses are then impossible because love is all there is.

Practicing unconditional love involves being able to find love for yourself, even whilst experiencing or expressing your negative patterns. This alone – the act of sending love in response to negativity – is probably the biggest hurdle that will stand between you and real spiritual transformation. However, if you are able to accomplish it, even just once, you will discover that love has the power to transform your inner world and diffuse all negativity. It is like introducing light into a dark environment; darkness simply cannot exist in its presence.

Every new day provides innumerable new possibilities to accept more of who we really are and practice loving *all* that we find. If we can approach life with a willingness to be forgiving and compassionate whenever we can, both towards ourselves and others, our vibration will shift to resonate at a higher frequency. When combined with patience and trust in our Divine nature, spiritual unfoldment and the passage to higher-functioning aspects of your personality is not just likely, it is assured.

Merging into Oneness

There will be a point in our spiritual unfoldment when it is no longer difficult to stay on track. We no longer have to remind ourselves to stay present, mindful and open to opportunities for growth; instead, our state of expanded awareness becomes so habitual that the 'lampshades' that used to prevent our inner light from shining just fade away.

As this 'negative' false self falls away, what is left is our Shining Self, gleaming and perfect in every way. By allowing ourselves to be connected to this eternally positive aspect of self, the vibration of our consciousness shifts to an extremely high frequency. When this occurs, the edges of our character begin to soften and become less distinct as we begin to merge into the experience of Oneness.

This state of Being is the very essence of being high-functioning. When you have reached this place, you will find yourself content to *be* rather than feeling compelled to *do*. You will no longer see yourself as separate from others and your environment but interconnected with all things. No life experiences will seem ordinary or mundane; everything looks bright and meaningful. You become open to everything and attached to nothing, and every aspect of your life, even that which you once considered negative or bad, is seen for what it is: the joyously diverse expression of the one infinite, loving Source. You will suffer spontaneous bouts of smiling and laughter, just because of the heartfelt gratitude you feel for all aspects of your glorious life experience. And most importantly of all, you will finally fall deeply in love with who you are and who you are constantly becoming.

Veronica Croft, B.Sc., Dip. Ed., is a highly experienced Enneagram teacher, a renowned public speaker and teacher of emotional therapy techniques. She has devoted the whole of her working life to helping people improve their sense of self, and empowering them to change their lives so that they may reach their potential. Veronica lives and works in Devon with her husband, cats and chickens.

Chris Croft, B.A., has an extensive background in design and has developed and taught many self-development courses. As well as his work with the Enneagram, he teaches ashtanga vinyasa yoga and is the founder of The Ashtanga Yoga Workshop, Exeter's only purpose-built yoga studio. Chris also lives and works in Devon with his partner and daughter.

Veronica and Chris have been teaching Enneagram courses since 2005. These in-depth courses provide information and insights into the Enneagram and the personality unavailable anywhere else in the world, enabling each participant to find their own path to becoming their best self.

For information about courses go to: www.enneagrampathways.com
                                       info@enneagrampathways.com

Printed in the United States
By Bookmasters